SWORD ART ONLINE: GIRLS' OPS 5

ART: NEKO NEKOBYOU
ORIGINAL STORY: REKI KAWAHARA
CHARACTER DESIGN: abec

Translation: Stephen Paul
Lettering: Brndn Blakeslee

SWORD ART ONLINE: GIRLS' OPS
© REKI KAWAHARA/NEKO NEKOBYOU 2018
First published in Japan in 2018 by KADOKAWA CORPORATION, Tokyo.
English translation rights arranged with KADOKAWA CORPORATION, Tokyo, through Tuttle-Mori Agency, Inc., Tokyo.

English translation © 2019 by Yen Press, LLC

Yen Press
1290 Avenue of the Americas
New York, NY 10104

Visit us at yenpress.com
facebook.com/yenpress
twitter.com/yenpress
yenpress.tumblr.com
instagram.com/yenpress

First Yen Press Edition: March 2019

Yen Press is an imprint of Yen Press, LLC.
The Yen Press name and logo are trademarks of Yen Press, LLC.

The publisher is not responsible for websites (or their content) that are not owned by the publisher.

Library of Congress Control Number: 2015952589

ISBNs: 978-1-9753-0375-4 (paperback)
        978-1-9753-5680-4 (ebook)

10 9 8 7 6 5 4 3 2 1

WOR

Printed in the United States of America

Special Thanks!

YAJI

REKI KAWAHARA-SENSEI

ABEC-SENSEI

SHINGO NAGAI-SENSEI

KAZUMI MIKI-SAMA

TOMOYUKI TSUCHIYA-SAMA

EVERYONE WHO
READ THIS
BOOK!

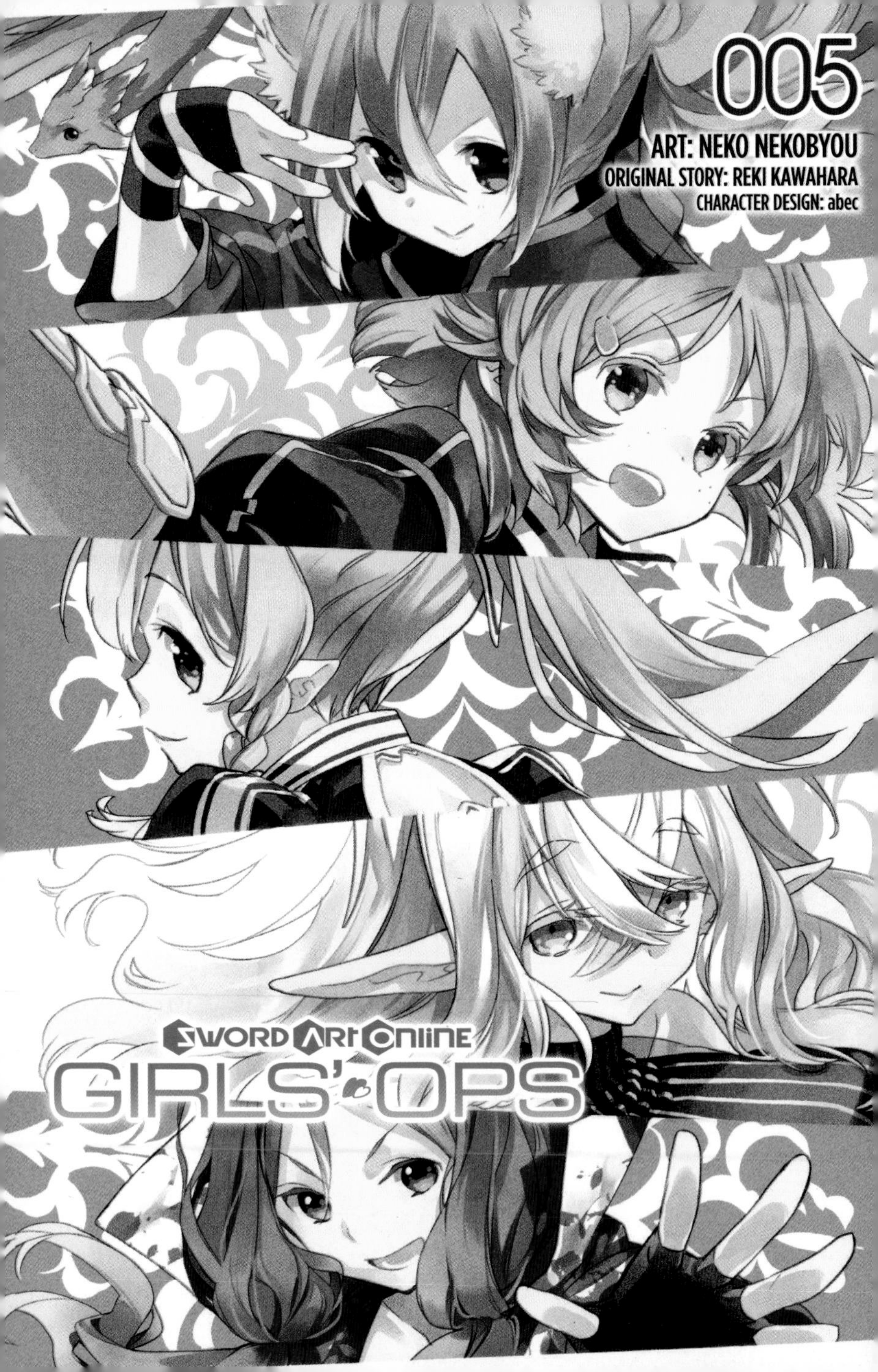
005
ART: NEKO NEKOBYOU
ORIGINAL STORY: REKI KAWAHARA
CHARACTER DESIGN: abec
SWORD ART ONLINE
GIRLS' OPS

005

SWORD ART ONLINE
GIRLS' OPERATIONS

art: Neko Nekobyou
original story: Reki Kawahara
character design: abec

Contents

KIRITO IS COOLEST WHEN...

SWORD ART ONLINE
GIRLS' OPS 005

SWORD ART ONLINE
GIRLS' OPERATIONS

ART: NEKO NEKOBYOU
ORIGINAL STORY: REKI KAWAHARA
CHARACTER DESIGN: abec

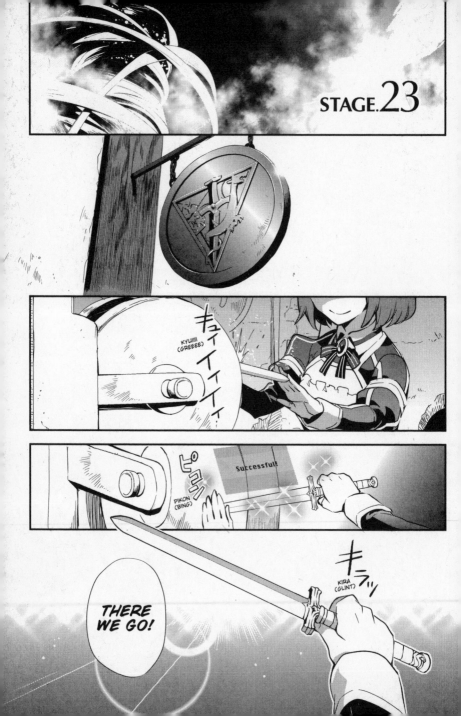

STAGE.23

KYUIIII
(GREEEE)

PIKON
(BING)

Successful!

KIRA
(GLINT)

THERE
WE GO!

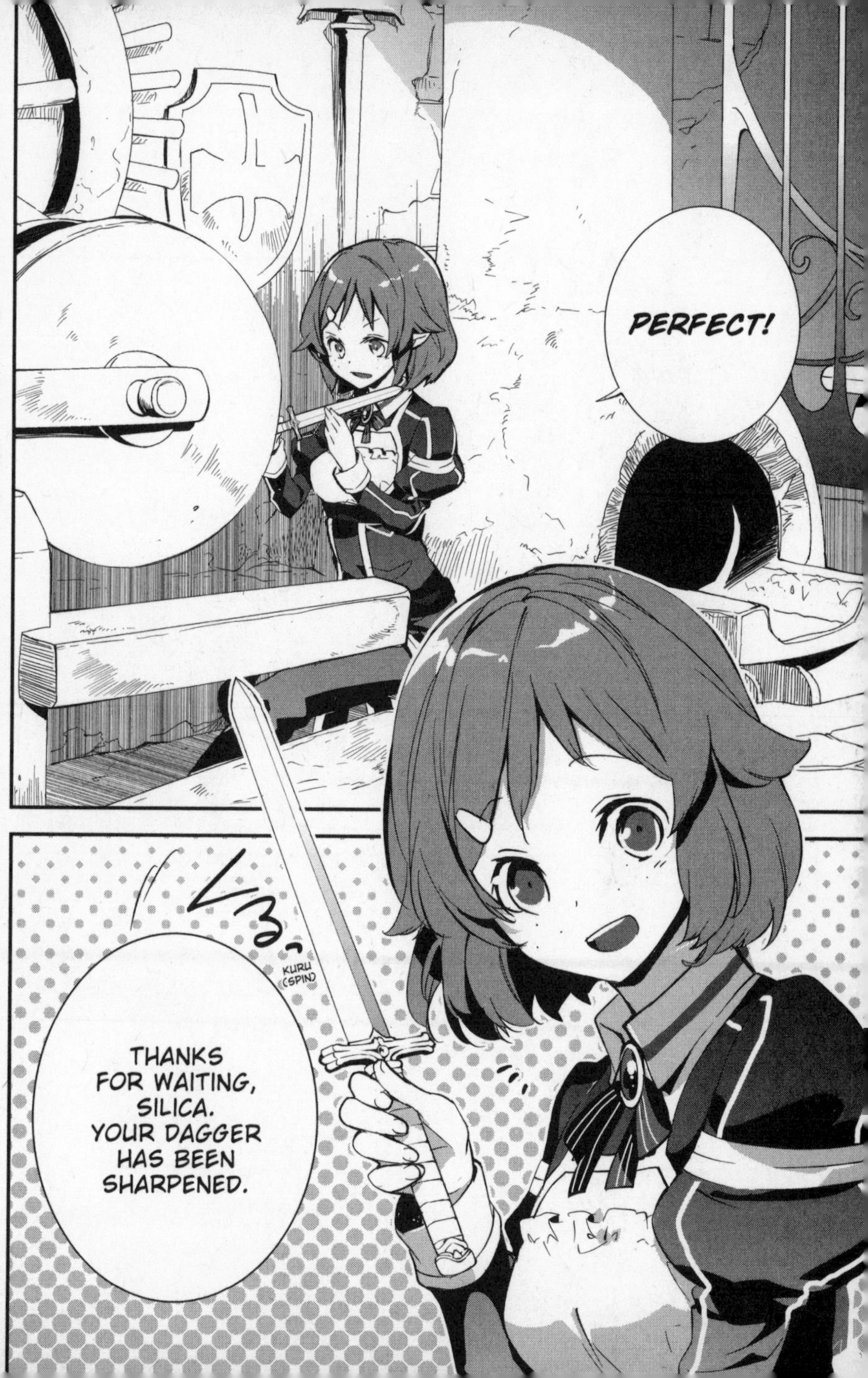
PERFECT!
KURU (SPIN)
THANKS FOR WAITING, SILICA. YOUR DAGGER HAS BEEN SHARPENED.

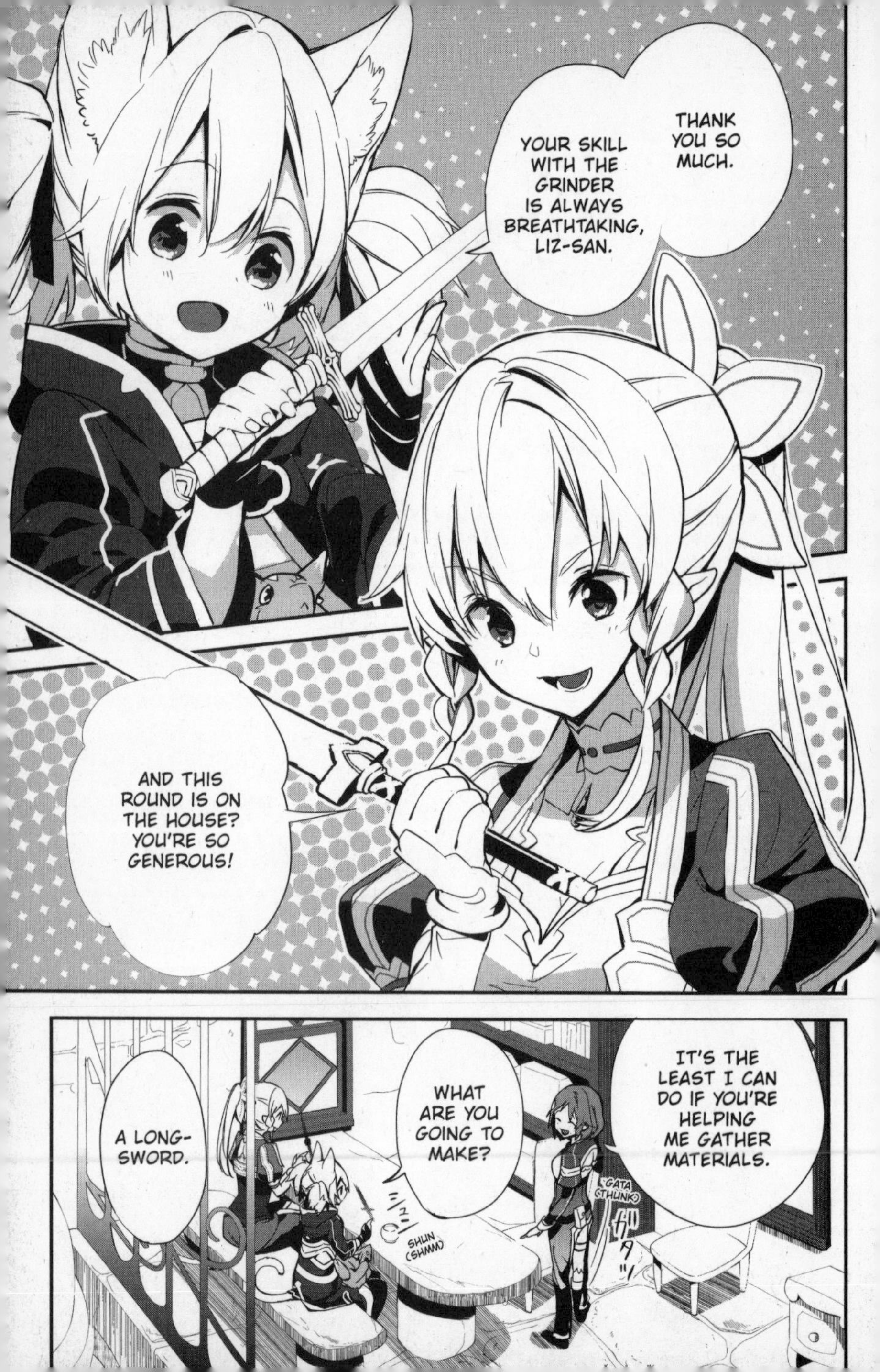
THANK YOU SO MUCH.
YOUR SKILL WITH THE GRINDER IS ALWAYS BREATHTAKING, LIZ-SAN.
AND THIS ROUND IS ON THE HOUSE? YOU'RE SO GENEROUS!
IT'S THE LEAST I CAN DO IF YOU'RE HELPING ME GATHER MATERIALS.
GATA (THUNK)
WHAT ARE YOU GOING TO MAKE?
SHUN (SHMM)
A LONG-SWORD.

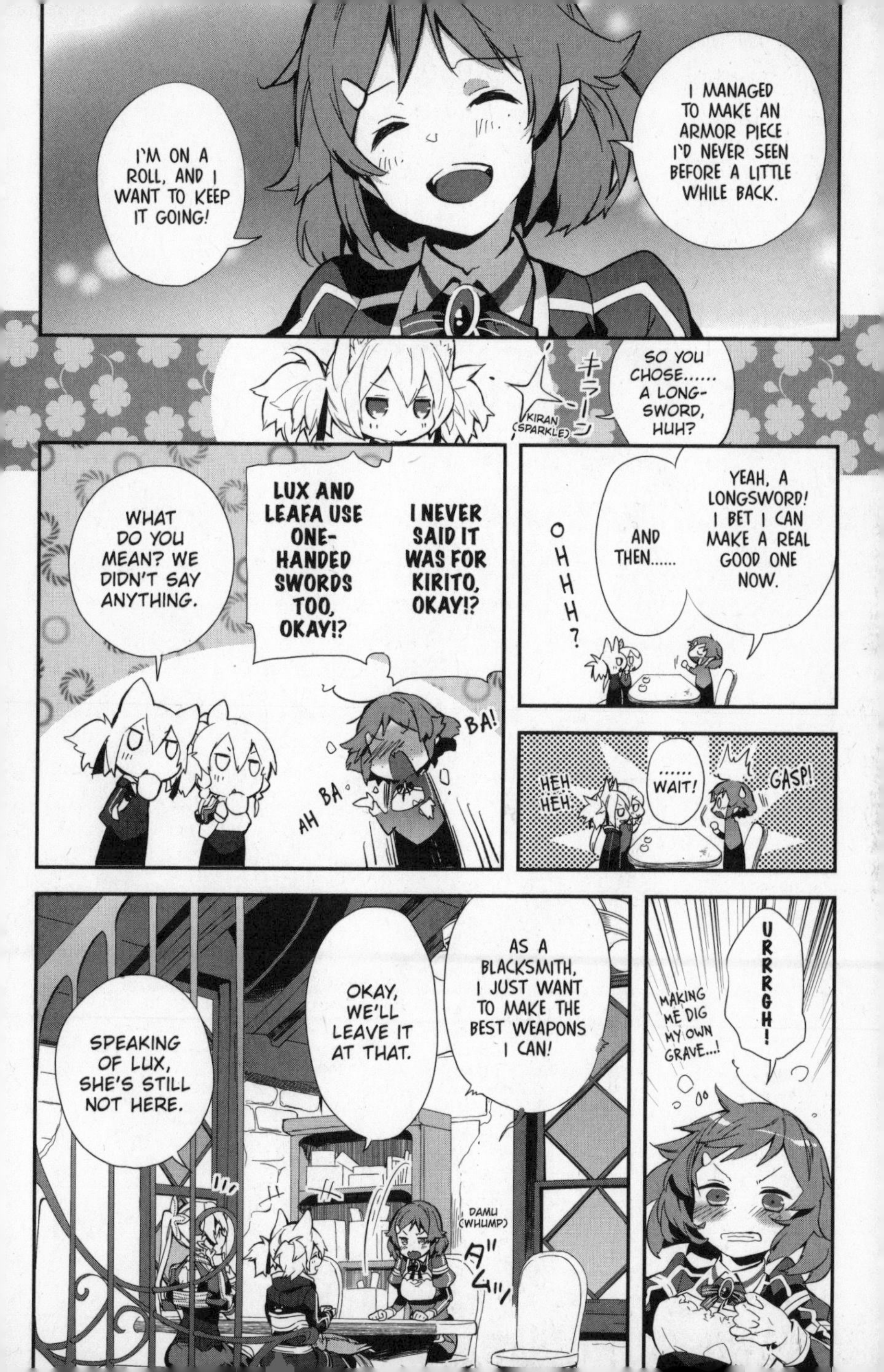
I MANAGED TO MAKE AN ARMOR PIECE I'D NEVER SEEN BEFORE A LITTLE WHILE BACK.
I'M ON A ROLL, AND I WANT TO KEEP IT GOING!
SO YOU CHOSE...... A LONG-SWORD, HUH?
KIRAN (SPARKLE)
YEAH, A LONGSWORD! I BET I CAN MAKE A REAL GOOD ONE NOW.
AND THEN......
OHHHH?
I NEVER SAID IT WAS FOR KIRITO, OKAY!?
LUX AND LEAFA USE ONE-HANDED SWORDS TOO, OKAY!?
WHAT DO YOU MEAN? WE DIDN'T SAY ANYTHING.
BA!
BA
AH
GASP!
......WAIT!
HEH HEH
URRRGH!
MAKING ME DIG MY OWN GRAVE...!
AS A BLACKSMITH, I JUST WANT TO MAKE THE BEST WEAPONS I CAN!
OKAY, WE'LL LEAVE IT AT THAT.
DAMU (WHUMP)
SPEAKING OF LUX, SHE'S STILL NOT HERE.

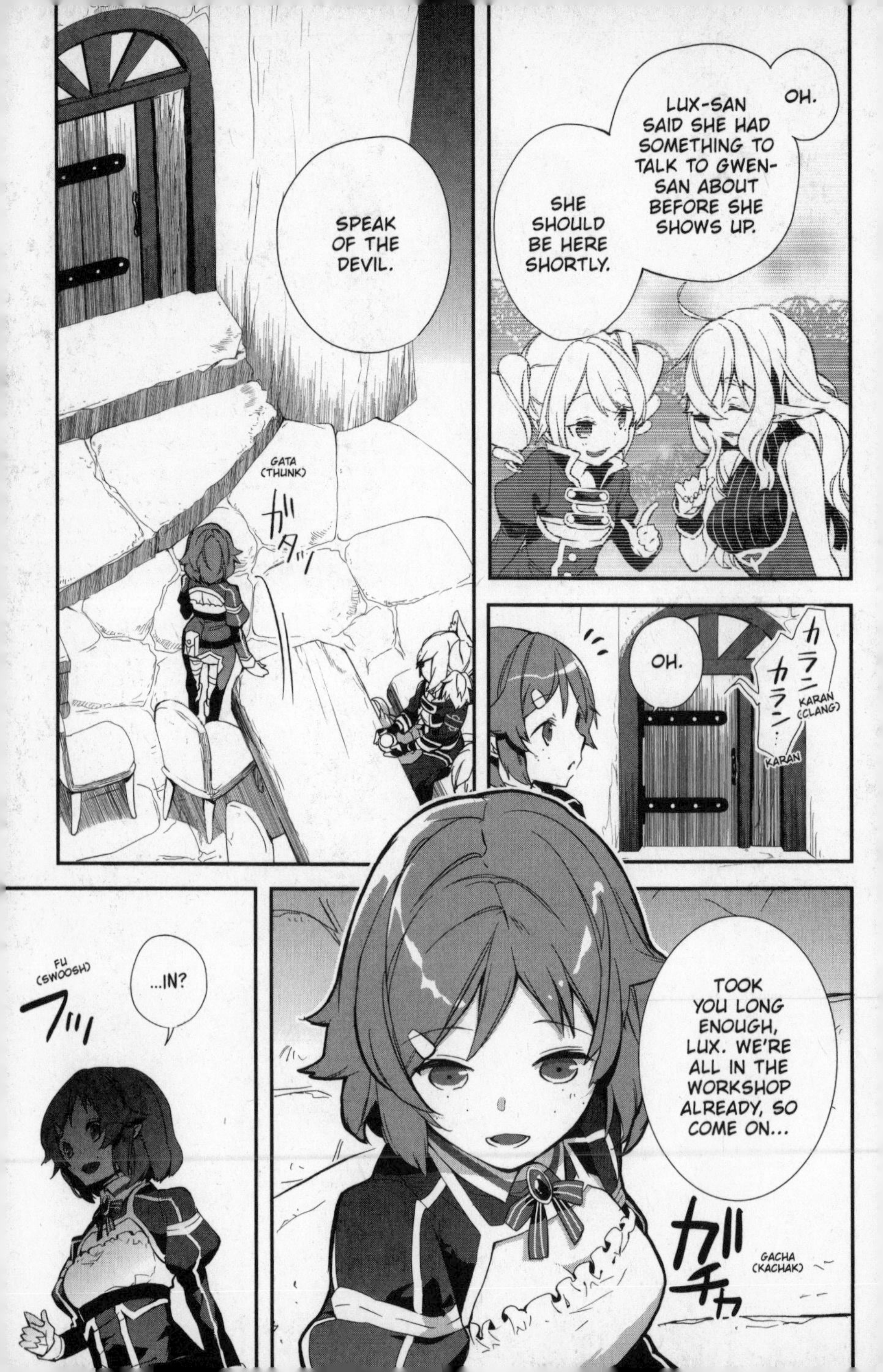

OH.
LUX-SAN SAID SHE HAD SOMETHING TO TALK TO GWEN-SAN ABOUT BEFORE SHE SHOWS UP.
SHE SHOULD BE HERE SHORTLY.
SPEAK OF THE DEVIL.
ガタッ
GATA (THUNK)
カラン カラン…
KARAN (CLANG)
KARAN
OH.
TOOK YOU LONG ENOUGH, LUX. WE'RE ALL IN THE WORKSHOP ALREADY, SO COME ON...
ガチャ
GACHA (KACHAK)
...IN?
フッ
FU (SWOOSH)

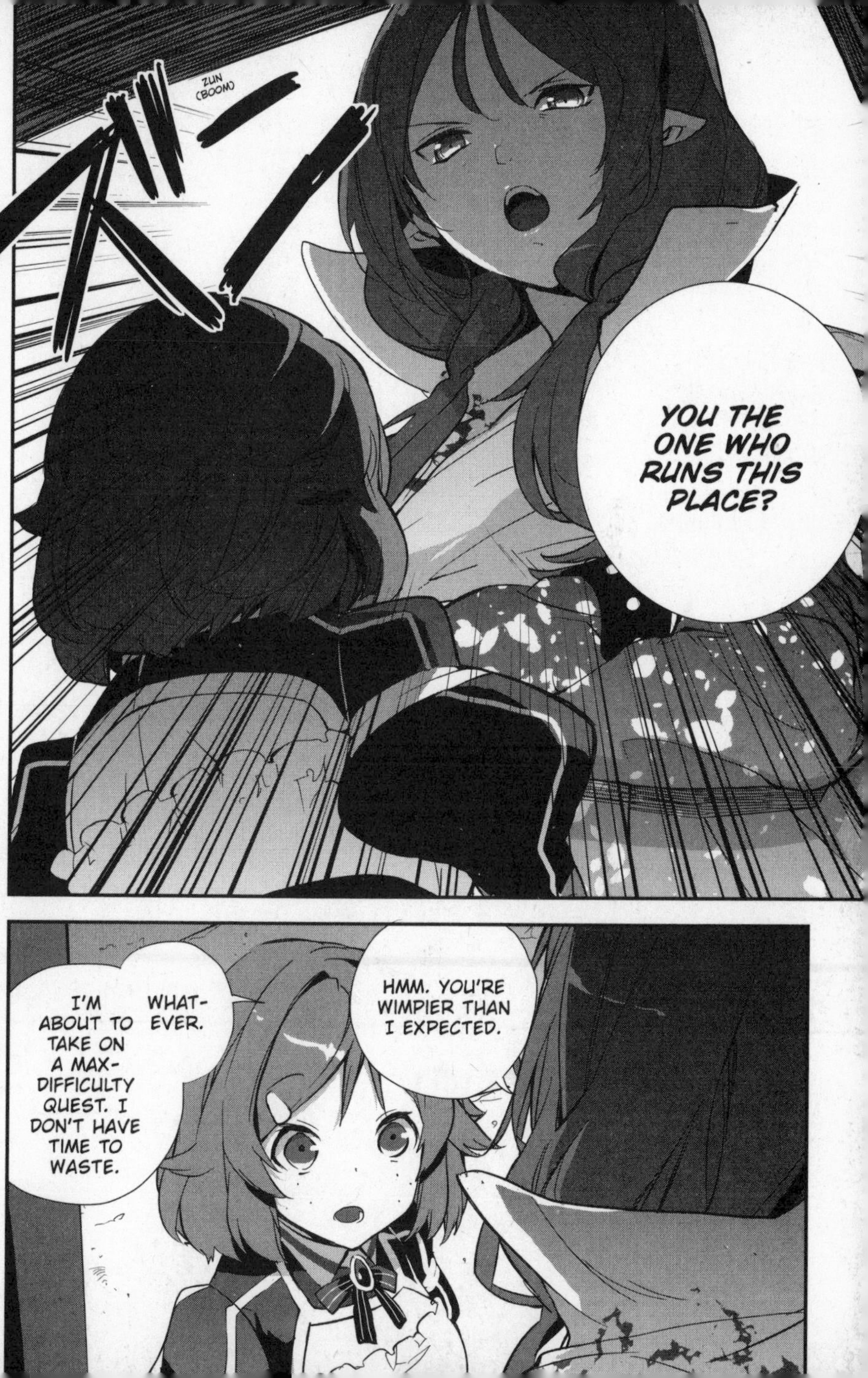
ZUN (BOOM)
YOU THE ONE WHO RUNS THIS PLACE?
HMM. YOU'RE WIMPIER THAN I EXPECTED.
WHAT-EVER.
I'M ABOUT TO TAKE ON A MAX-DIFFICULTY QUEST. I DON'T HAVE TIME TO WASTE.

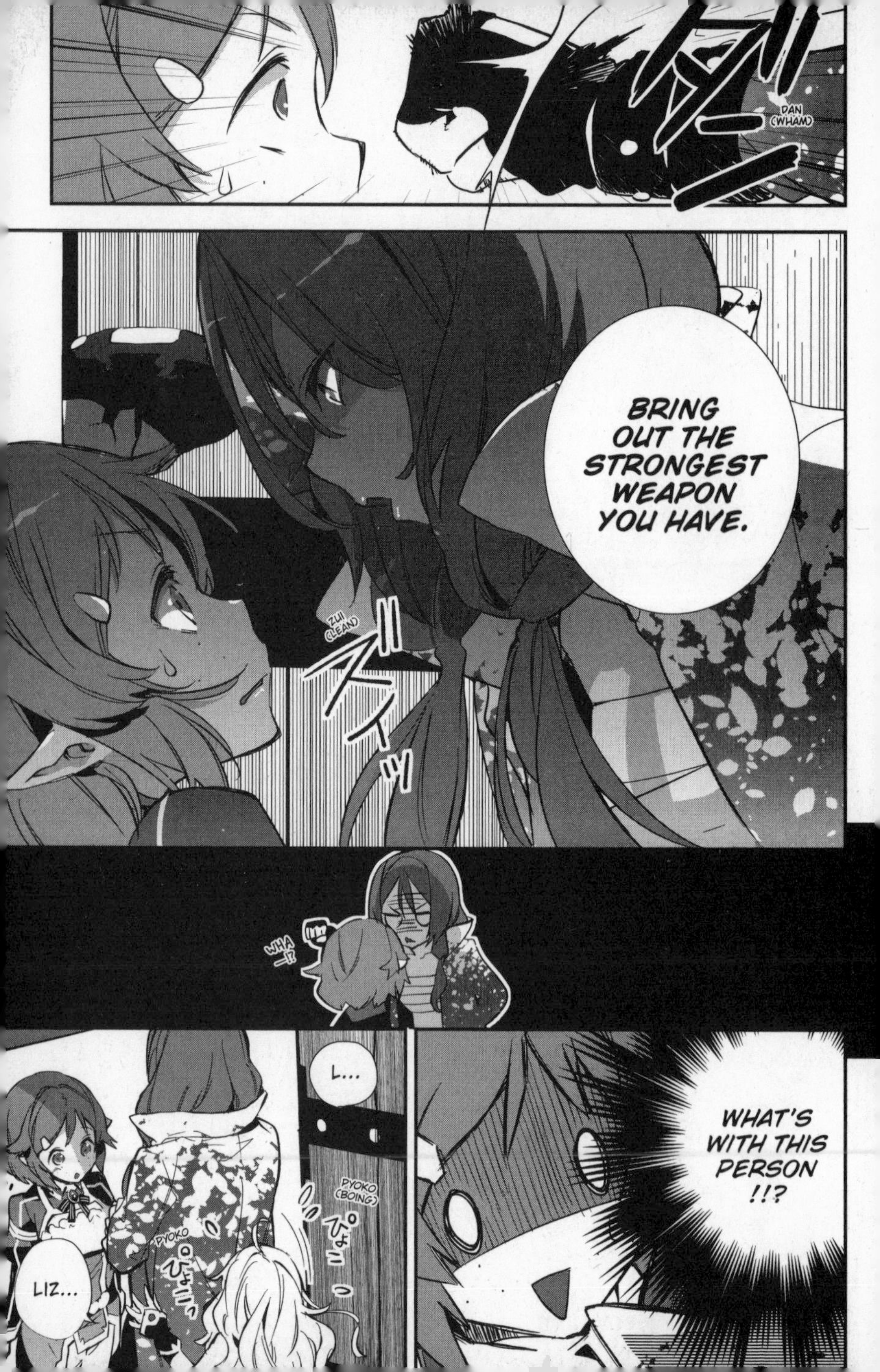

DAN (WHAM)
BRING OUT THE STRONGEST WEAPON YOU HAVE.
ZUI (LEAN)
WHA—!?
WHAT'S WITH THIS PERSON !!?
L...
PYOKO (BOING)
PYOKO
LIZ...

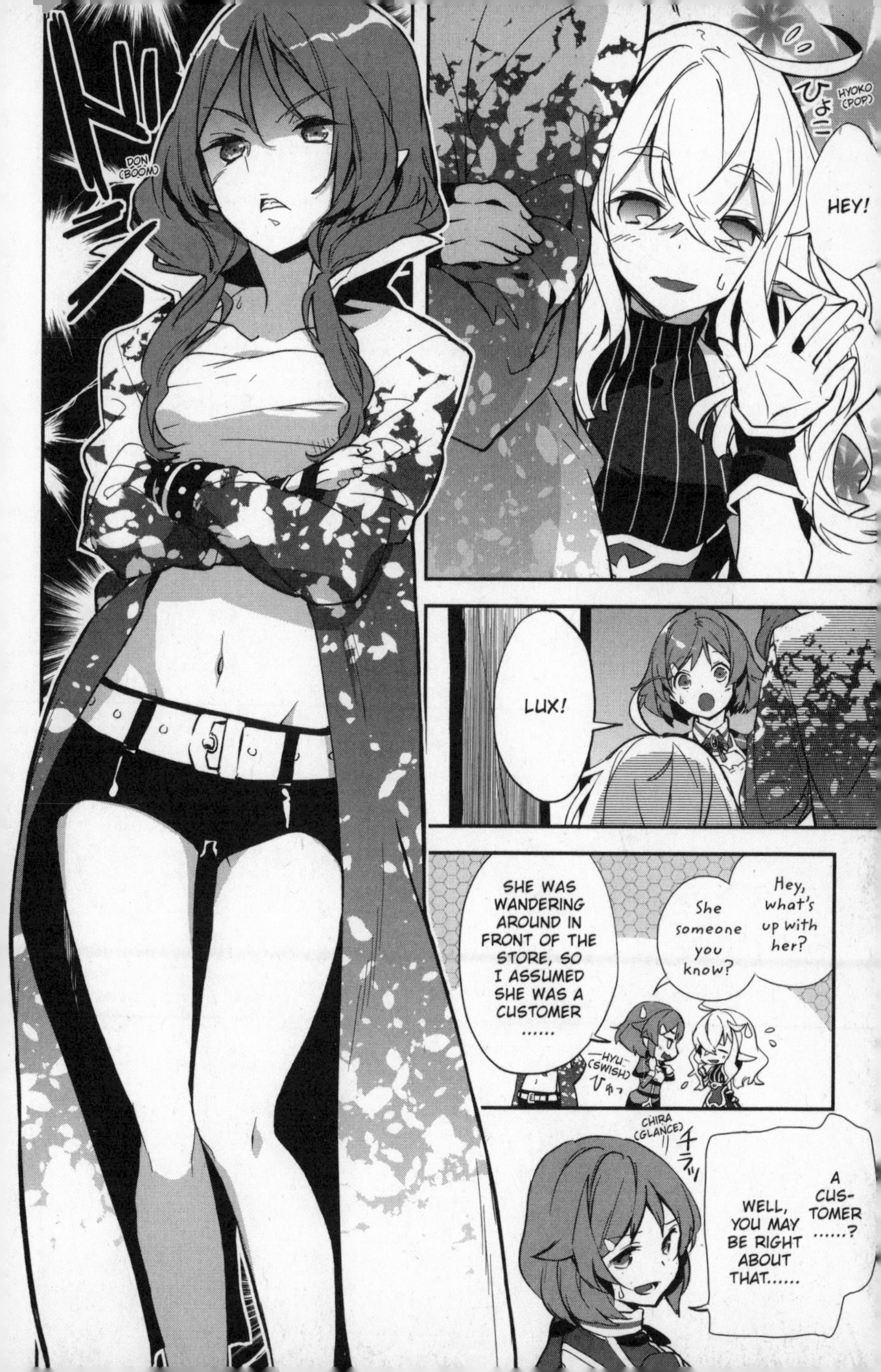
HYOKO (POP)
HEY!
DON (BOOM)
LUX!
Hey, what's up with her?
She someone you know?
SHE WAS WANDERING AROUND IN FRONT OF THE STORE, SO I ASSUMED SHE WAS A CUSTOMER ......
HYU (SWISH)
CHIRA (GLANCE)
A CUS-TOMER ......?
WELL, YOU MAY BE RIGHT ABOUT THAT......

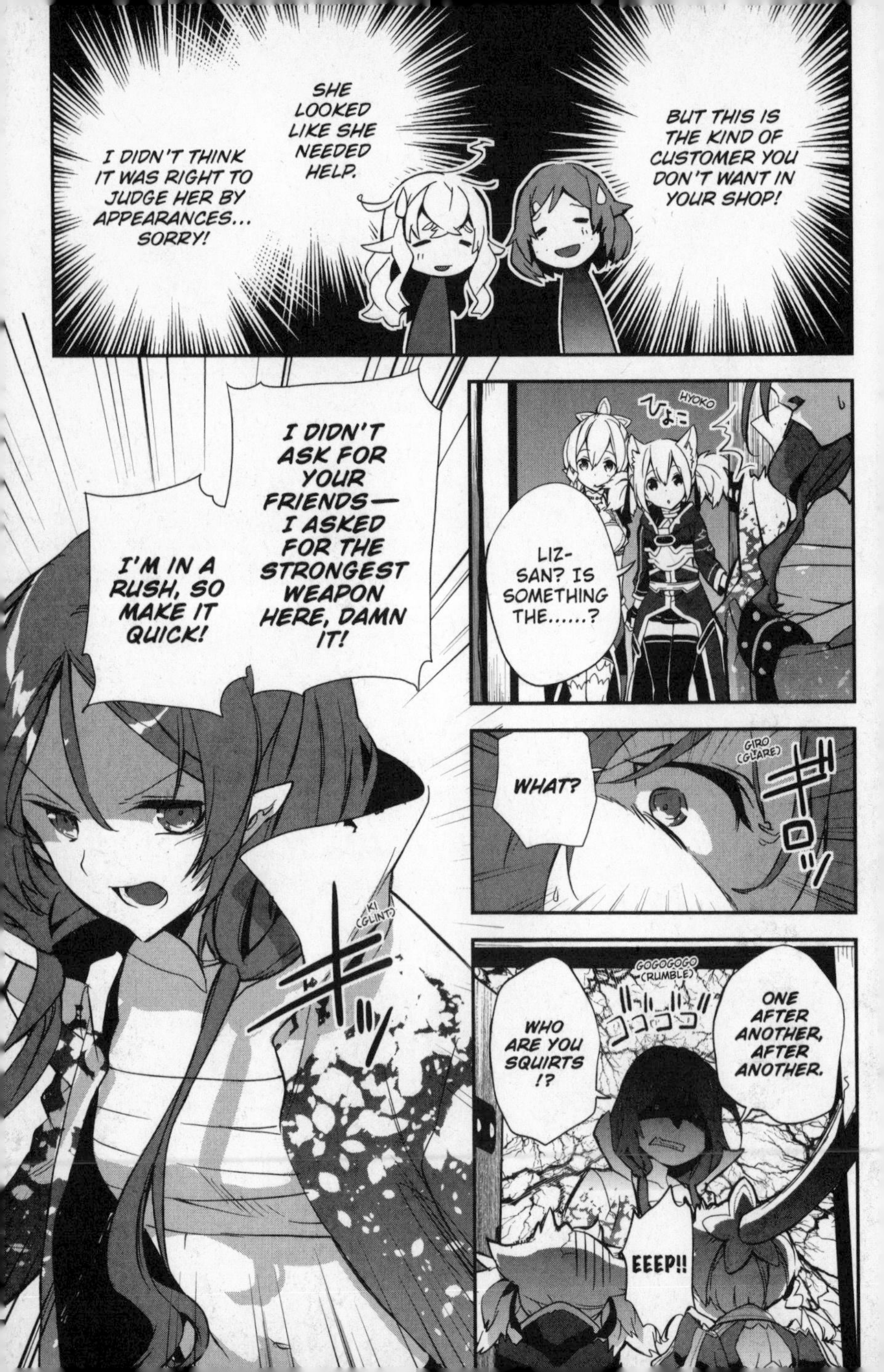
BUT THIS IS THE KIND OF CUSTOMER YOU DON'T WANT IN YOUR SHOP!
SHE LOOKED LIKE SHE NEEDED HELP.
I DIDN'T THINK IT WAS RIGHT TO JUDGE HER BY APPEARANCES... SORRY!
HYOKO
LIZ-SAN? IS SOMETHING THE......?
I DIDN'T ASK FOR YOUR FRIENDS— I ASKED FOR THE STRONGEST WEAPON HERE, DAMN IT!
I'M IN A RUSH, SO MAKE IT QUICK!
GIRO (GLARE)
WHAT?
KI (GLINT)
GOGOGOGO (RUMBLE)
ONE AFTER ANOTHER, AFTER ANOTHER.
WHO ARE YOU SQUIRTS!?
EEEP!!

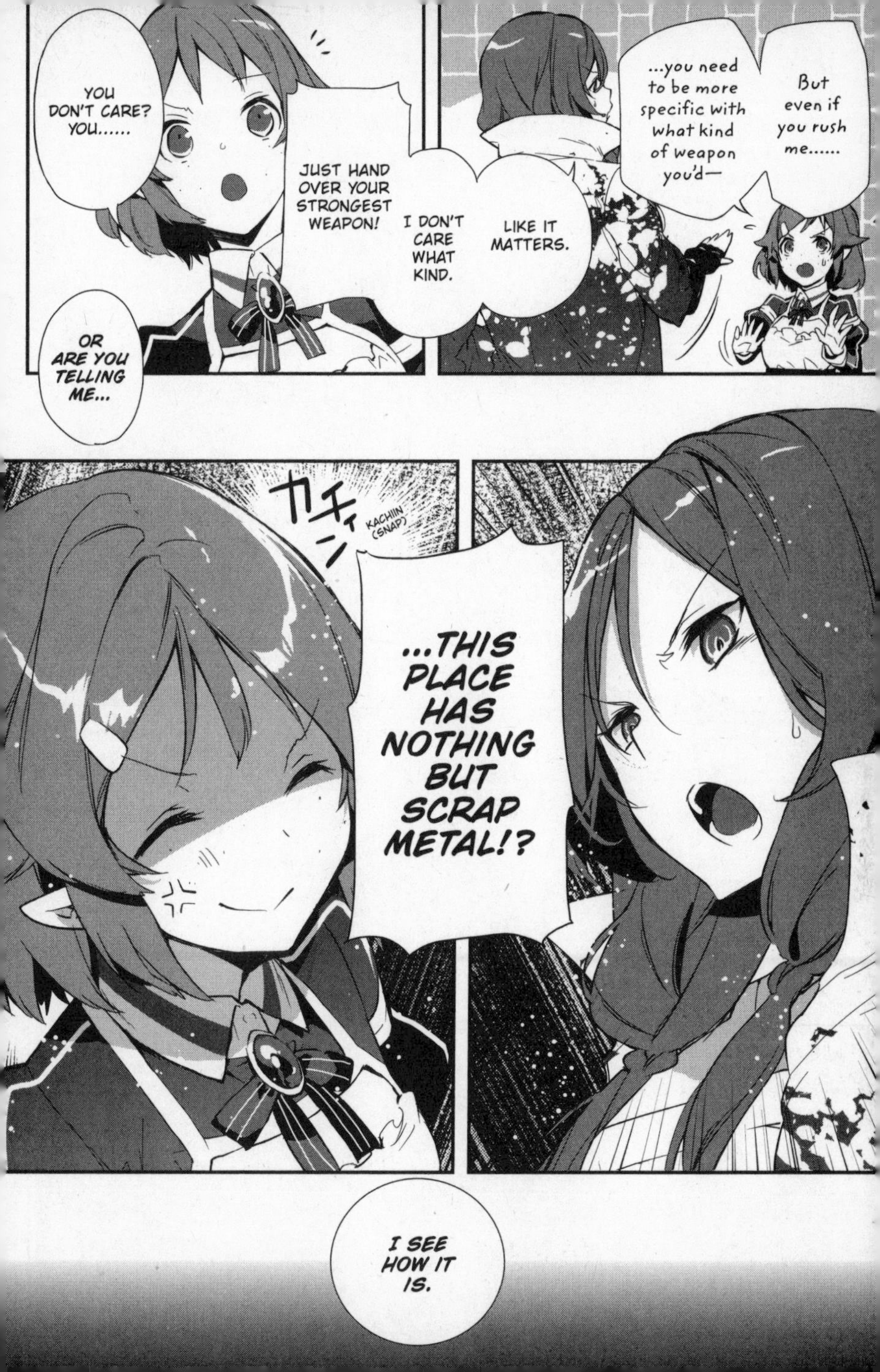
But even if you rush me......
...you need to be more specific with what kind of weapon you'd—
LIKE IT MATTERS.
I DON'T CARE WHAT KIND.
JUST HAND OVER YOUR STRONGEST WEAPON!
YOU DON'T CARE? YOU......
OR ARE YOU TELLING ME...
カチィン
KACHIIN (SNAP)
...THIS PLACE HAS NOTHING BUT SCRAP METAL!?
I SEE HOW IT IS.

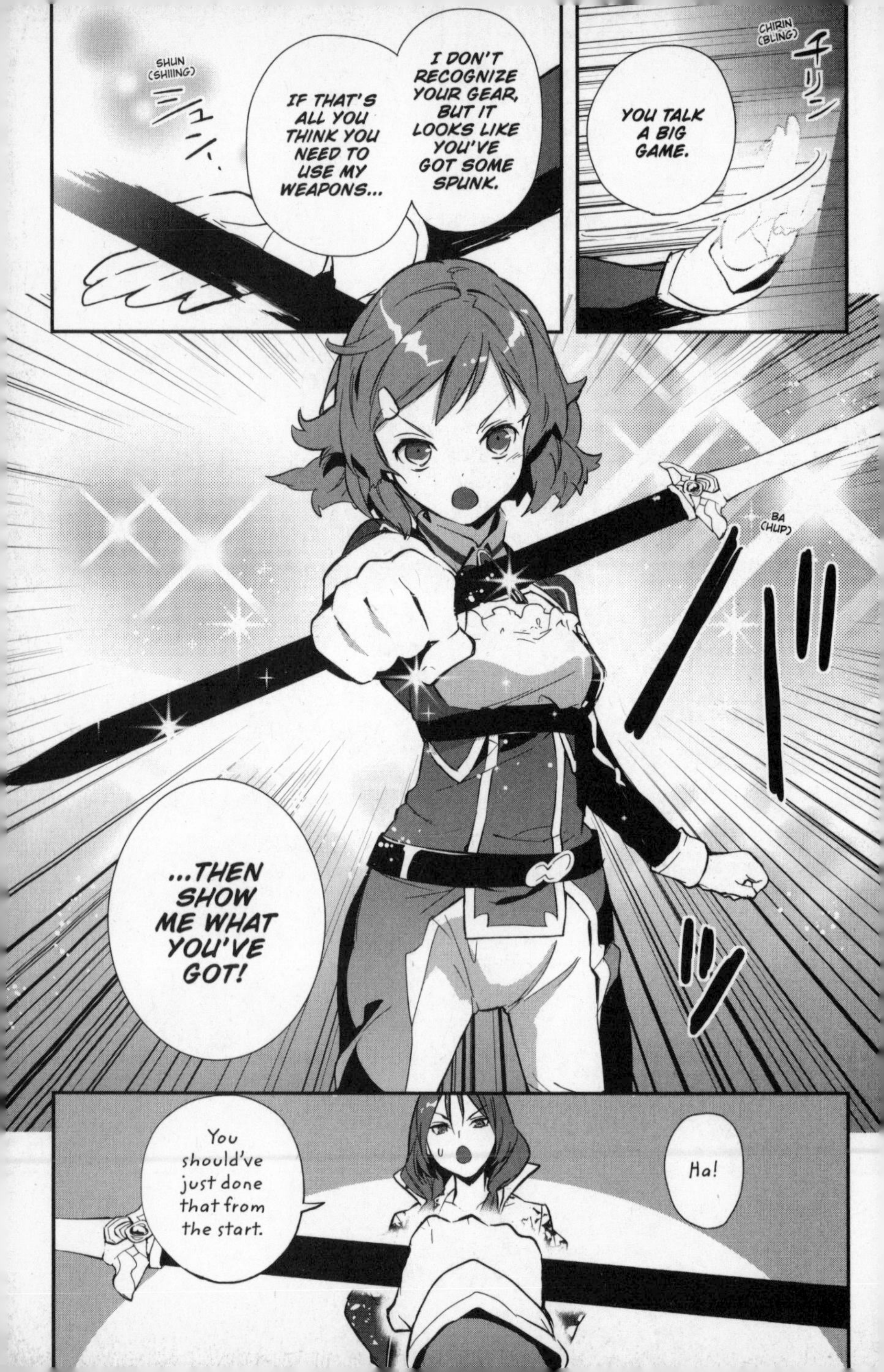

CHIRIN (BLING)
チリン
YOU TALK A BIG GAME.
I DON'T RECOGNIZE YOUR GEAR, BUT IT LOOKS LIKE YOU'VE GOT SOME SPUNK.
IF THAT'S ALL YOU THINK YOU NEED TO USE MY WEAPONS...
SHUN (SHIIING)
シュン
...THEN SHOW ME WHAT YOU'VE GOT!
BA (HUP)
バッ
Ha!
You should've just done that from the start.

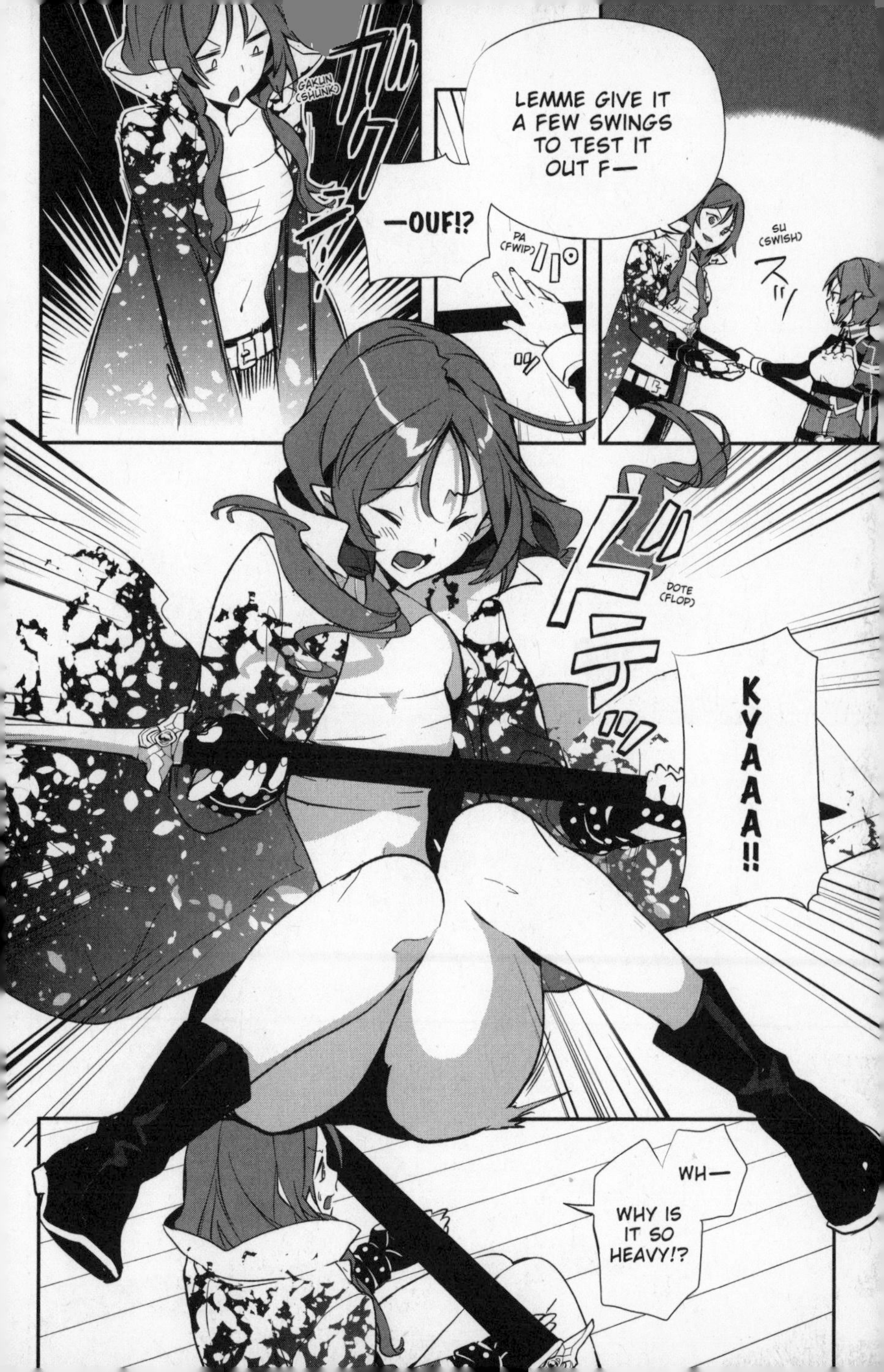
LEMME GIVE IT A FEW SWINGS TO TEST IT OUT F—
SU (SWISH)
PA (FWIP)
—OUF!?
GAKUN (SHUNK)
DOTE (FLOP)
KYAAA!!
WH—
WHY IS IT SO HEAVY!?

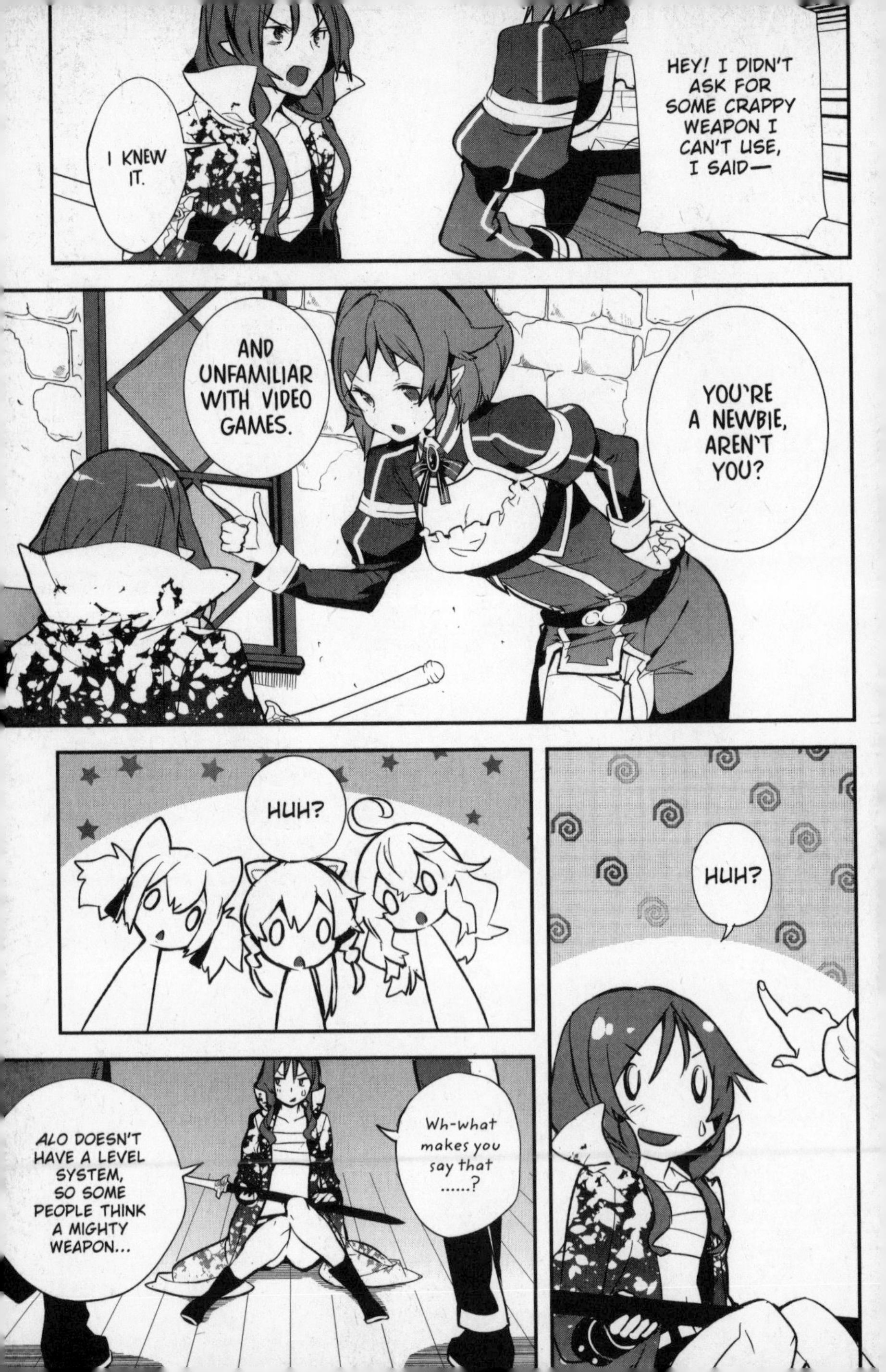
HEY! I DIDN'T ASK FOR SOME CRAPPY WEAPON I CAN'T USE, I SAID—
I KNEW IT.
YOU'RE A NEWBIE, AREN'T YOU?
AND UNFAMILIAR WITH VIDEO GAMES.
HUH?
HUH?
Wh-what makes you say that......?
ALO DOESN'T HAVE A LEVEL SYSTEM, SO SOME PEOPLE THINK A MIGHTY WEAPON...

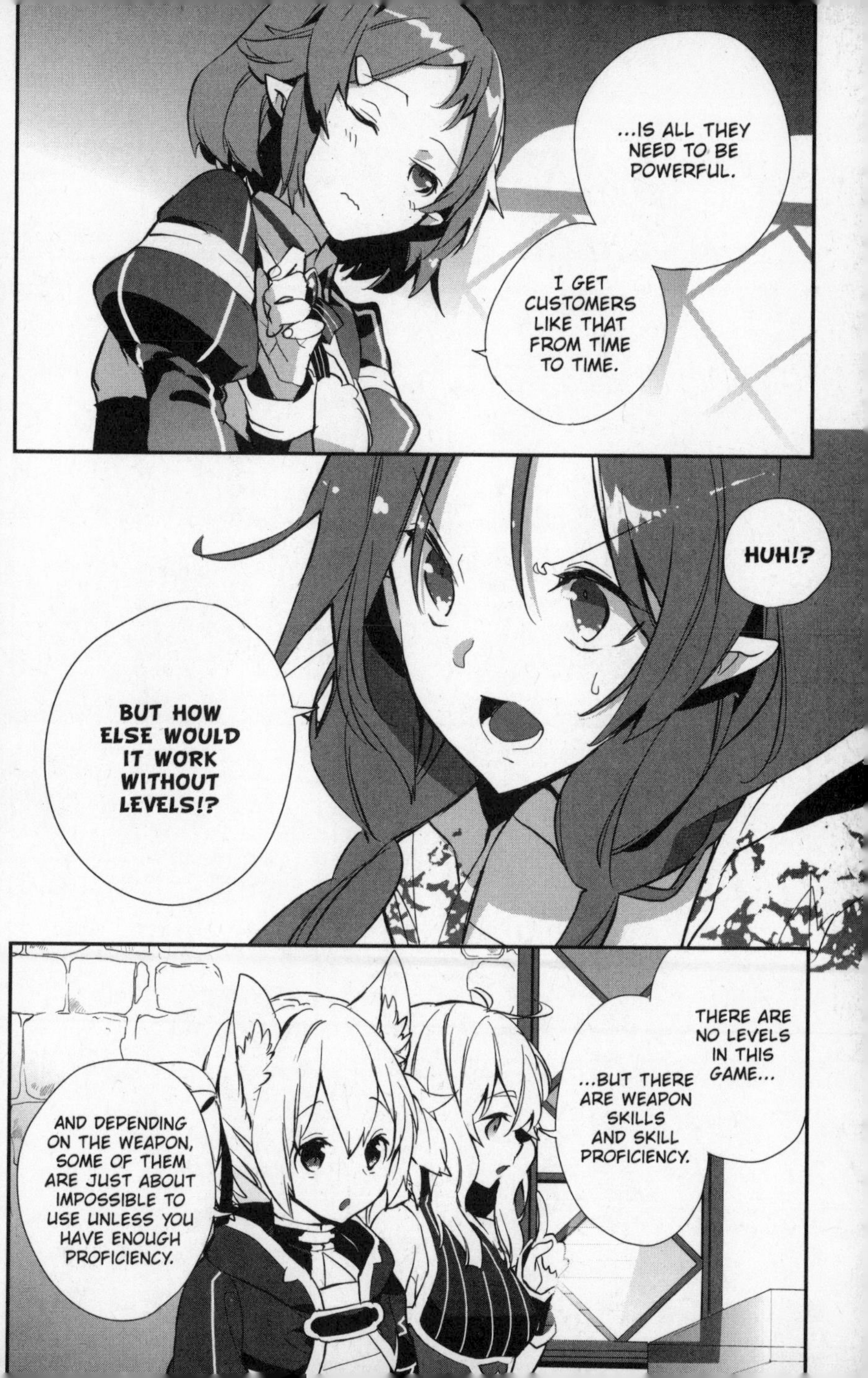
...IS ALL THEY NEED TO BE POWERFUL.
I GET CUSTOMERS LIKE THAT FROM TIME TO TIME.
HUH!?
BUT HOW ELSE WOULD IT WORK WITHOUT LEVELS!?
THERE ARE NO LEVELS IN THIS GAME...
...BUT THERE ARE WEAPON SKILLS AND SKILL PROFICIENCY.
AND DEPENDING ON THE WEAPON, SOME OF THEM ARE JUST ABOUT IMPOSSIBLE TO USE UNLESS YOU HAVE ENOUGH PROFICIENCY.

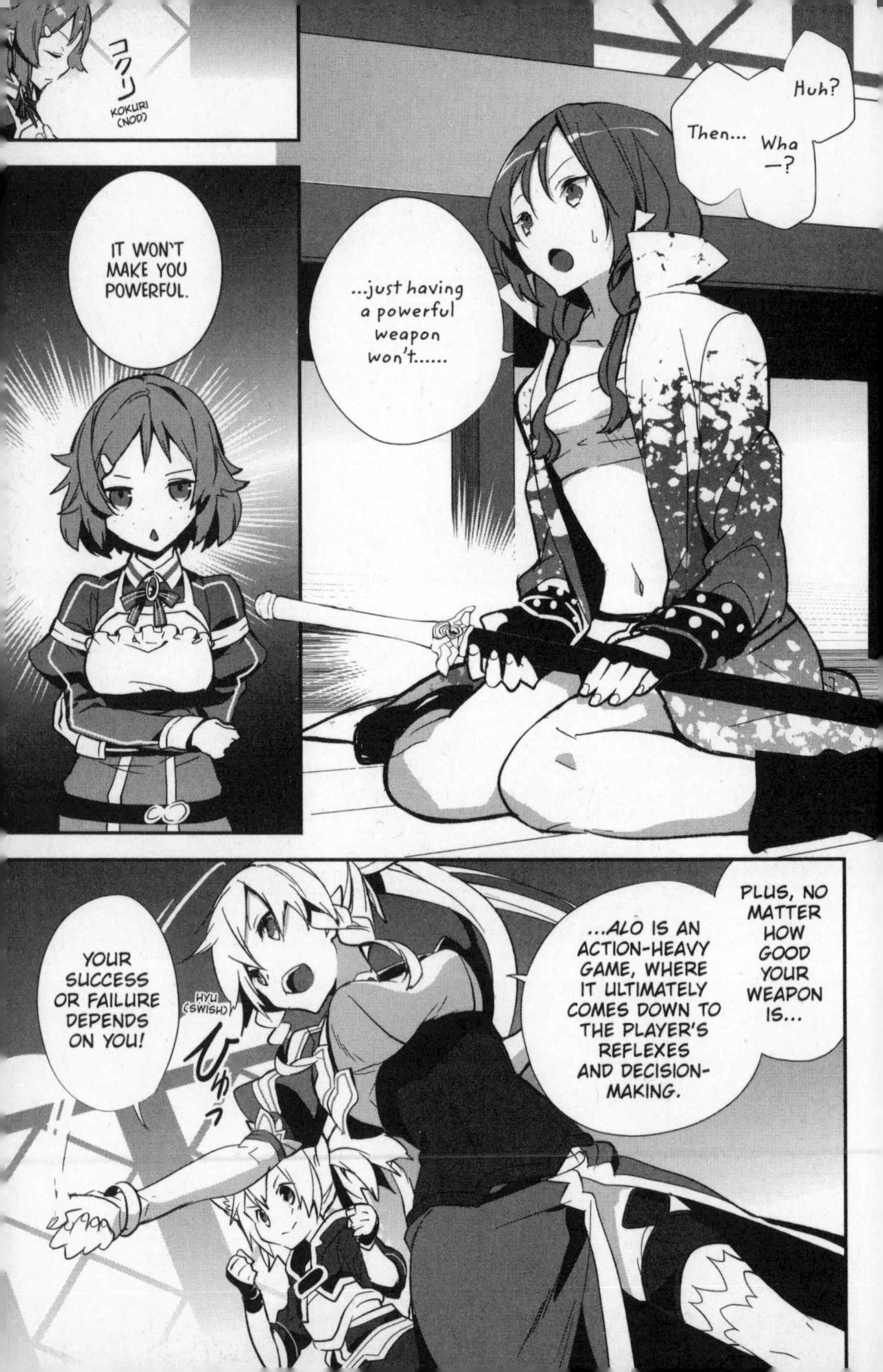
コクリ
KOKURI (NOD)
Huh?
Wha—?
Then...
...just having a powerful weapon won't......
IT WON'T MAKE YOU POWERFUL.
PLUS, NO MATTER HOW GOOD YOUR WEAPON IS...
...ALO IS AN ACTION-HEAVY GAME, WHERE IT ULTIMATELY COMES DOWN TO THE PLAYER'S REFLEXES AND DECISION-MAKING.
HYU (SWISH)
YOUR SUCCESS OR FAILURE DEPENDS ON YOU!

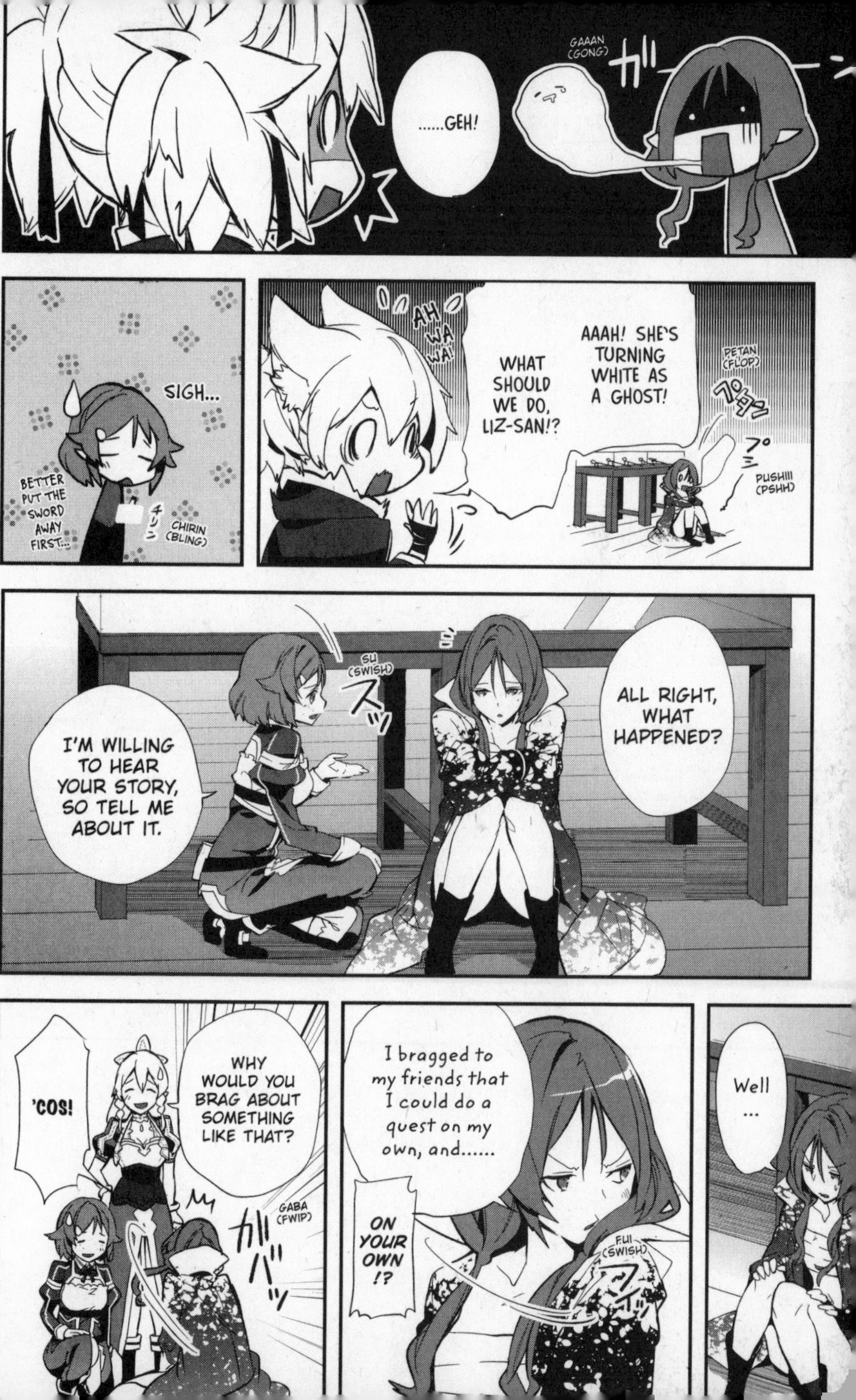
GAAAN (GONG)
......GEH!
AAAH! SHE'S TURNING WHITE AS A GHOST!
WHAT SHOULD WE DO, LIZ-SAN!?
AH WA WA!
PETAN (FLOP)
PUSHIII (PSHH)
SIGH...
BETTER PUT THE SWORD AWAY FIRST...
CHIRIN (BLING)
ALL RIGHT, WHAT HAPPENED?
SU (SWISH)
I'M WILLING TO HEAR YOUR STORY, SO TELL ME ABOUT IT.
Well ...
I bragged to my friends that I could do a quest on my own, and......
FUI (SWISH)
ON YOUR OWN!?
WHY WOULD YOU BRAG ABOUT SOMETHING LIKE THAT?
GABA (FWIP)
'COS!

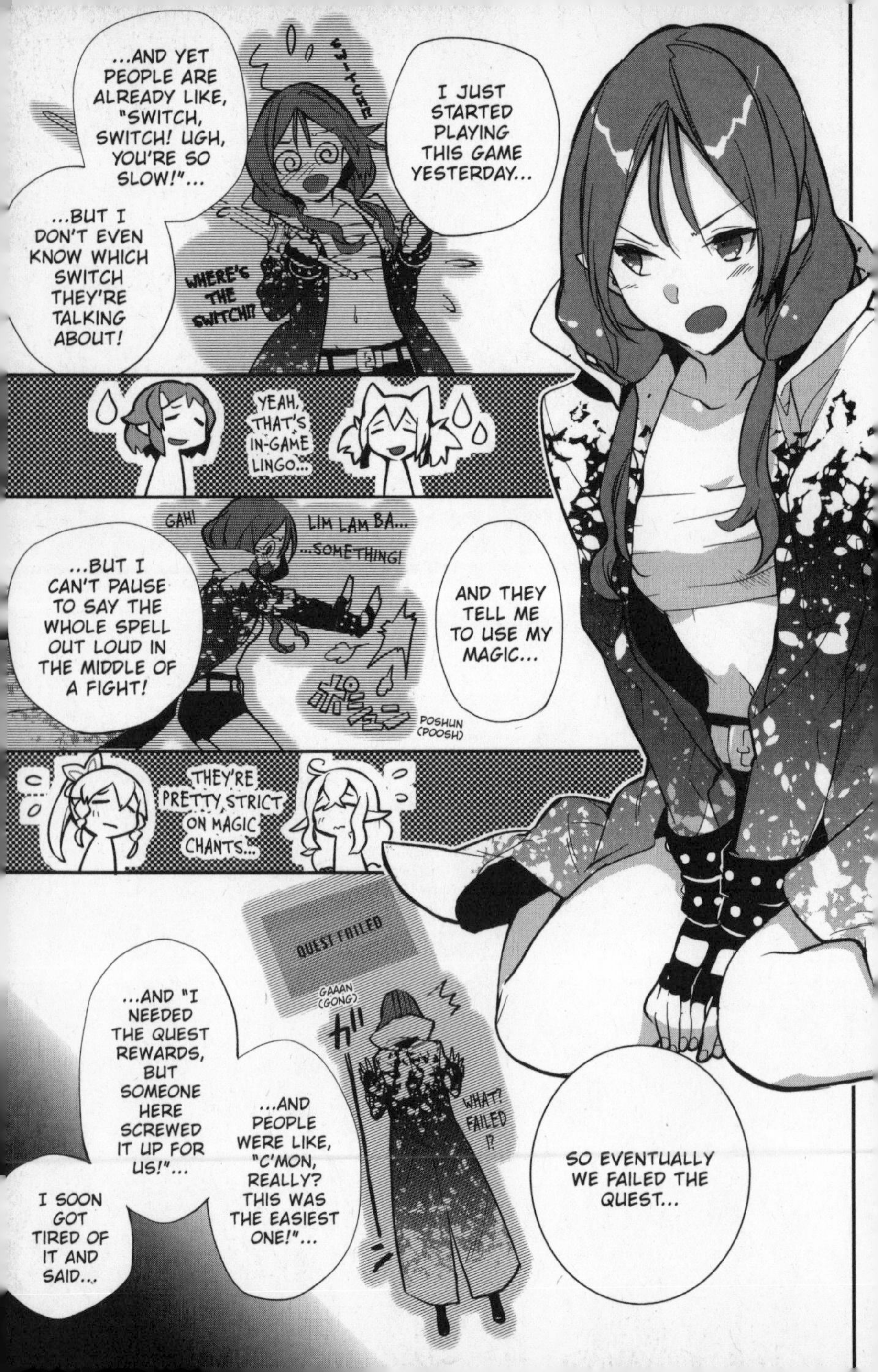
I JUST STARTED PLAYING THIS GAME YESTERDAY...
...AND YET PEOPLE ARE ALREADY LIKE, "SWITCH, SWITCH! UGH, YOU'RE SO SLOW!"...
...BUT I DON'T EVEN KNOW WHICH SWITCH THEY'RE TALKING ABOUT!
WHERE'S THE SWITCH!?
YEAH, THAT'S IN-GAME LINGO...
AND THEY TELL ME TO USE MY MAGIC...
GAH!
LIM LAM BA... ...SOMETHING!
...BUT I CAN'T PAUSE TO SAY THE WHOLE SPELL OUT LOUD IN THE MIDDLE OF A FIGHT!
POSHUN (POOSH)
THEY'RE PRETTY STRICT ON MAGIC CHANTS...
QUEST FAILED
SO EVENTUALLY WE FAILED THE QUEST...
GAAAN (GONG)
WHAT? FAILED !?
...AND PEOPLE WERE LIKE, "C'MON, REALLY? THIS WAS THE EASIEST ONE!"...
...AND "I NEEDED THE QUEST REWARDS, BUT SOMEONE HERE SCREWED IT UP FOR US!"...
I SOON GOT TIRED OF IT AND SAID...

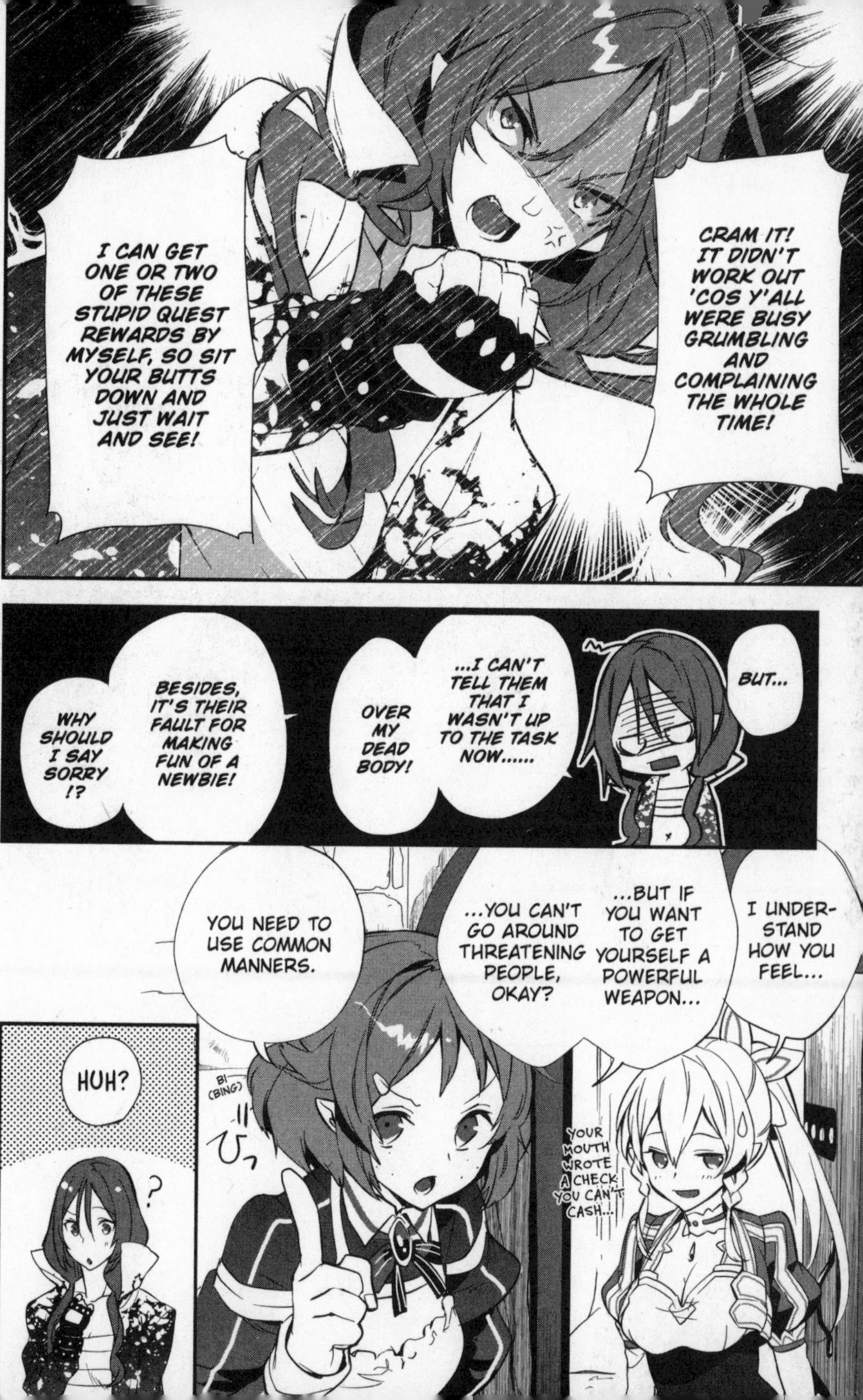
CRAM IT! IT DIDN'T WORK OUT 'COS Y'ALL WERE BUSY GRUMBLING AND COMPLAINING THE WHOLE TIME!
I CAN GET ONE OR TWO OF THESE STUPID QUEST REWARDS BY MYSELF, SO SIT YOUR BUTTS DOWN AND JUST WAIT AND SEE!
BUT...
...I CAN'T TELL THEM THAT I WASN'T UP TO THE TASK NOW......
OVER MY DEAD BODY!
BESIDES, IT'S THEIR FAULT FOR MAKING FUN OF A NEWBIE!
WHY SHOULD I SAY SORRY!?
I UNDER-STAND HOW YOU FEEL...
...BUT IF YOU WANT TO GET YOURSELF A POWERFUL WEAPON...
...YOU CAN'T GO AROUND THREATENING PEOPLE, OKAY?
YOU NEED TO USE COMMON MANNERS.
YOUR MOUTH WROTE A CHECK YOU CAN'T CASH...
BI (BING)
HUH?

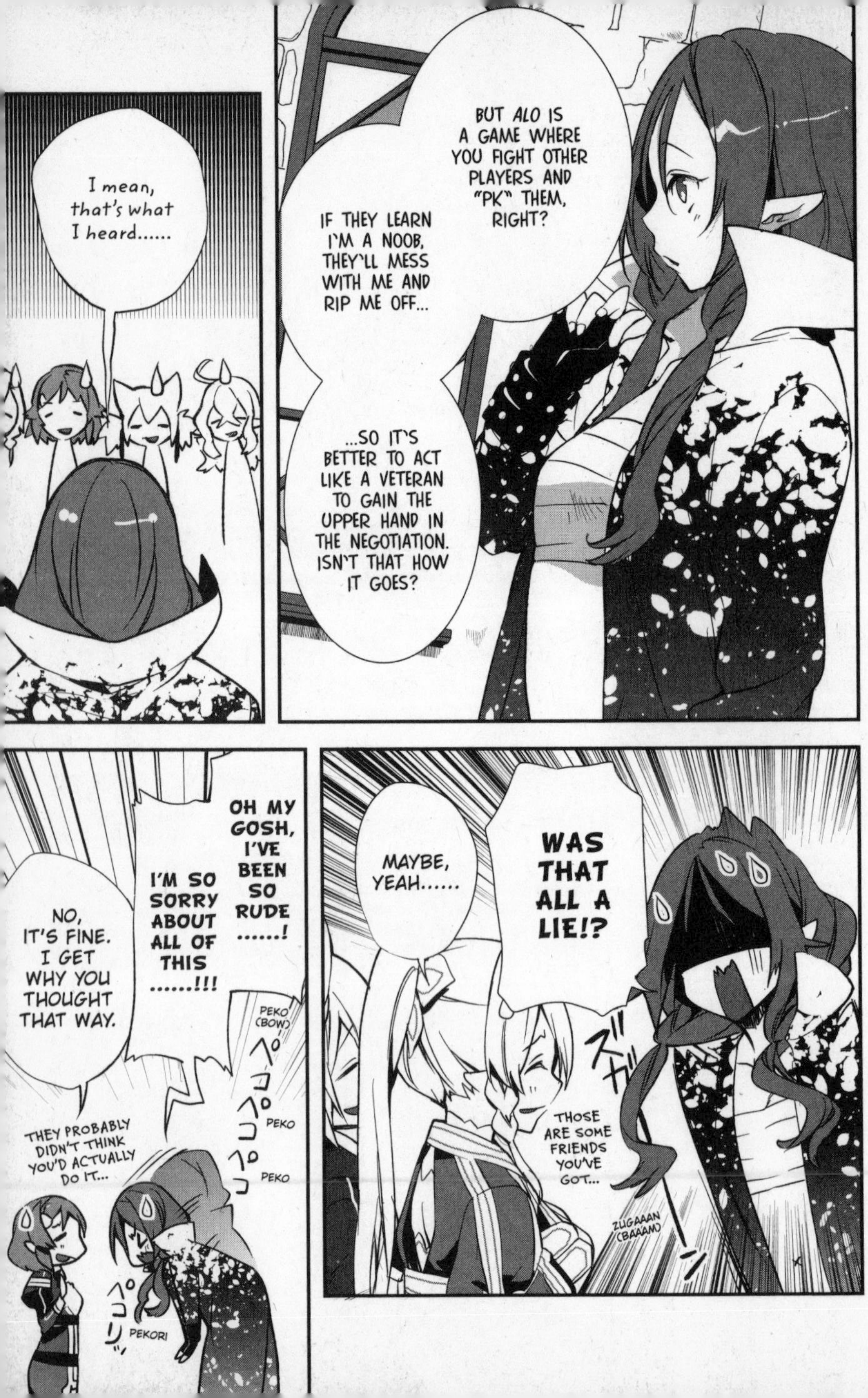
BUT ALO IS A GAME WHERE YOU FIGHT OTHER PLAYERS AND "PK" THEM, RIGHT?
IF THEY LEARN I'M A NOOB, THEY'LL MESS WITH ME AND RIP ME OFF...
...SO IT'S BETTER TO ACT LIKE A VETERAN TO GAIN THE UPPER HAND IN THE NEGOTIATION. ISN'T THAT HOW IT GOES?
I mean, that's what I heard......
WAS THAT ALL A LIE!?
MAYBE, YEAH......
ZUGAAAN (BAAAM)
THOSE ARE SOME FRIENDS YOU'VE GOT...
OH MY GOSH, I'VE BEEN SO RUDE ......!
I'M SO SORRY ABOUT ALL OF THIS ......!!!
PEKO (BOW)
PEKO
PEKO
NO, IT'S FINE. I GET WHY YOU THOUGHT THAT WAY.
THEY PROBABLY DIDN'T THINK YOU'D ACTUALLY DO IT...
PEKORI

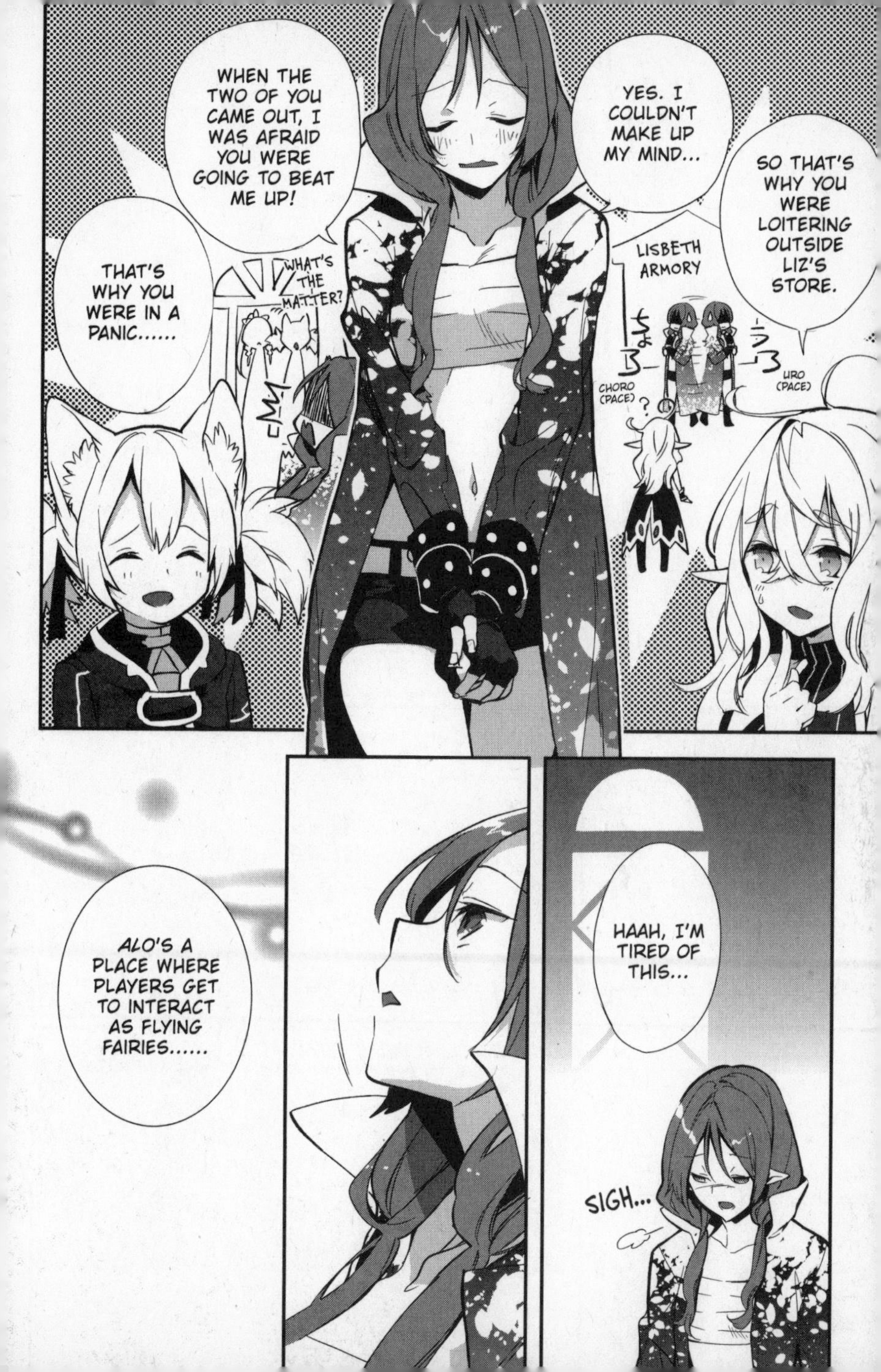
YES. I COULDN'T MAKE UP MY MIND...
SO THAT'S WHY YOU WERE LOITERING OUTSIDE LIZ'S STORE.
LISBETH ARMORY
URO (PACE)
CHORO (PACE)
?
WHEN THE TWO OF YOU CAME OUT, I WAS AFRAID YOU WERE GOING TO BEAT ME UP!
WHAT'S THE MATTER?
THAT'S WHY YOU WERE IN A PANIC......
HAAH, I'M TIRED OF THIS...
SIGH...
ALO'S A PLACE WHERE PLAYERS GET TO INTERACT AS FLYING FAIRIES......

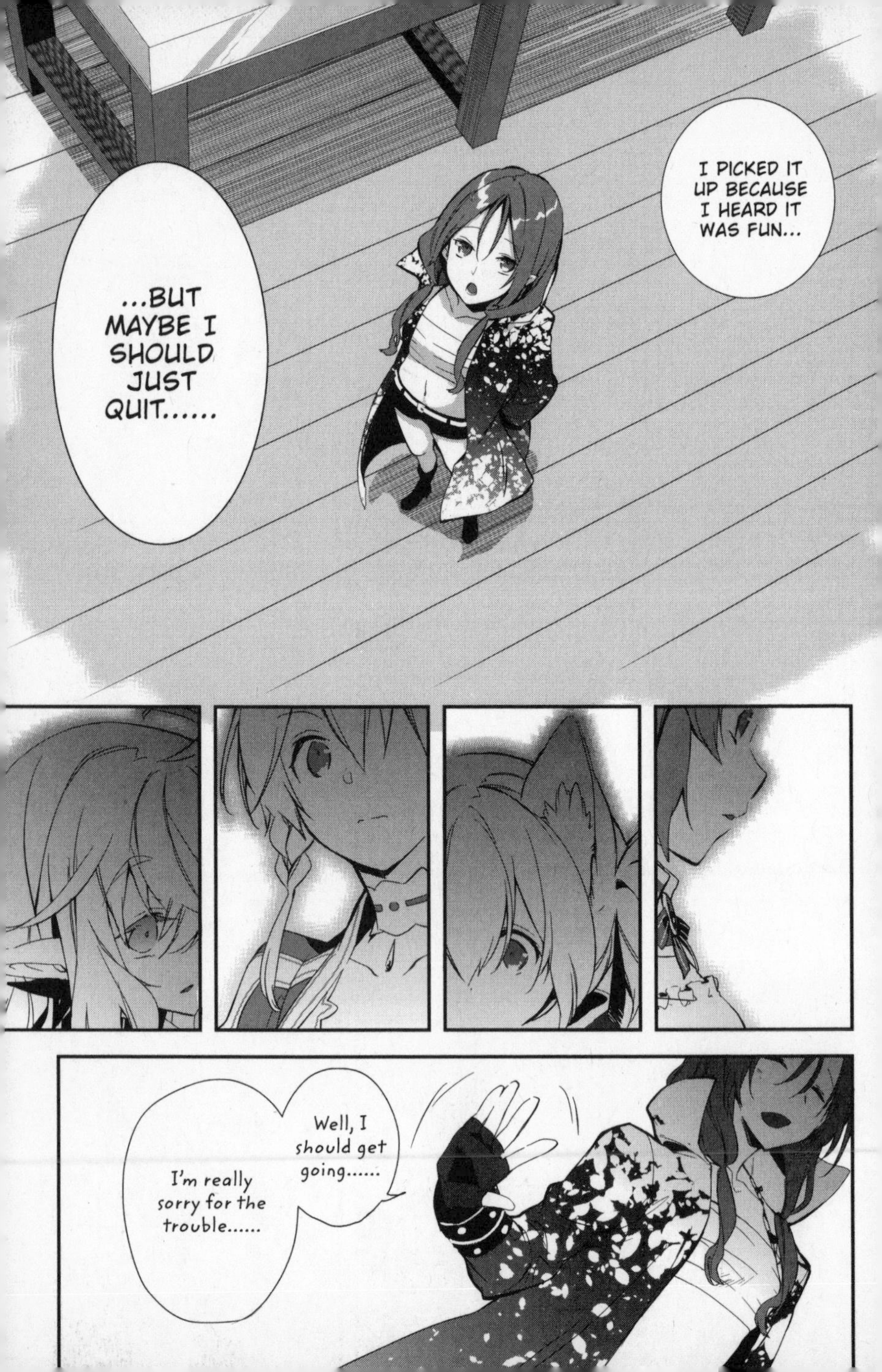
I PICKED IT UP BECAUSE I HEARD IT WAS FUN...
...BUT MAYBE I SHOULD JUST QUIT......
Well, I should get going......
I'm really sorry for the trouble......

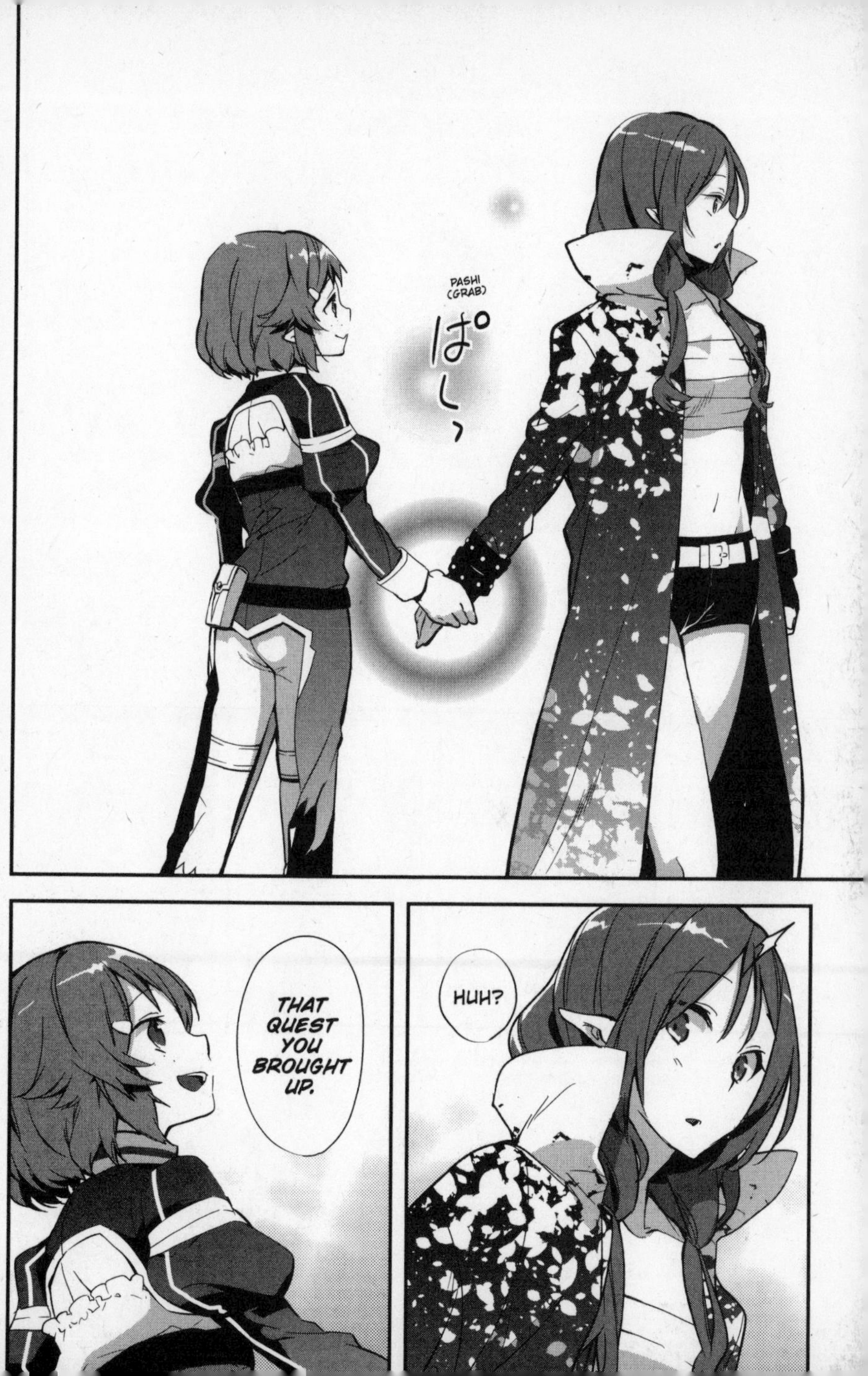
PASHI (GRAB)
ぱしっ
THAT QUEST YOU BROUGHT UP.
HUH?

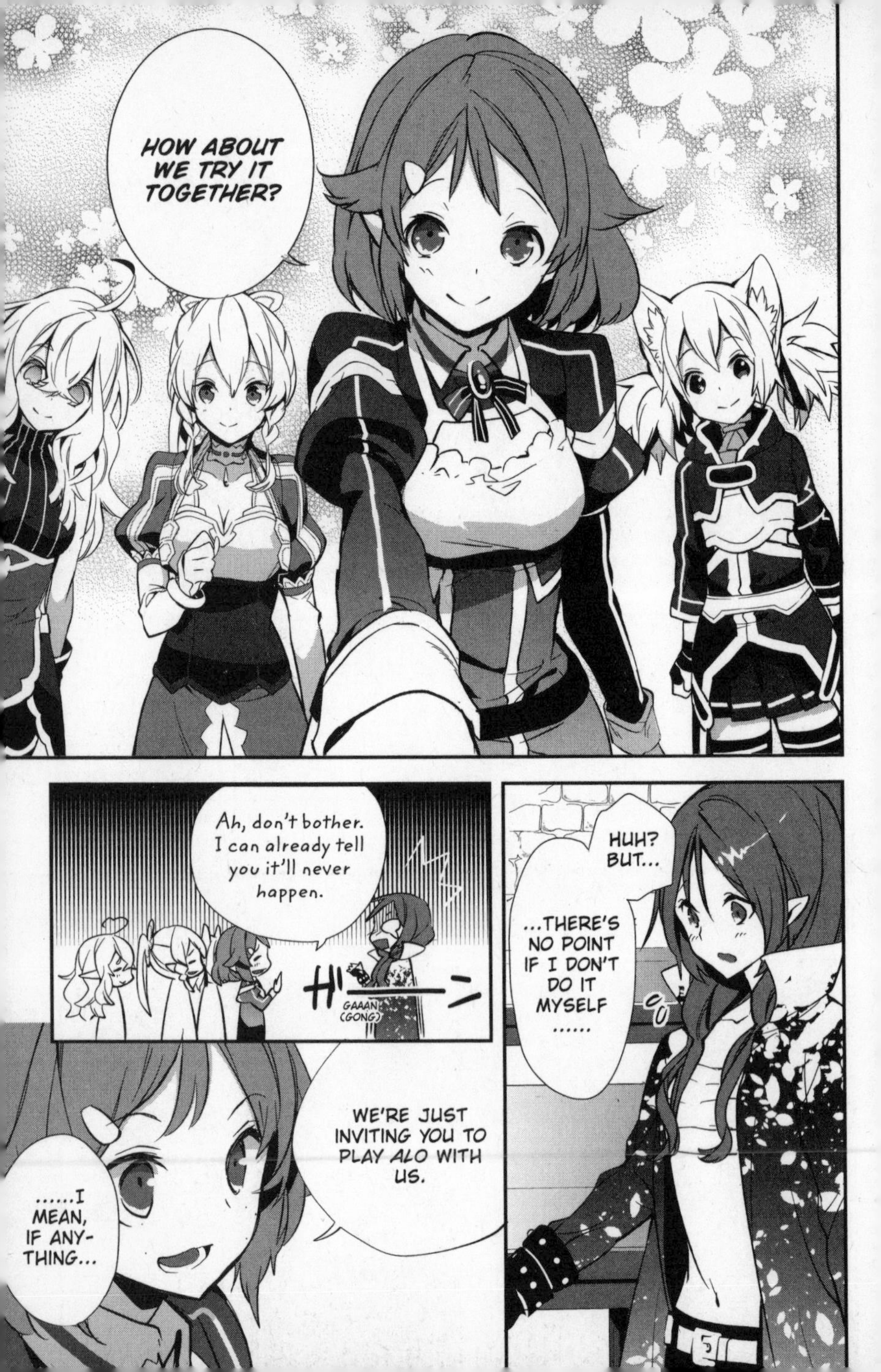
HOW ABOUT WE TRY IT TOGETHER?
HUH? BUT...
...THERE'S NO POINT IF I DON'T DO IT MYSELF ......
Ah, don't bother. I can already tell you it'll never happen.
GAAAN (GONG)
WE'RE JUST INVITING YOU TO PLAY ALO WITH US.
......I MEAN, IF ANY-THING...

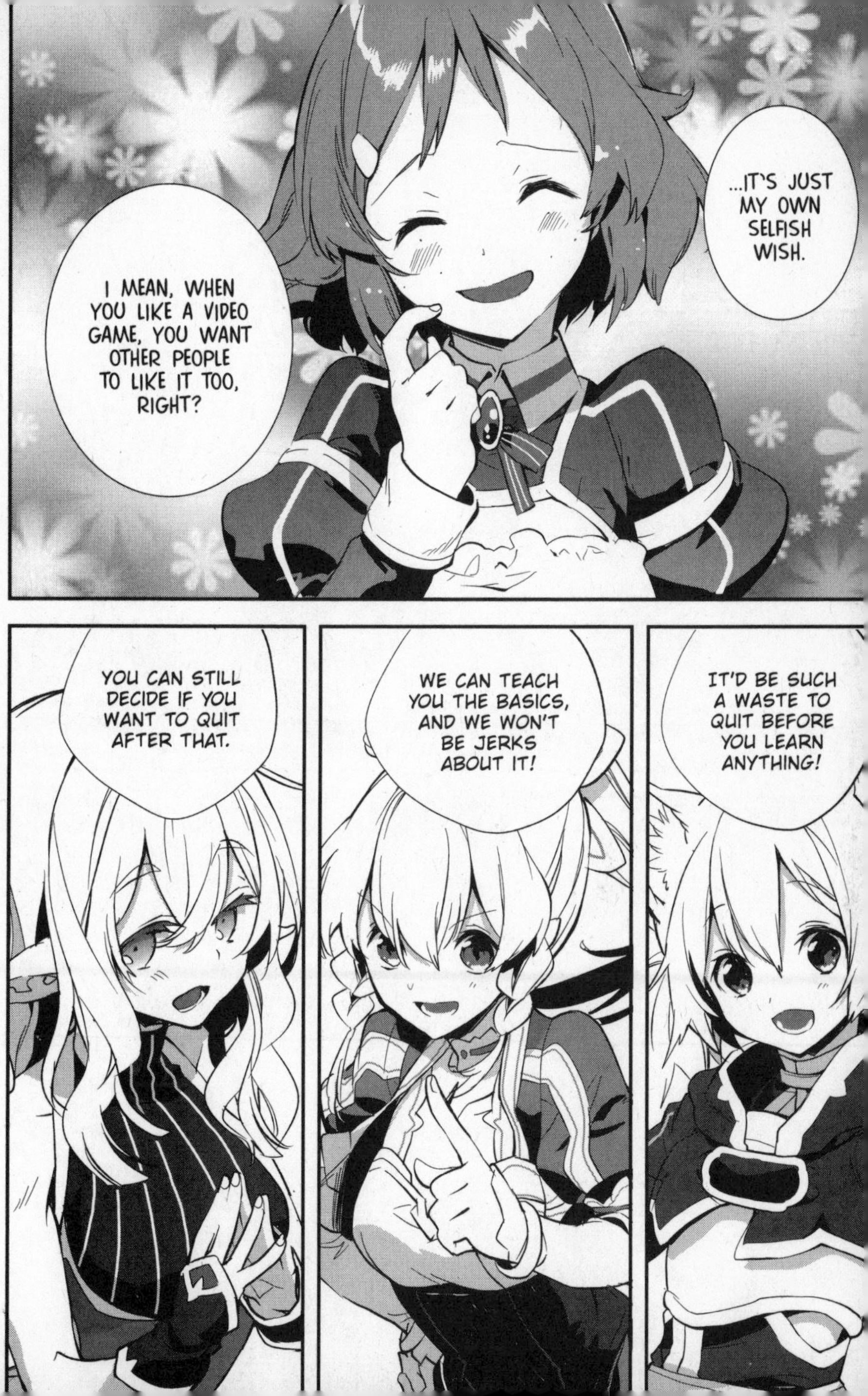
...IT'S JUST MY OWN SELFISH WISH.
I MEAN, WHEN YOU LIKE A VIDEO GAME, YOU WANT OTHER PEOPLE TO LIKE IT TOO, RIGHT?
IT'D BE SUCH A WASTE TO QUIT BEFORE YOU LEARN ANYTHING!
WE CAN TEACH YOU THE BASICS, AND WE WON'T BE JERKS ABOUT IT!
YOU CAN STILL DECIDE IF YOU WANT TO QUIT AFTER THAT.

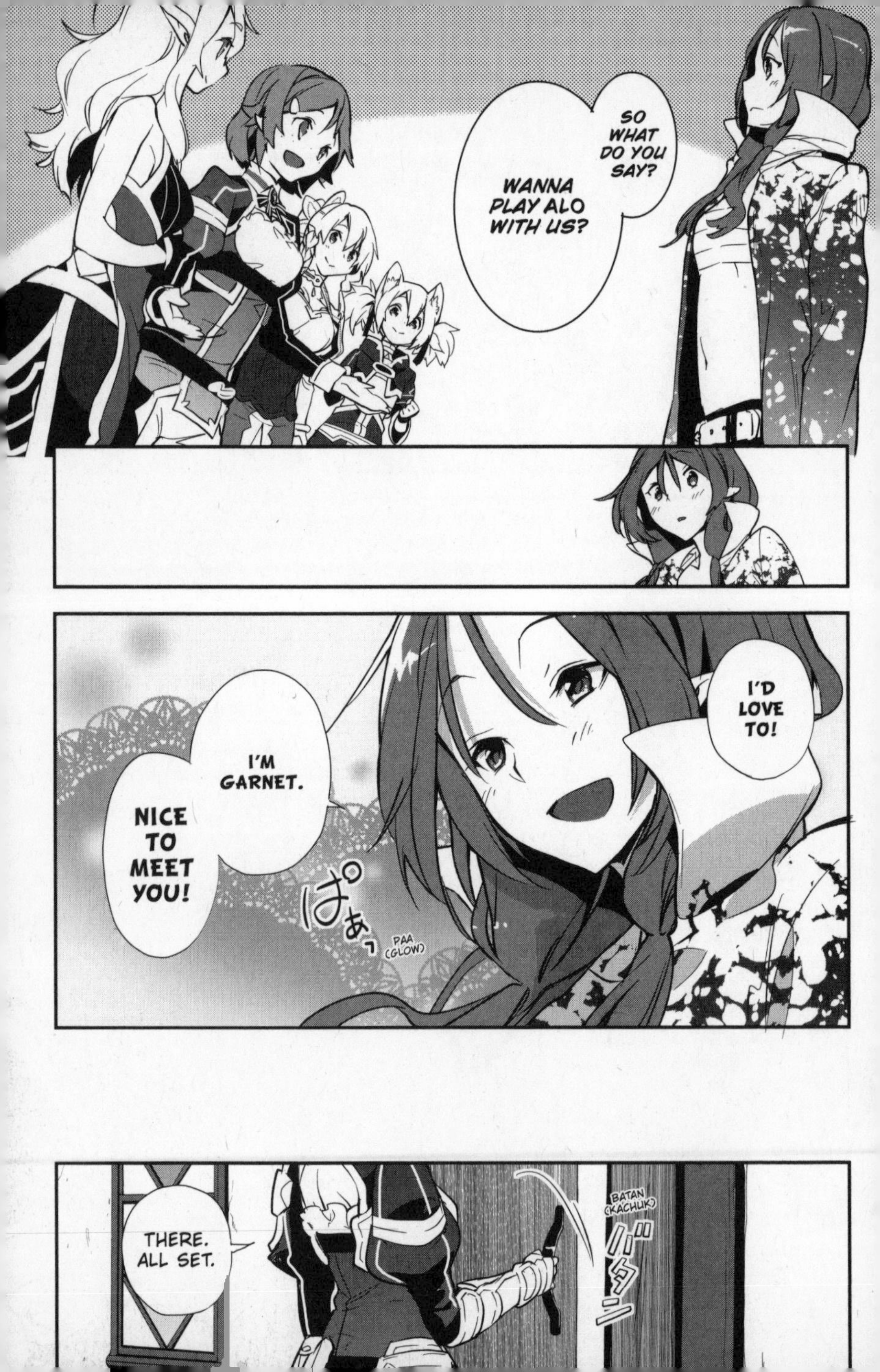
SO WHAT DO YOU SAY?
WANNA PLAY ALO WITH US?
I'D LOVE TO!
I'M GARNET.
NICE TO MEET YOU!
ぱぁっ
PAA (GLOW)
BATAN (KACHUK)
バタン
THERE. ALL SET.

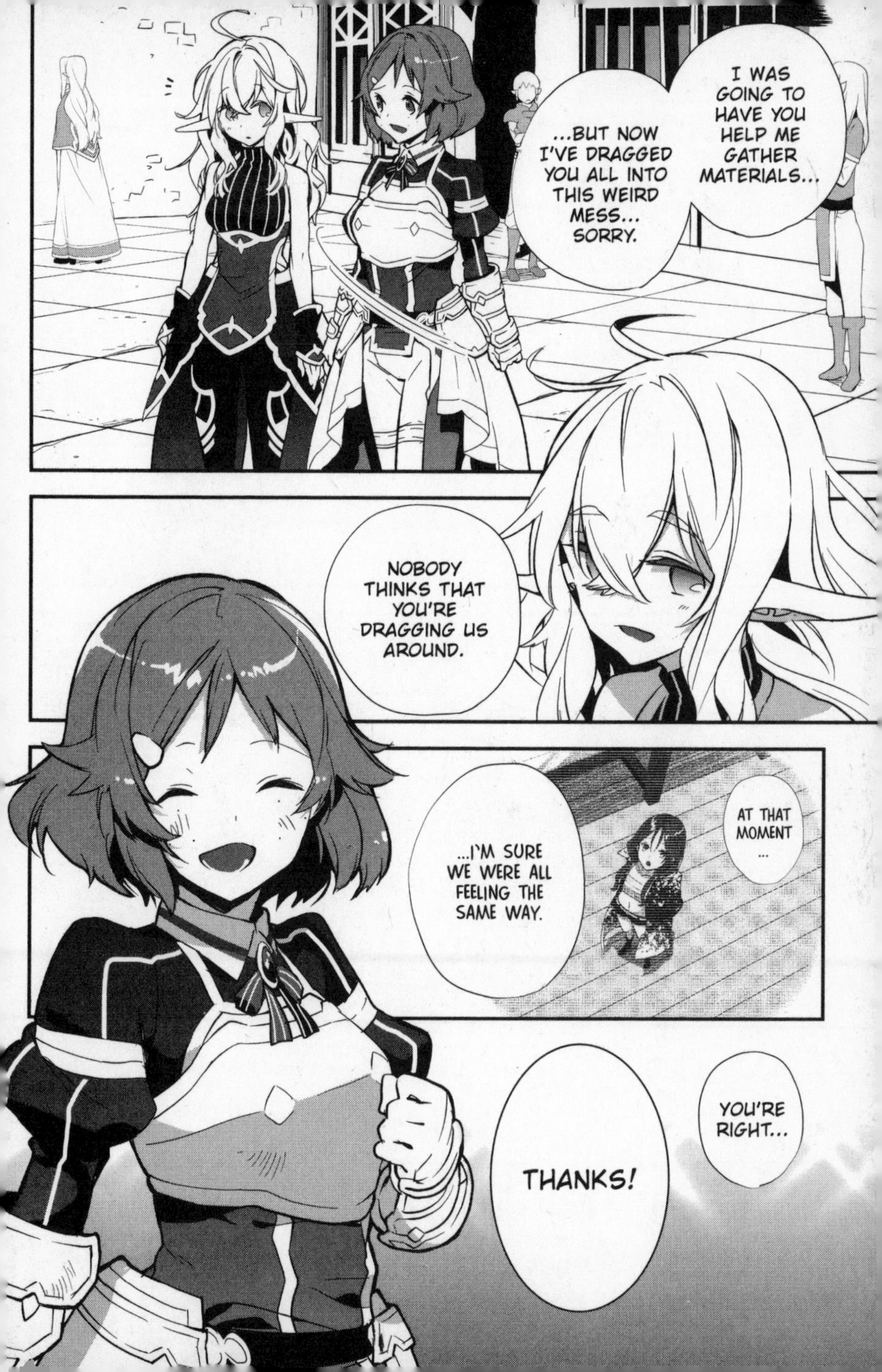
I WAS GOING TO HAVE YOU HELP ME GATHER MATERIALS...
...BUT NOW I'VE DRAGGED YOU ALL INTO THIS WEIRD MESS... SORRY.
NOBODY THINKS THAT YOU'RE DRAGGING US AROUND.
AT THAT MOMENT ...
...I'M SURE WE WERE ALL FEELING THE SAME WAY.
YOU'RE RIGHT...
THANKS!

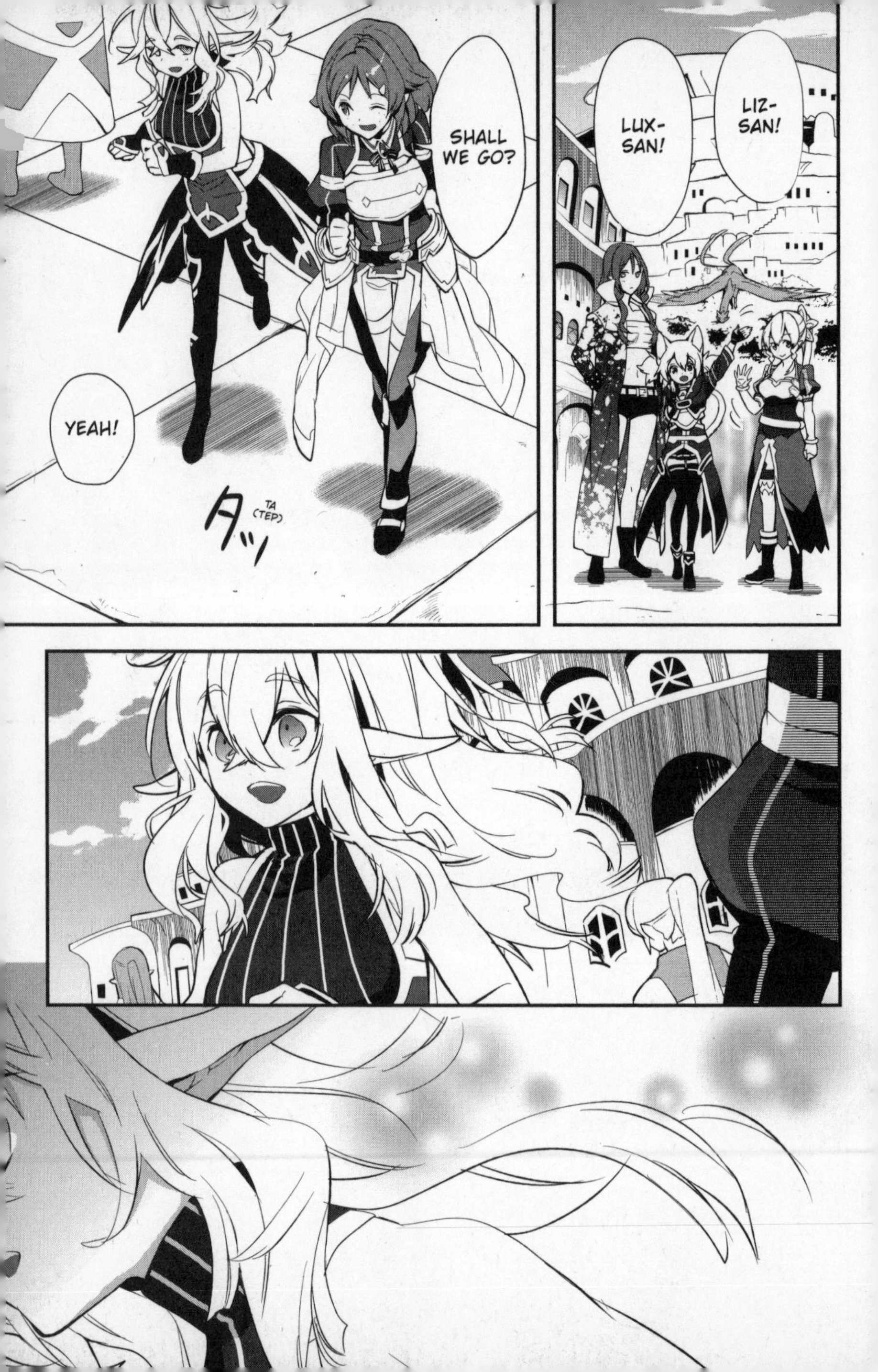
LIZ-SAN!
LUX-SAN!
SHALL WE GO?
YEAH!
タッ
TA (TEP)

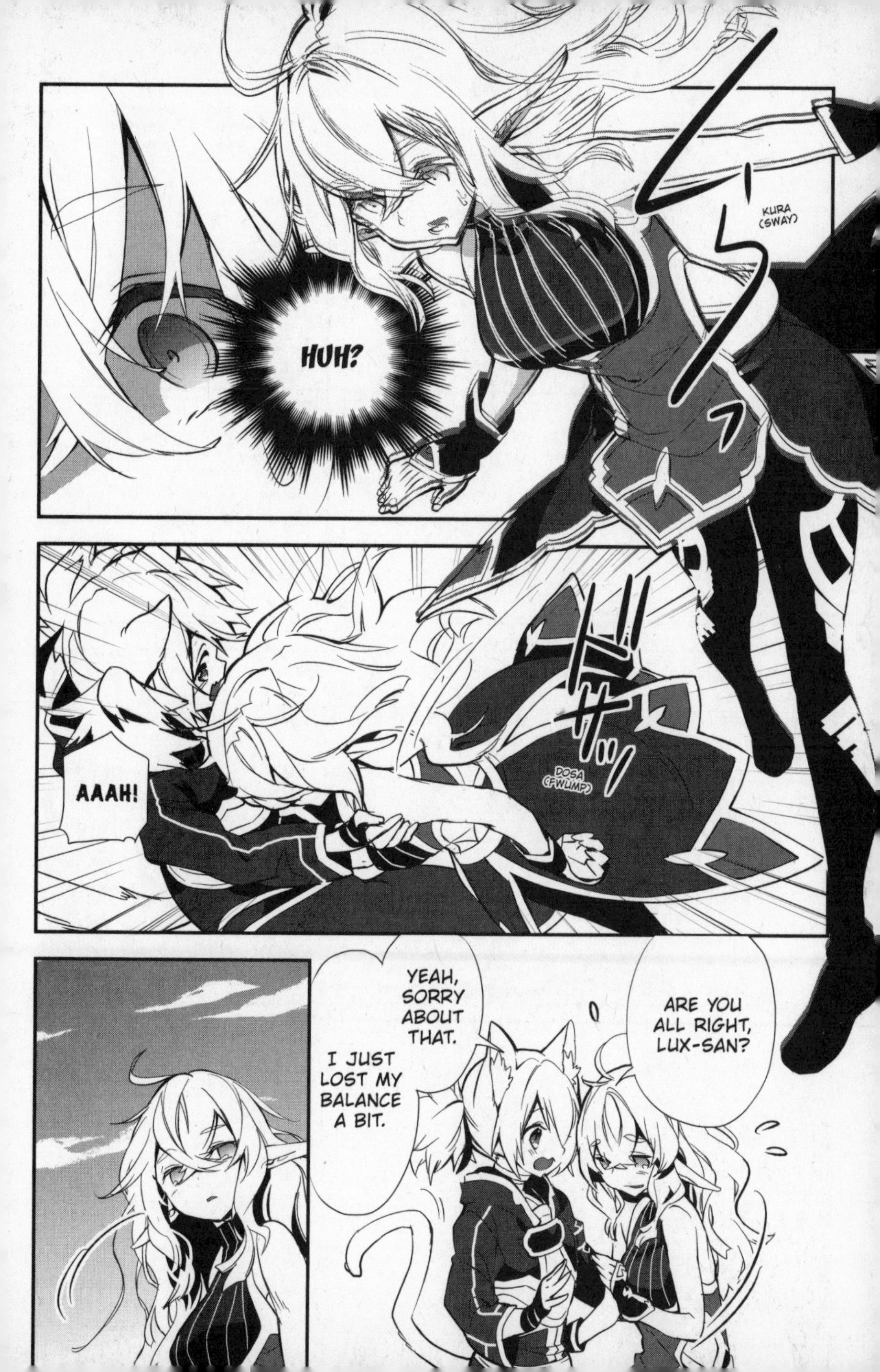
KURA (SWAY)
HUH?
DOSA (FWUMP)
AAAH!
ARE YOU ALL RIGHT, LUX-SAN?
YEAH, SORRY ABOUT THAT.
I JUST LOST MY BALANCE A BIT.

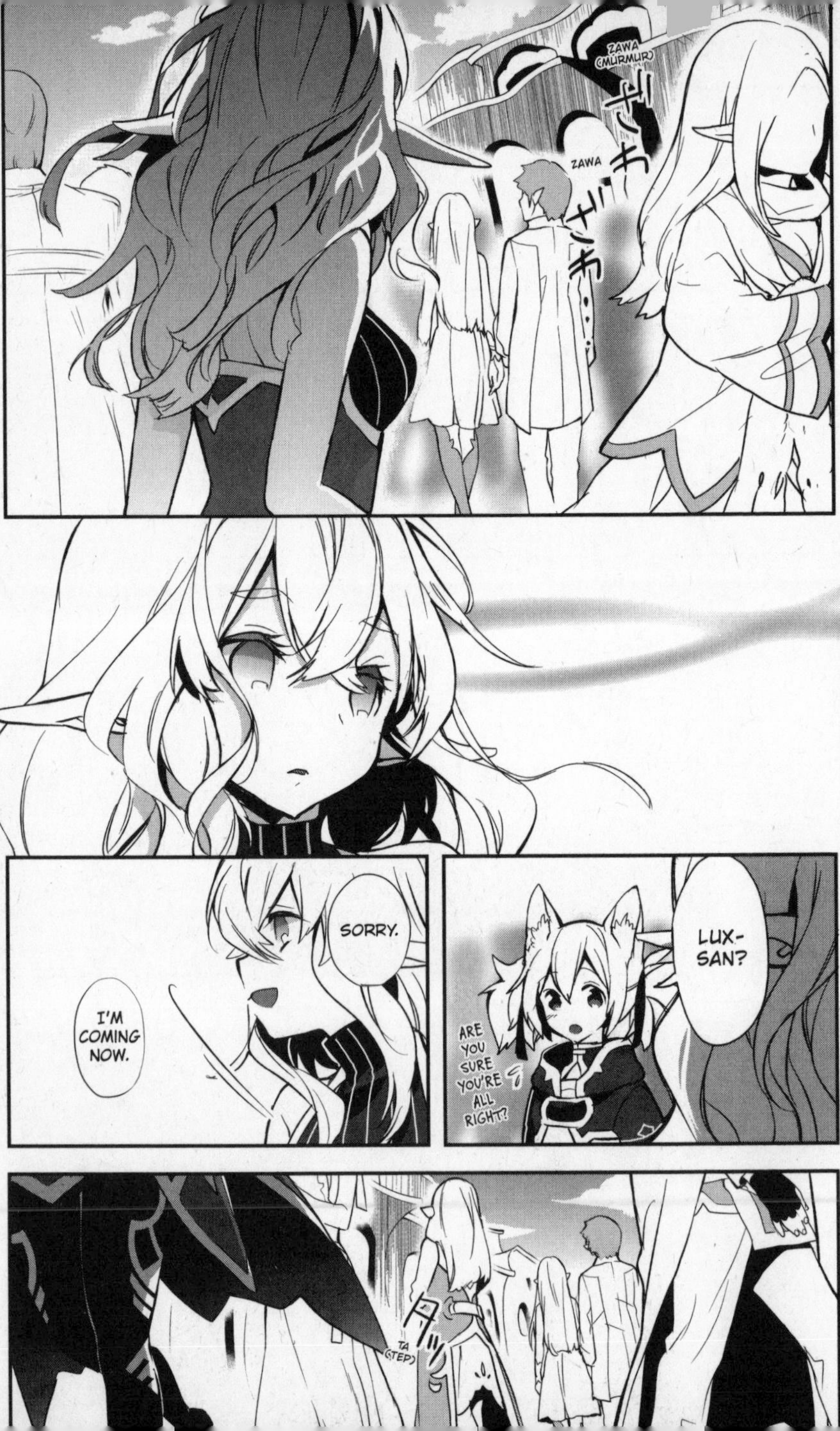
ZAWA (MURMUR)
ZAWA
SORRY.
I'M COMING NOW.
LUX-SAN?
ARE YOU SURE YOU'RE ALL RIGHT?
TA (STEP)

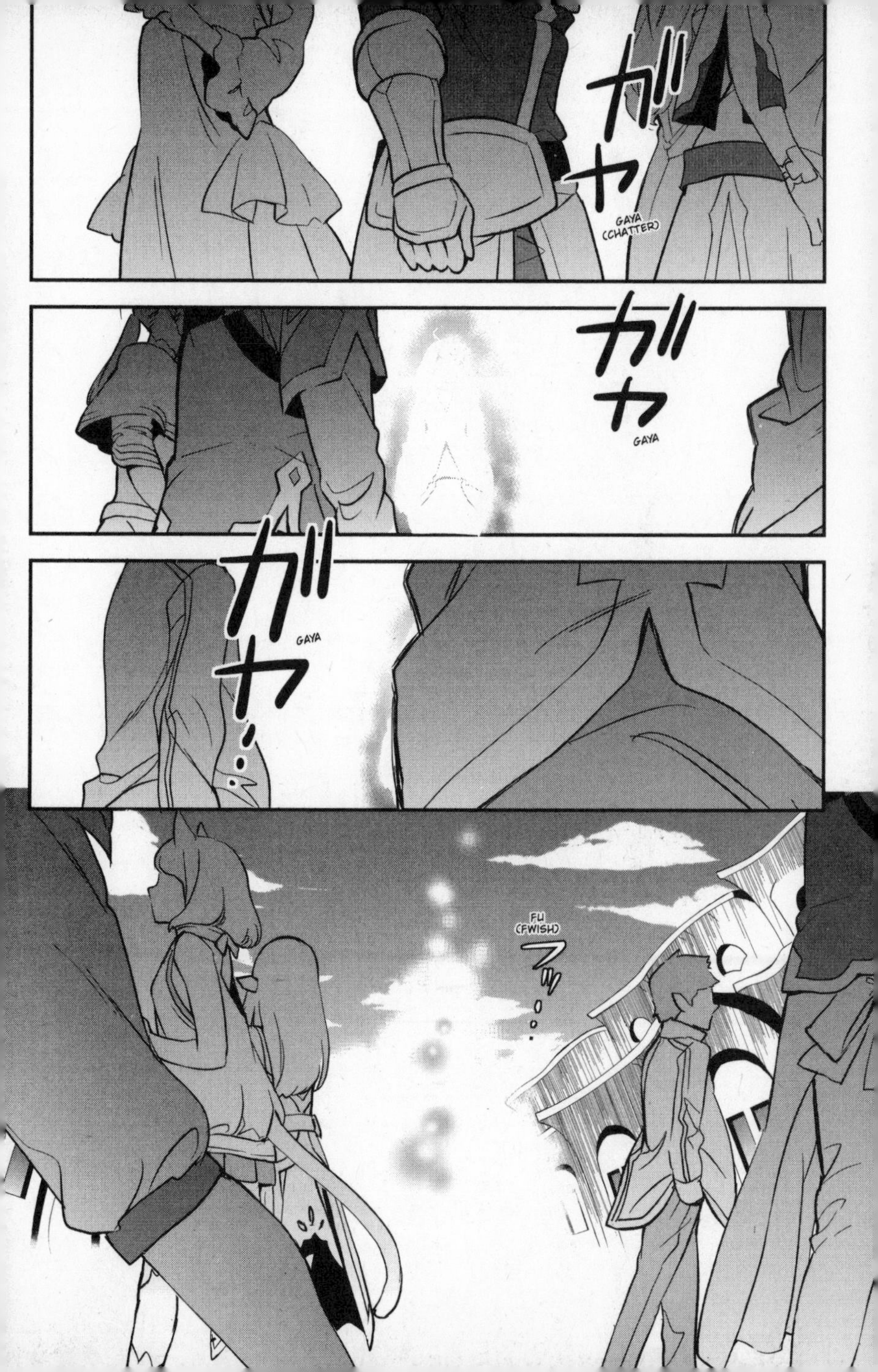
ガヤ
GAYA (CHATTER)
ガヤ
GAYA
ガヤ…
GAYA
FU (FWISH)
フッ…

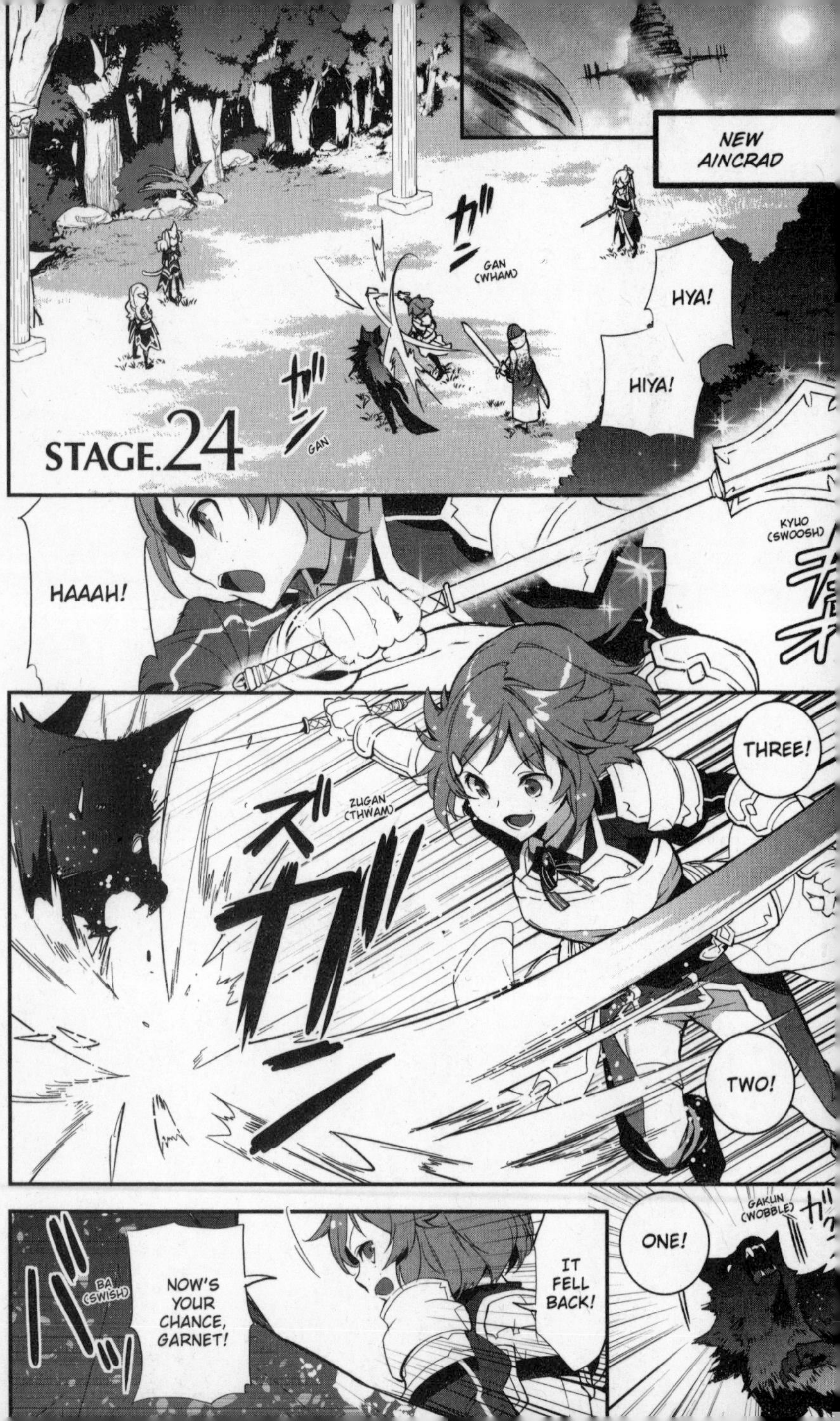
NEW AINCRAD
HYA!
HIYA!
GAN (WHAM)
GAN
STAGE.24
KYUO (SWOOSH)
HAAAH!
THREE!
TWO!
ZUGAN (THWAM)
GAKUN (WOBBLE)
ONE!
IT FELL BACK!
NOW'S YOUR CHANCE, GARNET!
BA (SWISH)

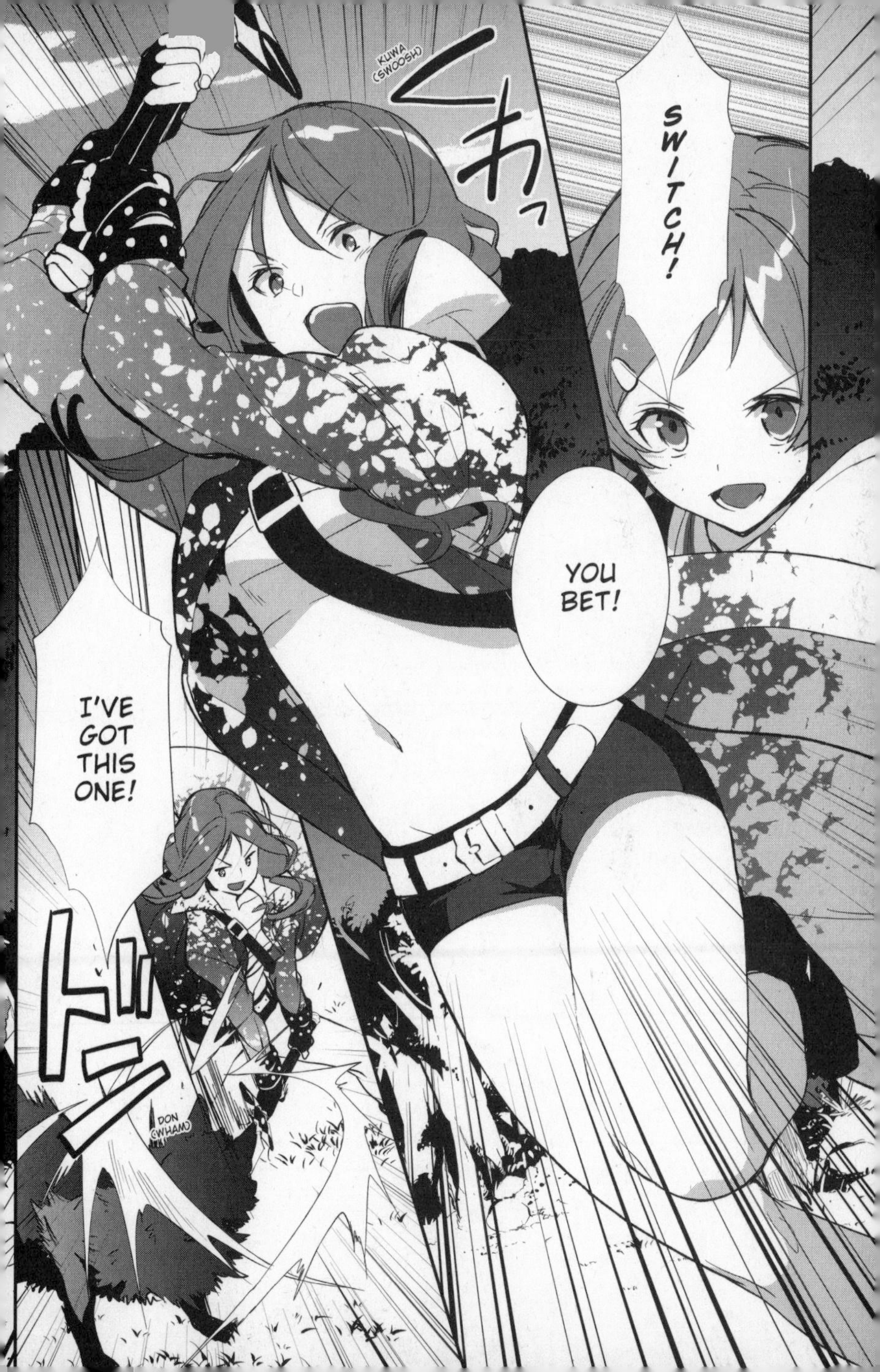
SWITCH!
KUWA (SWOOSH)
YOU BET!
I'VE GOT THIS ONE!
DON (WHAM)

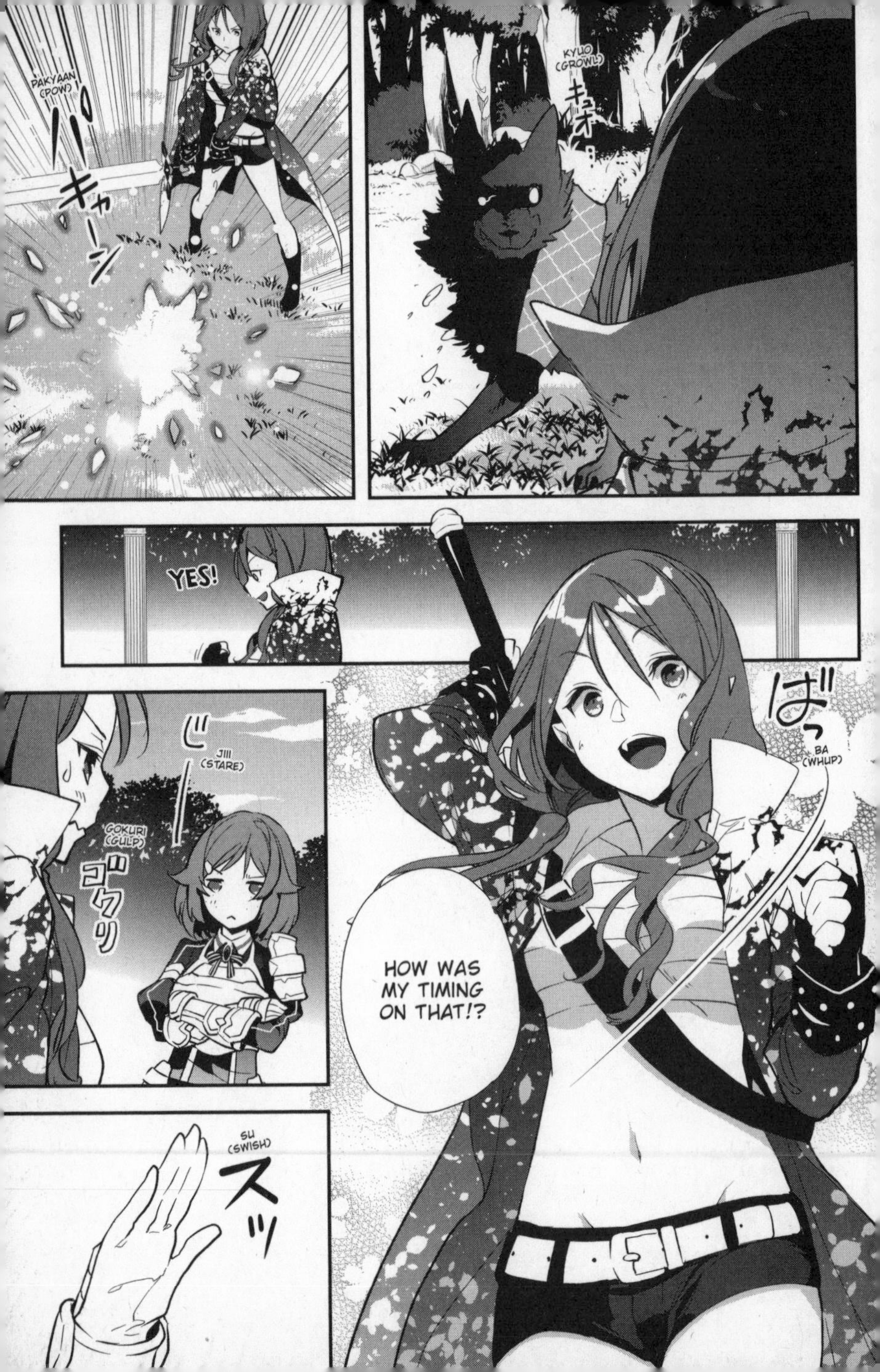
KYUO (GROWL)
キュオ…
PAKYAAN (POW)
パキャーン
YES!
BA (WHUP)
ばっ
HOW WAS MY TIMING ON THAT!?
JIII (STARE)
じー
GOKURI (GULP)
ゴクリ
SU (SWISH)
スッ

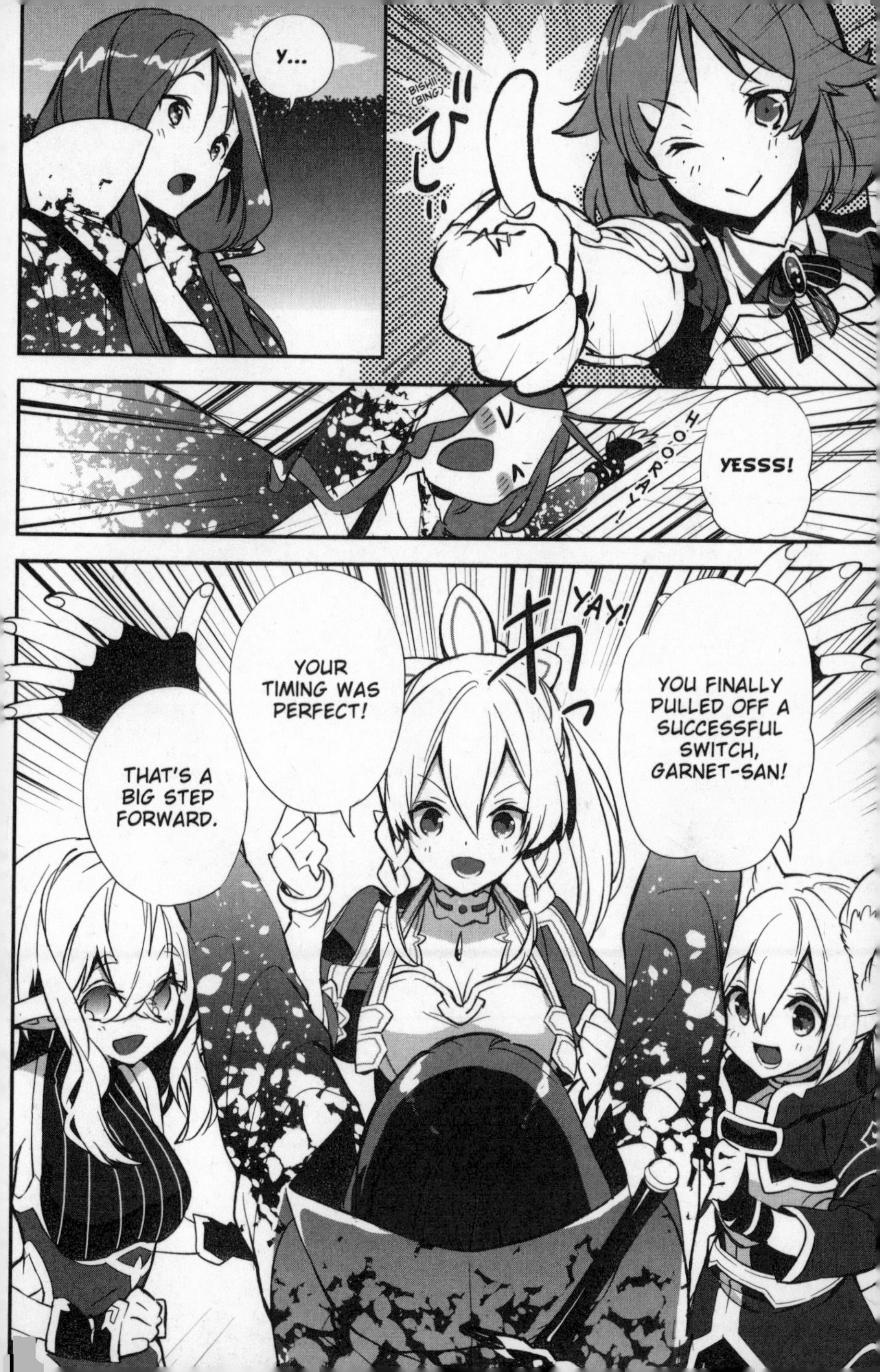
BISHI!! (BING)
Y...
YESSS!
HOORAY!!
YAY!
YOU FINALLY PULLED OFF A SUCCESSFUL SWITCH, GARNET-SAN!
YOUR TIMING WAS PERFECT!
THAT'S A BIG STEP FORWARD.

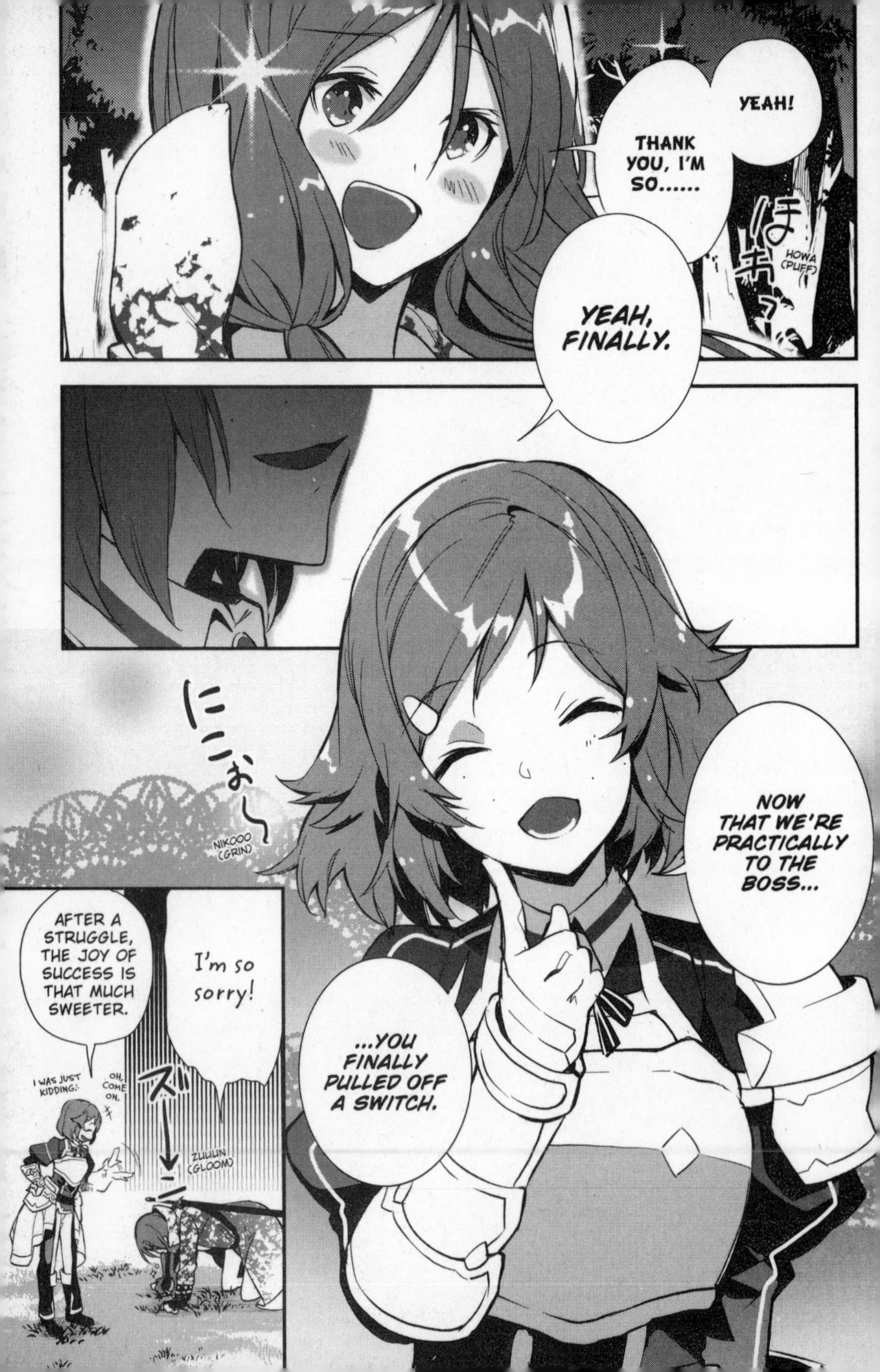
YEAH!
THANK YOU, I'M SO......
ほわ
HOWA (PUFF)
YEAH, FINALLY.
NOW THAT WE'RE PRACTICALLY TO THE BOSS...
...YOU FINALLY PULLED OFF A SWITCH.
にこぉ～
NIKOOO (GRIN)
I'm so sorry!
ズーン
ZUUUN (GLOOM)
AFTER A STRUGGLE, THE JOY OF SUCCESS IS THAT MUCH SWEETER.
OH, COME ON.
I WAS JUST KIDDING!

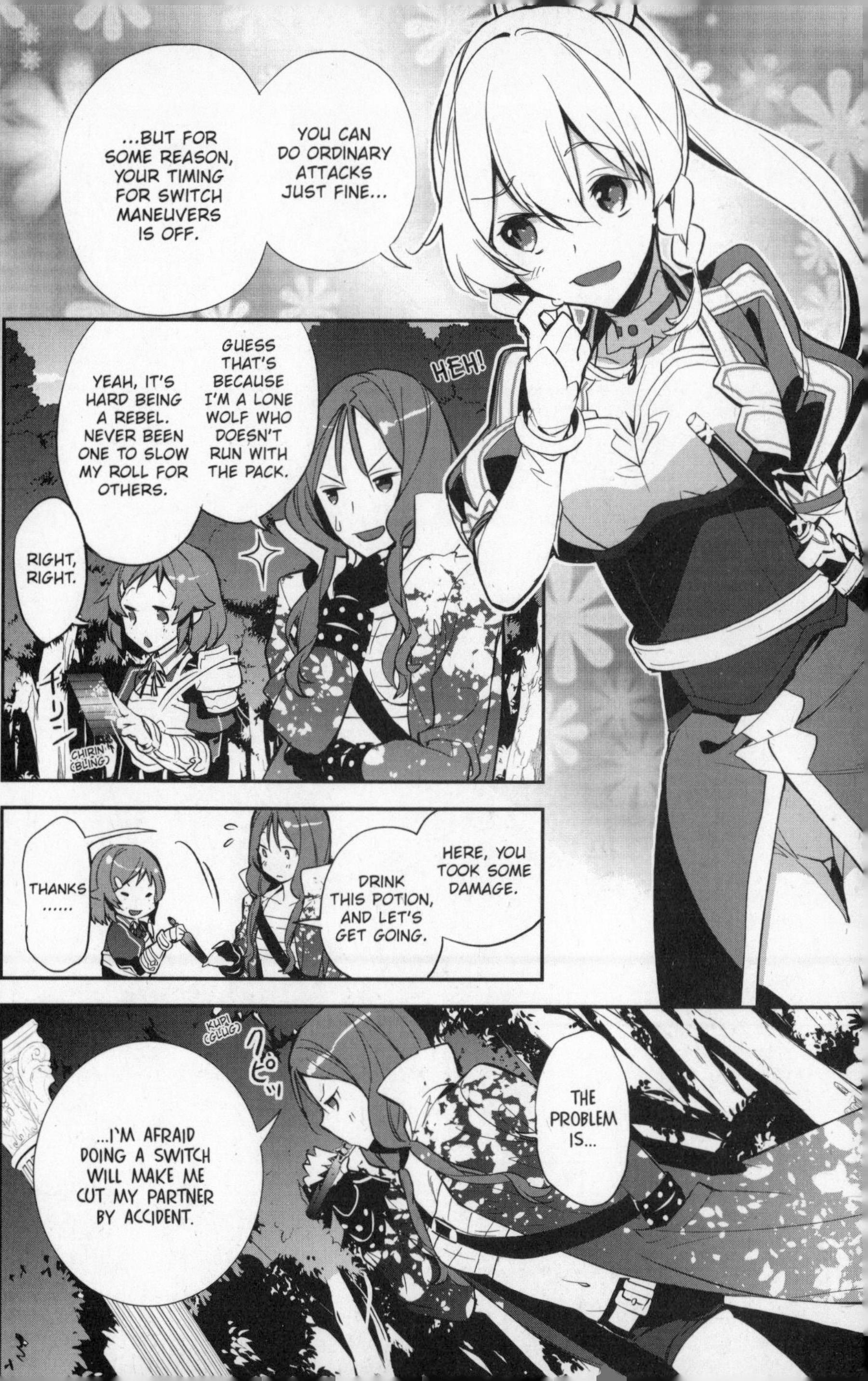
YOU CAN DO ORDINARY ATTACKS JUST FINE...
...BUT FOR SOME REASON, YOUR TIMING FOR SWITCH MANEUVERS IS OFF.
HEH!
GUESS THAT'S BECAUSE I'M A LONE WOLF WHO DOESN'T RUN WITH THE PACK.
YEAH, IT'S HARD BEING A REBEL. NEVER BEEN ONE TO SLOW MY ROLL FOR OTHERS.
RIGHT, RIGHT.
CHIRIN (BLING)
HERE, YOU TOOK SOME DAMAGE.
DRINK THIS POTION, AND LET'S GET GOING.
THANKS ......
KUPI (GLUG)
THE PROBLEM IS...
...I'M AFRAID DOING A SWITCH WILL MAKE ME CUT MY PARTNER BY ACCIDENT.

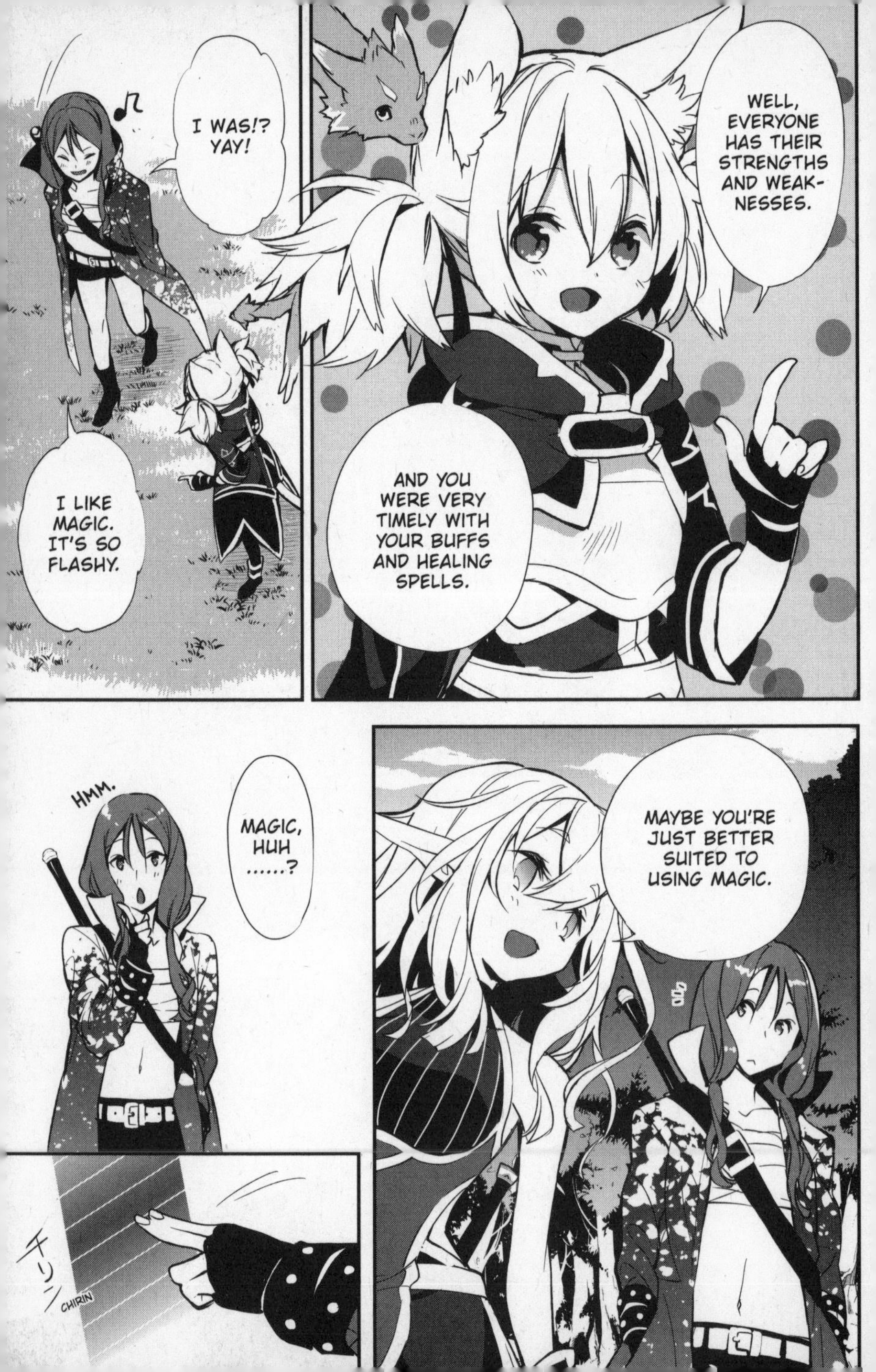
WELL, EVERYONE HAS THEIR STRENGTHS AND WEAK-NESSES.
AND YOU WERE VERY TIMELY WITH YOUR BUFFS AND HEALING SPELLS.
I WAS!? YAY!
I LIKE MAGIC. IT'S SO FLASHY.
MAYBE YOU'RE JUST BETTER SUITED TO USING MAGIC.
HMM.
MAGIC, HUH ......?
チリン
CHIRIN

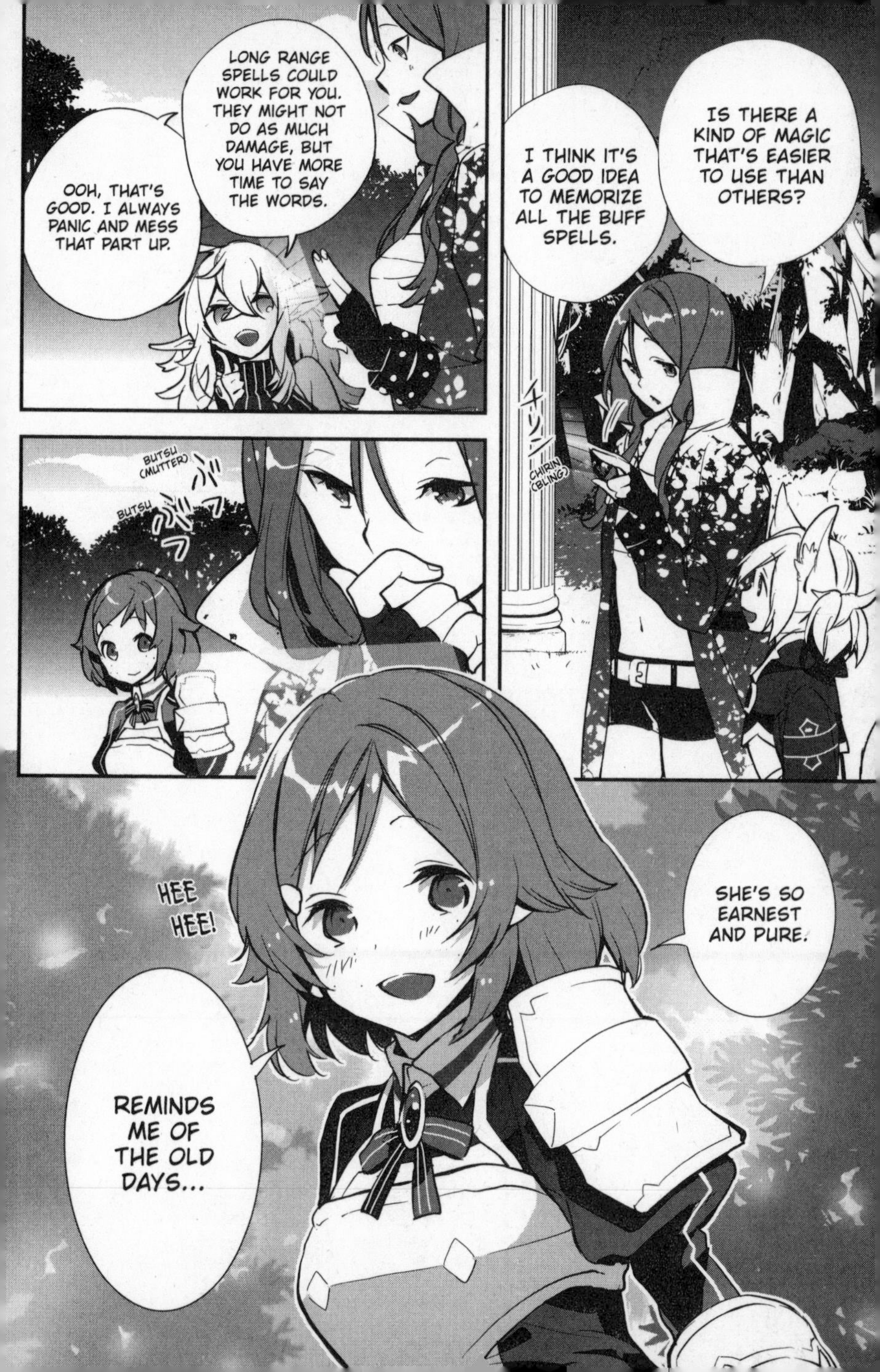
IS THERE A KIND OF MAGIC THAT'S EASIER TO USE THAN OTHERS?
I THINK IT'S A GOOD IDEA TO MEMORIZE ALL THE BUFF SPELLS.
CHIRIN (BLING)
LONG RANGE SPELLS COULD WORK FOR YOU. THEY MIGHT NOT DO AS MUCH DAMAGE, BUT YOU HAVE MORE TIME TO SAY THE WORDS.
OOH, THAT'S GOOD. I ALWAYS PANIC AND MESS THAT PART UP.
BUTSU (MUTTER)
BUTSU
SHE'S SO EARNEST AND PURE.
HEE HEE!
REMINDS ME OF THE OLD DAYS...

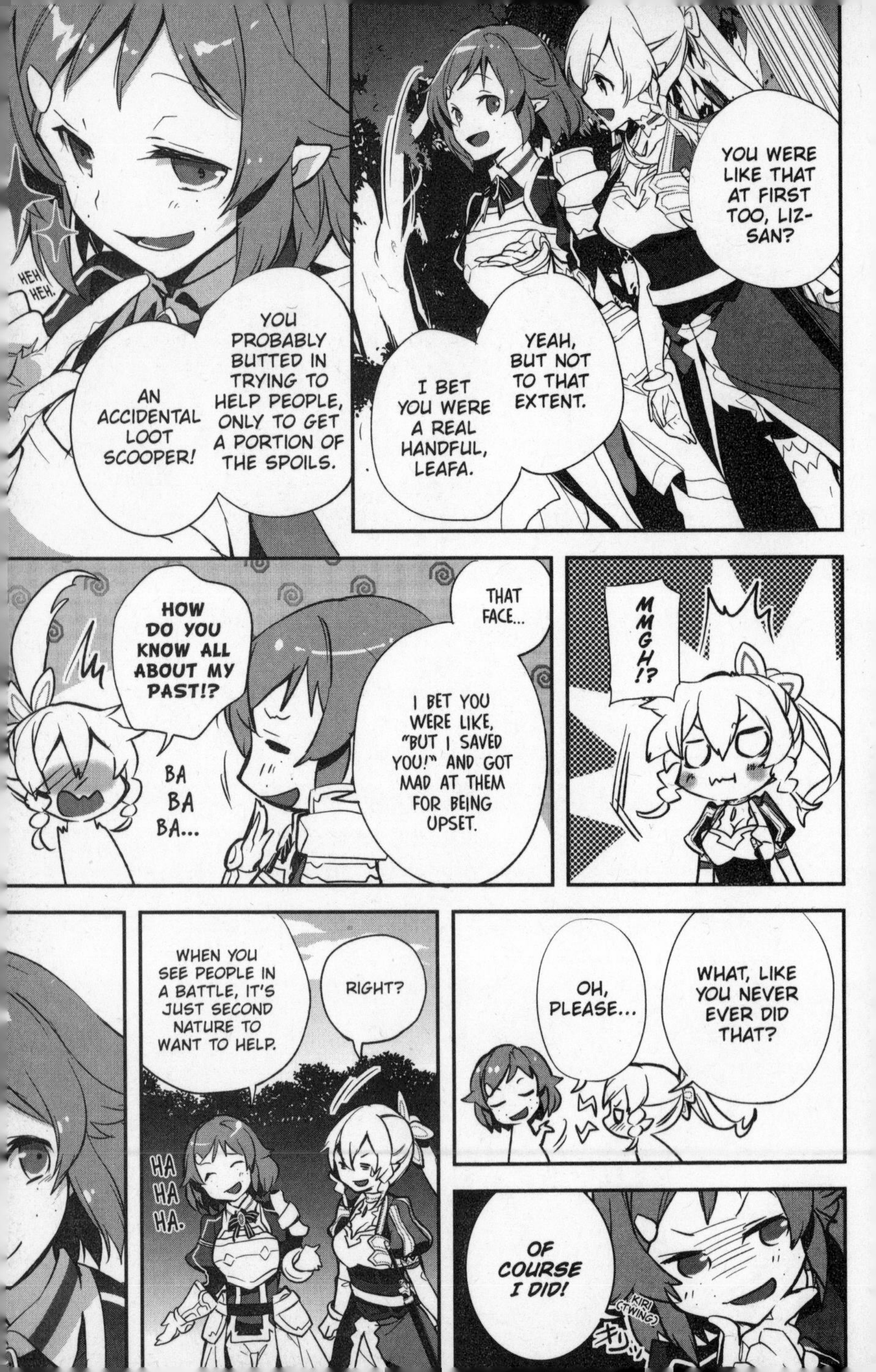
YOU WERE LIKE THAT AT FIRST TOO, LIZ-SAN?
YEAH, BUT NOT TO THAT EXTENT.
I BET YOU WERE A REAL HANDFUL, LEAFA.
YOU PROBABLY BUTTED IN TRYING TO HELP PEOPLE, ONLY TO GET A PORTION OF THE SPOILS.
AN ACCIDENTAL LOOT SCOOPER!
HEH HEH.
MMGH!?
THAT FACE...
I BET YOU WERE LIKE, "BUT I SAVED YOU!" AND GOT MAD AT THEM FOR BEING UPSET.
HOW DO YOU KNOW ALL ABOUT MY PAST!?
BA BA BA...
WHAT, LIKE YOU NEVER EVER DID THAT?
OH, PLEASE...
OF COURSE I DID!
KIRI (TWING)
RIGHT?
WHEN YOU SEE PEOPLE IN A BATTLE, IT'S JUST SECOND NATURE TO WANT TO HELP.
HA HA HA.

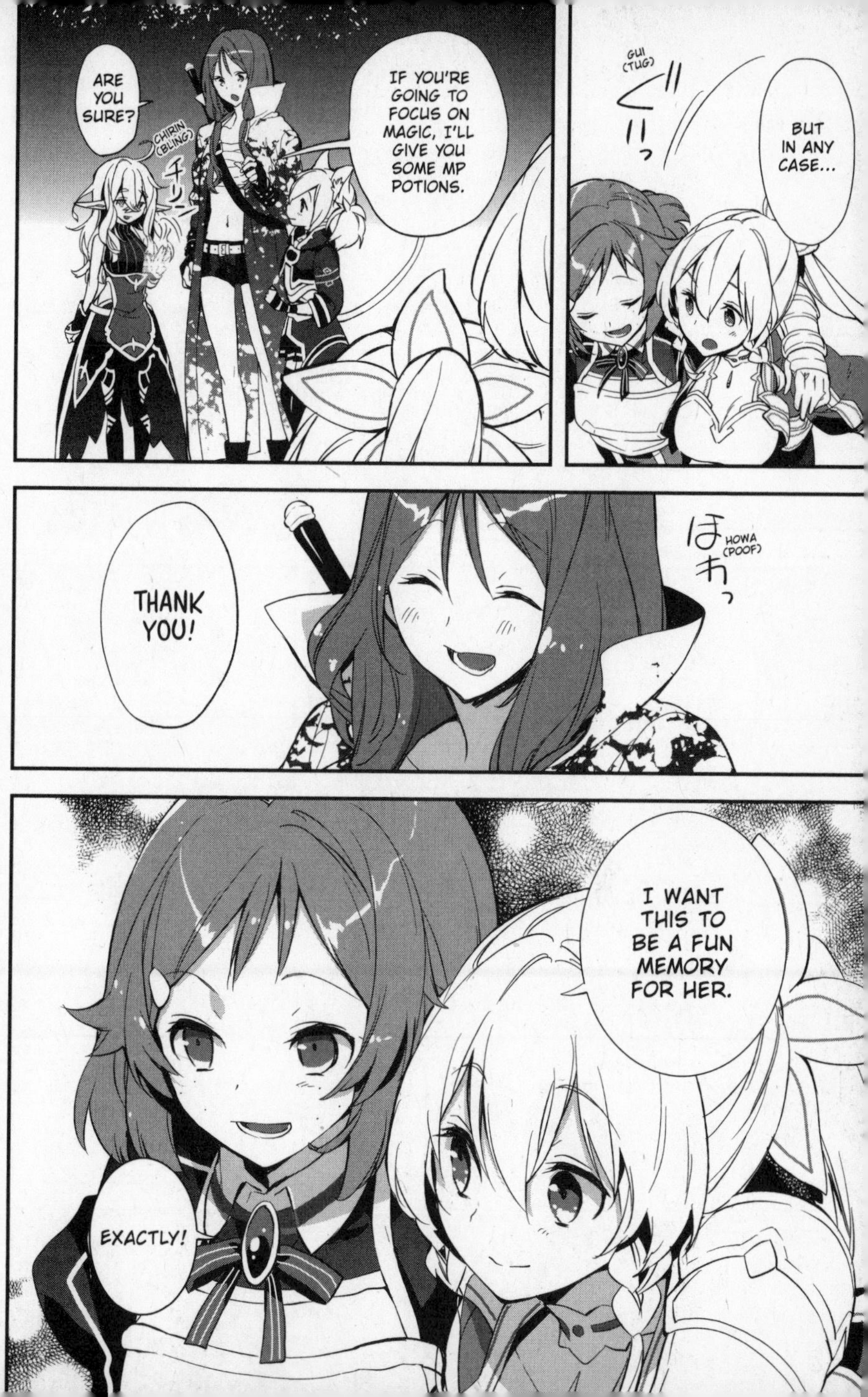
GUI (TUG)
BUT IN ANY CASE...
IF YOU'RE GOING TO FOCUS ON MAGIC, I'LL GIVE YOU SOME MP POTIONS.
ARE YOU SURE?
CHIRIN (BLING)
HOWA (POOF)
THANK YOU!
I WANT THIS TO BE A FUN MEMORY FOR HER.
EXACTLY!

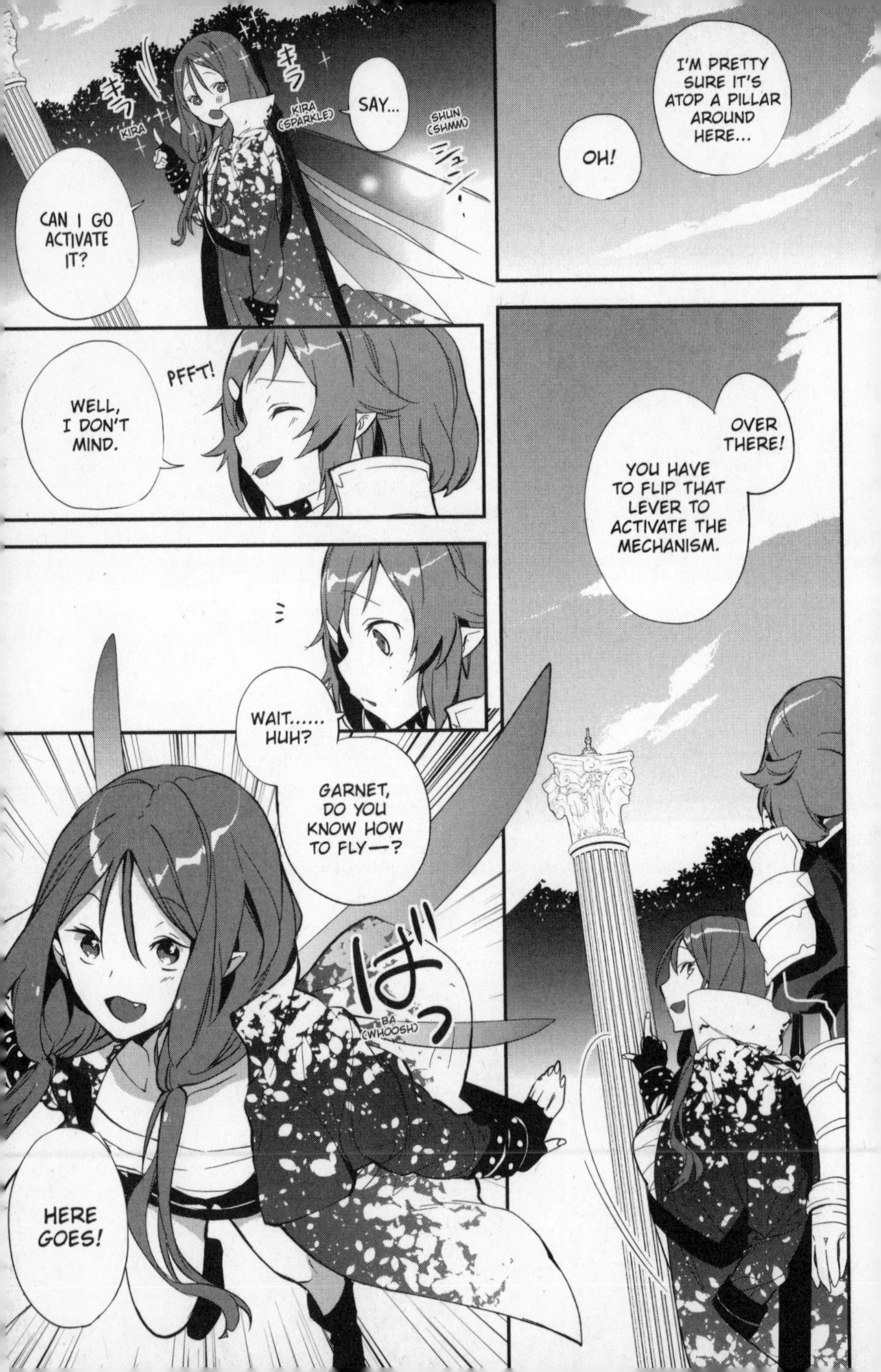
I'M PRETTY SURE IT'S ATOP A PILLAR AROUND HERE...
OH!
OVER THERE!
YOU HAVE TO FLIP THAT LEVER TO ACTIVATE THE MECHANISM.
シュン
SHUN (SHMM)
キラ
KIRA (SPARKLE)
SAY...
キラ
KIRA
CAN I GO ACTIVATE IT?
PFFT!
WELL, I DON'T MIND.
WAIT...... HUH?
GARNET, DO YOU KNOW HOW TO FLY—?
ばっ
BA (WHOOSH)
HERE GOES!

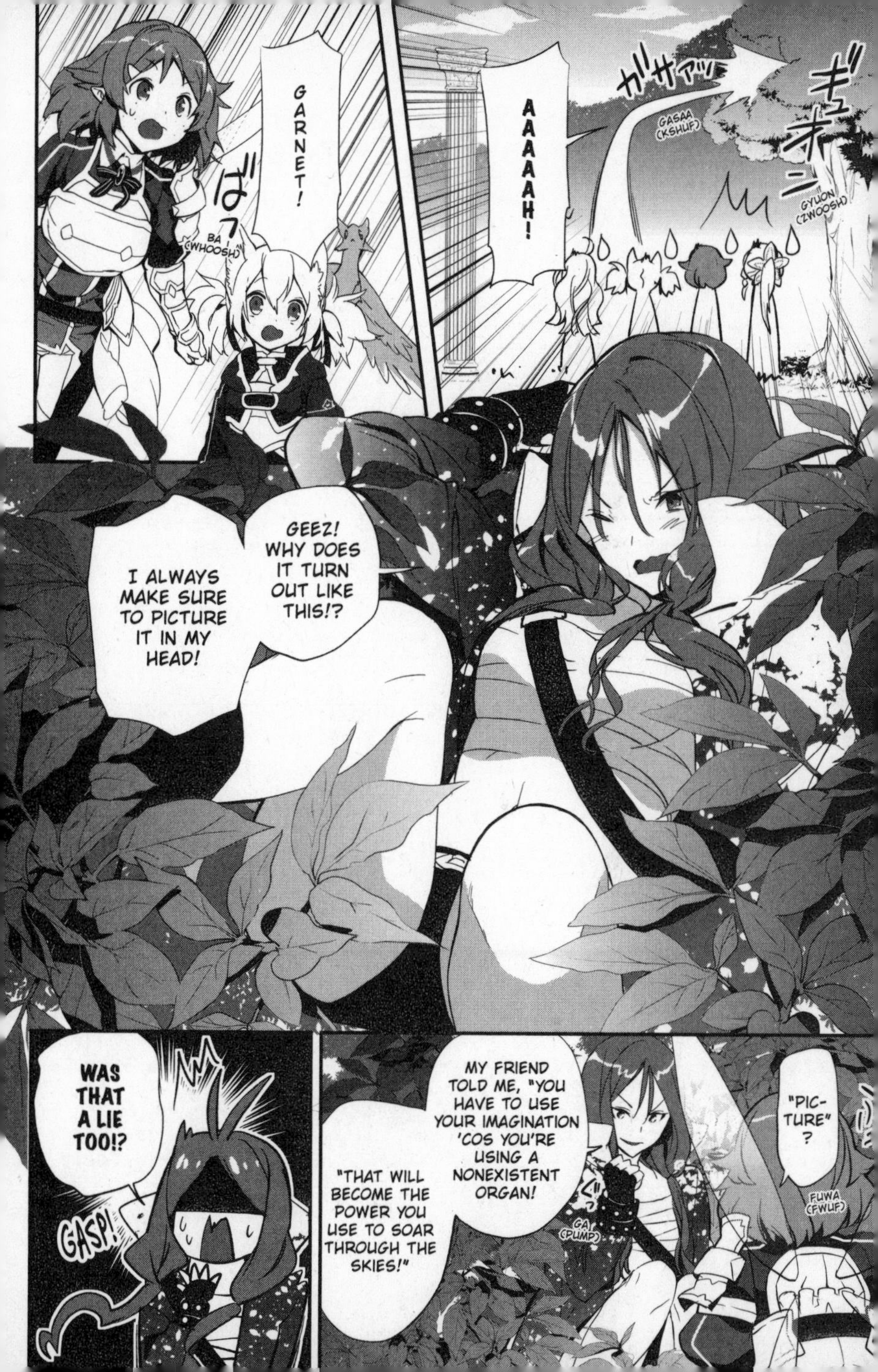
GASAA (KSHUF)
GYUON (ZWOOSH)
AAAAAAH!
GARNET!
BA (WHOOSH)
GEEZ! WHY DOES IT TURN OUT LIKE THIS!?
I ALWAYS MAKE SURE TO PICTURE IT IN MY HEAD!
"PIC-TURE"?
FUWA (FWUF)
MY FRIEND TOLD ME, "YOU HAVE TO USE YOUR IMAGINATION 'COS YOU'RE USING A NONEXISTENT ORGAN!
GA (PUMP)
"THAT WILL BECOME THE POWER YOU USE TO SOAR THROUGH THE SKIES!"
WAS THAT A LIE TOO!?
GASP!

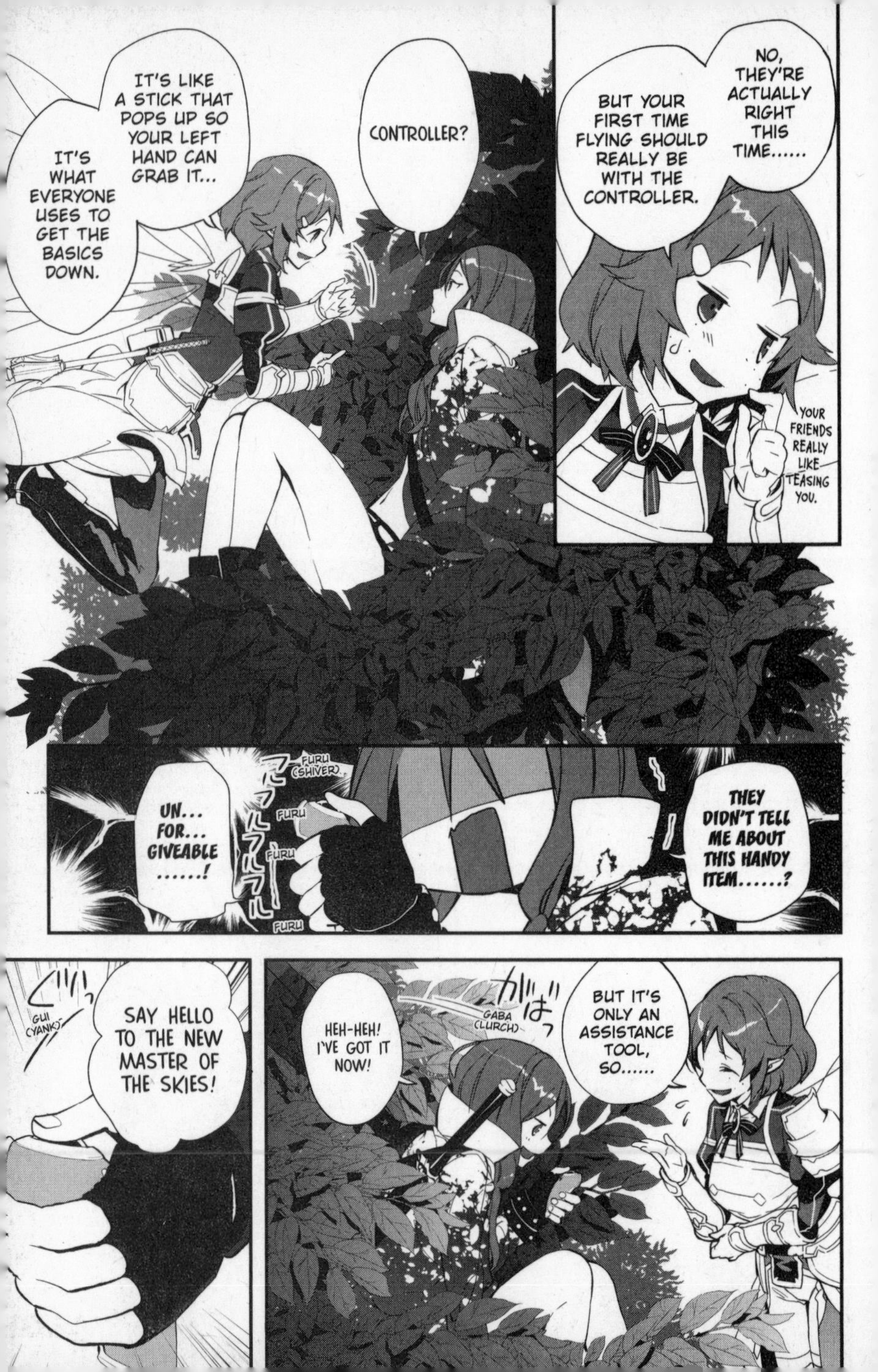
NO, THEY'RE ACTUALLY RIGHT THIS TIME......
BUT YOUR FIRST TIME FLYING SHOULD REALLY BE WITH THE CONTROLLER.
YOUR FRIENDS REALLY LIKE TEASING YOU.
CONTROLLER?
IT'S LIKE A STICK THAT POPS UP SO YOUR LEFT HAND CAN GRAB IT...
IT'S WHAT EVERYONE USES TO GET THE BASICS DOWN.
THEY DIDN'T TELL ME ABOUT THIS HANDY ITEM......?
FURU (SHIVER)
FURU
FURU
FURU
UN... FOR... GIVEABLE ......!
BUT IT'S ONLY AN ASSISTANCE TOOL, SO......
GABA (LURCH)
HEH-HEH! I'VE GOT IT NOW!
GUI (YANK)
SAY HELLO TO THE NEW MASTER OF THE SKIES!

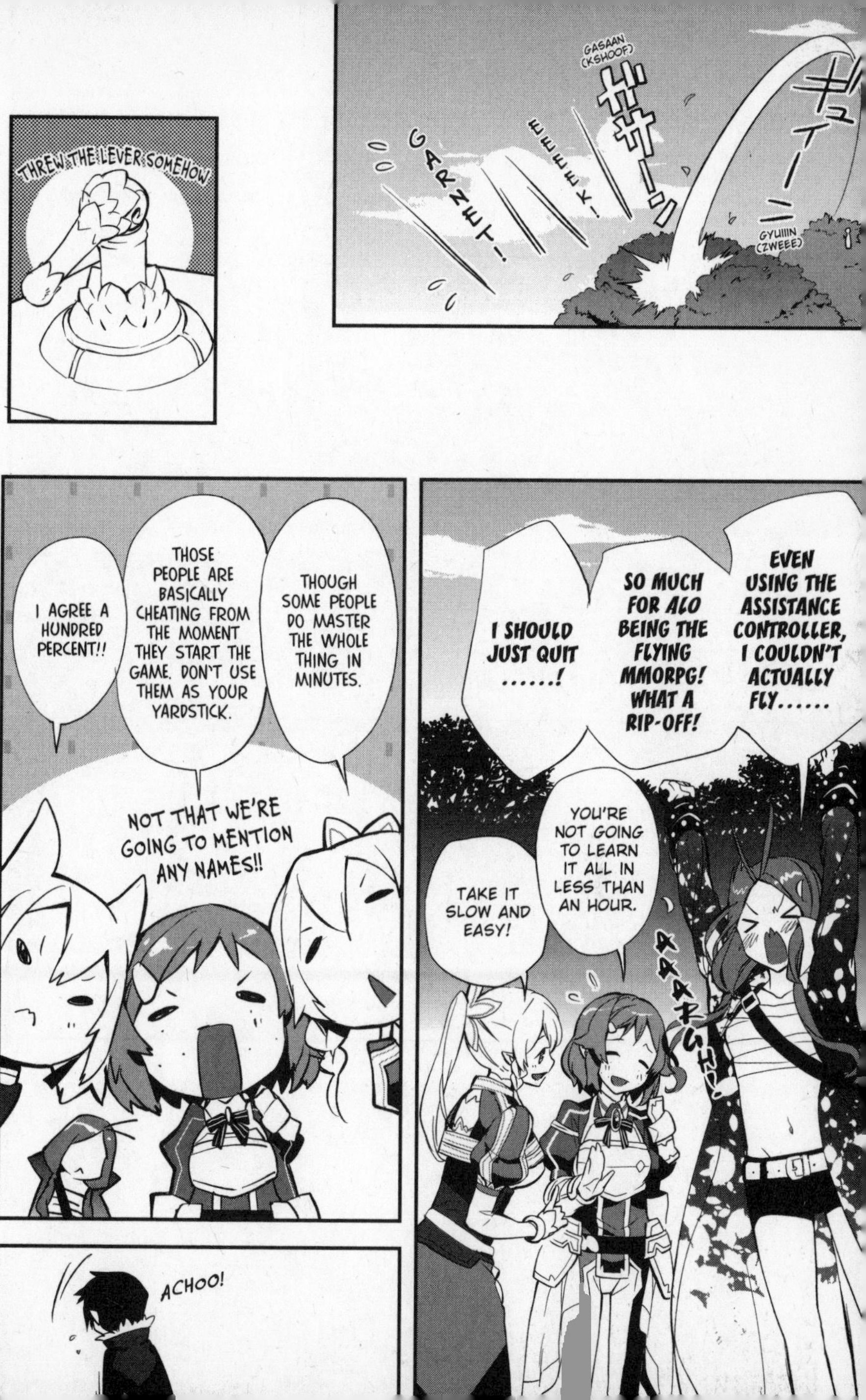
GASAAN (KSHOOF)
GYUIIIN (ZWEEE)
EEEEEK!
GARNET!
THREW THE LEVER SOMEHOW
EVEN USING THE ASSISTANCE CONTROLLER, I COULDN'T ACTUALLY FLY......
SO MUCH FOR ALO BEING THE FLYING MMORPG! WHAT A RIP-OFF!
I SHOULD JUST QUIT......!
YOU'RE NOT GOING TO LEARN IT ALL IN LESS THAN AN HOUR.
TAKE IT SLOW AND EASY!
AAARGH!
THOUGH SOME PEOPLE DO MASTER THE WHOLE THING IN MINUTES.
THOSE PEOPLE ARE BASICALLY CHEATING FROM THE MOMENT THEY START THE GAME. DON'T USE THEM AS YOUR YARDSTICK.
I AGREE A HUNDRED PERCENT!!
NOT THAT WE'RE GOING TO MENTION ANY NAMES!!
ACHOO!

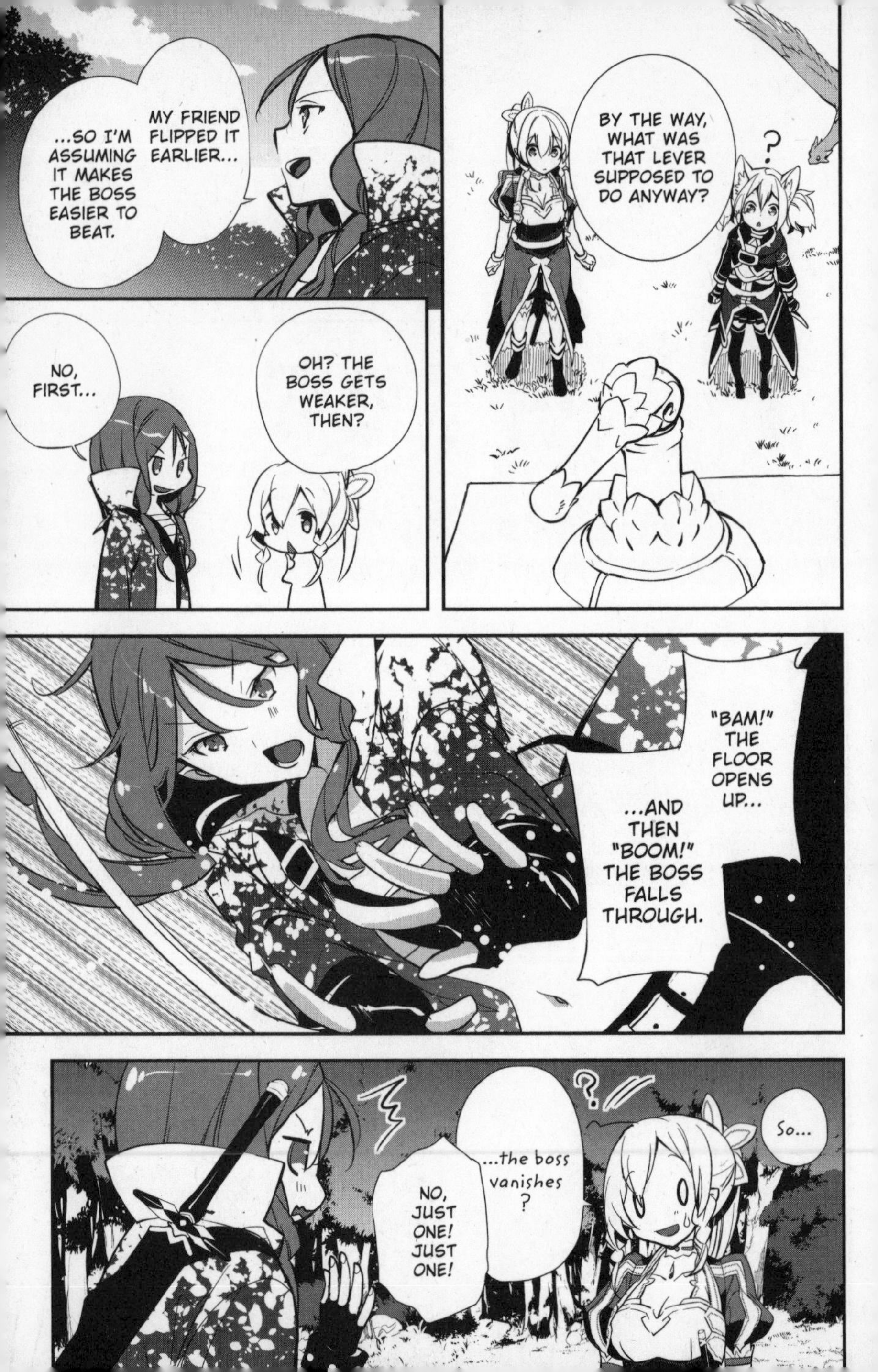
BY THE WAY, WHAT WAS THAT LEVER SUPPOSED TO DO ANYWAY?
?
MY FRIEND FLIPPED IT EARLIER...
...SO I'M ASSUMING IT MAKES THE BOSS EASIER TO BEAT.
OH? THE BOSS GETS WEAKER, THEN?
NO, FIRST...
"BAM!" THE FLOOR OPENS UP...
...AND THEN "BOOM!" THE BOSS FALLS THROUGH.
So...
...the boss vanishes ?
NO, JUST ONE! JUST ONE!

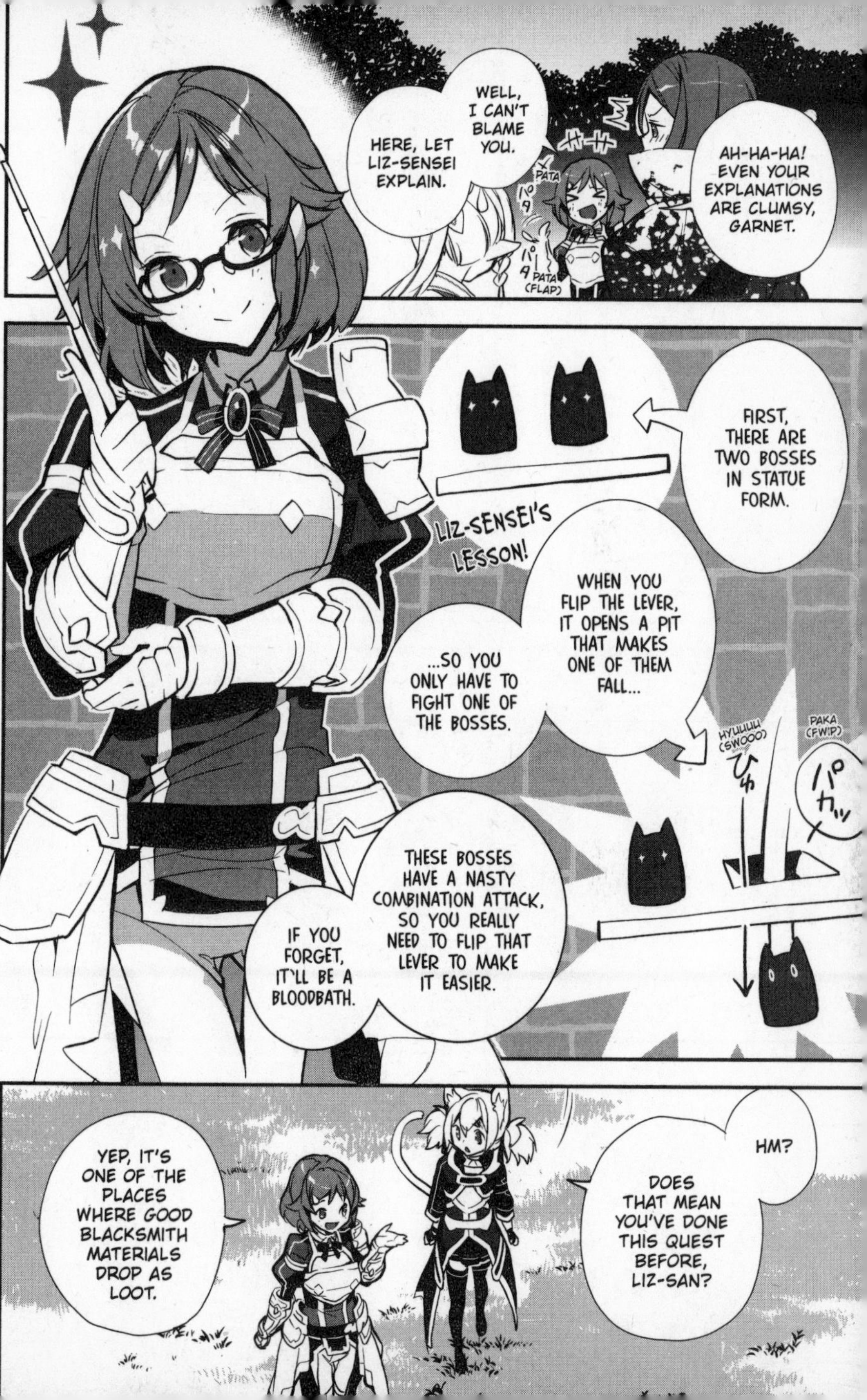
AH-HA-HA! EVEN YOUR EXPLANATIONS ARE CLUMSY, GARNET.
WELL, I CAN'T BLAME YOU.
HERE, LET LIZ-SENSEI EXPLAIN.
PATA
PATA (FLAP)
FIRST, THERE ARE TWO BOSSES IN STATUE FORM.
LIZ-SENSEI'S LESSON!
WHEN YOU FLIP THE LEVER, IT OPENS A PIT THAT MAKES ONE OF THEM FALL...
...SO YOU ONLY HAVE TO FIGHT ONE OF THE BOSSES.
PAKA (FWIP)
HYUUUU (SWOOO)
THESE BOSSES HAVE A NASTY COMBINATION ATTACK, SO YOU REALLY NEED TO FLIP THAT LEVER TO MAKE IT EASIER.
IF YOU FORGET, IT'LL BE A BLOODBATH.
HM?
DOES THAT MEAN YOU'VE DONE THIS QUEST BEFORE, LIZ-SAN?
YEP, IT'S ONE OF THE PLACES WHERE GOOD BLACKSMITH MATERIALS DROP AS LOOT.

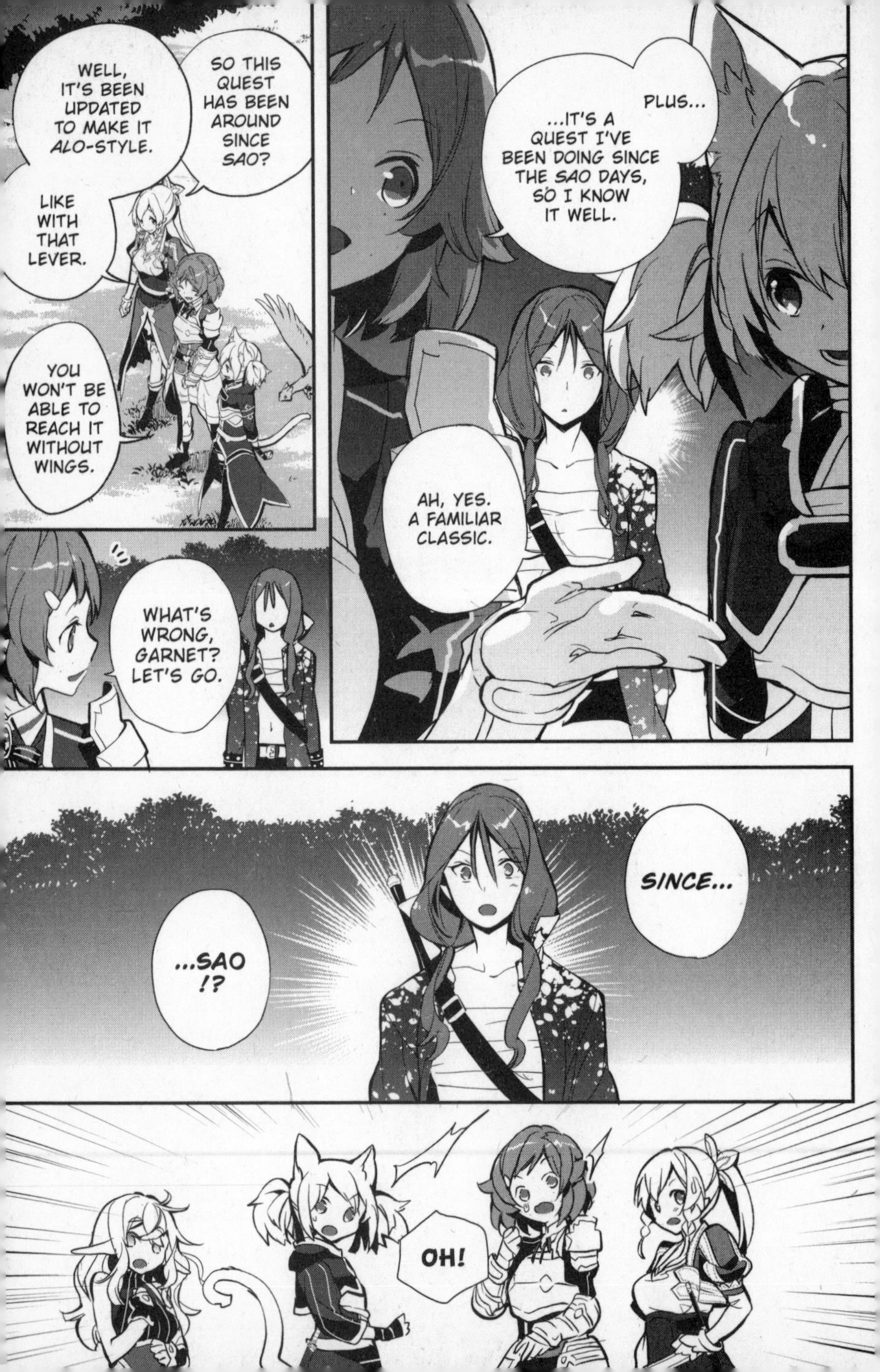
PLUS... ...IT'S A QUEST I'VE BEEN DOING SINCE THE SAO DAYS, SO I KNOW IT WELL.
AH, YES. A FAMILIAR CLASSIC.
SO THIS QUEST HAS BEEN AROUND SINCE SAO?
WELL, IT'S BEEN UPDATED TO MAKE IT ALO-STYLE.
LIKE WITH THAT LEVER.
YOU WON'T BE ABLE TO REACH IT WITHOUT WINGS.
WHAT'S WRONG, GARNET? LET'S GO.
SINCE...
...SAO !?
OH!

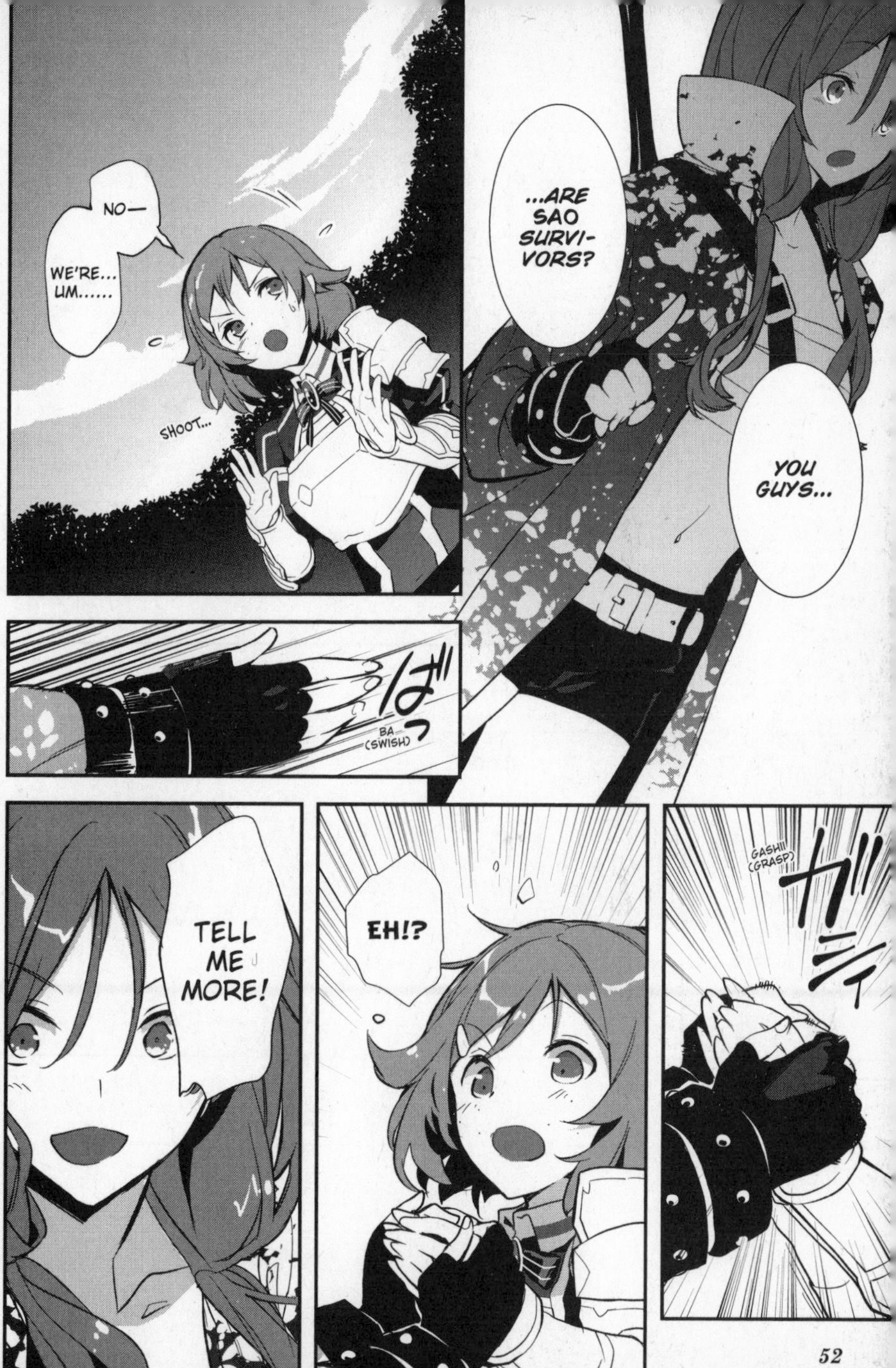
YOU GUYS...
...ARE SAO SURVIVORS?
NO—
WE'RE... UM......
SHOOT...
ばっ
BA (SWISH)
ガシィ
GASHII (GRASP)
EH!?
TELL ME MORE!

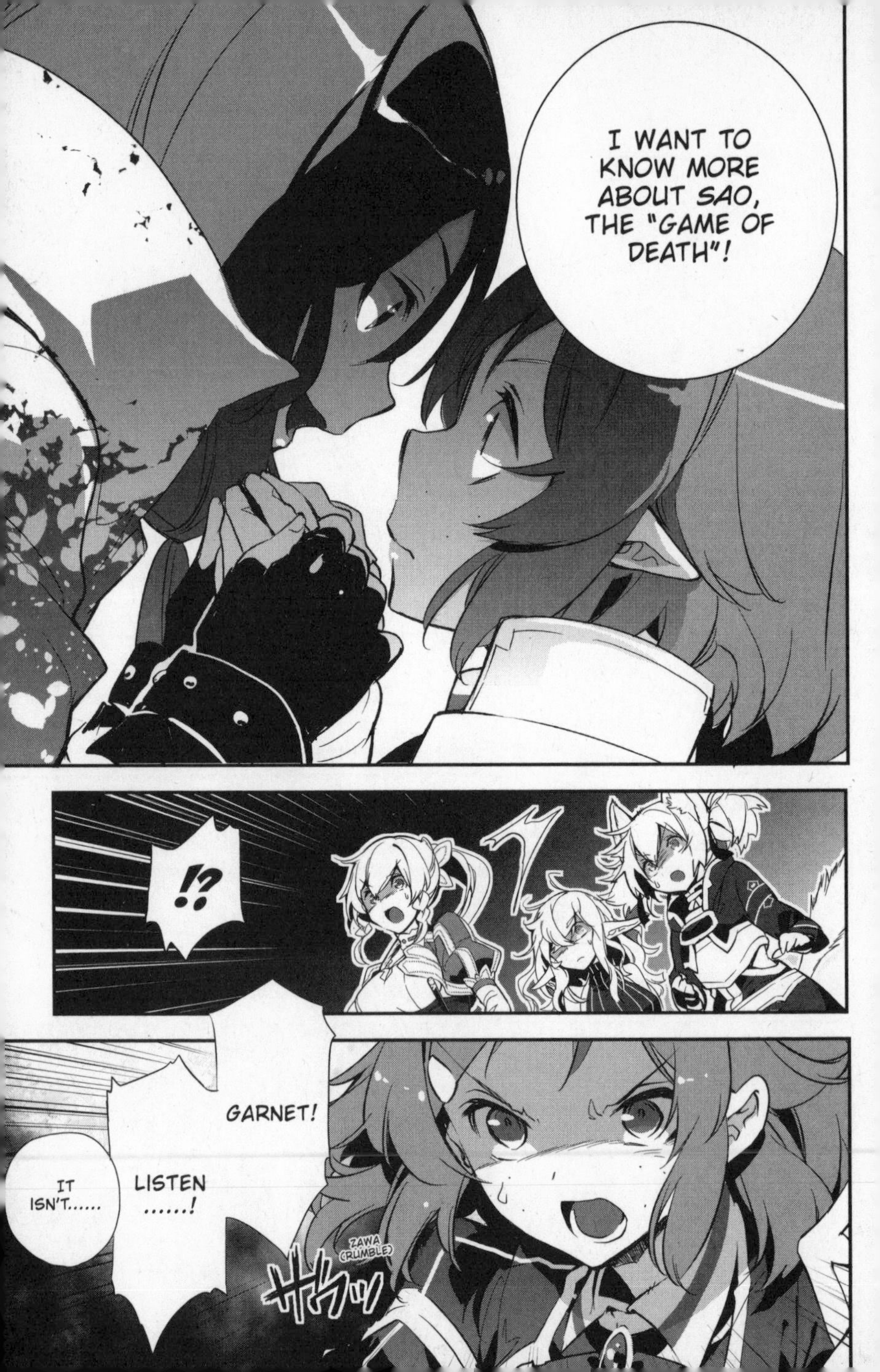
I WANT TO KNOW MORE ABOUT SAO, THE "GAME OF DEATH"!
!?
GARNET!
LISTEN ......!
IT ISN'T......
ZAWA (RUMBLE)

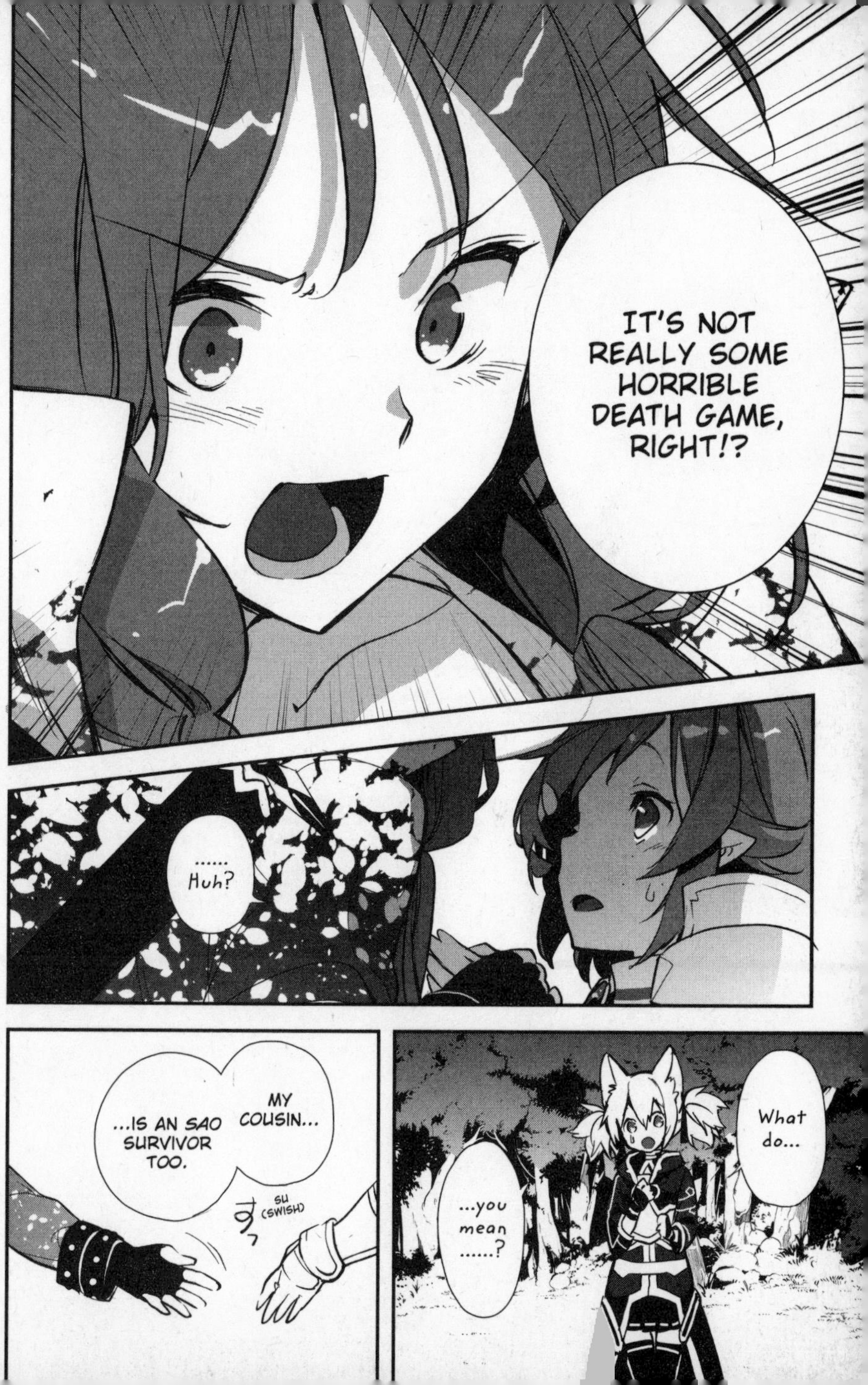
IT'S NOT REALLY SOME HORRIBLE DEATH GAME, RIGHT!?
......Huh?
What do...
...you mean ......?
MY COUSIN...
...IS AN SAO SURVIVOR TOO.
す SU (SWISH)

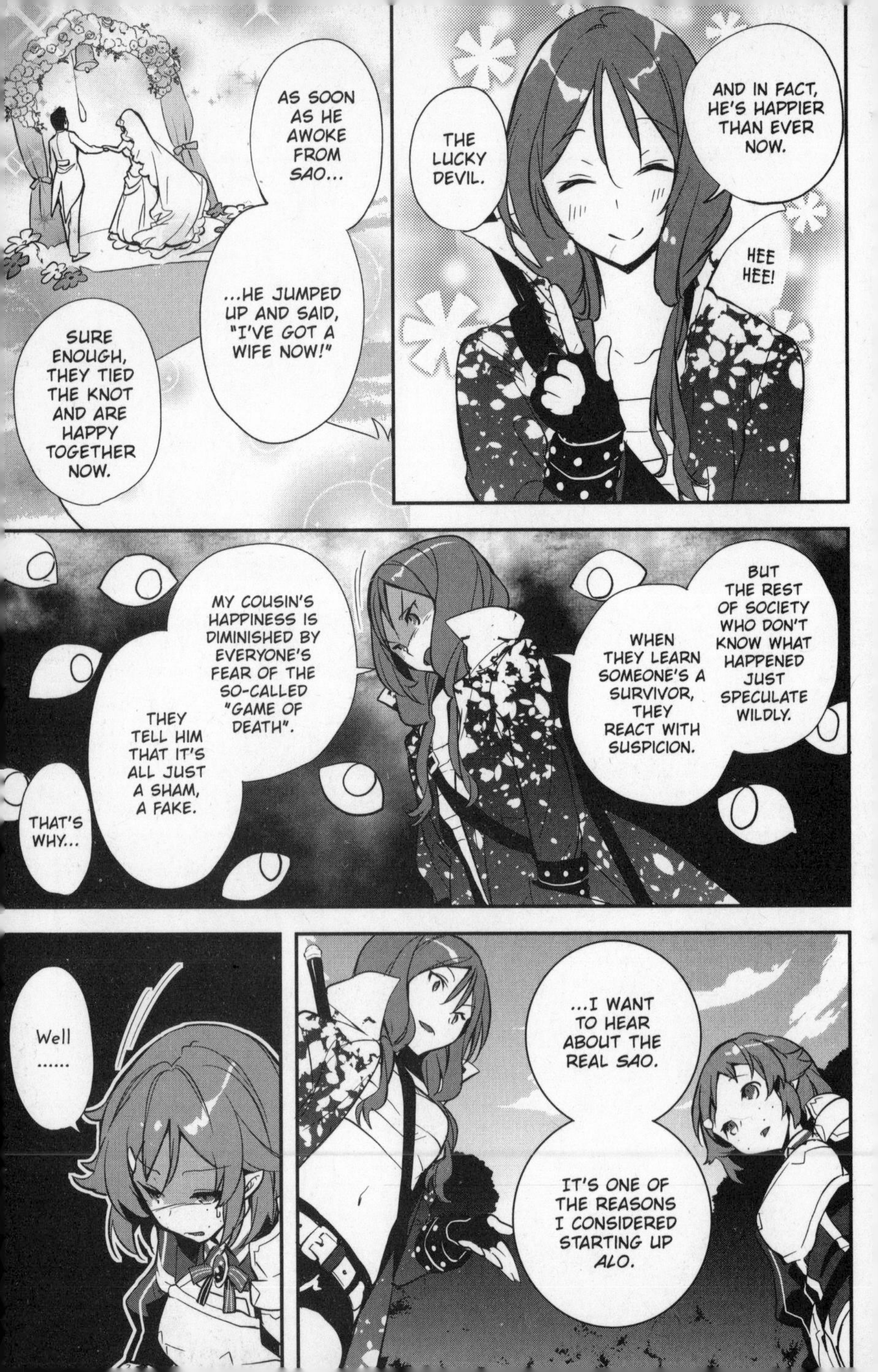

AND IN FACT, HE'S HAPPIER THAN EVER NOW.
THE LUCKY DEVIL.
HEE HEE!
AS SOON AS HE AWOKE FROM SAO...
...HE JUMPED UP AND SAID, "I'VE GOT A WIFE NOW!"
SURE ENOUGH, THEY TIED THE KNOT AND ARE HAPPY TOGETHER NOW.
BUT THE REST OF SOCIETY WHO DON'T KNOW WHAT HAPPENED JUST SPECULATE WILDLY.
WHEN THEY LEARN SOMEONE'S A SURVIVOR, THEY REACT WITH SUSPICION.
MY COUSIN'S HAPPINESS IS DIMINISHED BY EVERYONE'S FEAR OF THE SO-CALLED "GAME OF DEATH".
THEY TELL HIM THAT IT'S ALL JUST A SHAM, A FAKE.
THAT'S WHY...
...I WANT TO HEAR ABOUT THE REAL SAO.
IT'S ONE OF THE REASONS I CONSIDERED STARTING UP ALO.
Well ......

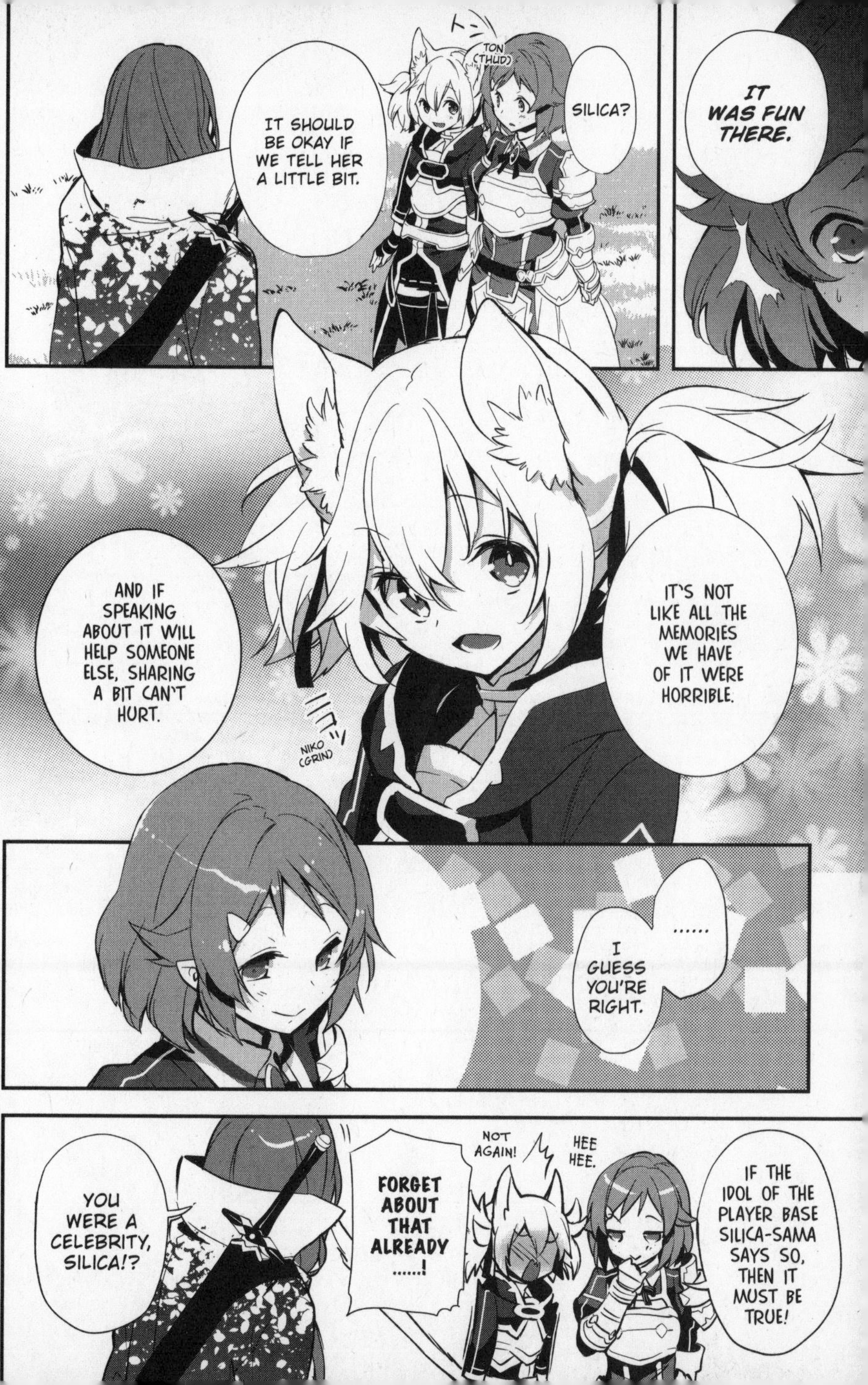
IT WAS FUN THERE.
SILICA?
TON (THUD)
IT SHOULD BE OKAY IF WE TELL HER A LITTLE BIT.
IT'S NOT LIKE ALL THE MEMORIES WE HAVE OF IT WERE HORRIBLE.
NIKO (GRIN)
AND IF SPEAKING ABOUT IT WILL HELP SOMEONE ELSE, SHARING A BIT CAN'T HURT.
......
I GUESS YOU'RE RIGHT.
IF THE IDOL OF THE PLAYER BASE SILICA-SAMA SAYS SO, THEN IT MUST BE TRUE!
HEE HEE.
NOT AGAIN!
FORGET ABOUT THAT ALREADY ......!
YOU WERE A CELEBRITY, SILICA!?

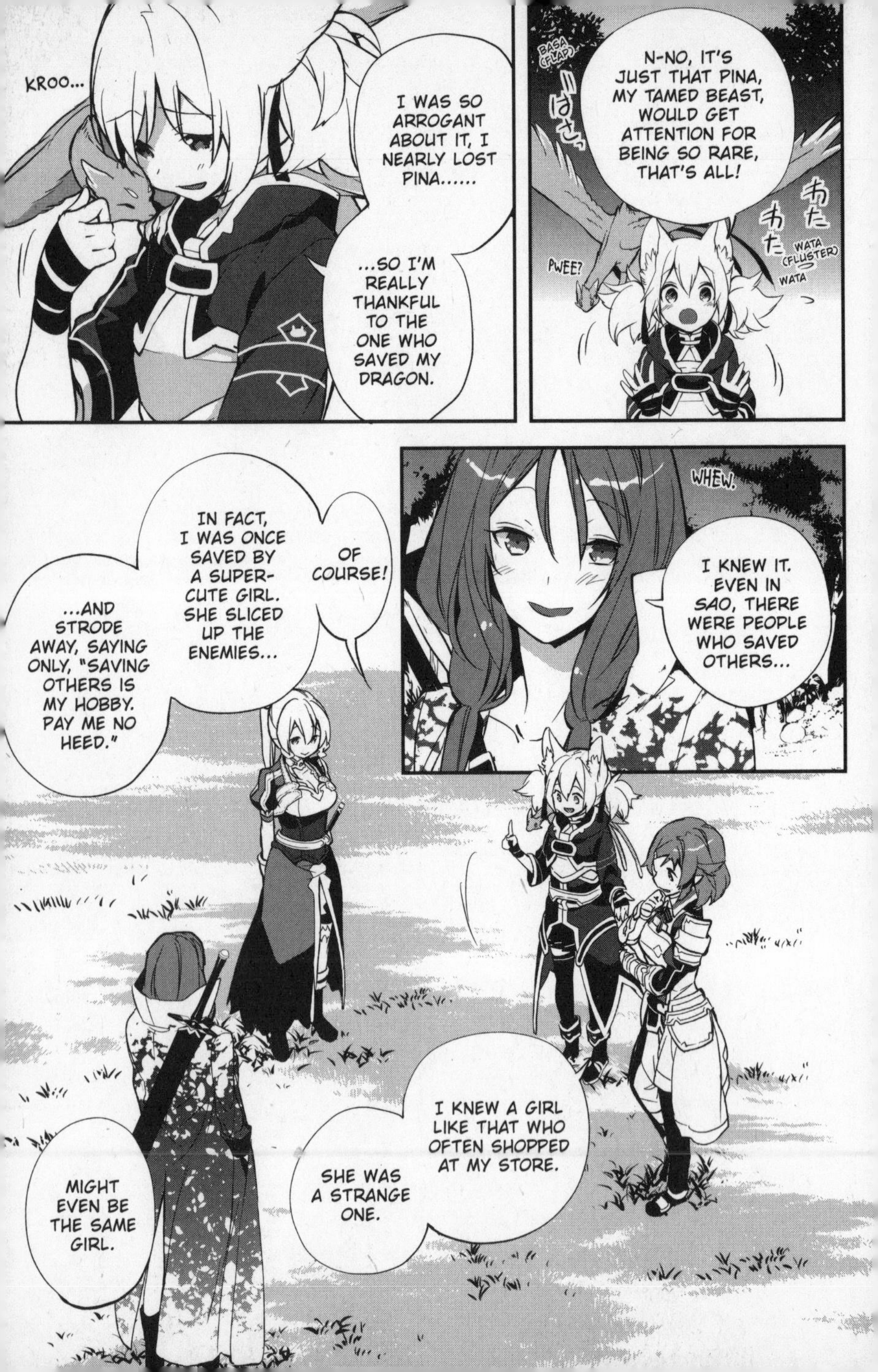
BASA (FLAP)
N-NO, IT'S JUST THAT PINA, MY TAMED BEAST, WOULD GET ATTENTION FOR BEING SO RARE, THAT'S ALL!
WATA (FLUSTER) WATA
PWEE?
I WAS SO ARROGANT ABOUT IT, I NEARLY LOST PINA......
KROO...
...SO I'M REALLY THANKFUL TO THE ONE WHO SAVED MY DRAGON.
WHEW.
I KNEW IT. EVEN IN SAO, THERE WERE PEOPLE WHO SAVED OTHERS...
OF COURSE!
IN FACT, I WAS ONCE SAVED BY A SUPER-CUTE GIRL. SHE SLICED UP THE ENEMIES...
...AND STRODE AWAY, SAYING ONLY, "SAVING OTHERS IS MY HOBBY. PAY ME NO HEED."
I KNEW A GIRL LIKE THAT WHO OFTEN SHOPPED AT MY STORE.
SHE WAS A STRANGE ONE.
MIGHT EVEN BE THE SAME GIRL.

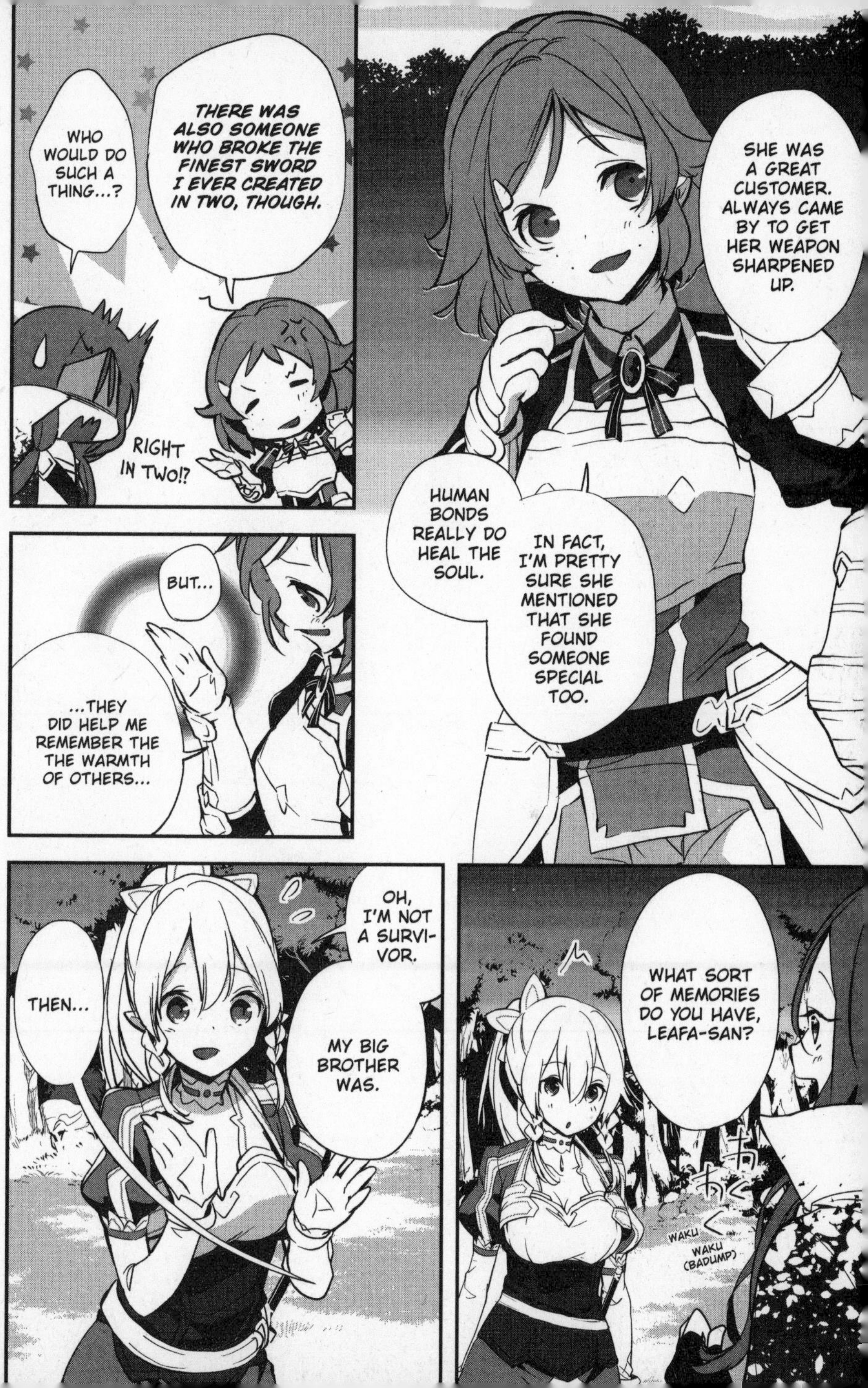
SHE WAS A GREAT CUSTOMER. ALWAYS CAME BY TO GET HER WEAPON SHARPENED UP.
IN FACT, I'M PRETTY SURE SHE MENTIONED THAT SHE FOUND SOMEONE SPECIAL TOO.
THERE WAS ALSO SOMEONE WHO BROKE THE FINEST SWORD I EVER CREATED IN TWO, THOUGH.
WHO WOULD DO SUCH A THING...?
RIGHT IN TWO!?
HUMAN BONDS REALLY DO HEAL THE SOUL.
BUT...
...THEY DID HELP ME REMEMBER THE THE WARMTH OF OTHERS...
WHAT SORT OF MEMORIES DO YOU HAVE, LEAFA-SAN?
WAKU WAKU (BADUMP)
OH, I'M NOT A SURVIVOR.
THEN...
MY BIG BROTHER WAS.

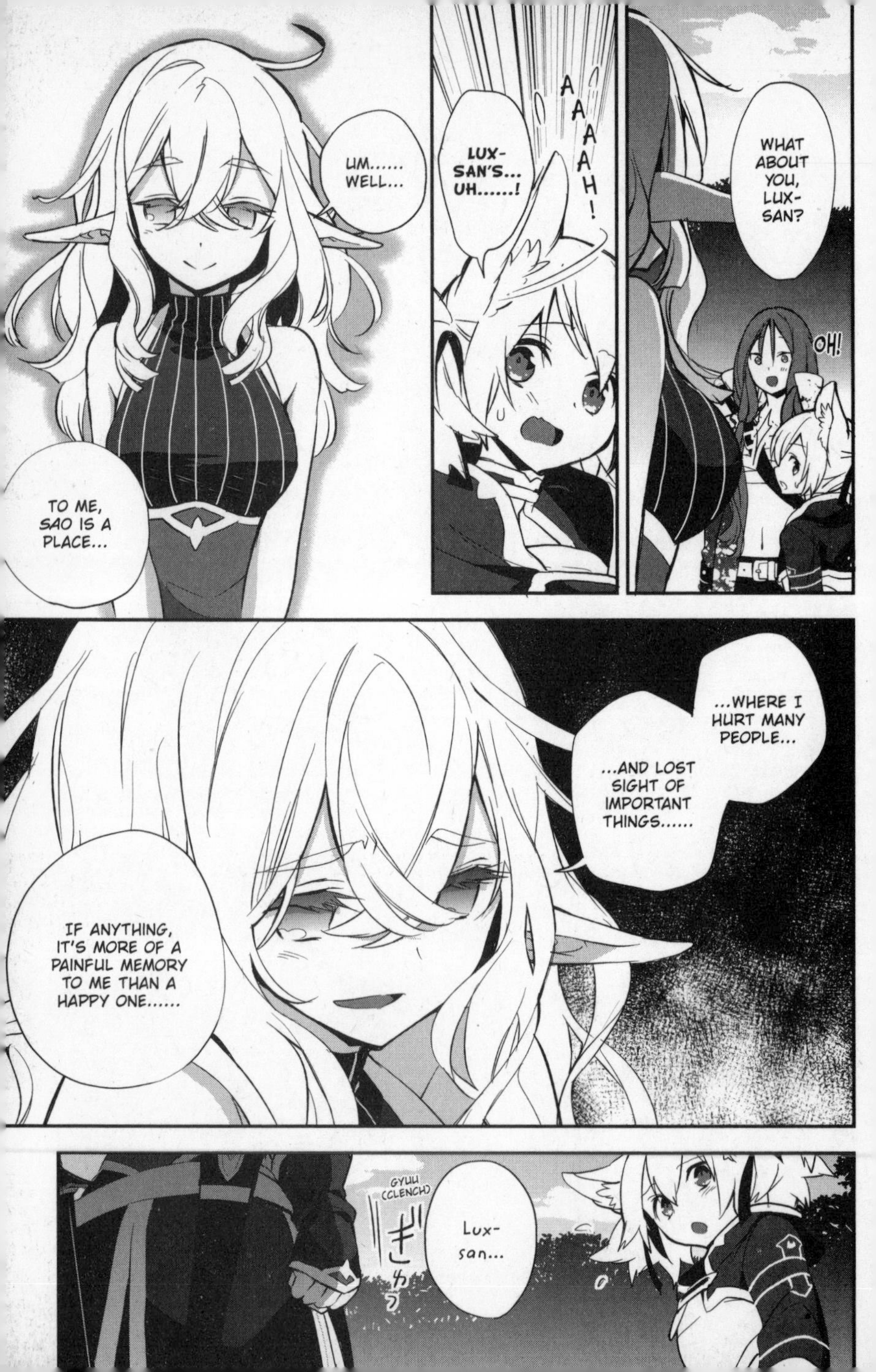
WHAT ABOUT YOU, LUX-SAN?
OH!
AAAAH!
LUX-SAN'S... UH......!
UM...... WELL...
TO ME, SAO IS A PLACE...
...WHERE I HURT MANY PEOPLE...
...AND LOST SIGHT OF IMPORTANT THINGS......
IF ANYTHING, IT'S MORE OF A PAINFUL MEMORY TO ME THAN A HAPPY ONE......
Lux-san...
GYUU (CLENCH)
ぎゅっ

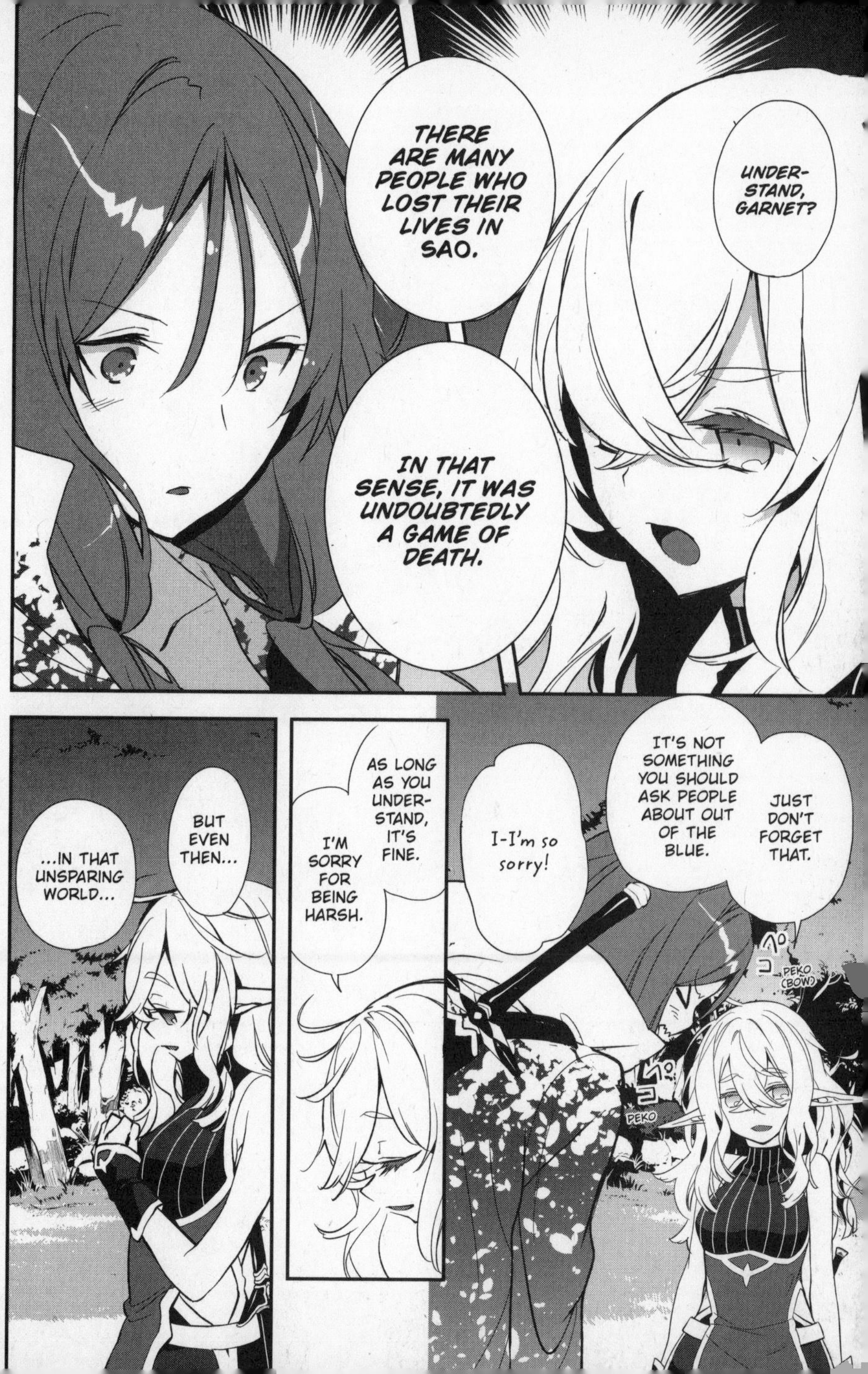
UNDER-STAND, GARNET?
THERE ARE MANY PEOPLE WHO LOST THEIR LIVES IN SAO.
IN THAT SENSE, IT WAS UNDOUBTEDLY A GAME OF DEATH.
JUST DON'T FORGET THAT.
IT'S NOT SOMETHING YOU SHOULD ASK PEOPLE ABOUT OUT OF THE BLUE.
I-I'm so sorry!
PEKO (BOW)
PEKO
AS LONG AS YOU UNDER-STAND, IT'S FINE.
I'M SORRY FOR BEING HARSH.
BUT EVEN THEN...
...IN THAT UNSPARING WORLD...

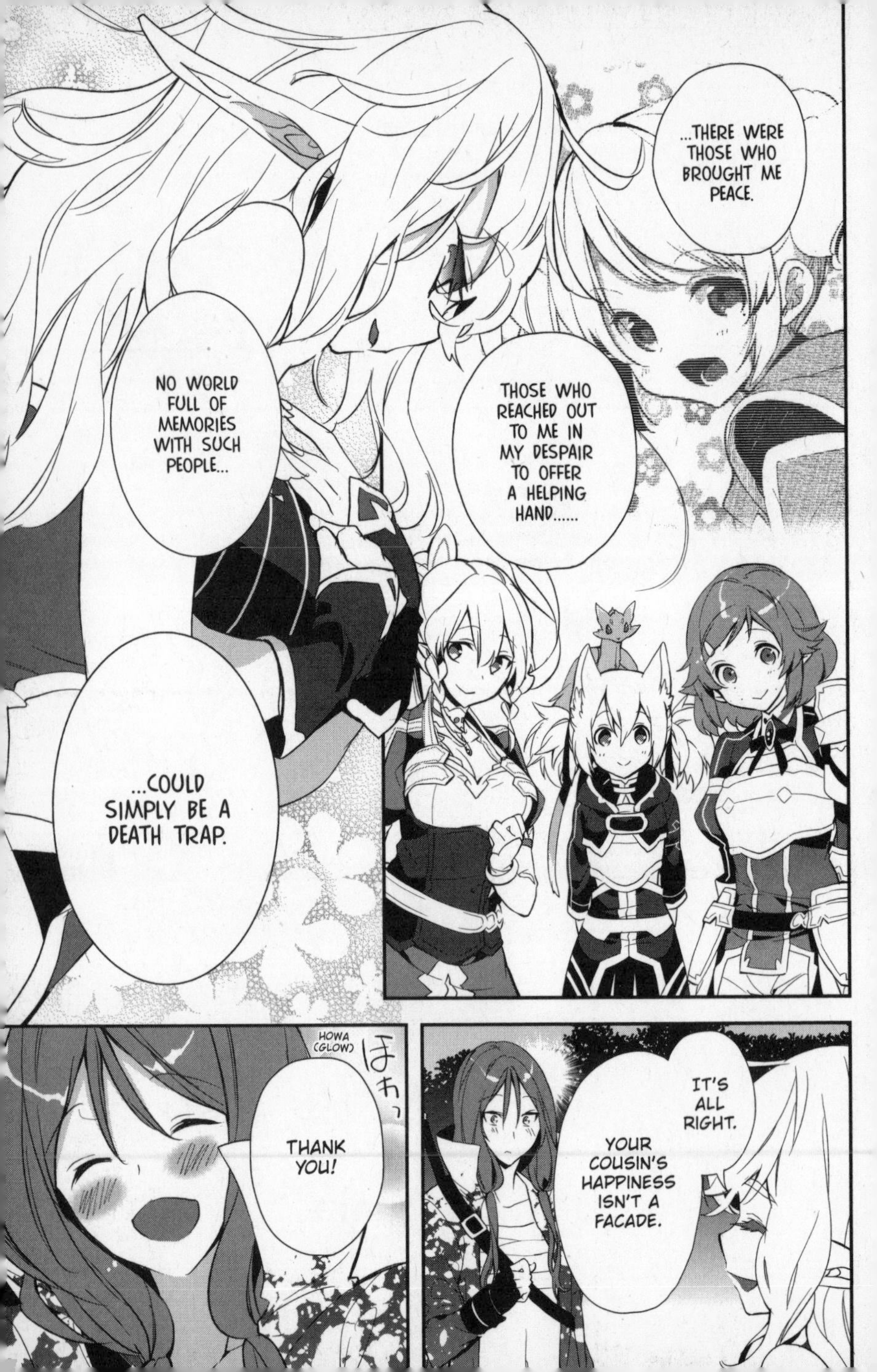
...THERE WERE THOSE WHO BROUGHT ME PEACE.
THOSE WHO REACHED OUT TO ME IN MY DESPAIR TO OFFER A HELPING HAND......
NO WORLD FULL OF MEMORIES WITH SUCH PEOPLE...
...COULD SIMPLY BE A DEATH TRAP.
IT'S ALL RIGHT.
YOUR COUSIN'S HAPPINESS ISN'T A FACADE.
ほわっ
HOWA (GLOW)
THANK YOU!

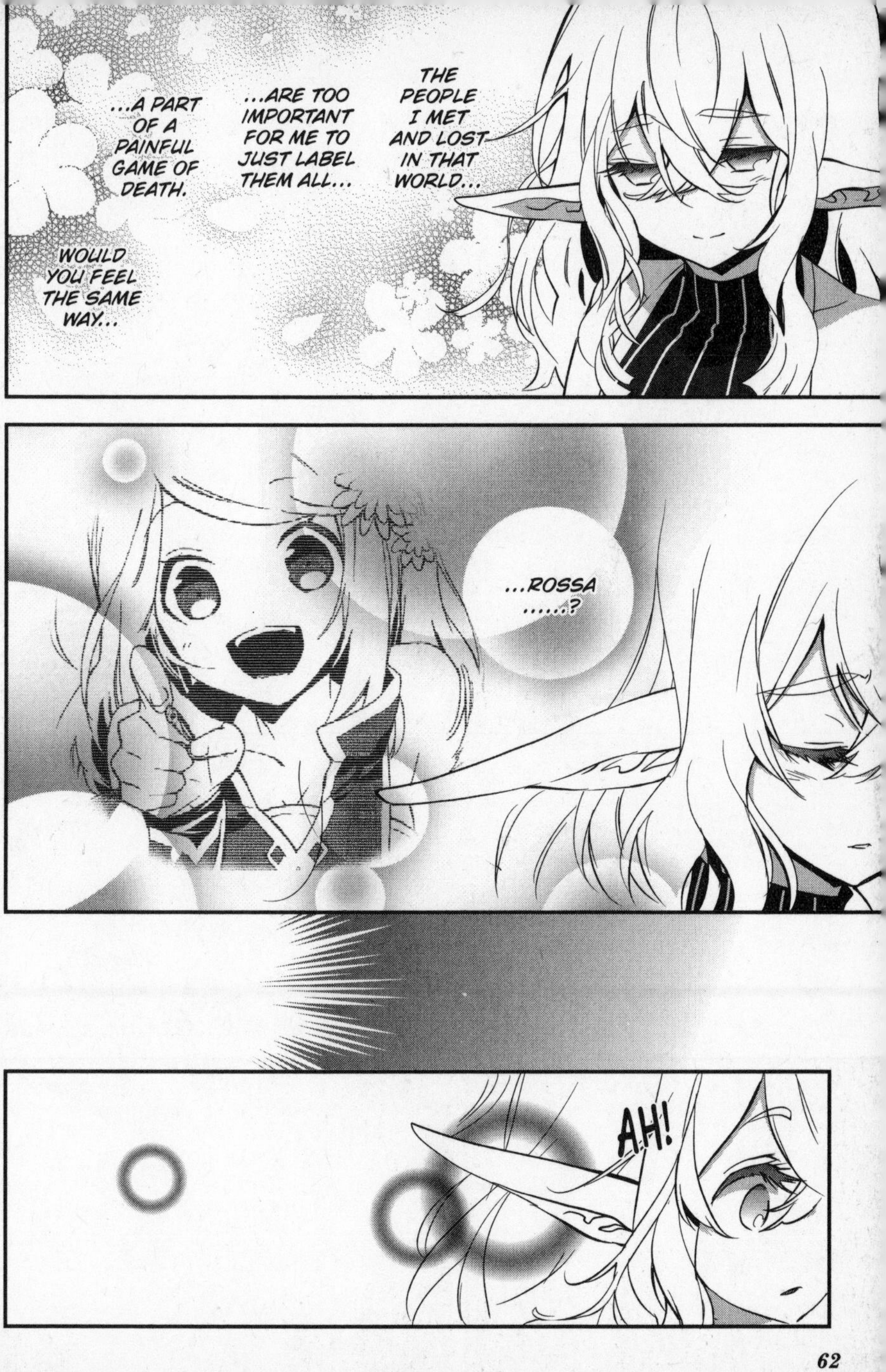
THE PEOPLE I MET AND LOST IN THAT WORLD...
...ARE TOO IMPORTANT FOR ME TO JUST LABEL THEM ALL...
...A PART OF A PAINFUL GAME OF DEATH.
WOULD YOU FEEL THE SAME WAY...
...ROSSA ......?
AH!

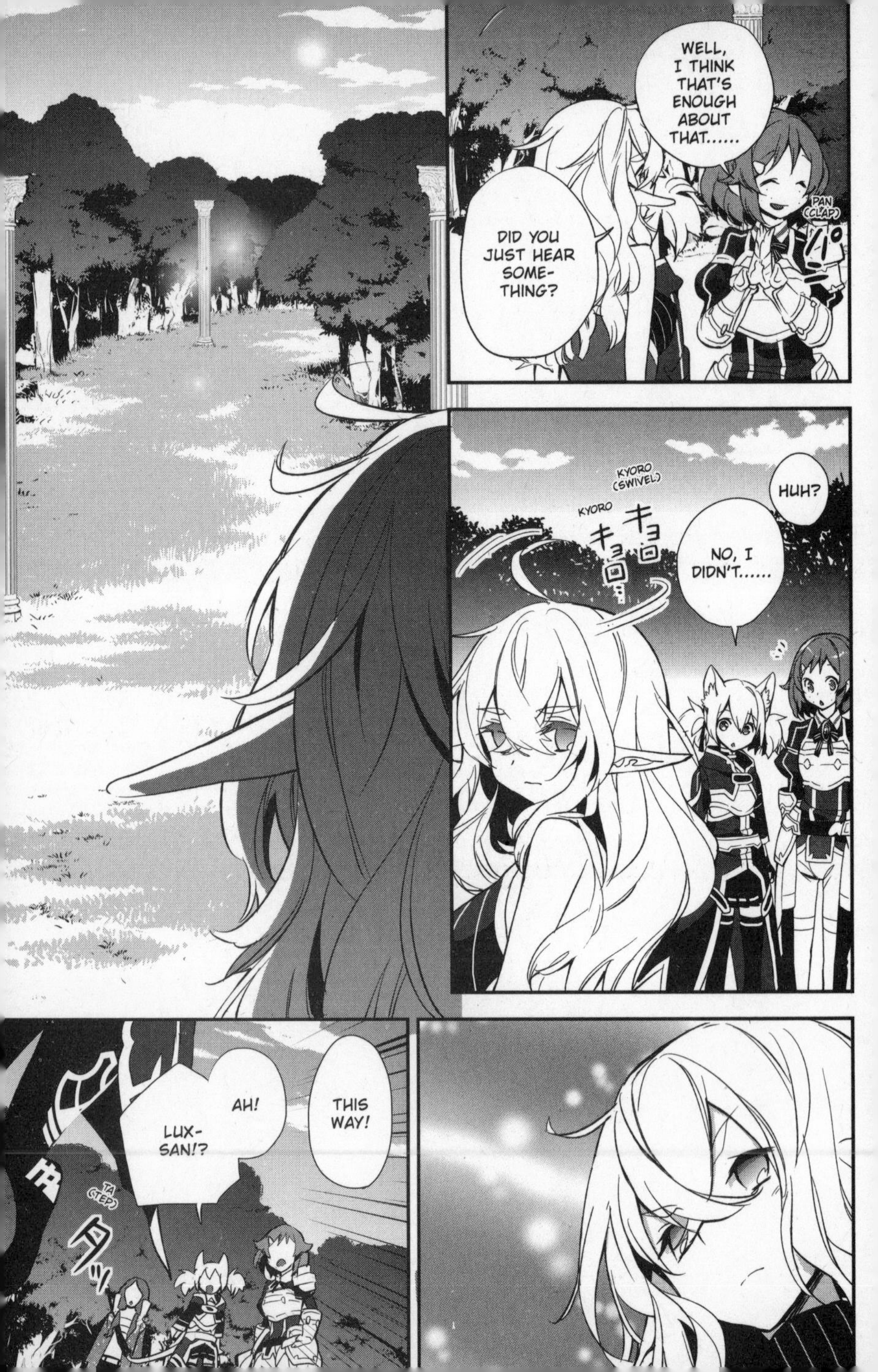
WELL, I THINK THAT'S ENOUGH ABOUT THAT......
PAN (CLAP)
DID YOU JUST HEAR SOME-THING?
HUH?
NO, I DIDN'T......
KYORO (SWIVEL)
KYORO
キョロキョロ
THIS WAY!
AH!
LUX-SAN!?
TA (TEP)
タッ

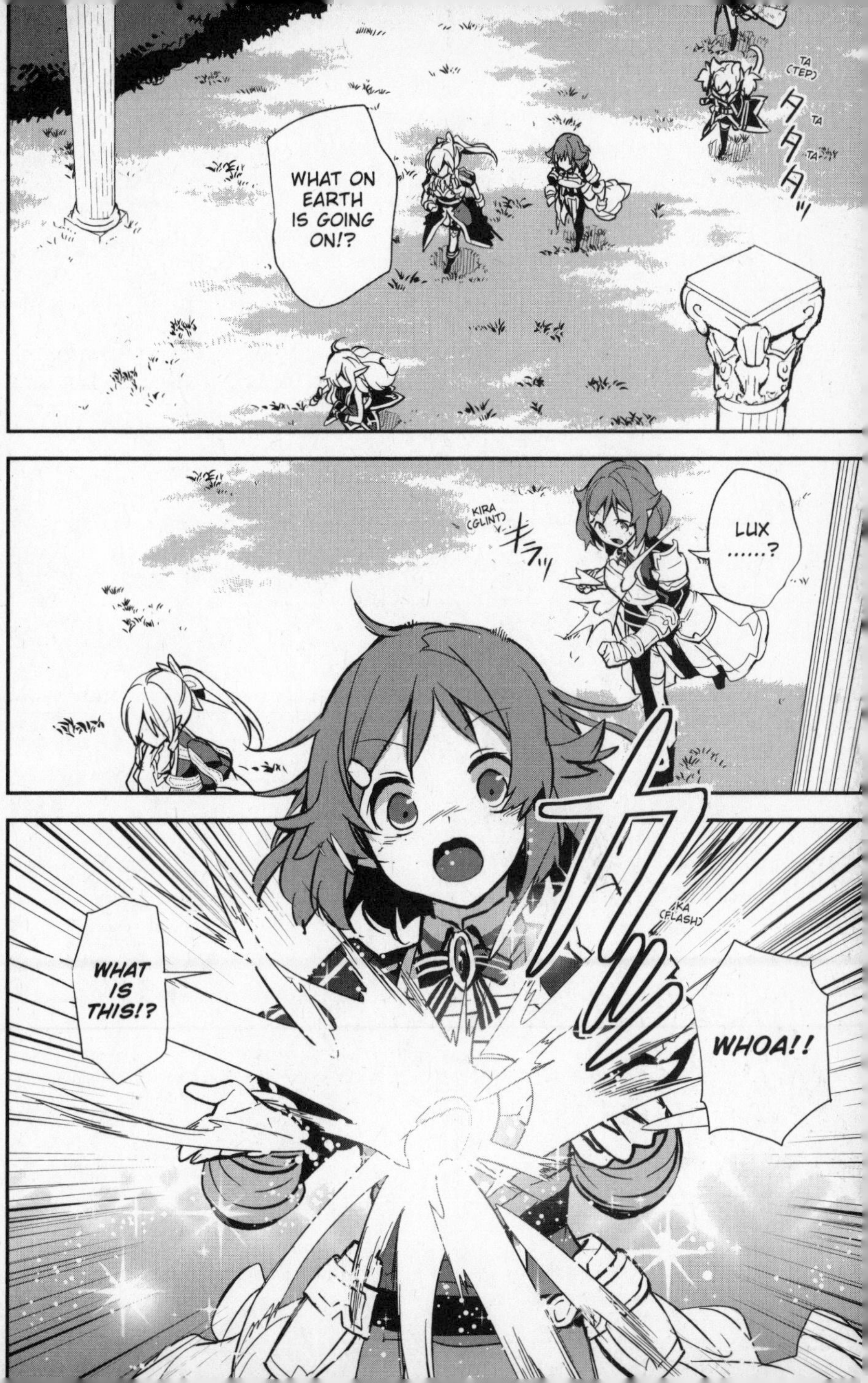

TA (TEP)
TA
TA
WHAT ON EARTH IS GOING ON!?
LUX ......?
KIRA (GLINT)
KA (FLASH)
WHOA!!
WHAT IS THIS!?

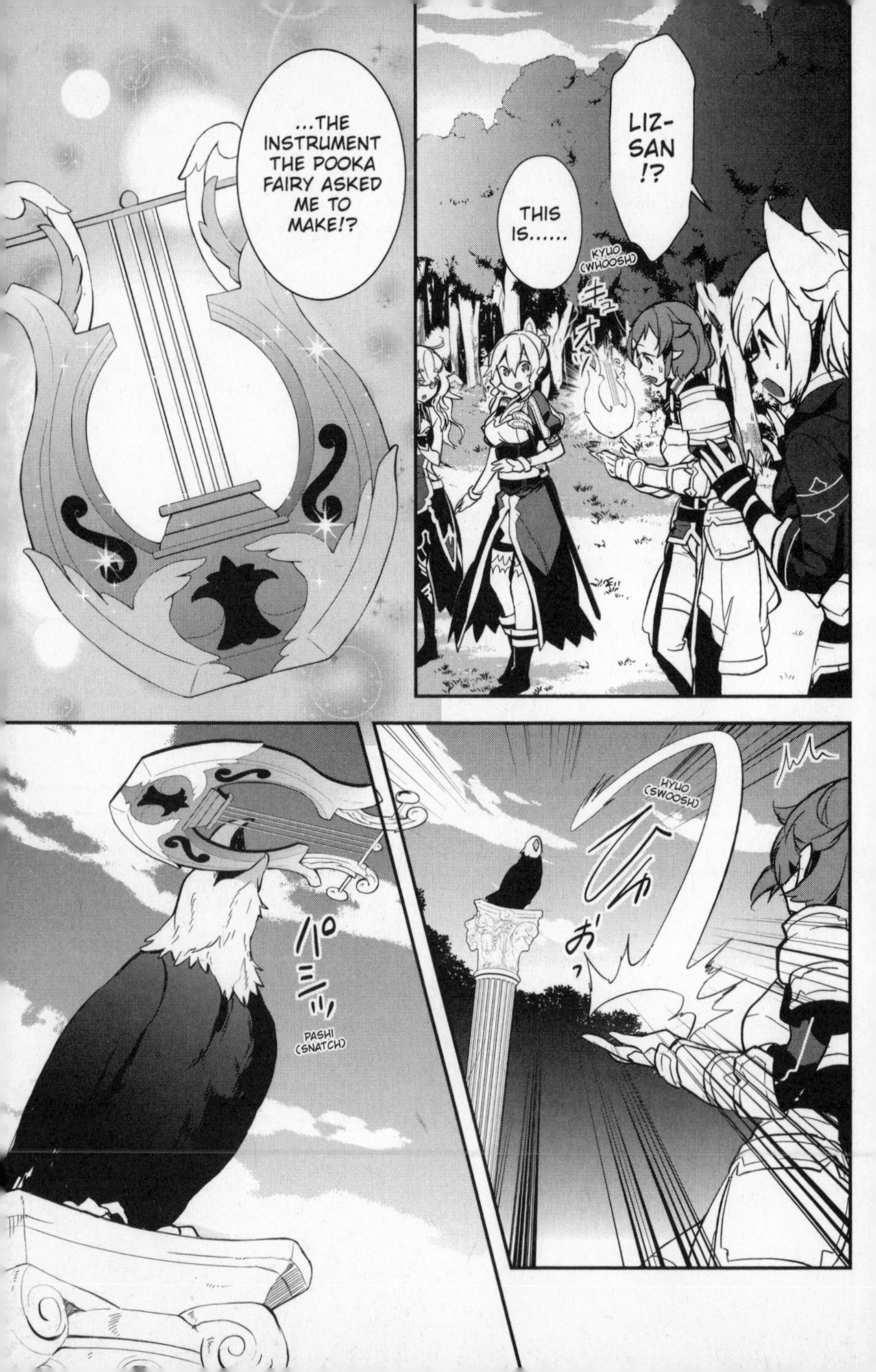
LIZ-SAN!?
THIS IS......
KYUO (WHOOSH)
...THE INSTRUMENT THE POOKA FAIRY ASKED ME TO MAKE!?
HYUO (SWOOSH)
PASHI (SNATCH)

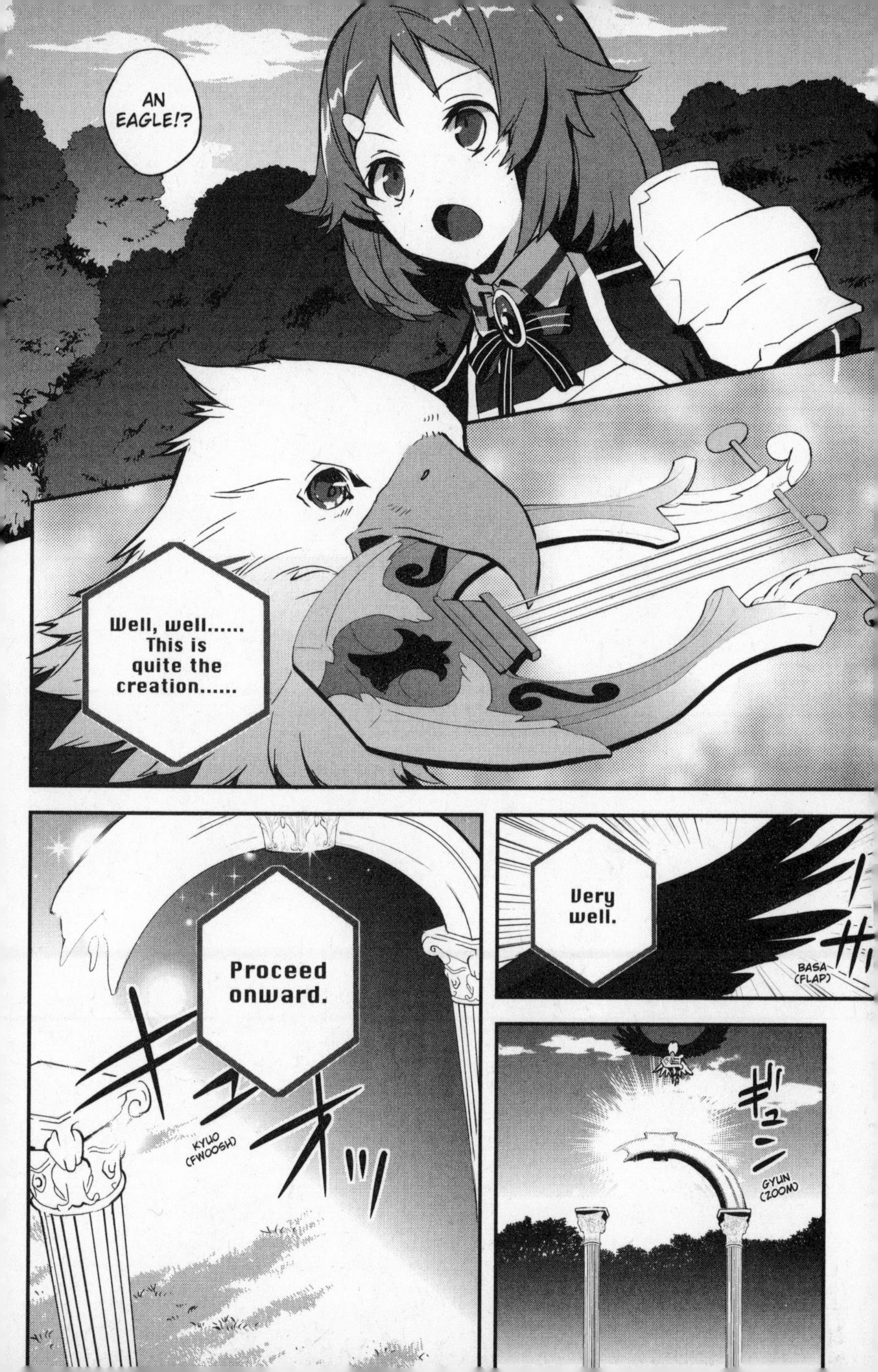
AN EAGLE!?
Well, well...... This is quite the creation......
Very well.
BASA (FLAP)
Proceed onward.
KYUO (FWOOSH)
GYUN (ZOOM)

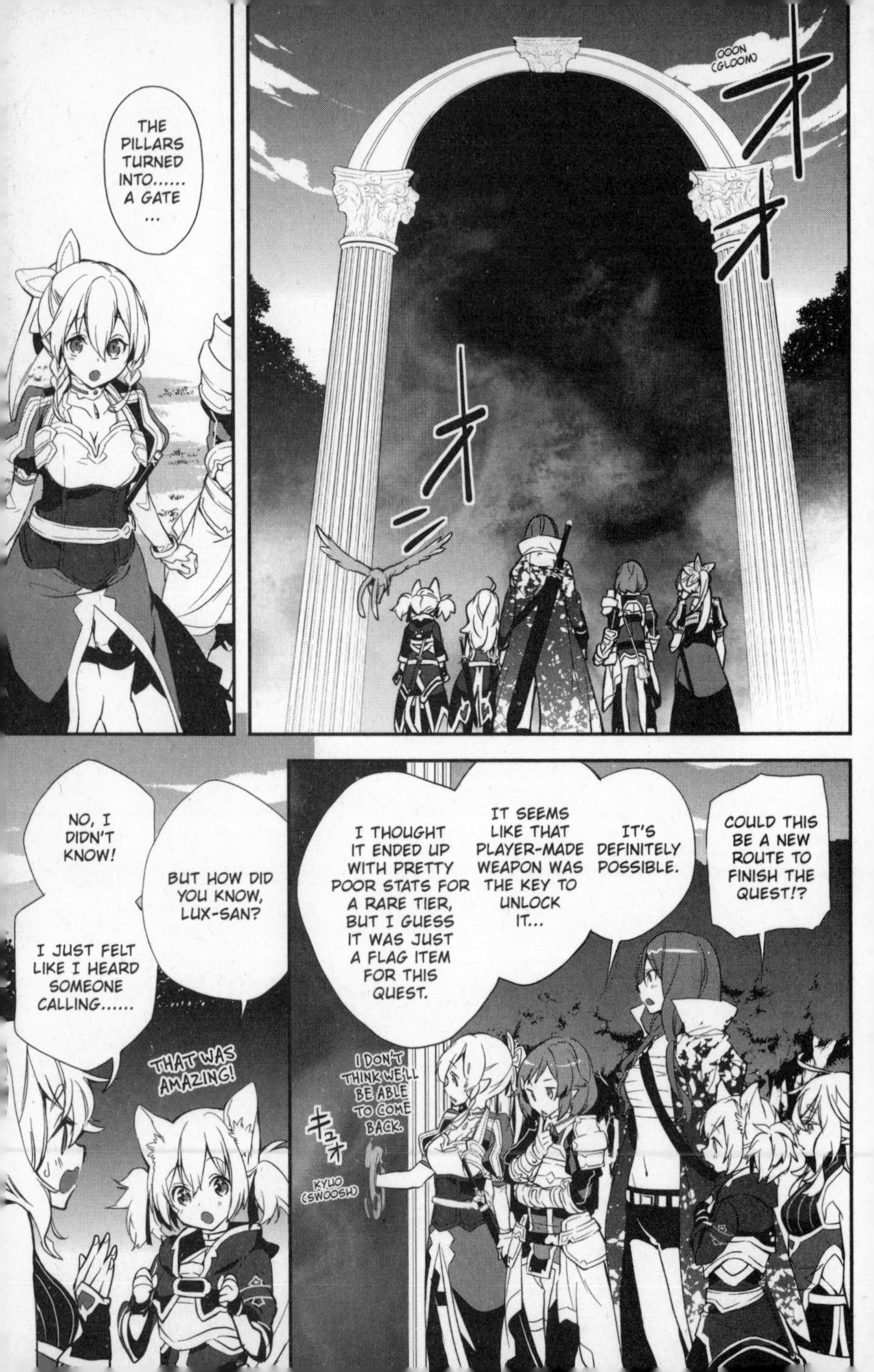
OOON (GLOOM)
THE PILLARS TURNED INTO...... A GATE ...
COULD THIS BE A NEW ROUTE TO FINISH THE QUEST!?
IT'S DEFINITELY POSSIBLE.
IT SEEMS LIKE THAT PLAYER-MADE WEAPON WAS THE KEY TO UNLOCK IT...
I THOUGHT IT ENDED UP WITH PRETTY POOR STATS FOR A RARE TIER, BUT I GUESS IT WAS JUST A FLAG ITEM FOR THIS QUEST.
I DON'T THINK WE'LL BE ABLE TO COME BACK.
KYUO (SWOOSH)
BUT HOW DID YOU KNOW, LUX-SAN?
NO, I DIDN'T KNOW!
I JUST FELT LIKE I HEARD SOMEONE CALLING......
THAT WAS AMAZING!

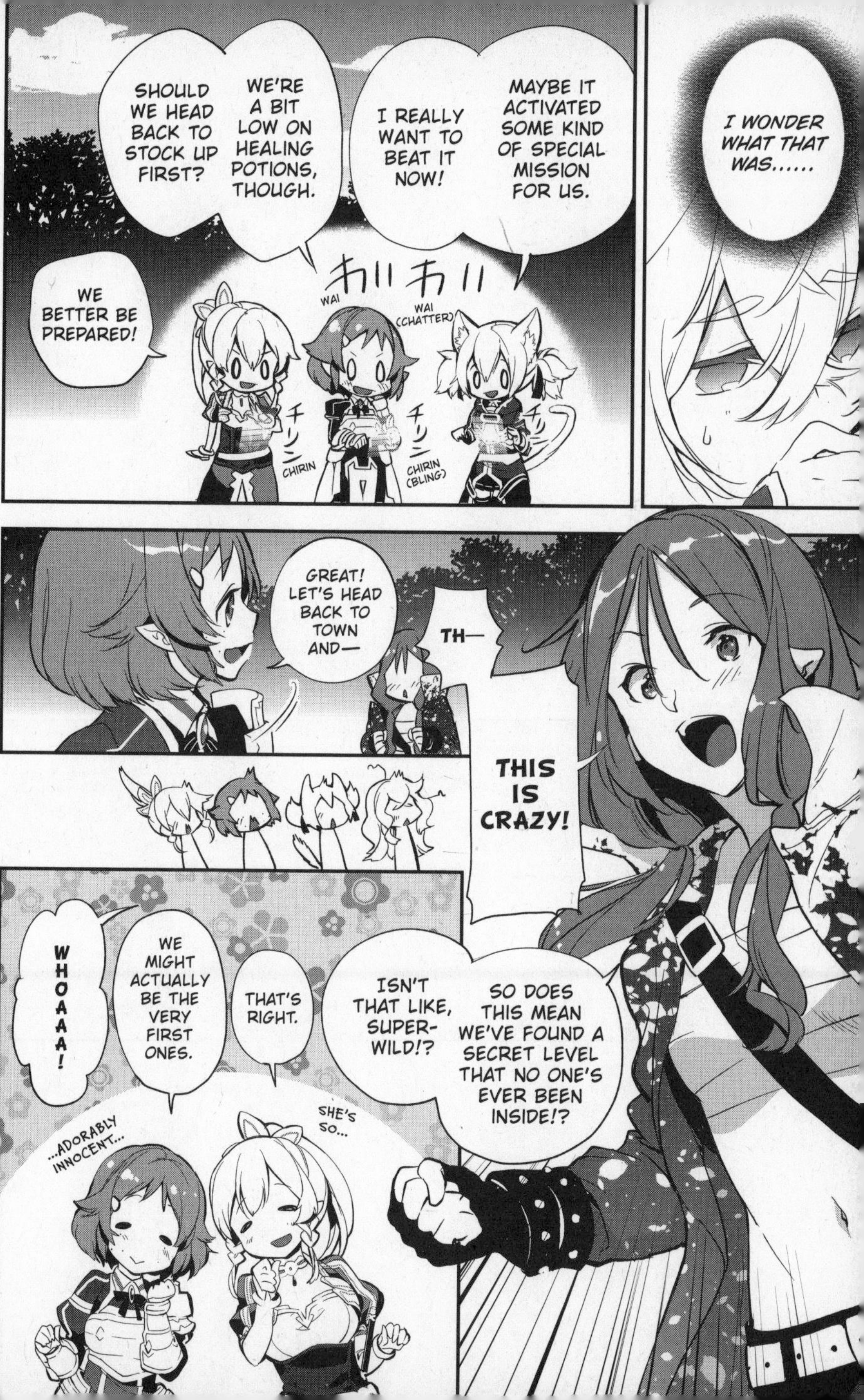
I WONDER WHAT THAT WAS......
MAYBE IT ACTIVATED SOME KIND OF SPECIAL MISSION FOR US.
I REALLY WANT TO BEAT IT NOW!
WE'RE A BIT LOW ON HEALING POTIONS, THOUGH.
SHOULD WE HEAD BACK TO STOCK UP FIRST?
わいわい
WAI WAI (CHATTER)
WE BETTER BE PREPARED!
チリン チリン
CHIRIN CHIRIN (BLING)
GREAT! LET'S HEAD BACK TO TOWN AND—
TH—
THIS IS CRAZY!
SO DOES THIS MEAN WE'VE FOUND A SECRET LEVEL THAT NO ONE'S EVER BEEN INSIDE!?
ISN'T THAT LIKE, SUPER-WILD!?
THAT'S RIGHT.
WE MIGHT ACTUALLY BE THE VERY FIRST ONES.
WHOAAAA!
SHE'S SO...
...ADORABLY INNOCENT...

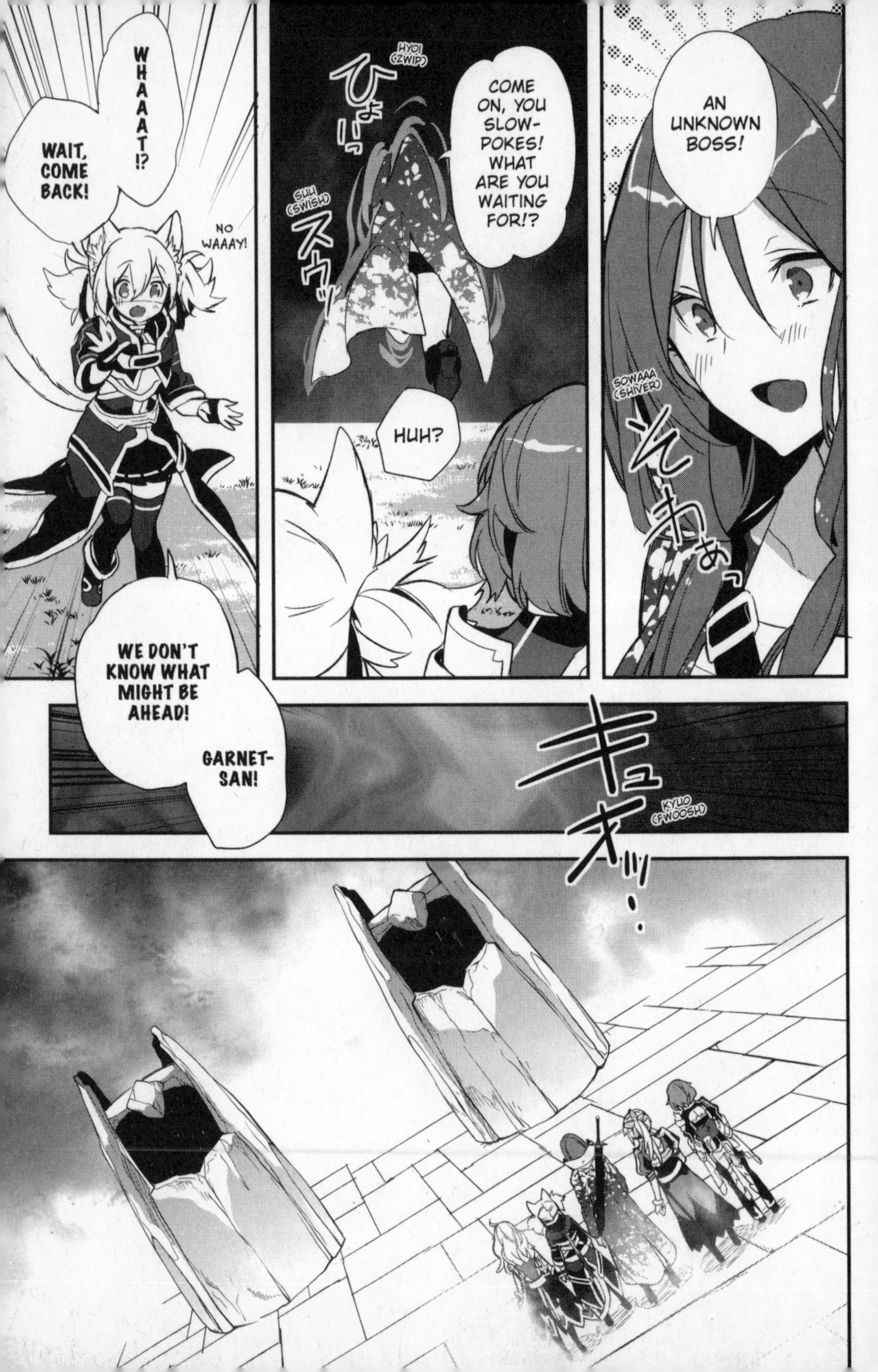
AN UNKNOWN BOSS!
SOWAAA (SHIVER)
HYOI (ZWIP)
COME ON, YOU SLOW-POKES! WHAT ARE YOU WAITING FOR!?
SUU (SWISH)
HUH?
WHAAAAT!?
WAIT, COME BACK!
NO WAAAY!
WE DON'T KNOW WHAT MIGHT BE AHEAD!
GARNET-SAN!
KYUO (FWOOSH)

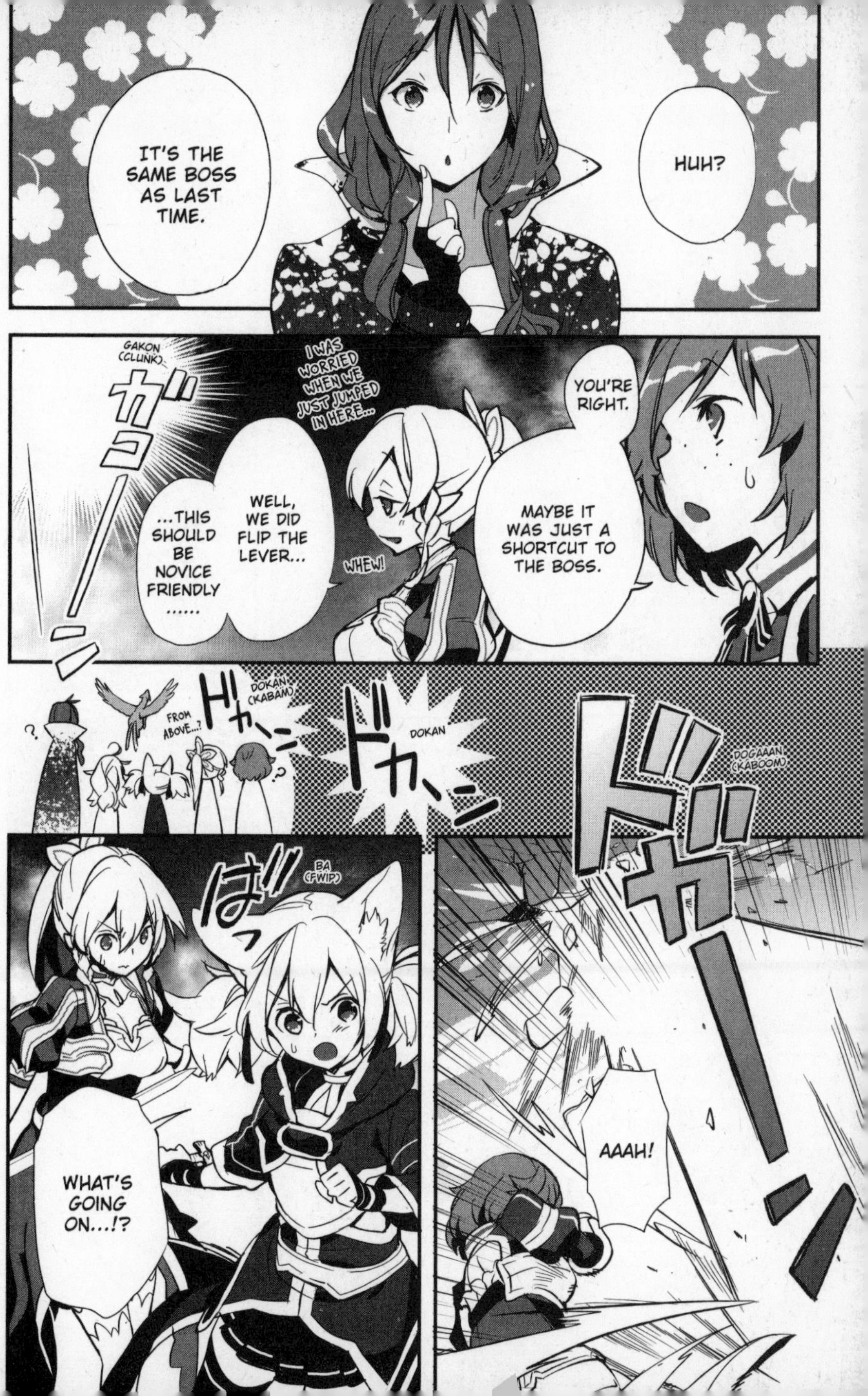
HUH?
IT'S THE SAME BOSS AS LAST TIME.
YOU'RE RIGHT.
MAYBE IT WAS JUST A SHORTCUT TO THE BOSS.
WHEW!
I WAS WORRIED WHEN WE JUST JUMPED IN HERE...
WELL, WE DID FLIP THE LEVER...
...THIS SHOULD BE NOVICE FRIENDLY ......
GAKON (CLUNK)
DOGAAAN (KABOOM)
DOKAN
DOKAN (KABAM)
FROM ABOVE...?
AAAH!
BA (FWIP)
WHAT'S GOING ON...!?

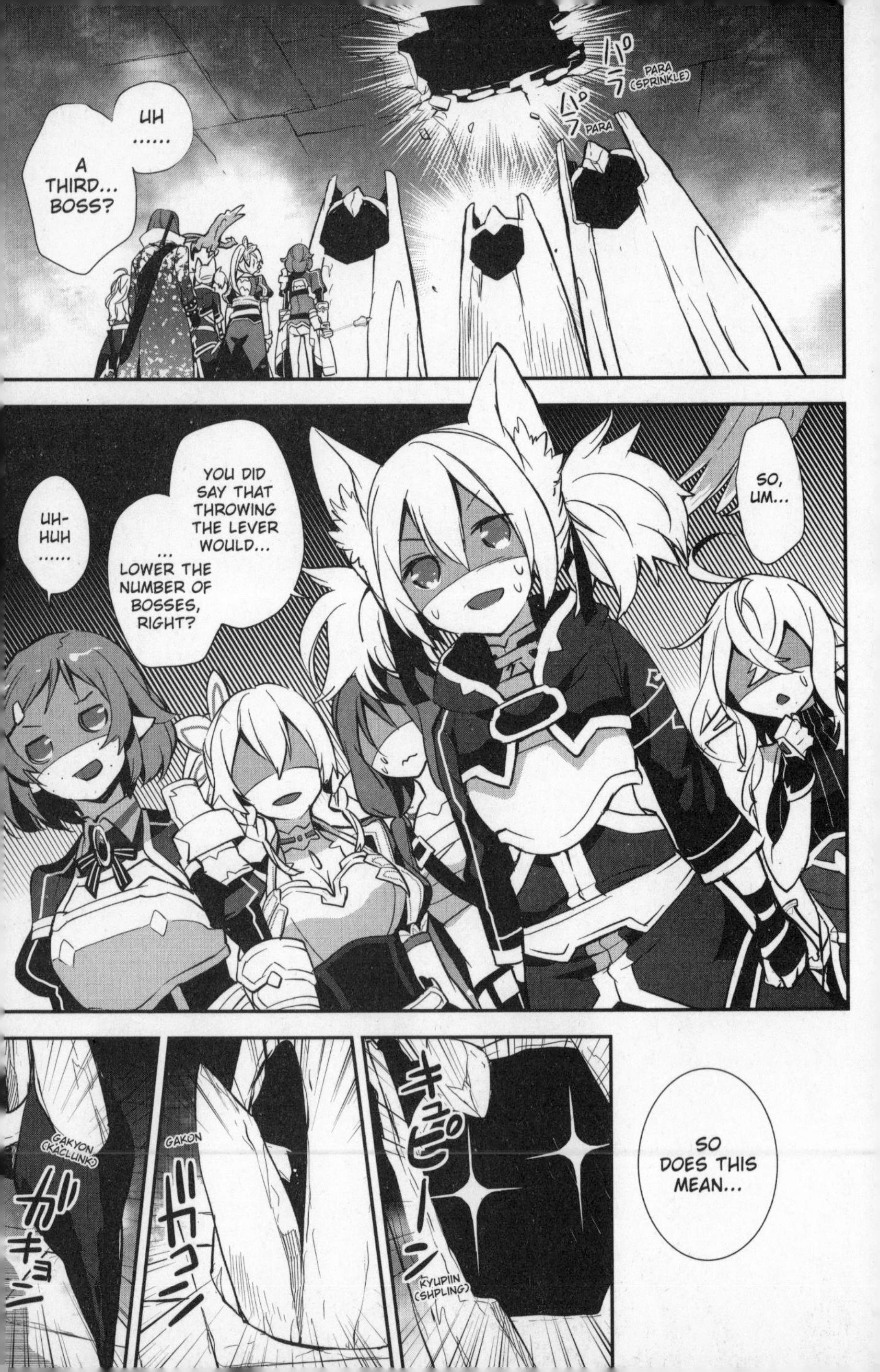
パラ
PARA (SPRINKLE)
パラ
PARA
UH ......
A THIRD... BOSS?
SO, UM...
YOU DID SAY THAT THROWING THE LEVER WOULD...
... LOWER THE NUMBER OF BOSSES, RIGHT?
UH-HUH ......
SO DOES THIS MEAN...
キュピーン
KYUPIIN (SHPLING)
ガコン
GAKON
がキョン
GAKYON (KACLUNK)

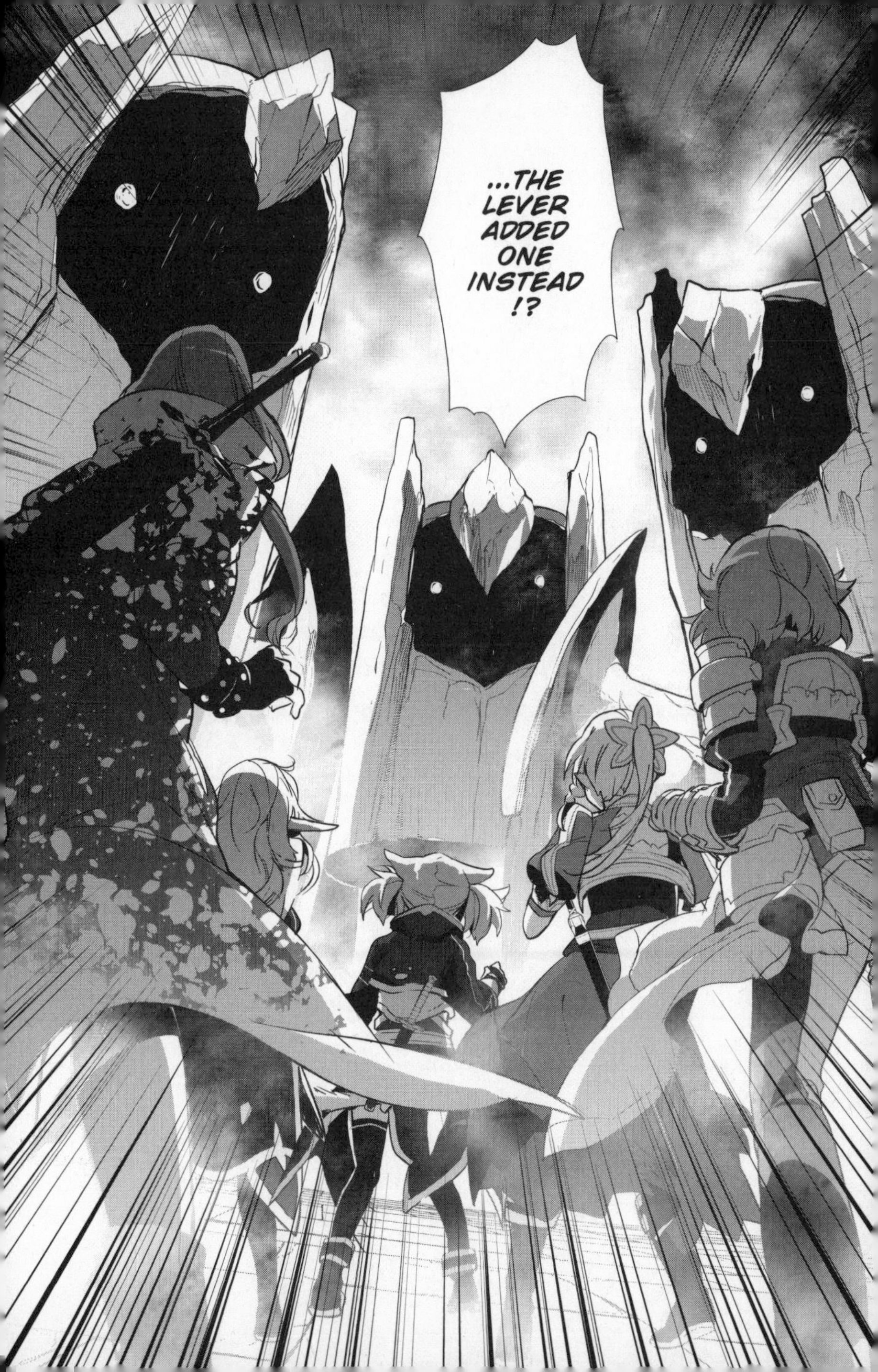
...THE LEVER ADDED ONE INSTEAD !?

SWORD ART ONLINE
GIRLS' OPS

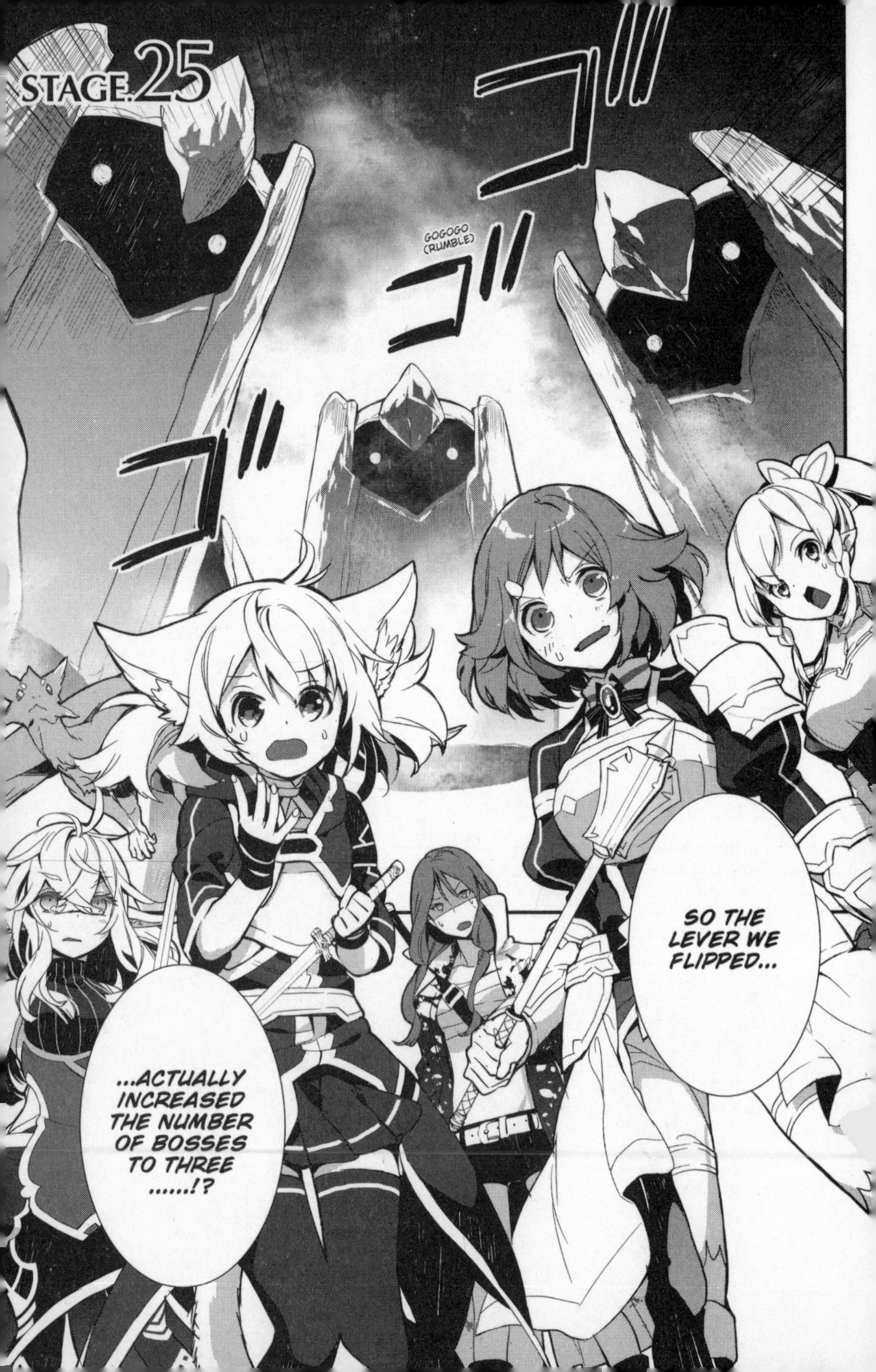
STAGE 25
GOGOGO (RUMBLE)
SO THE LEVER WE FLIPPED...
...ACTUALLY INCREASED THE NUMBER OF BOSSES TO THREE ......!?

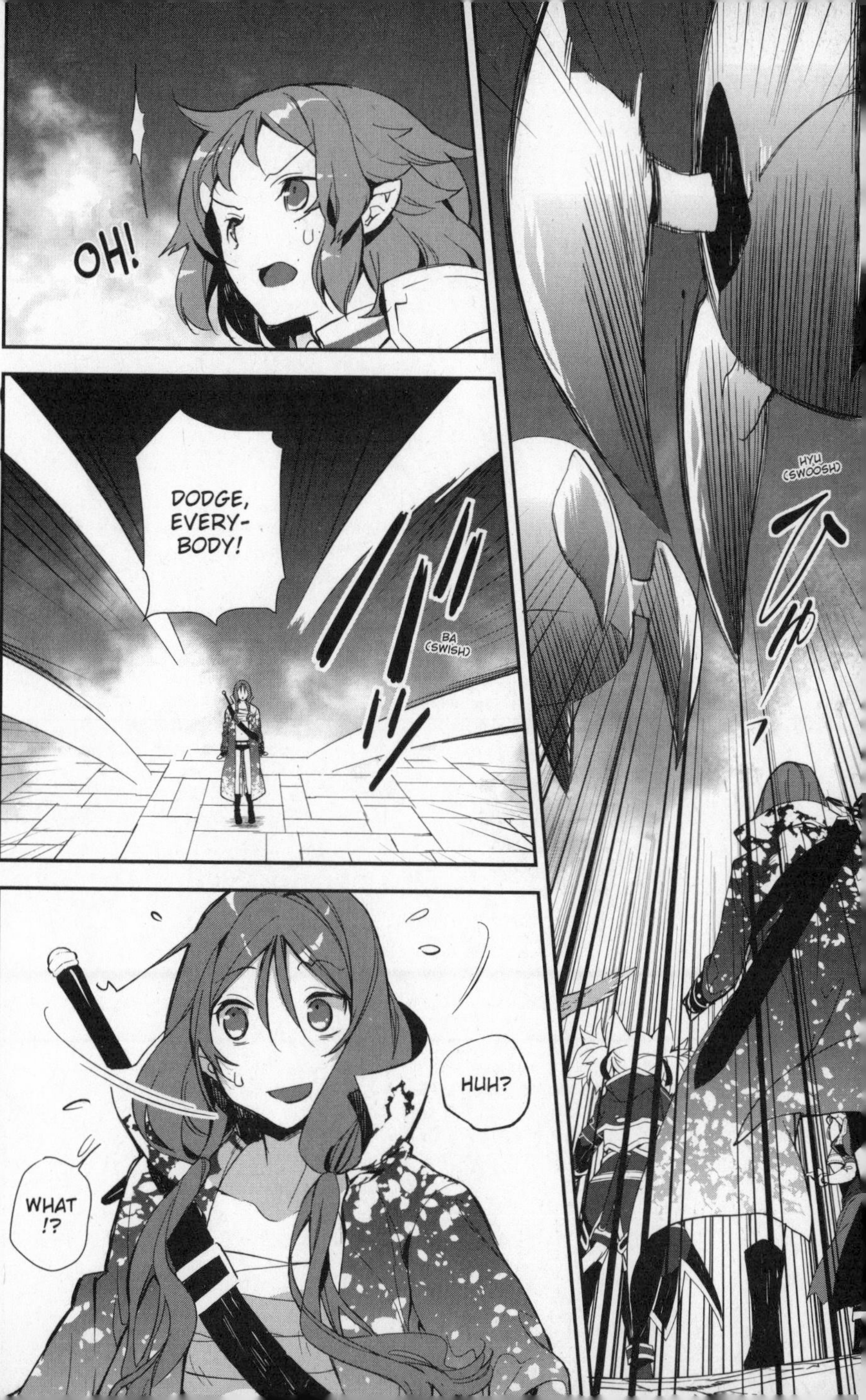
HYU
(SWOOSH)
OH!
DODGE, EVERY-BODY!
BA
(SWISH)
HUH?
WHAT!?

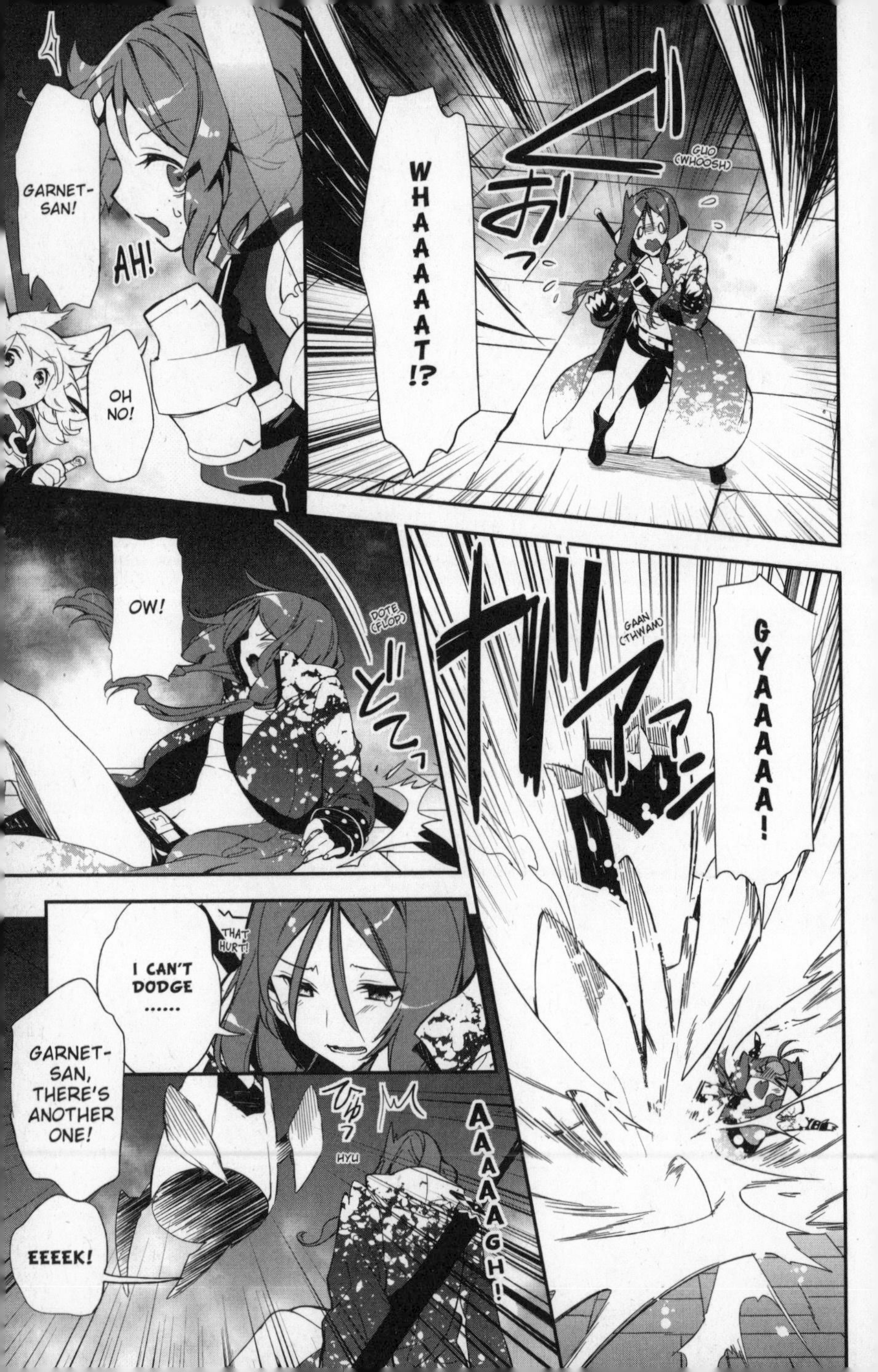
GUO (WHOOSH)
WHAAAAAAAT!?
GARNET-SAN!
AH!
OH NO!
GAAN (THWAM)
GYAAAAAA!
DOTE (FLOP)
OW!
THAT HURT!
I CAN'T DODGE ......
GARNET-SAN, THERE'S ANOTHER ONE!
HYU
AAAAAAAGH!
EEEEK!

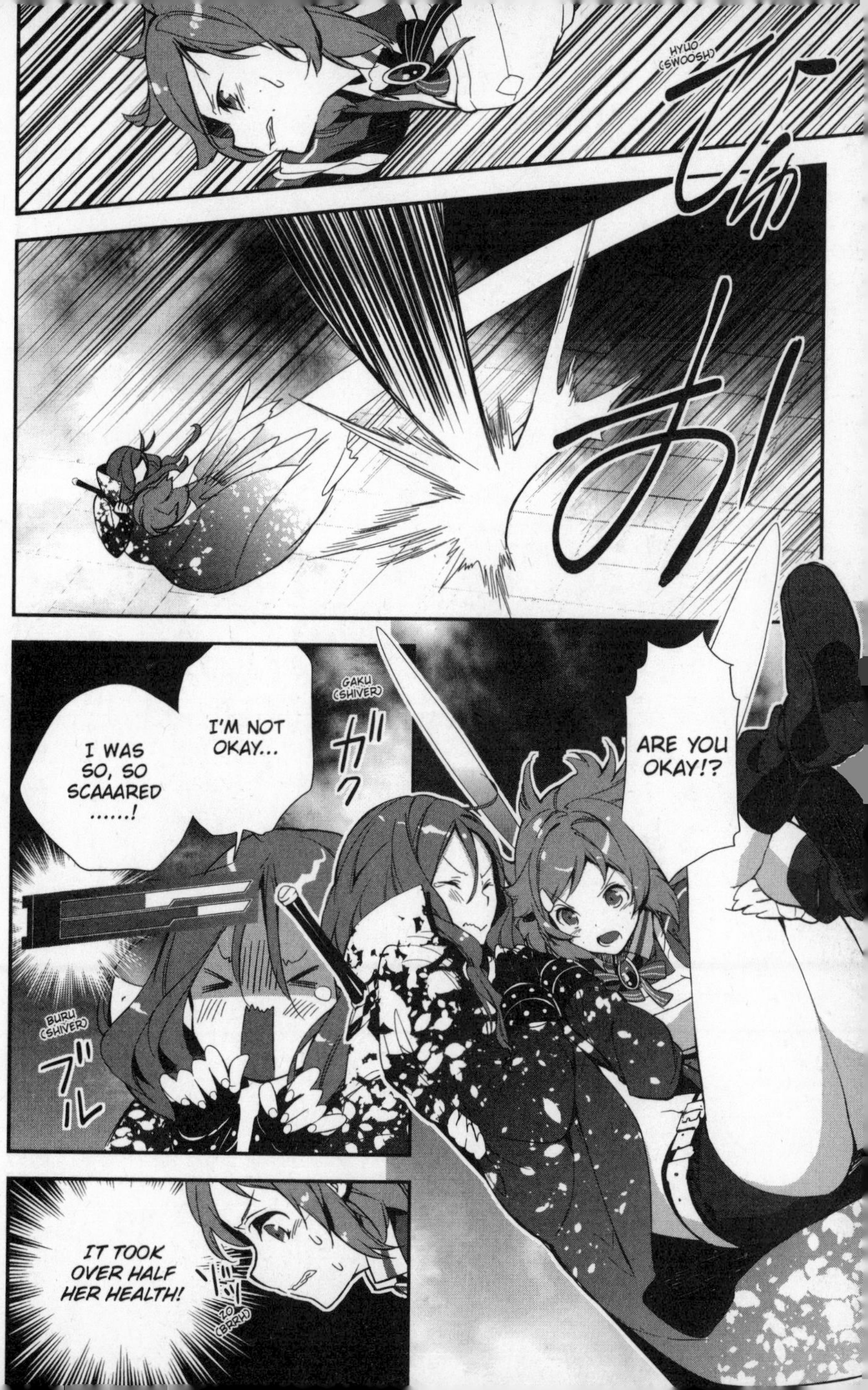
HYUO (SWOOSH)
ARE YOU OKAY!?
GAKU (SHIVER)
ガク
I'M NOT OKAY...
I WAS SO, SO SCAAARED ......!
BURU (SHIVER)
ブル
IT TOOK OVER HALF HER HEALTH!
ZO (BRRR)

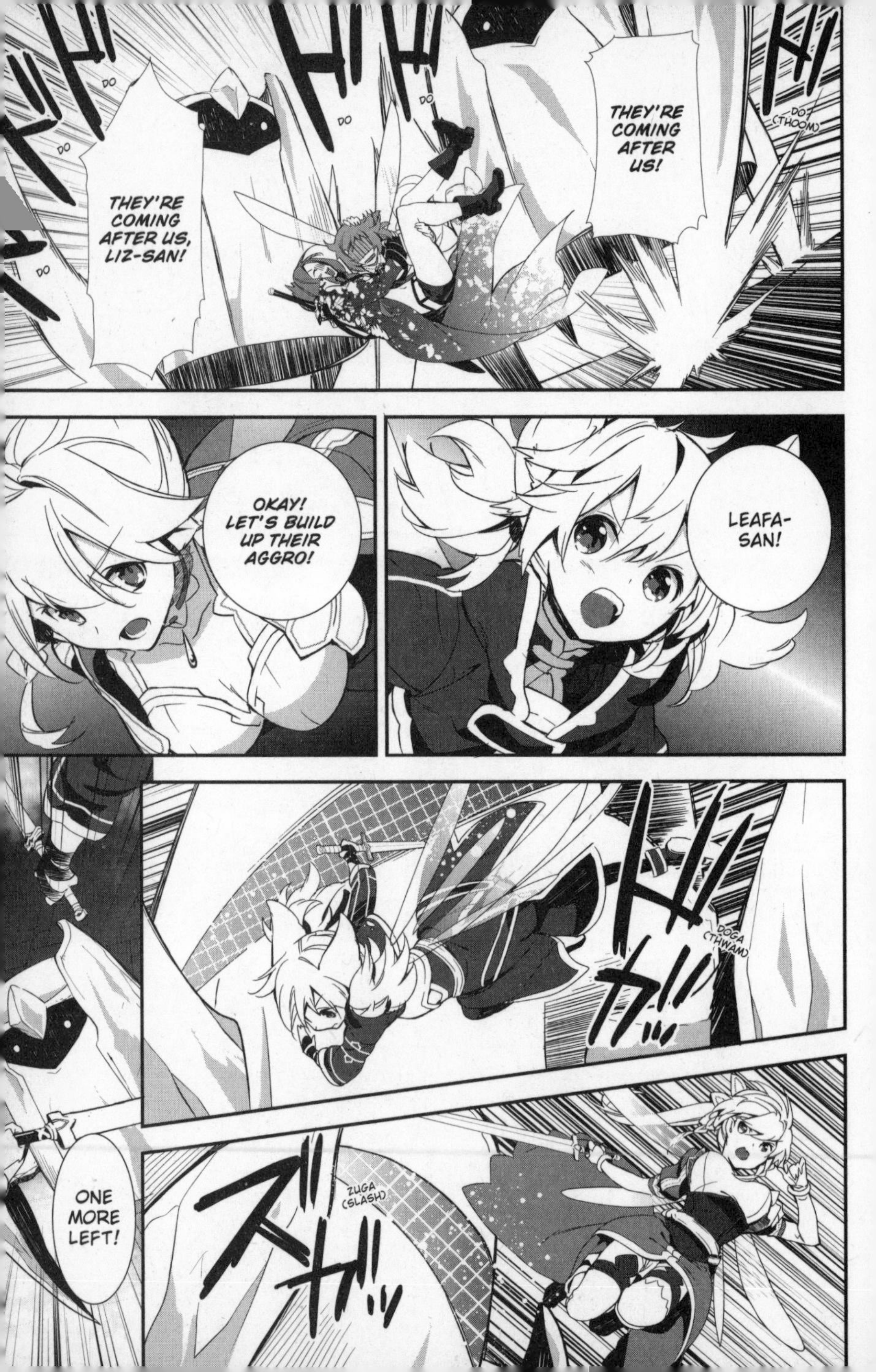
DO (THOOM)
THEY'RE COMING AFTER US!
DO
DO
THEY'RE COMING AFTER US, LIZ-SAN!
DO
DO
LEAFA-SAN!
OKAY! LET'S BUILD UP THEIR AGGRO!
DOGA (THWAM)
ZUGA (SLASH)
ONE MORE LEFT!

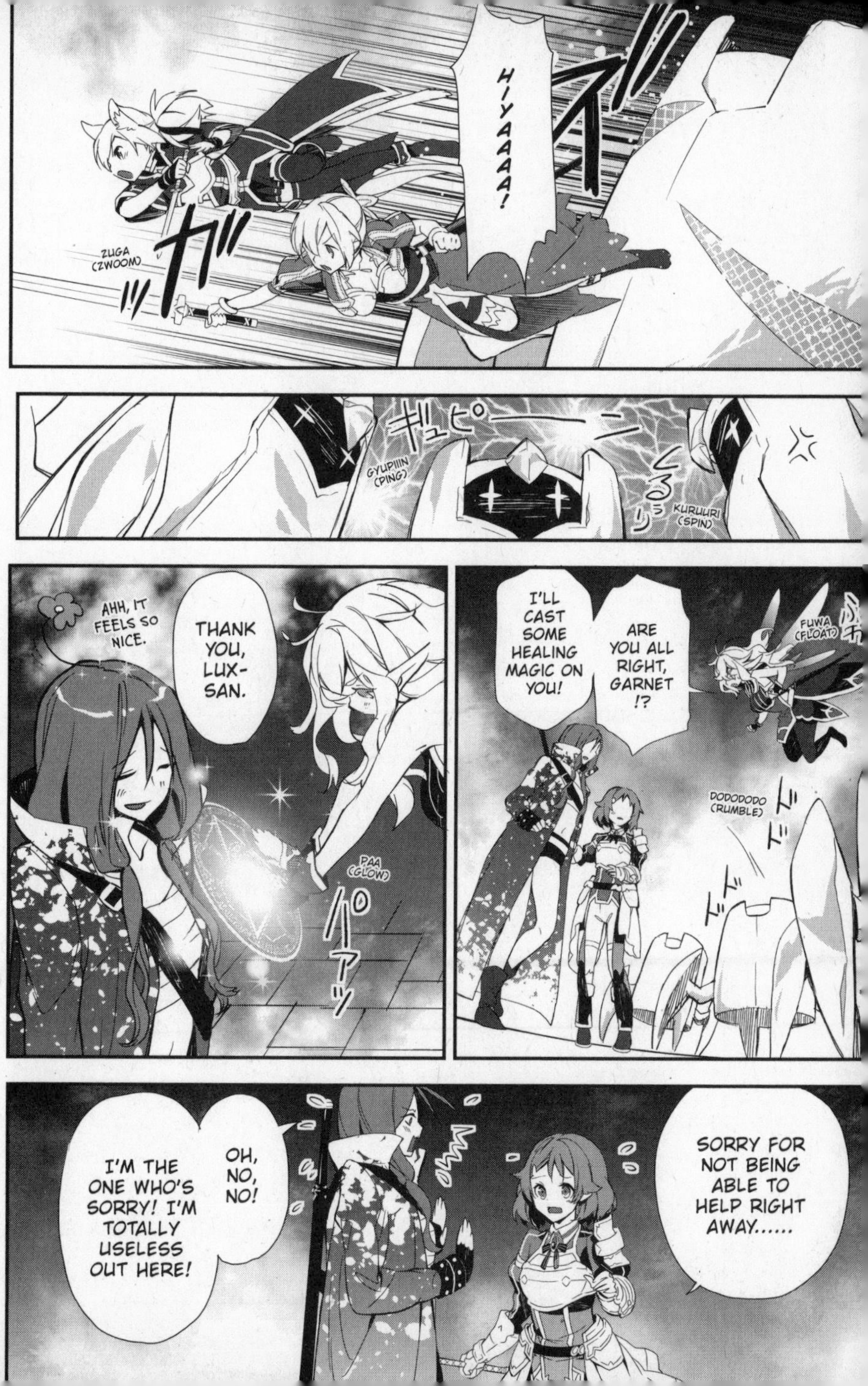
HIYAAAA!
ZUGA (ZWOOM)
GYUPIIIN (PING)
KURUURI (SPIN)
FUWA (FLOAT)
ARE YOU ALL RIGHT, GARNET!?
I'LL CAST SOME HEALING MAGIC ON YOU!
DODODODO (RUMBLE)
THANK YOU, LUX-SAN.
AHH, IT FEELS SO NICE.
PAA (GLOW)
SORRY FOR NOT BEING ABLE TO HELP RIGHT AWAY......
OH, NO, NO!
I'M THE ONE WHO'S SORRY! I'M TOTALLY USELESS OUT HERE!

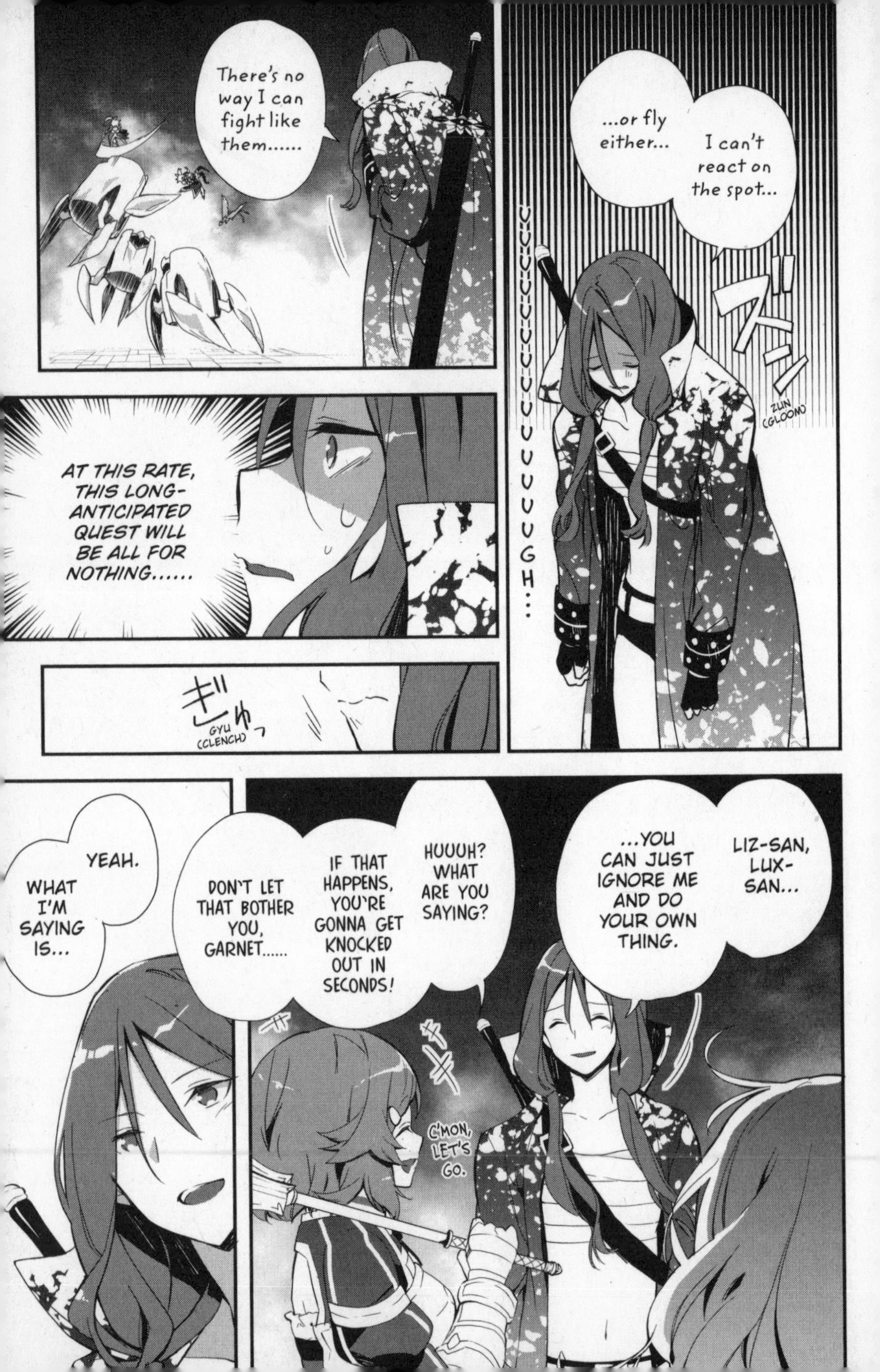

I can't react on the spot...
...or fly either...
UUUUUUUUUUUUUUUUUGH...
ズーン
ZUN (GLOOM)
There's no way I can fight like them......
AT THIS RATE, THIS LONG-ANTICIPATED QUEST WILL BE ALL FOR NOTHING......
ぎゅっ
GYU (CLENCH)
LIZ-SAN, LUX-SAN...
...YOU CAN JUST IGNORE ME AND DO YOUR OWN THING.
HUUUH? WHAT ARE YOU SAYING?
IF THAT HAPPENS, YOU'RE GONNA GET KNOCKED OUT IN SECONDS!
C'MON, LET'S GO.
DON'T LET THAT BOTHER YOU, GARNET......
YEAH.
WHAT I'M SAYING IS...

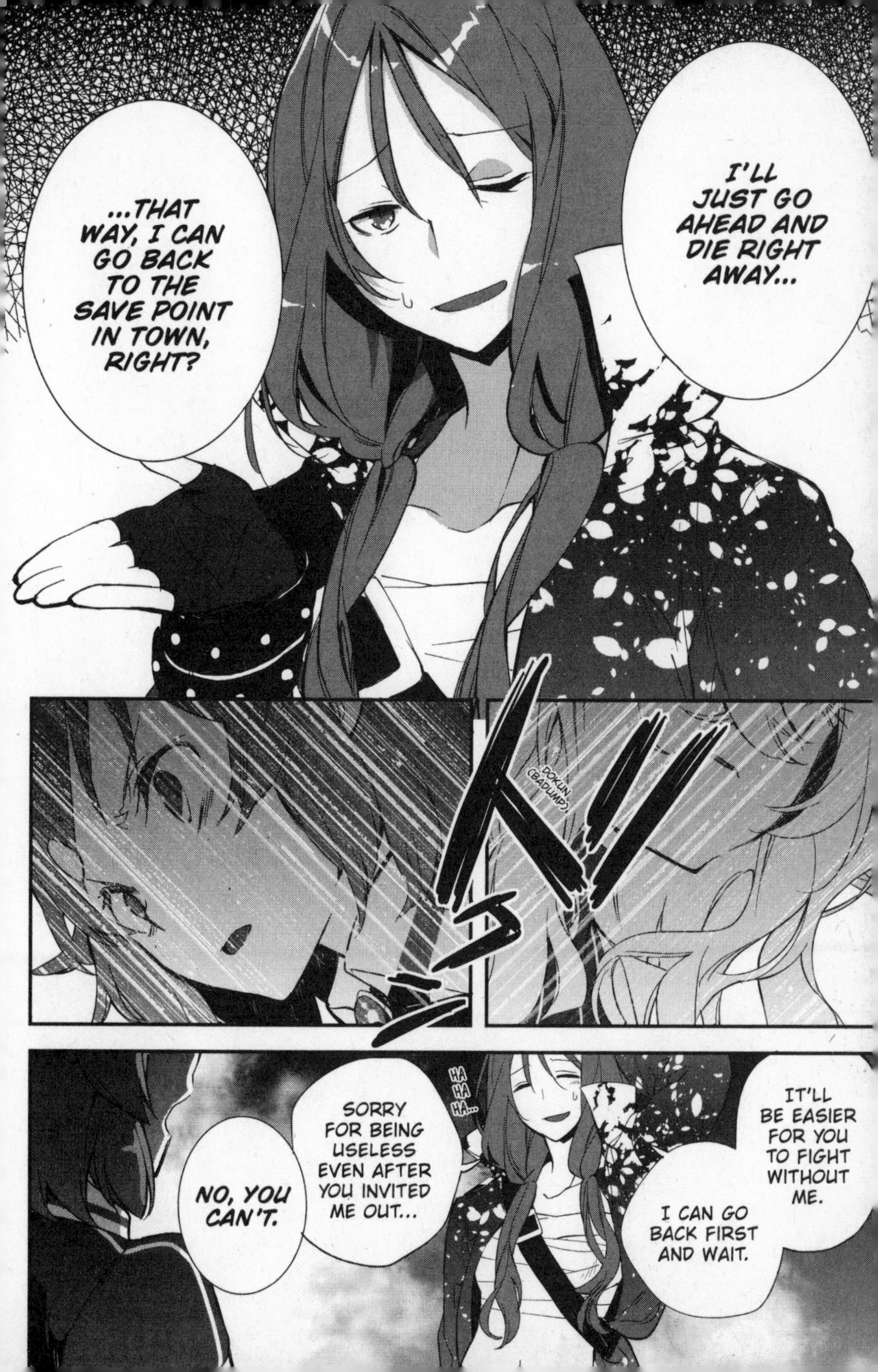
I'LL JUST GO AHEAD AND DIE RIGHT AWAY...
...THAT WAY, I CAN GO BACK TO THE SAVE POINT IN TOWN, RIGHT?
DOKUN (BADUMP)
IT'LL BE EASIER FOR YOU TO FIGHT WITHOUT ME.
I CAN GO BACK FIRST AND WAIT.
HA HA HA...
SORRY FOR BEING USELESS EVEN AFTER YOU INVITED ME OUT...
NO, YOU CAN'T.

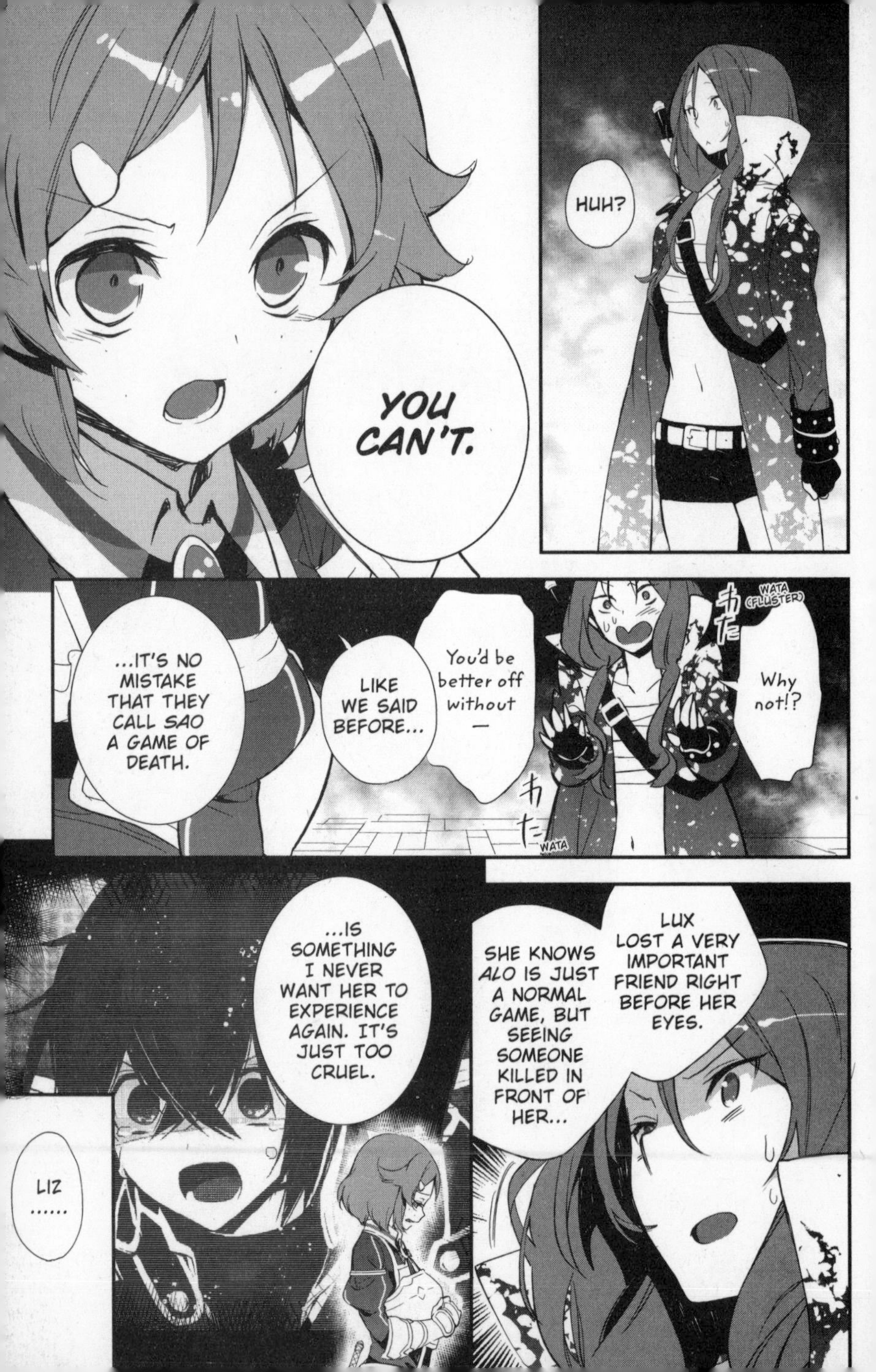
HUH?
YOU CAN'T.
WATA (FLUSTER)
Why not!?
You'd be better off without —
LIKE WE SAID BEFORE...
...IT'S NO MISTAKE THAT THEY CALL SAO A GAME OF DEATH.
WATA
LUX LOST A VERY IMPORTANT FRIEND RIGHT BEFORE HER EYES.
SHE KNOWS ALO IS JUST A NORMAL GAME, BUT SEEING SOMEONE KILLED IN FRONT OF HER...
...IS SOMETHING I NEVER WANT HER TO EXPERIENCE AGAIN. IT'S JUST TOO CRUEL.
LIZ ......

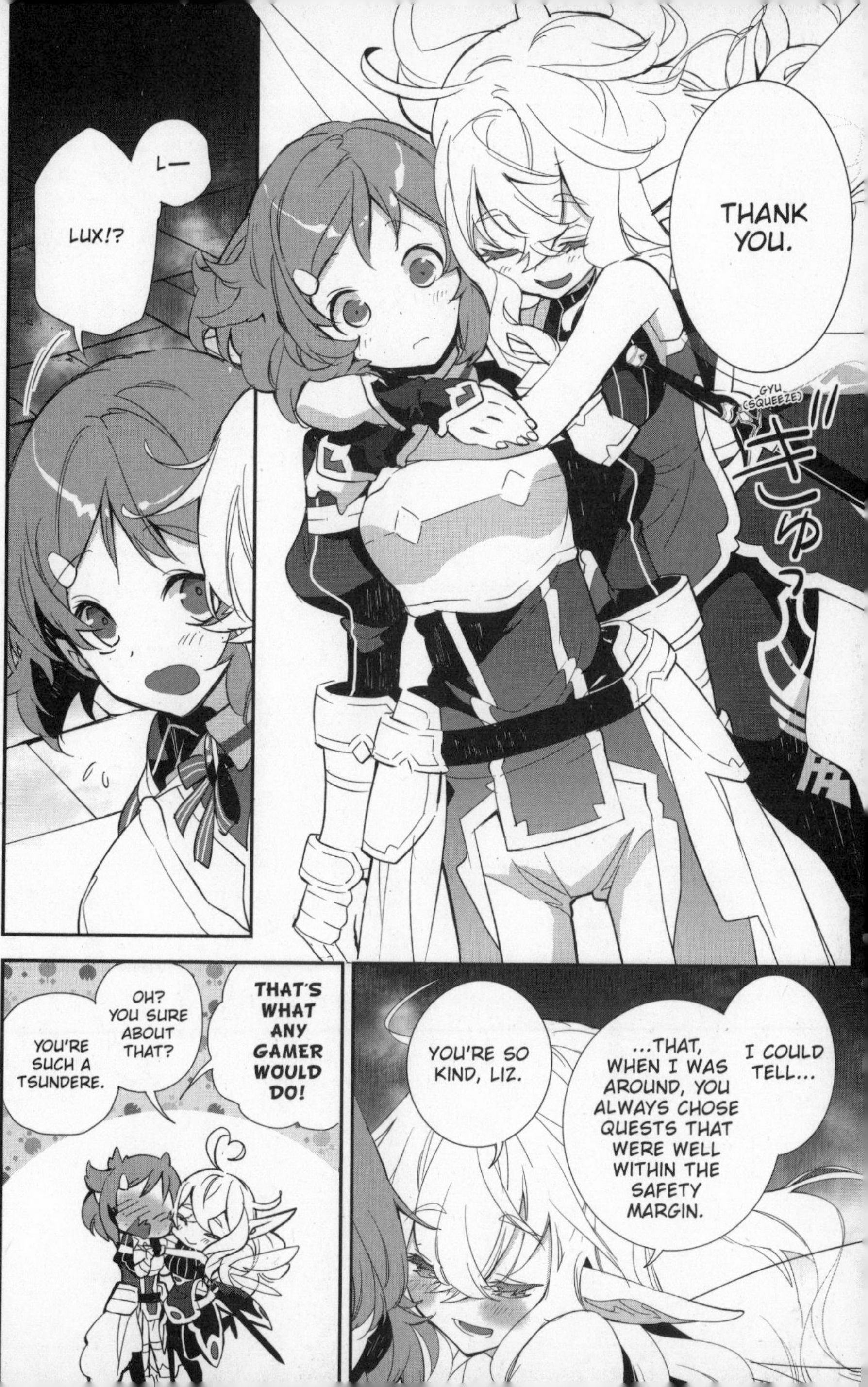
THANK YOU.
GYU (SQUEEZE)
L—
LUX!?
I COULD TELL...
...THAT, WHEN I WAS AROUND, YOU ALWAYS CHOSE QUESTS THAT WERE WELL WITHIN THE SAFETY MARGIN.
YOU'RE SO KIND, LIZ.
THAT'S WHAT ANY GAMER WOULD DO!
OH? YOU SURE ABOUT THAT?
YOU'RE SUCH A TSUNDERE.

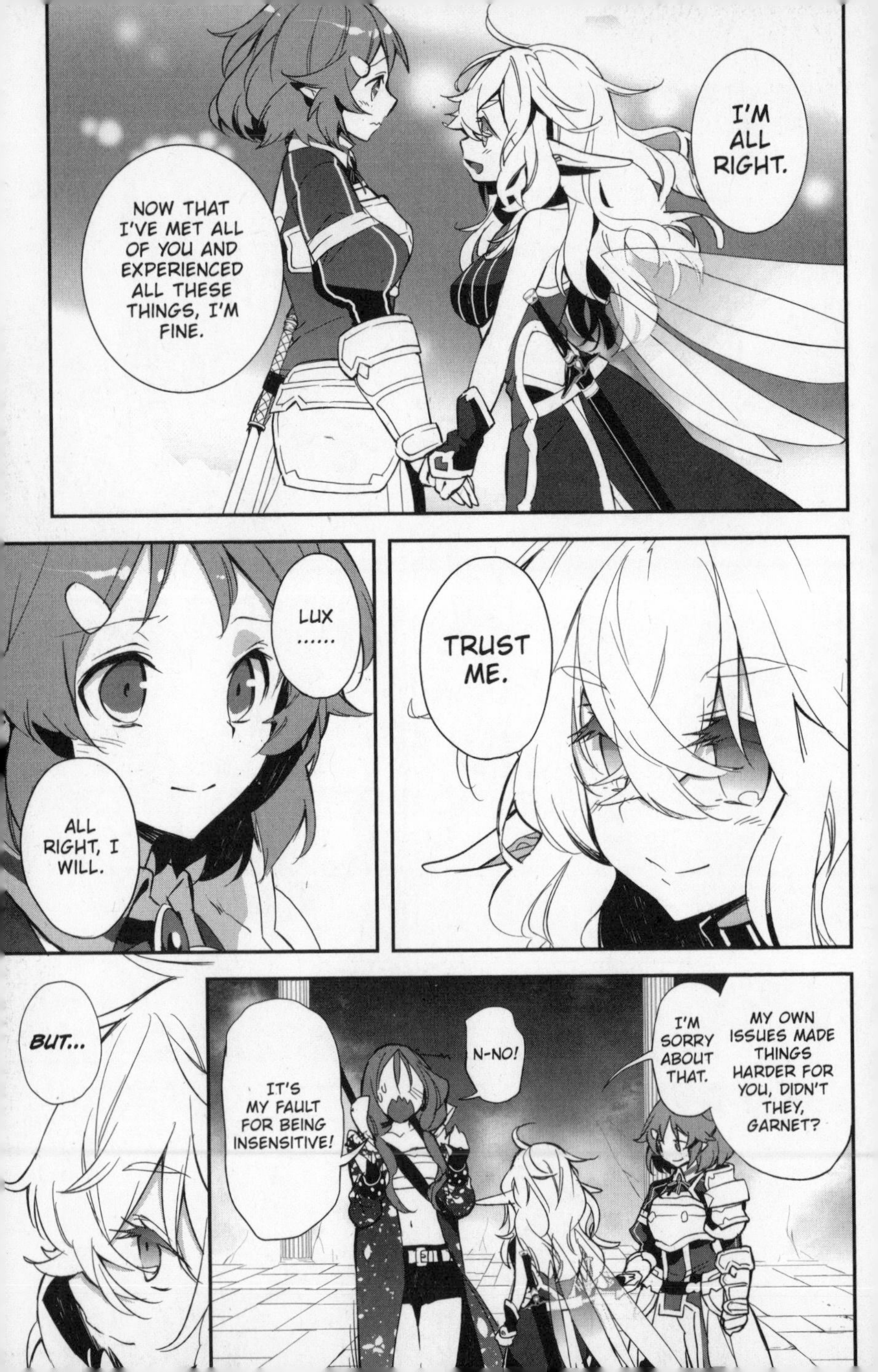
I'M ALL RIGHT.
NOW THAT I'VE MET ALL OF YOU AND EXPERIENCED ALL THESE THINGS, I'M FINE.
TRUST ME.
LUX ......
ALL RIGHT, I WILL.
MY OWN ISSUES MADE THINGS HARDER FOR YOU, DIDN'T THEY, GARNET?
I'M SORRY ABOUT THAT.
N-NO!
IT'S MY FAULT FOR BEING INSENSITIVE!
BUT...

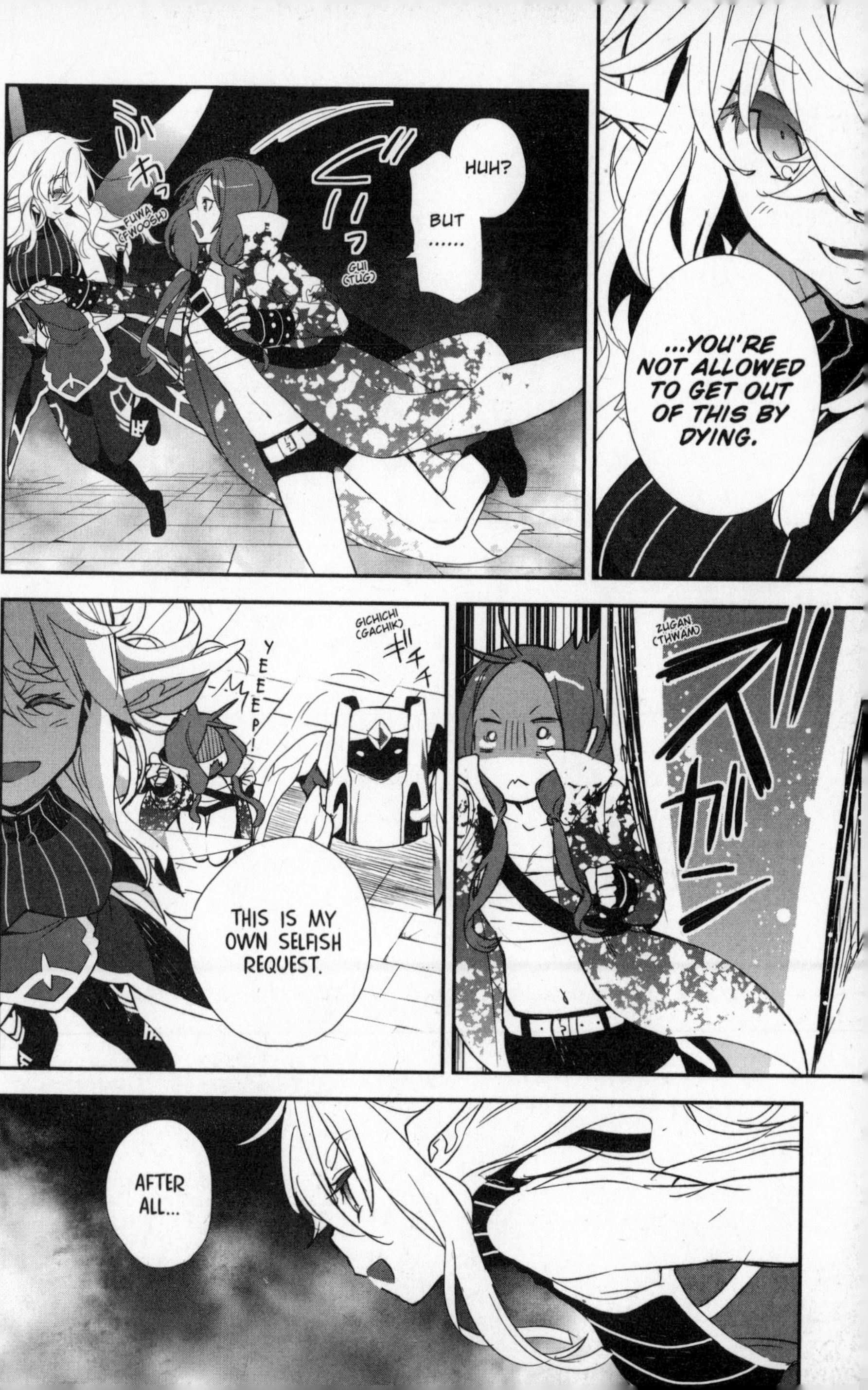
...YOU'RE NOT ALLOWED TO GET OUT OF THIS BY DYING.
FUWA (FWOOSH)
HUH?
BUT ......
GUI (TUG)
ZUGAN (THWAM)
GICHICHI (GACHIK)
YEEEP!
THIS IS MY OWN SELFISH REQUEST.
AFTER ALL...

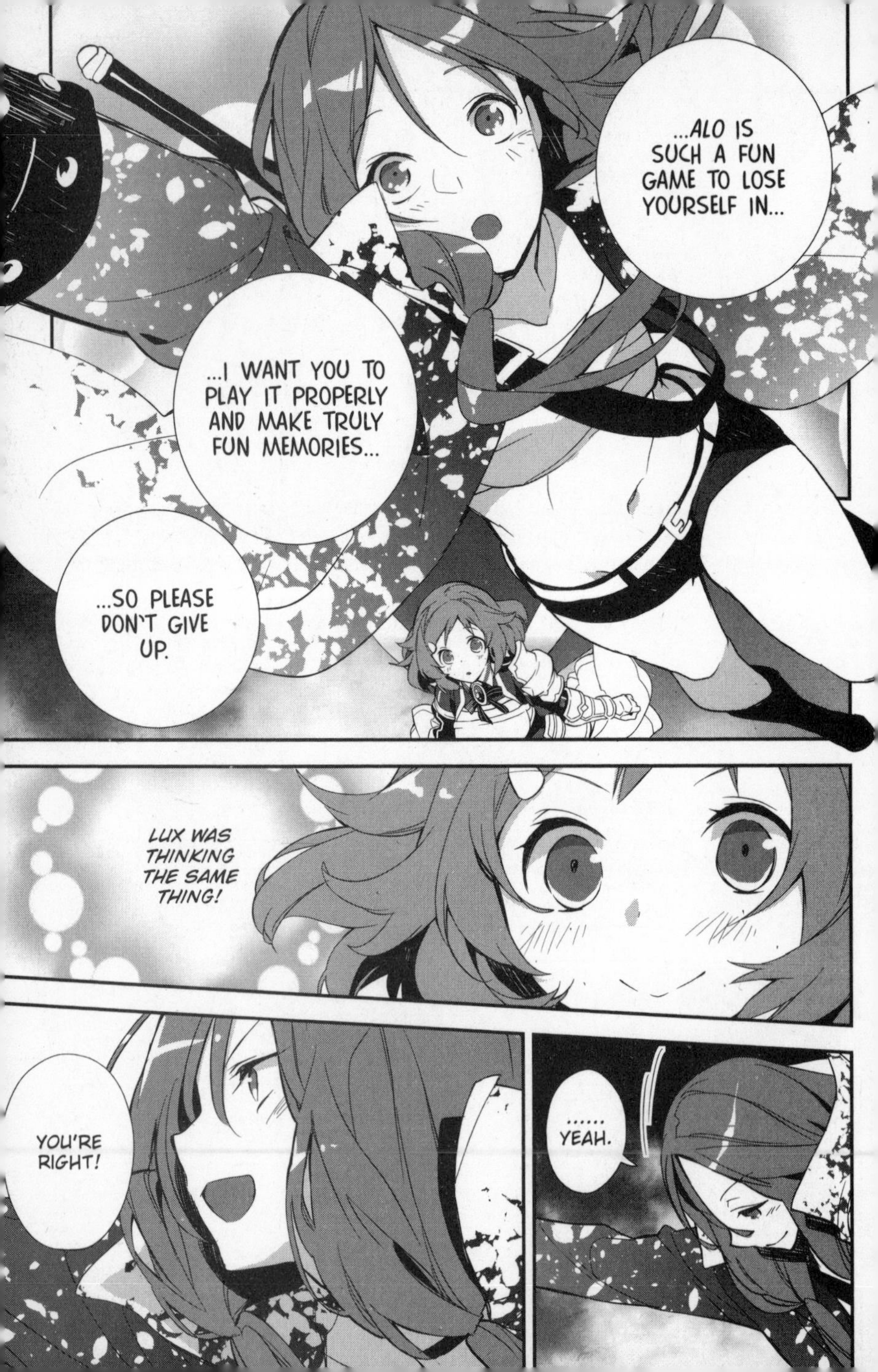
...ALO IS SUCH A FUN GAME TO LOSE YOURSELF IN...
...I WANT YOU TO PLAY IT PROPERLY AND MAKE TRULY FUN MEMORIES...
...SO PLEASE DON'T GIVE UP.
LUX WAS THINKING THE SAME THING!
......YEAH.
YOU'RE RIGHT!

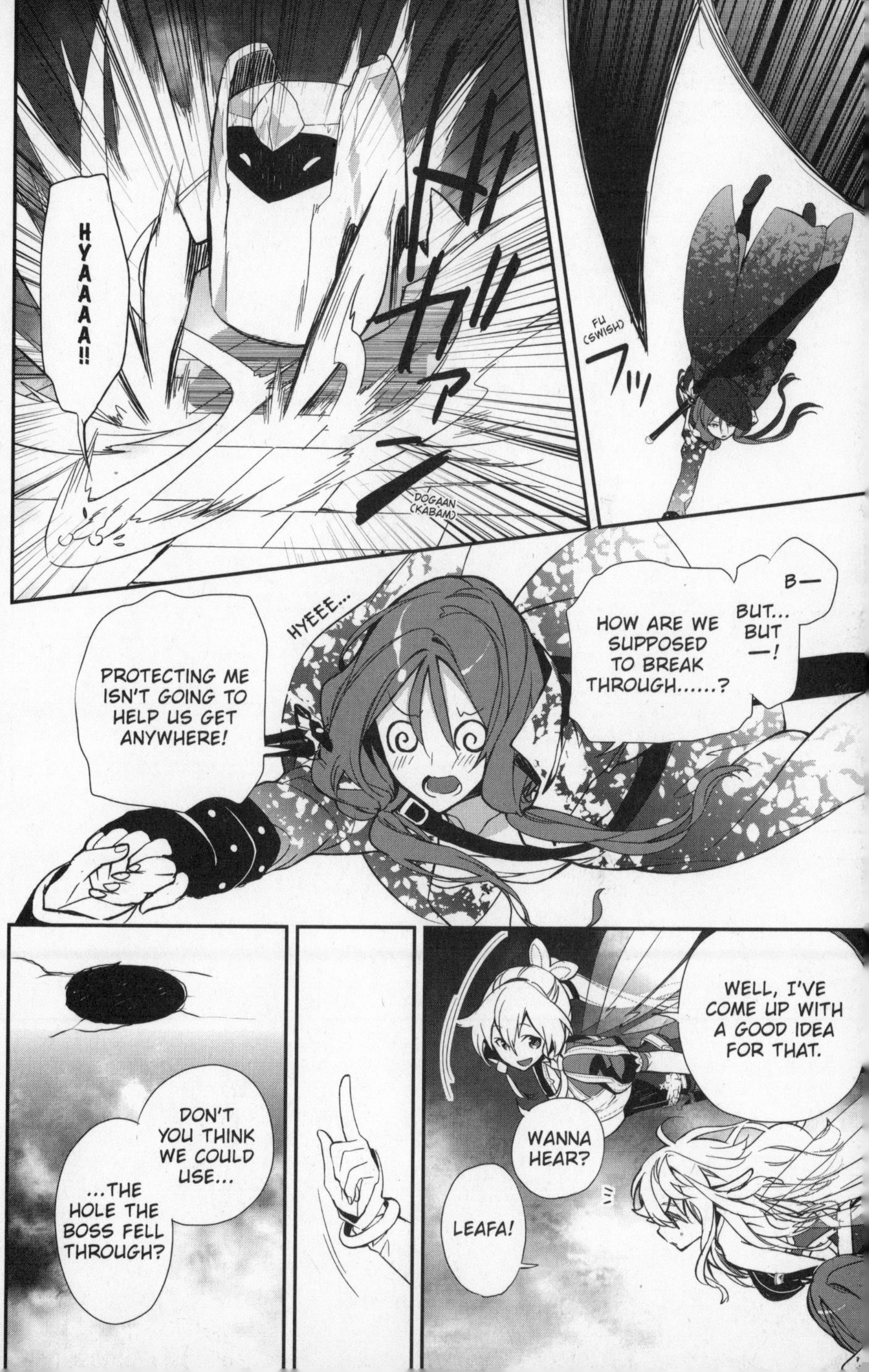
FU (SWISH)
HYAAAAA!!
DOGAAN (KABAM)
B— BUT... BUT —!
HOW ARE WE SUPPOSED TO BREAK THROUGH......?
HYEEE...
PROTECTING ME ISN'T GOING TO HELP US GET ANYWHERE!
WELL, I'VE COME UP WITH A GOOD IDEA FOR THAT.
WANNA HEAR?
LEAFA!
DON'T YOU THINK WE COULD USE...
...THE HOLE THE BOSS FELL THROUGH?

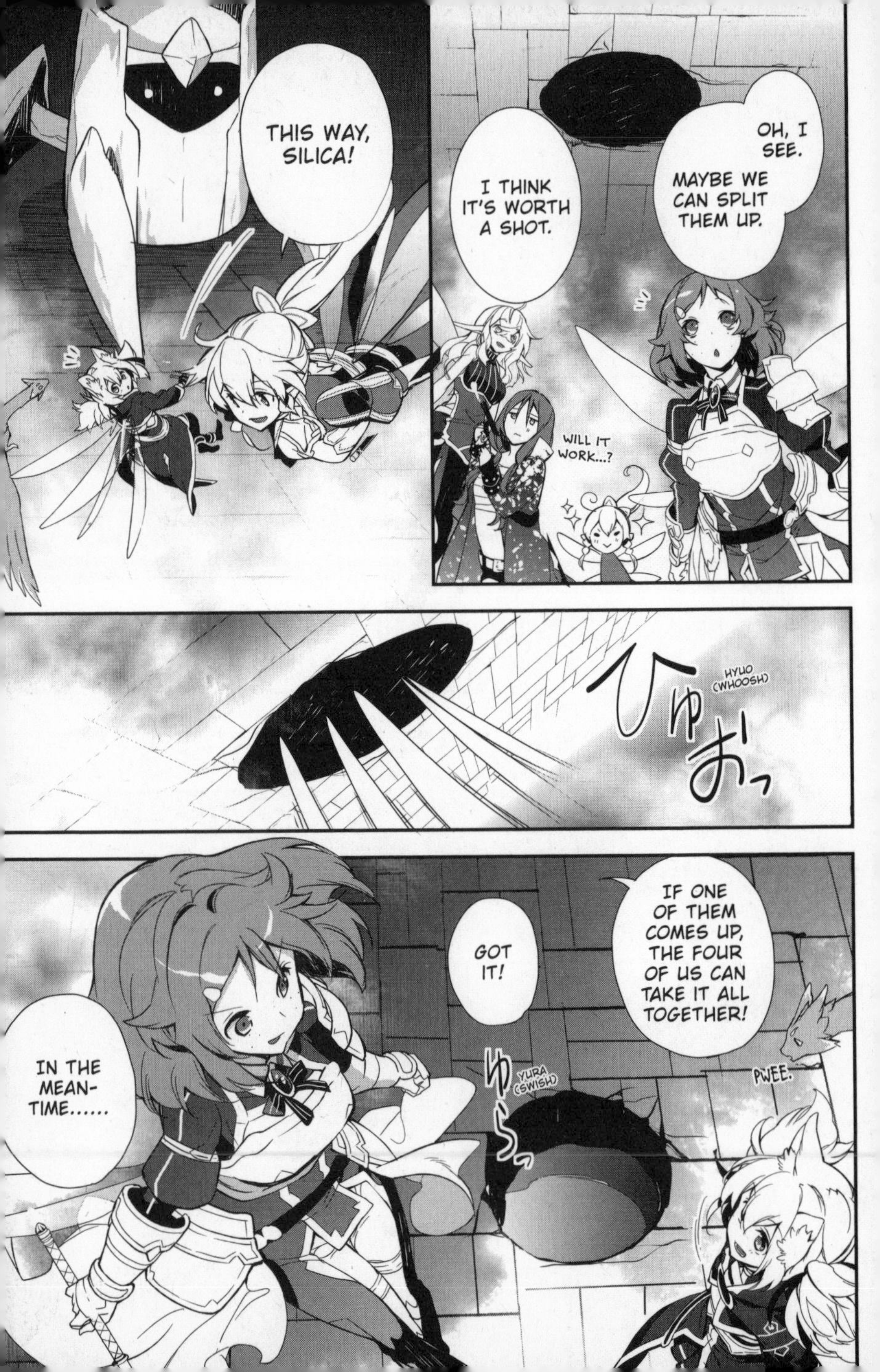
OH, I SEE.
MAYBE WE CAN SPLIT THEM UP.
I THINK IT'S WORTH A SHOT.
WILL IT WORK...?
THIS WAY, SILICA!
ひゅおっ
HYUO (WHOOSH)
IF ONE OF THEM COMES UP, THE FOUR OF US CAN TAKE IT ALL TOGETHER!
GOT IT!
PWEE.
ゆらっ
YURA (SWISH)
IN THE MEAN-TIME......

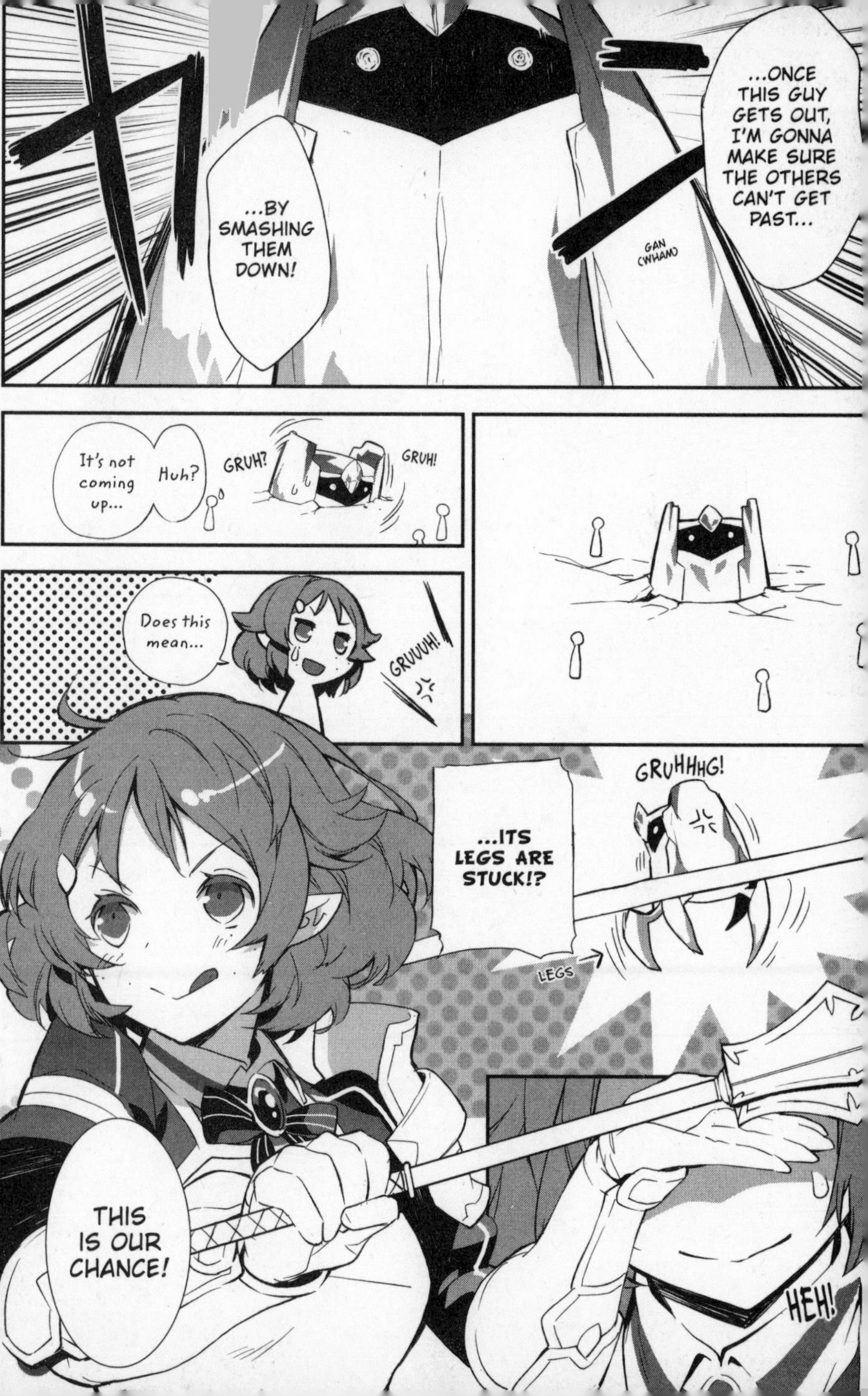
...ONCE THIS GUY GETS OUT, I'M GONNA MAKE SURE THE OTHERS CAN'T GET PAST...
GAN (WHAM)
...BY SMASHING THEM DOWN!
GRUH!
GRUH?
Huh?
It's not coming up...
Does this mean...
GRUUUH!
GRUHHHG!
...ITS LEGS ARE STUCK!?
LEGS
HEH!
THIS IS OUR CHANCE!

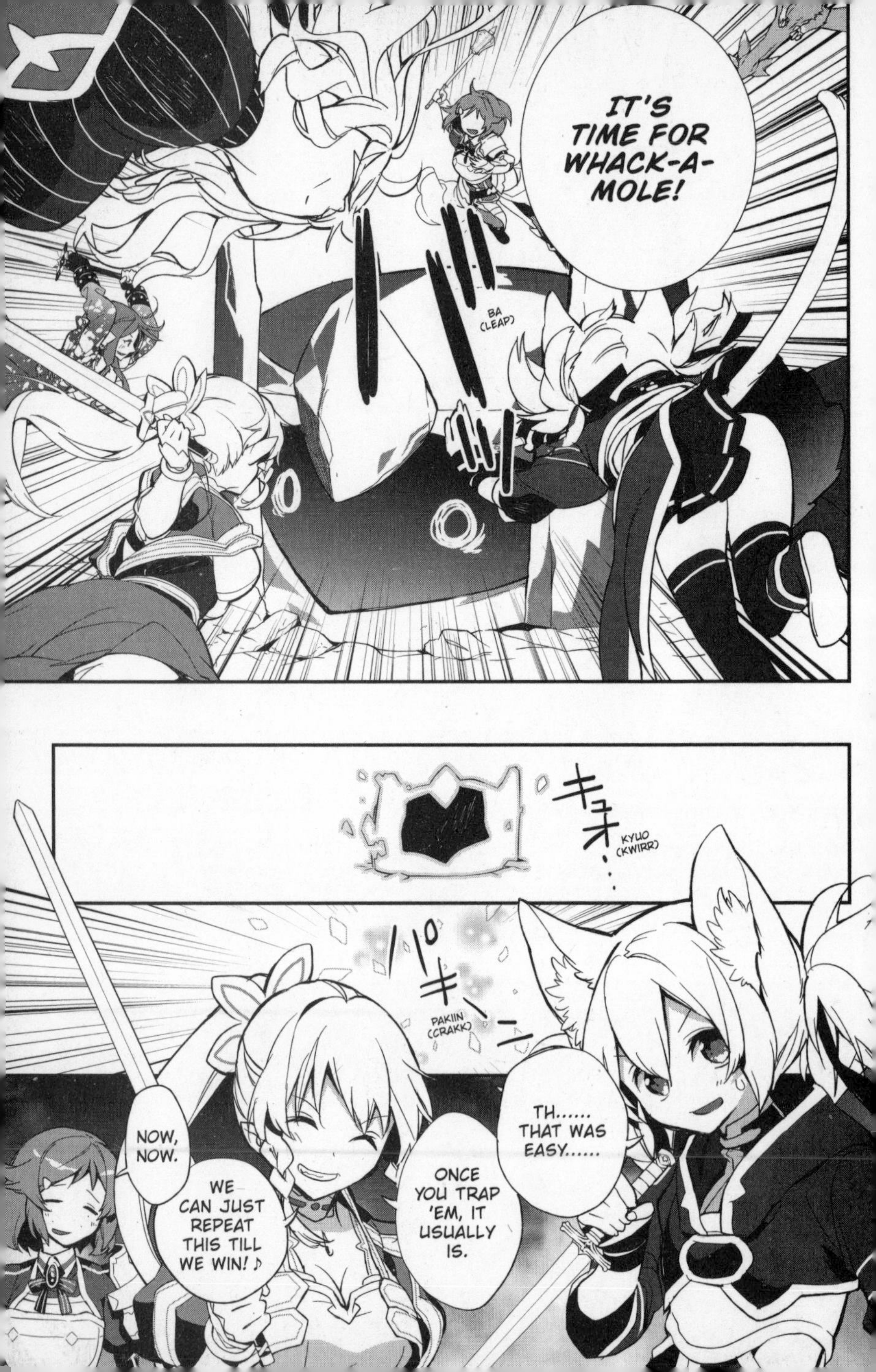
IT'S TIME FOR WHACK-A-MOLE!
BA (LEAP)
キュオ…
KYUO (KWIRR)
パキーン
PAKIIN (CRAKK)
TH...... THAT WAS EASY......
ONCE YOU TRAP 'EM, IT USUALLY IS.
NOW, NOW.
WE CAN JUST REPEAT THIS TILL WE WIN! ♪

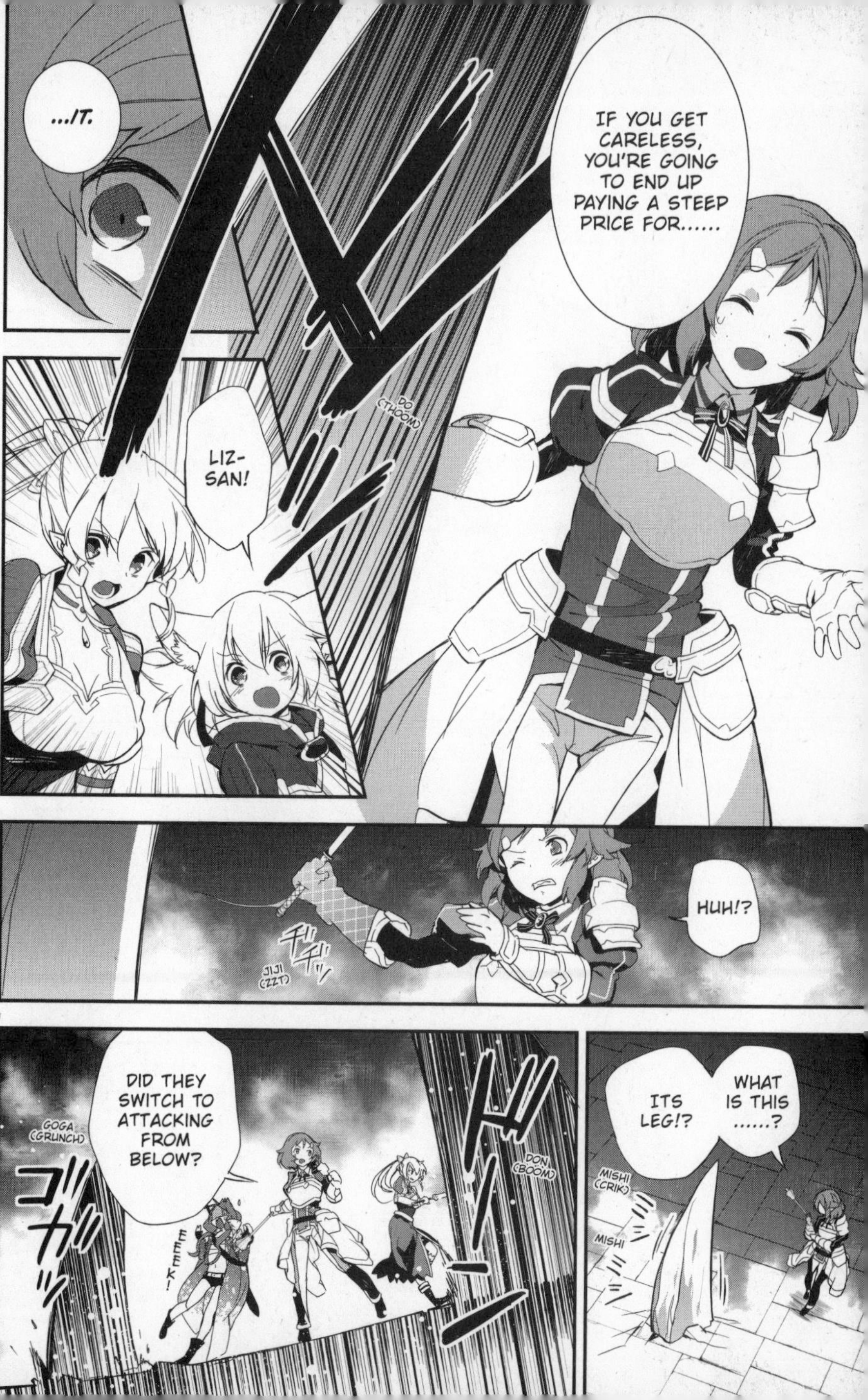
IF YOU GET CARELESS, YOU'RE GOING TO END UP PAYING A STEEP PRICE FOR......
...IT.
DO (THOOM)
LIZ-SAN!
HUH!?
JIJI (ZZZT)
WHAT IS THIS ......?
ITS LEG!?
MISHI (CRIK)
MISHI
DON (BOOM)
DID THEY SWITCH TO ATTACKING FROM BELOW?
EEEK!
GOGA (GRUNCH)

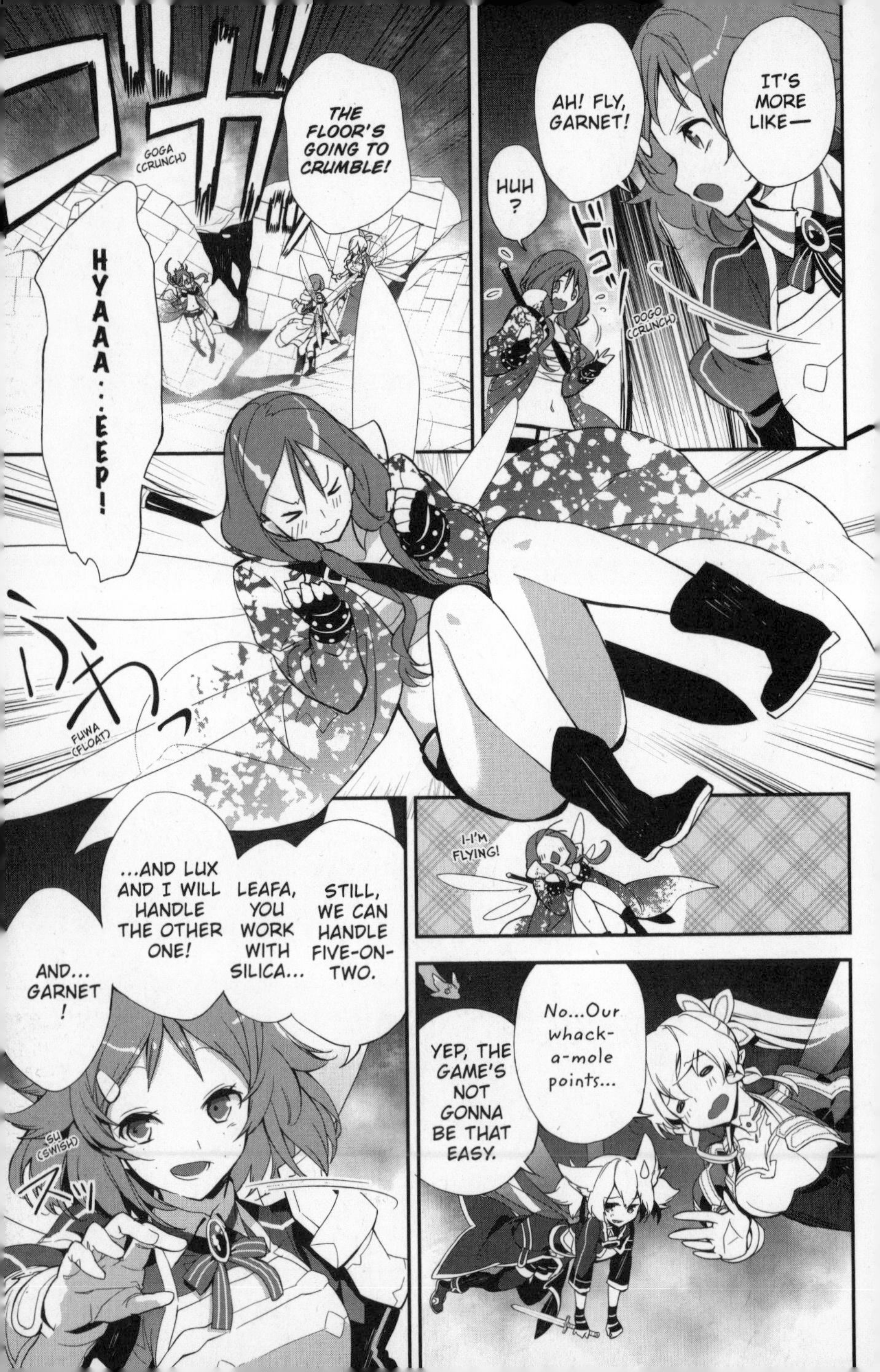
IT'S MORE LIKE—
AH! FLY, GARNET!
HUH?
DOGO (CRUNCH)
THE FLOOR'S GOING TO CRUMBLE!
GOGA (CRUNCH)
HYAAA...EEEP!
FUWA (FLOAT)
I-I'M FLYING!
No...Our whack-a-mole points...
YEP, THE GAME'S NOT GONNA BE THAT EASY.
STILL, WE CAN HANDLE FIVE-ON-TWO.
LEAFA, YOU WORK WITH SILICA...
...AND LUX AND I WILL HANDLE THE OTHER ONE!
AND... GARNET!
SU (SWISH)

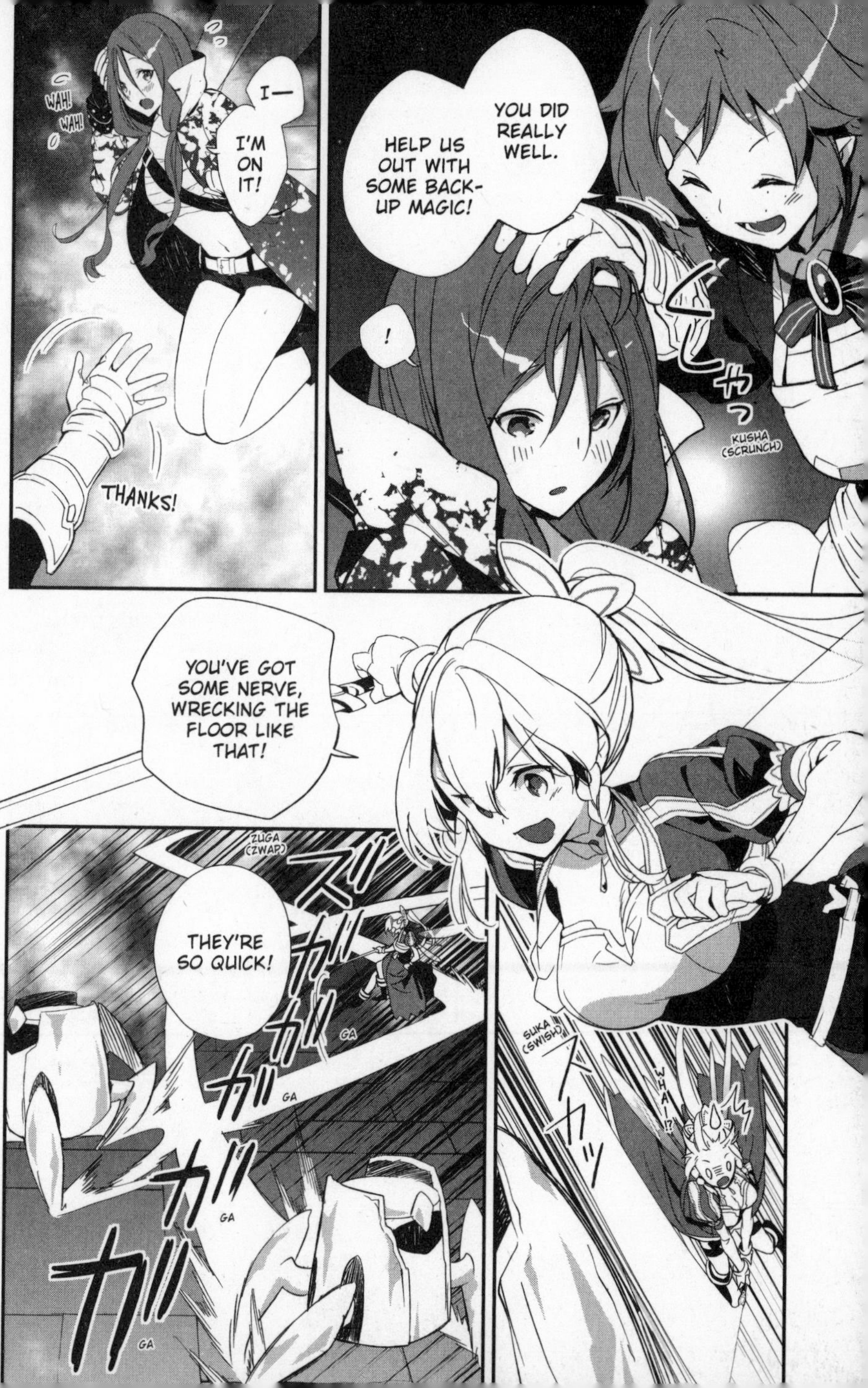
YOU DID REALLY WELL.
HELP US OUT WITH SOME BACK-UP MAGIC!
!
KUSHA (SCRUNCH)
I—
I'M ON IT!
WAH! WAH!
THANKS!
YOU'VE GOT SOME NERVE, WRECKING THE FLOOR LIKE THAT!
SUKA (SWISH)
WHA—!?
ZUGA (ZWAP)
THEY'RE SO QUICK!
GA
GA
GA
GA

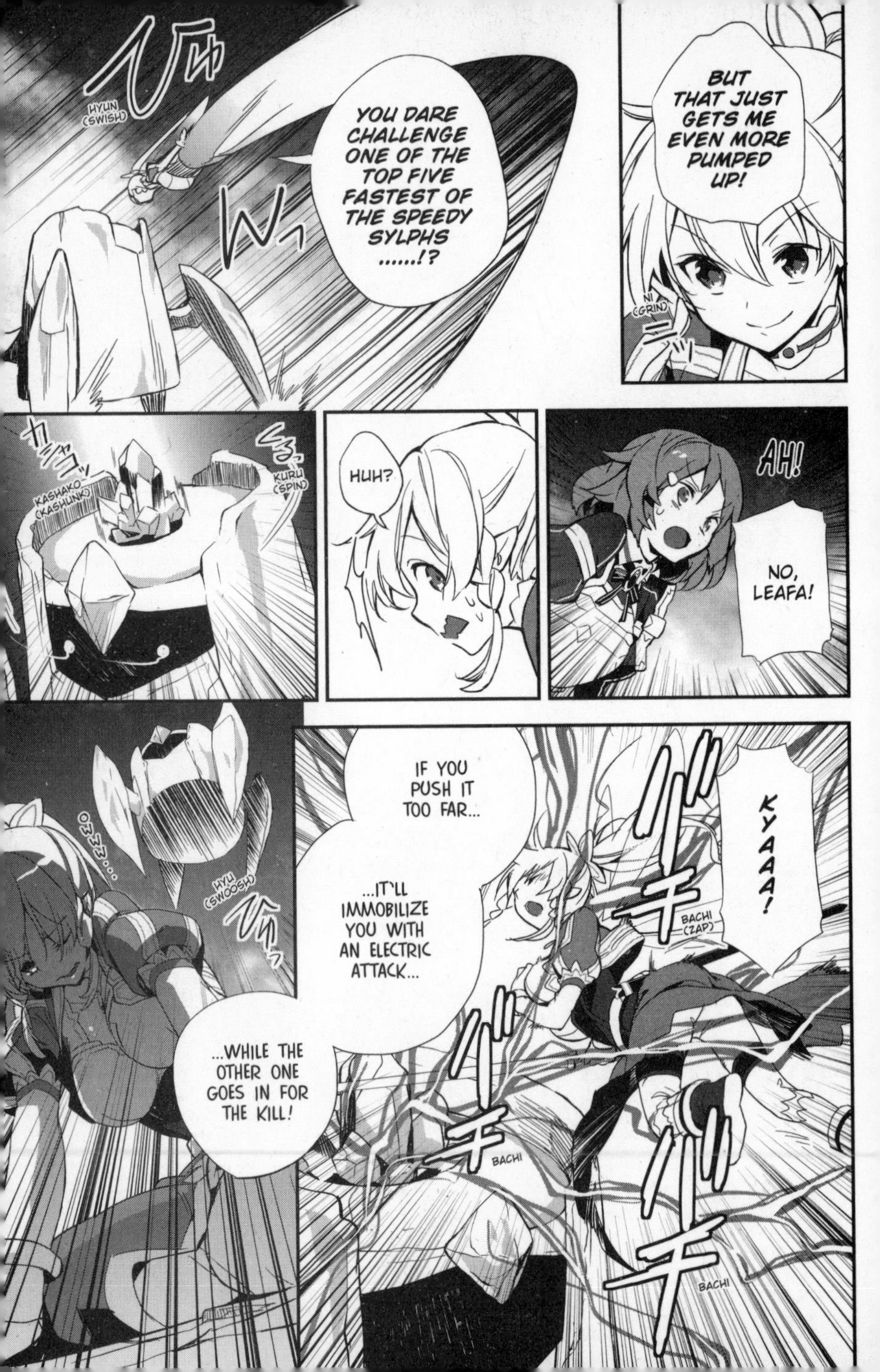
BUT THAT JUST GETS ME EVEN MORE PUMPED UP!
NI (GRIN)
YOU DARE CHALLENGE ONE OF THE TOP FIVE FASTEST OF THE SPEEDY SYLPHS ......!?
HYUN (SWISH)
AH!
NO, LEAFA!
HUH?
KURU (SPIN)
KASHAKO (KASHUNK)
KYAAAA!
BACHI (ZAP)
IF YOU PUSH IT TOO FAR...
...IT'LL IMMOBILIZE YOU WITH AN ELECTRIC ATTACK...
...WHILE THE OTHER ONE GOES IN FOR THE KILL!
BACHI
BACHI
HYU (SWOOSH)
OWWW...

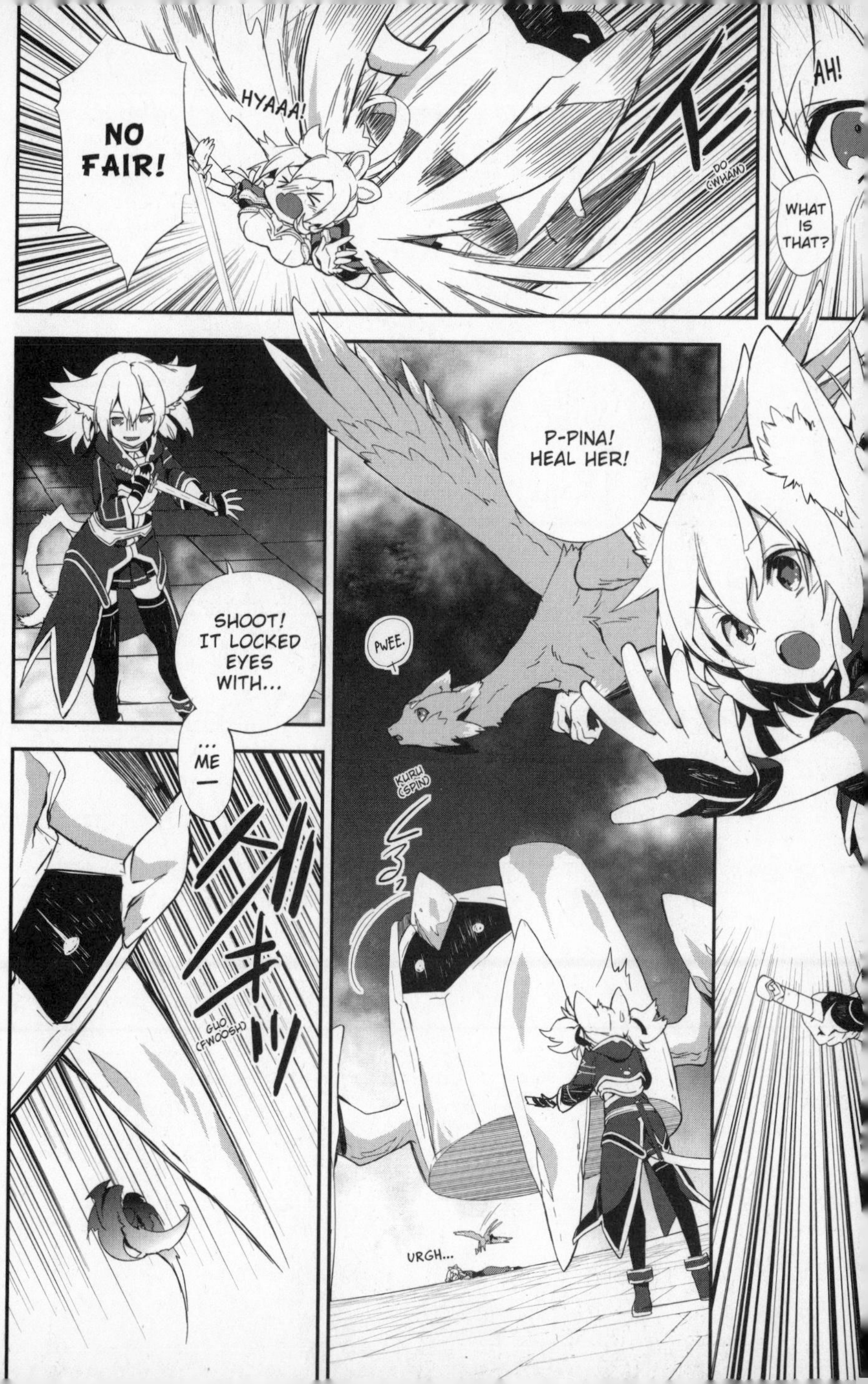
AH!
WHAT IS THAT?
DO (WHAM)
HYAAA!
NO FAIR!
P-PINA! HEAL HER!
PWEE.
SHOOT! IT LOCKED EYES WITH...
... ME —
KURU (SPIN)
GUO (FWOOSH)
URGH...

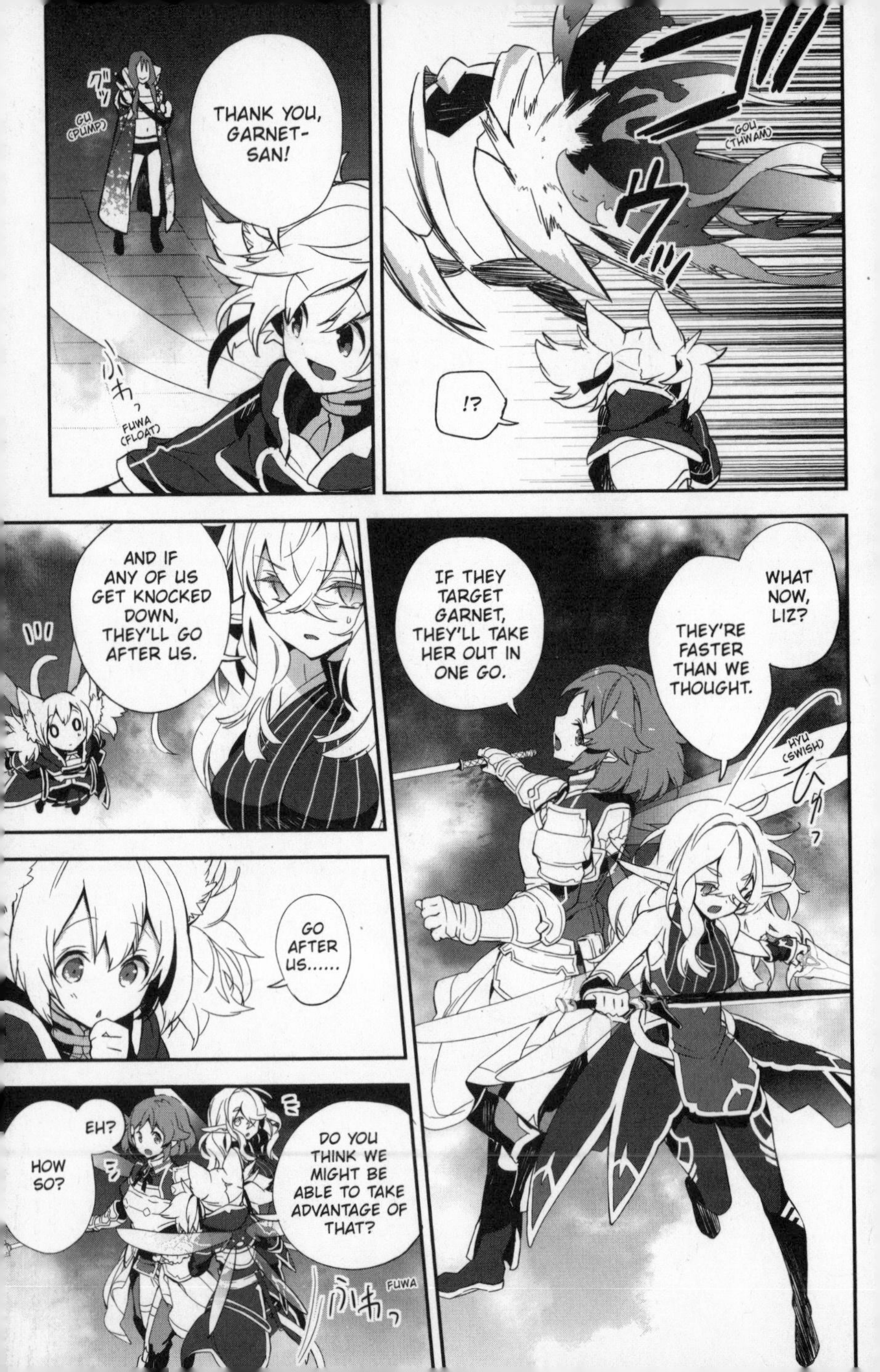
GOU (THWAM)
!?
GU (PUMP)
THANK YOU, GARNET-SAN!
FUWA (FLOAT)
WHAT NOW, LIZ?
THEY'RE FASTER THAN WE THOUGHT.
IF THEY TARGET GARNET, THEY'LL TAKE HER OUT IN ONE GO.
HYU (SWISH)
AND IF ANY OF US GET KNOCKED DOWN, THEY'LL GO AFTER US.
GO AFTER US......
DO YOU THINK WE MIGHT BE ABLE TO TAKE ADVANTAGE OF THAT?
EH?
HOW SO?
FUWA

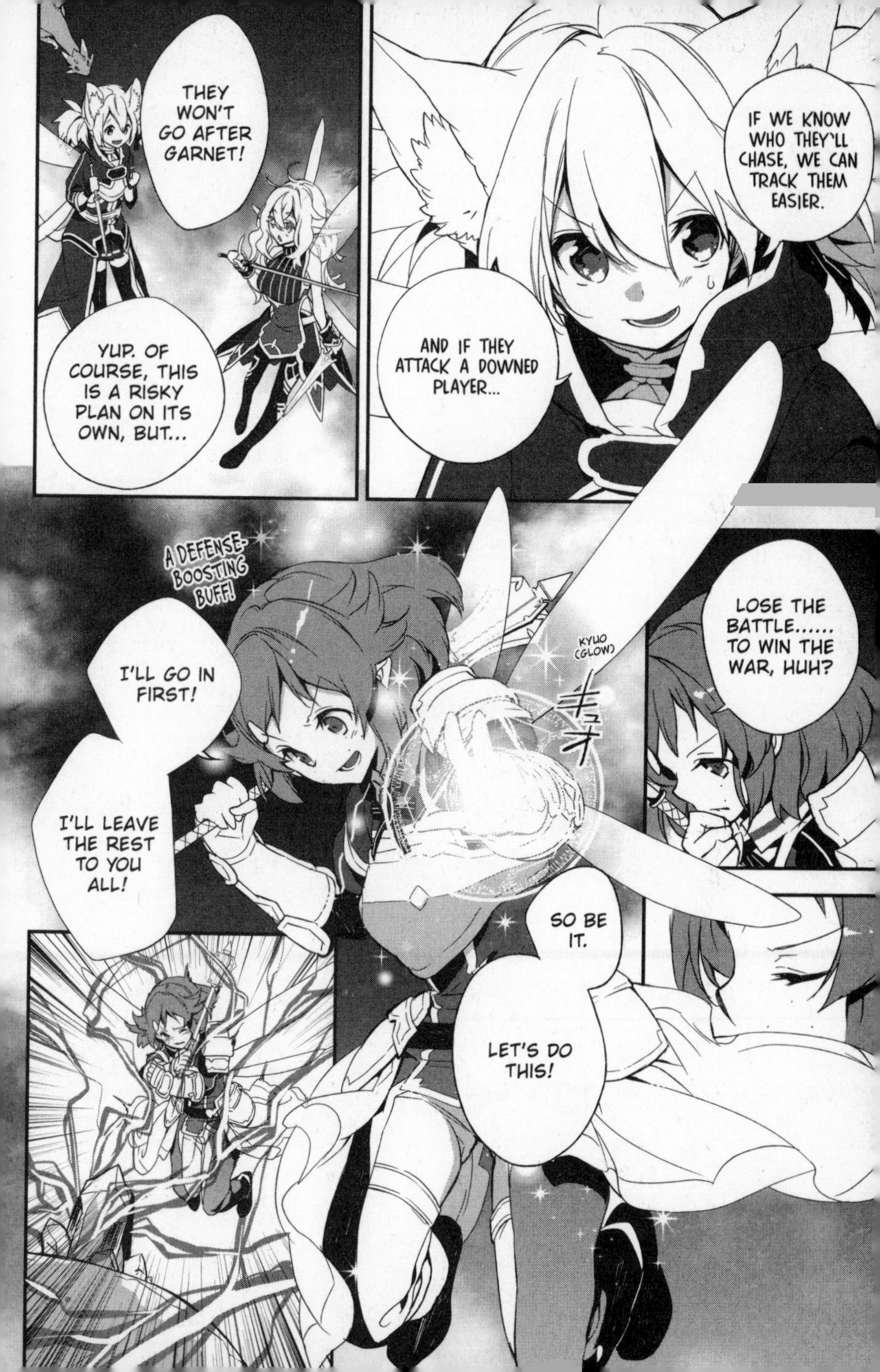
IF WE KNOW WHO THEY'LL CHASE, WE CAN TRACK THEM EASIER.
AND IF THEY ATTACK A DOWNED PLAYER...
THEY WON'T GO AFTER GARNET!
YUP. OF COURSE, THIS IS A RISKY PLAN ON ITS OWN, BUT...
LOSE THE BATTLE...... TO WIN THE WAR, HUH?
KYUO (GLOW)
A DEFENSE-BOOSTING BUFF!
I'LL GO IN FIRST!
I'LL LEAVE THE REST TO YOU ALL!
SO BE IT.
LET'S DO THIS!

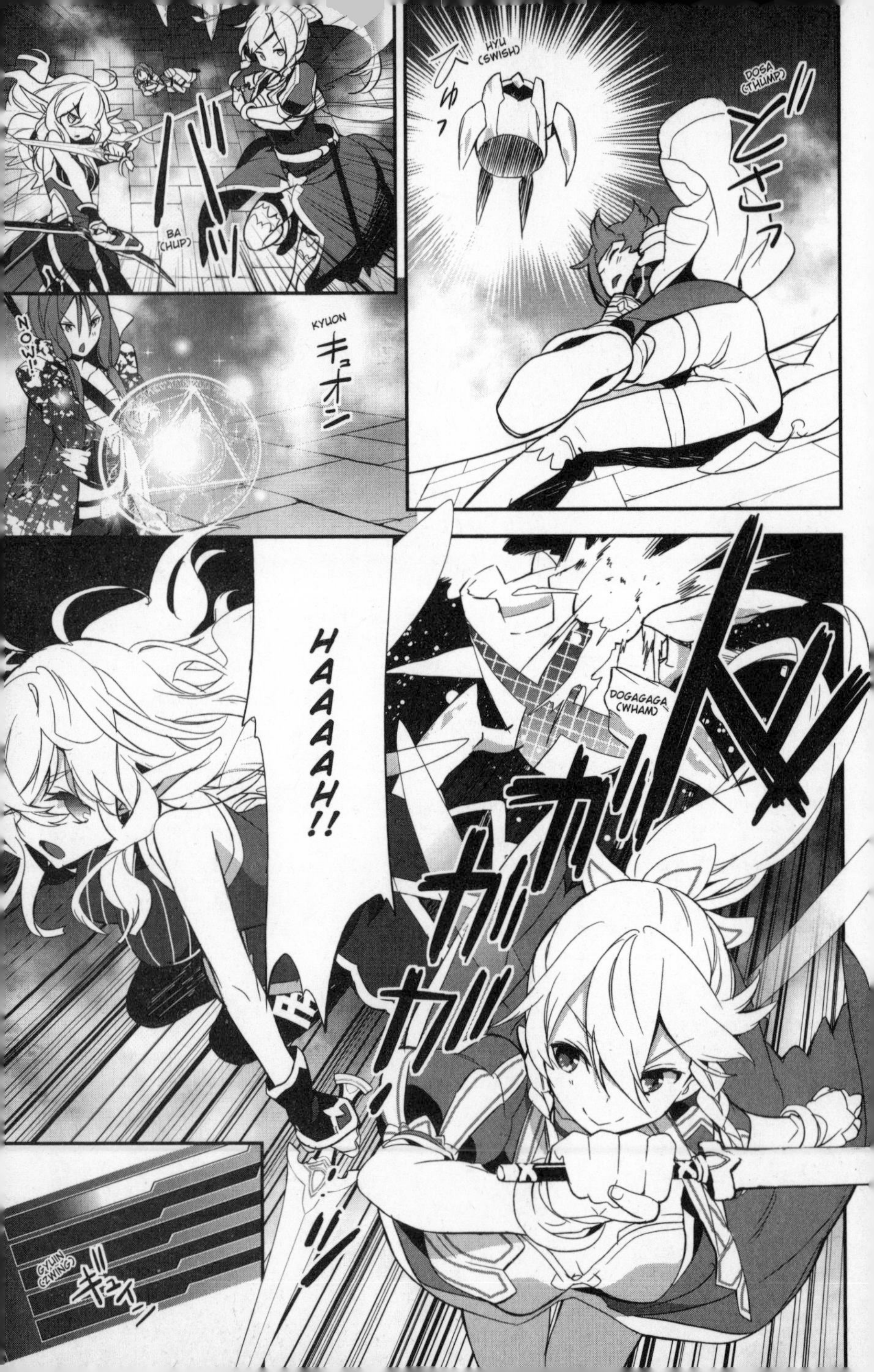
HYU (SWISH)
ひゅっ
DOSA (THUMP)
どしゃァ
BA (CHUP)
バッ
KYUON
キュオン
NOW!
DOGAGAGA (WHAM)
HAAAAAAH!!
GYUIN (ZWING)
ギュイン

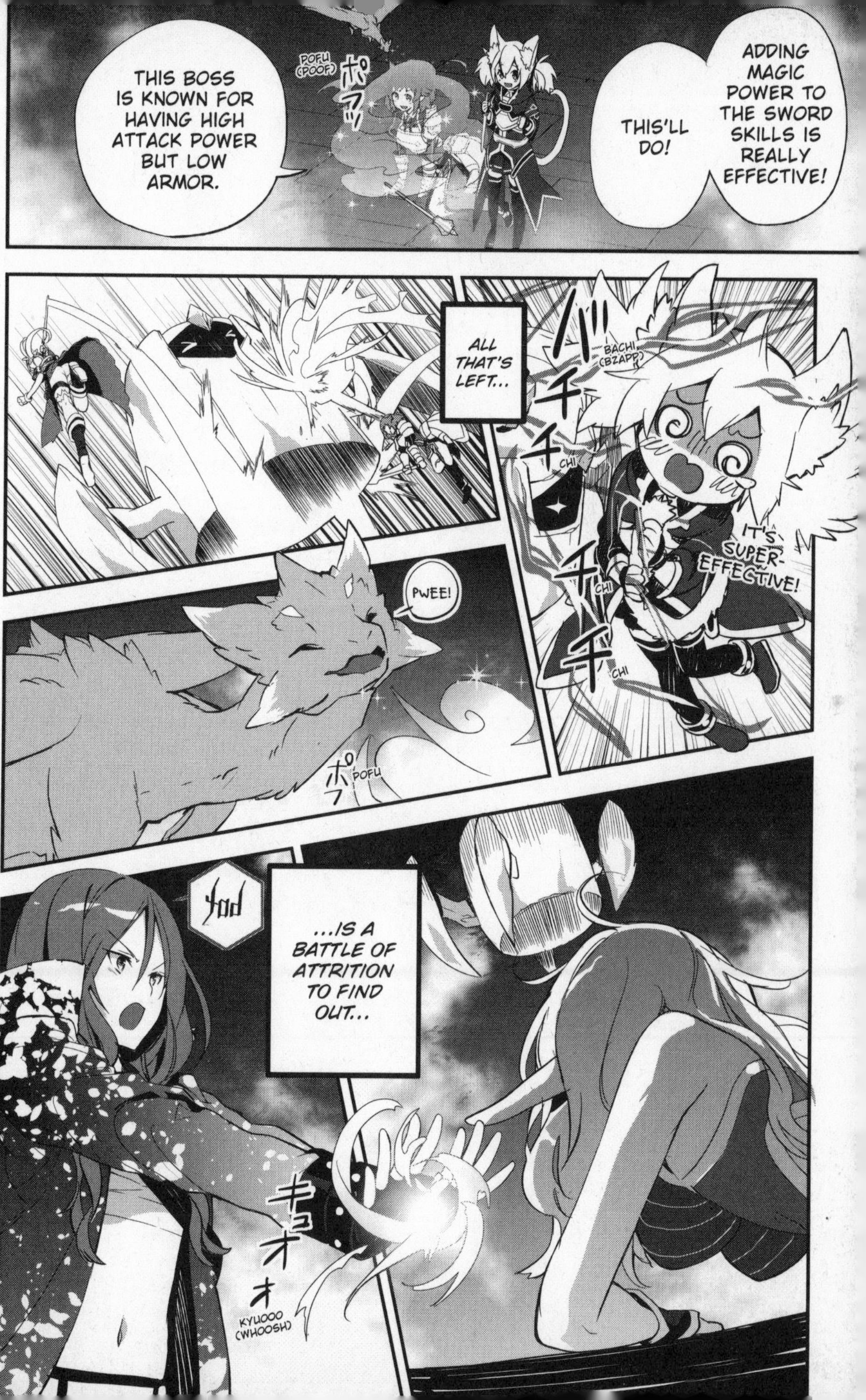
ADDING MAGIC POWER TO THE SWORD SKILLS IS REALLY EFFECTIVE!
THIS'LL DO!
POFU (POOF)
THIS BOSS IS KNOWN FOR HAVING HIGH ATTACK POWER BUT LOW ARMOR.
BACHI (BZAPP)
CHI
CHI
CHI
IT'S SUPER-EFFECTIVE!
ALL THAT'S LEFT...
PWEE!
POFU
...IS A BATTLE OF ATTRITION TO FIND OUT...
KYUOOO (WHOOSH)

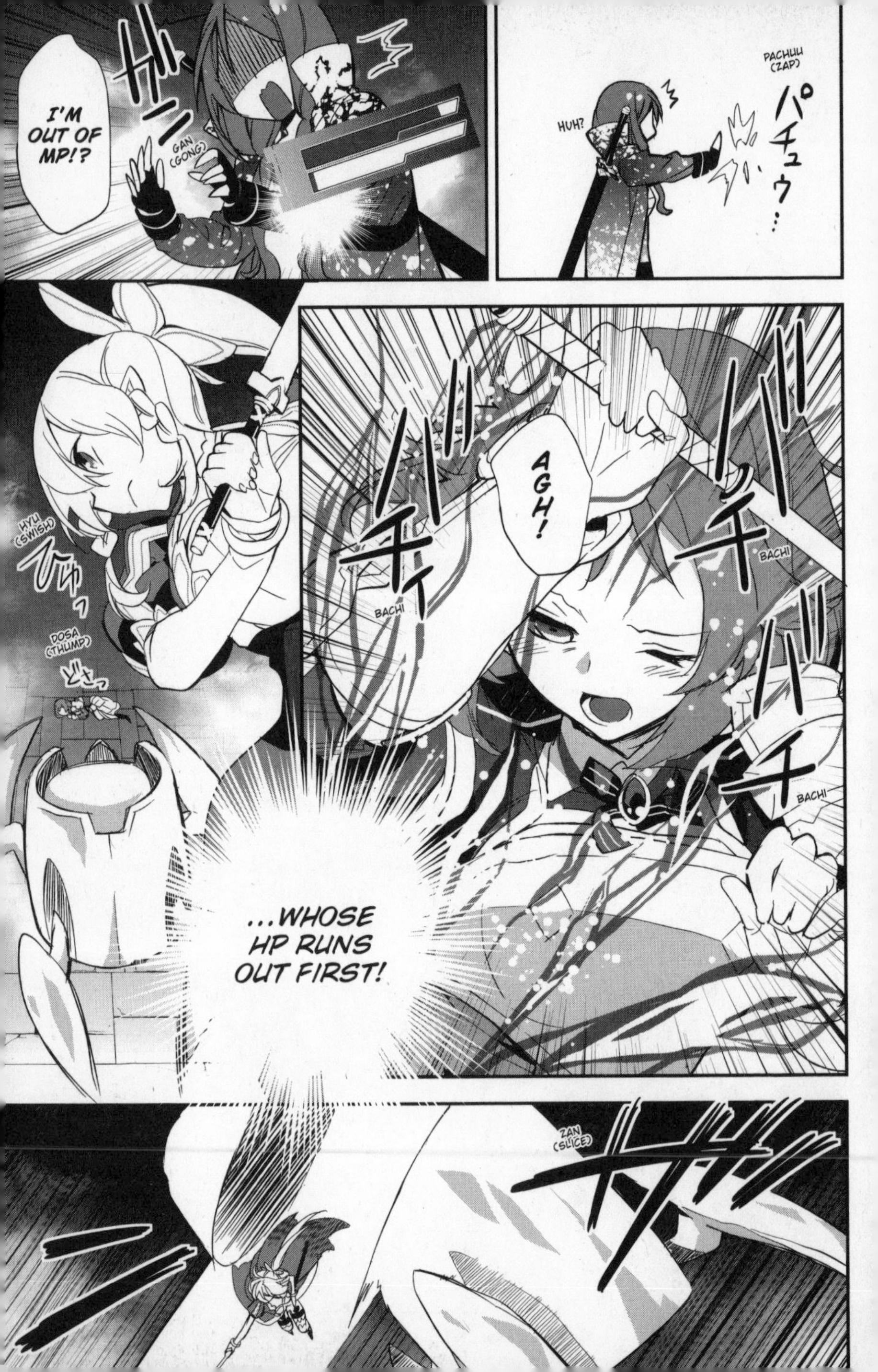
PACHUU (ZAP)
パチュウ…
HUH?
GAN (GONG)
ガーン
I'M OUT OF MP!?
バチ
BACHI
AGH!
バチィ
BACHI
バチ
BACHI
HYU (SWISH)
ひゅっ
DOSA (THUMP)
どさっ
...WHOSE HP RUNS OUT FIRST!
ZAN (SLICE)
ザン

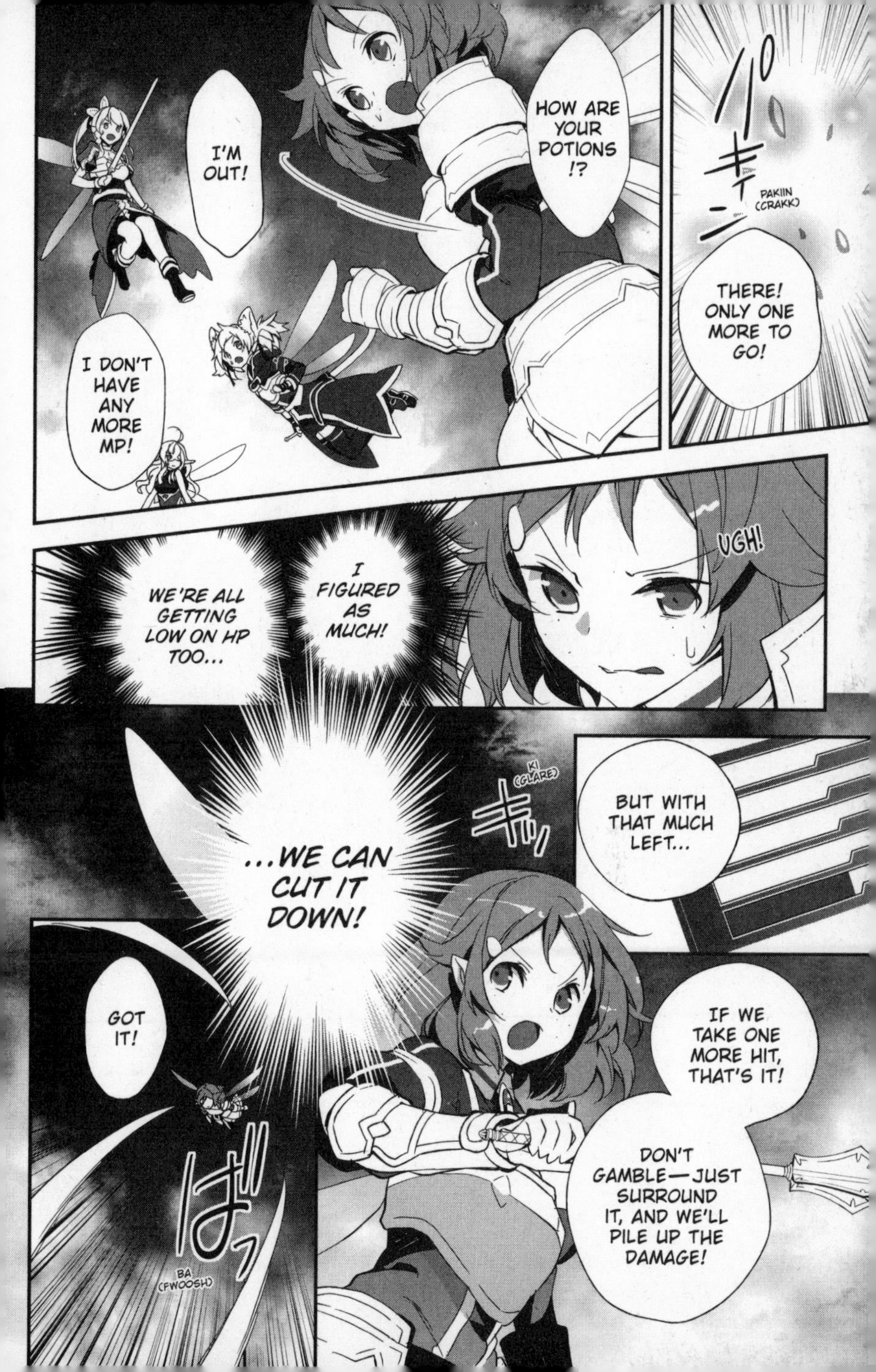

PAKIIN (CRAKK)
THERE! ONLY ONE MORE TO GO!
HOW ARE YOUR POTIONS !?
I'M OUT!
I DON'T HAVE ANY MORE MP!
UGH!
I FIGURED AS MUCH!
WE'RE ALL GETTING LOW ON HP TOO...
BUT WITH THAT MUCH LEFT...
KI (GLARE)
...WE CAN CUT IT DOWN!
IF WE TAKE ONE MORE HIT, THAT'S IT!
DON'T GAMBLE—JUST SURROUND IT, AND WE'LL PILE UP THE DAMAGE!
GOT IT!
BA (FWOOSH)

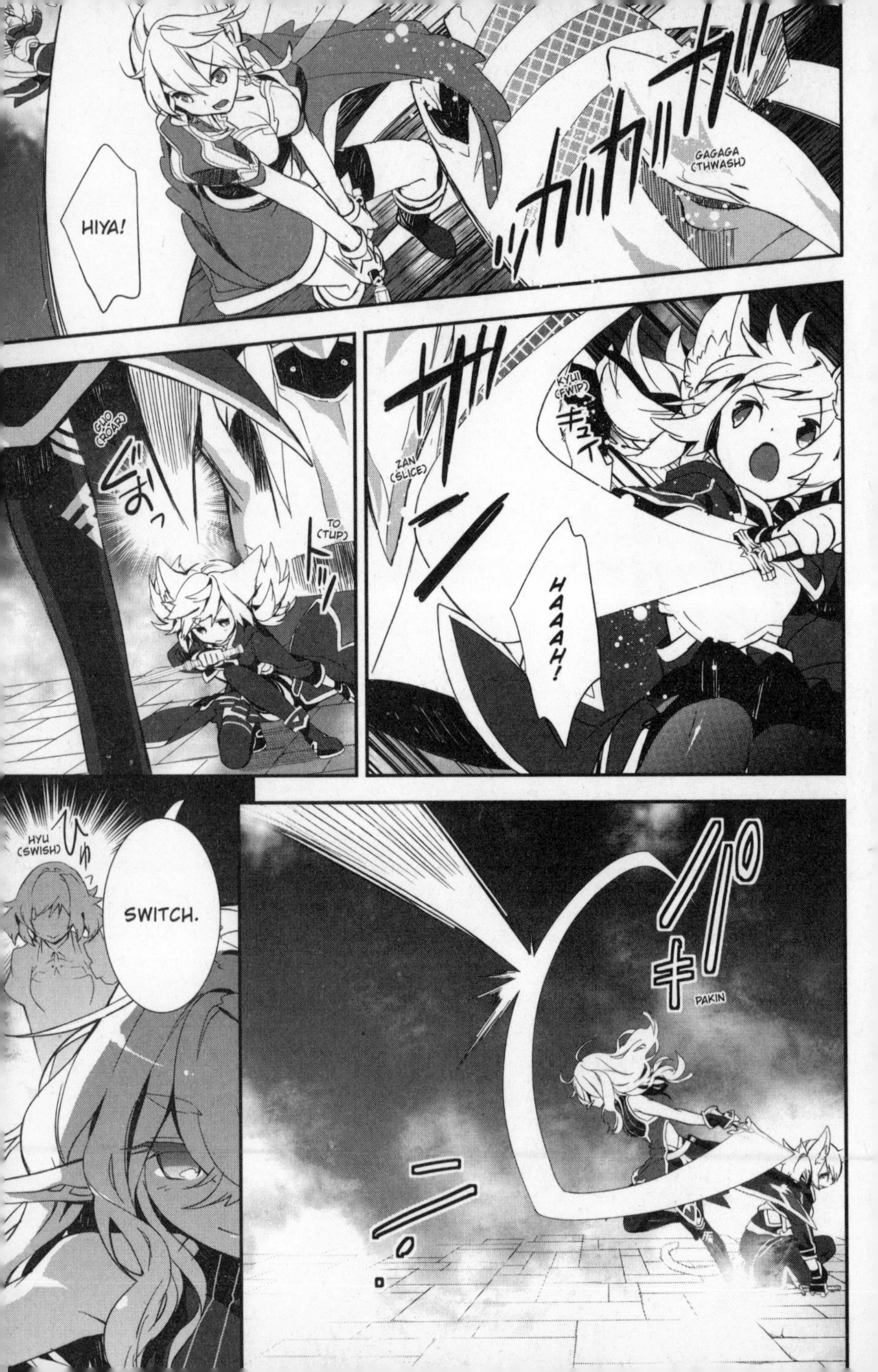
GAGAGA (THWASH)
HIYA!
KYUI (FWIP)
ZAN (SLICE)
HAAAAH!
GUO (ROAR)
TO (TUP)
PAKIN
HYU (SWISH)
SWITCH.

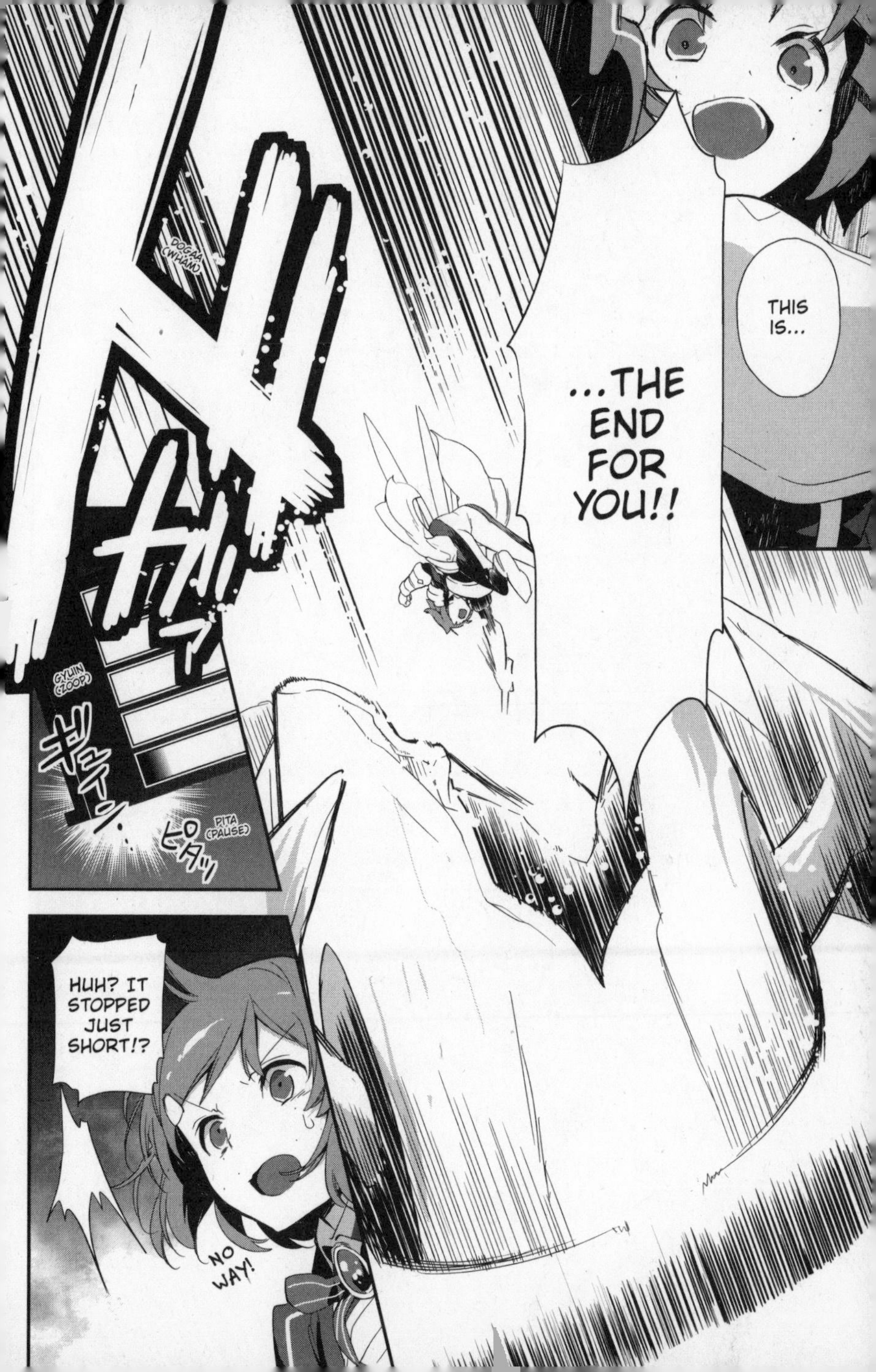
THIS IS...
...THE END FOR YOU!!
DOGAA (WHAM)
GYUIN (ZOOP)
PITA (PAUSE)
HUH? IT STOPPED JUST SHORT!?
NO WAY!

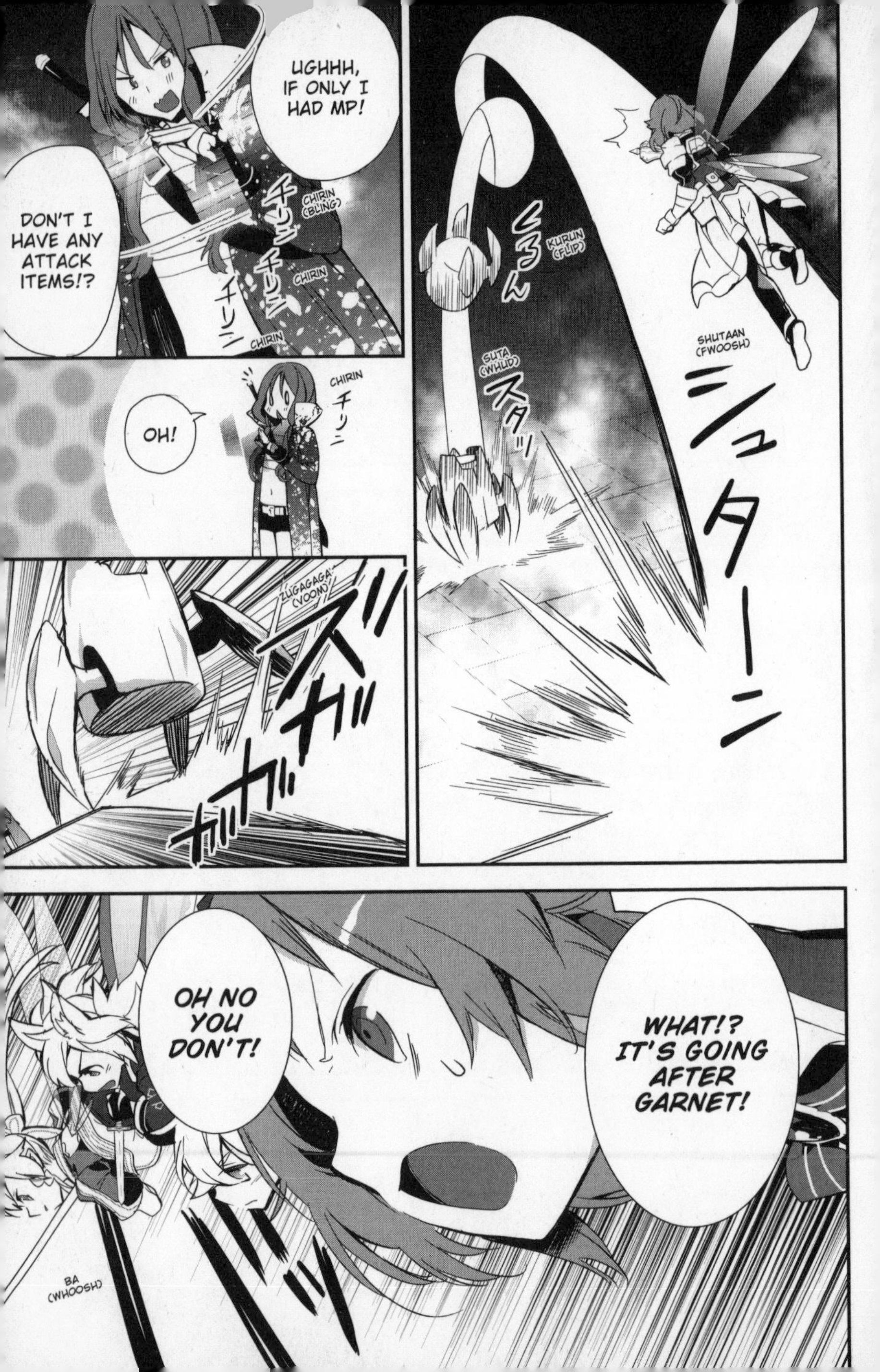

KURUN (FLIP)
くるん
SHUTAAN (FWOOSH)
シュターン
SUTA (WHUD)
スタッ
UGHHH, IF ONLY I HAD MP!
CHIRIN (BLING)
CHIRIN
CHIRIN
DON'T I HAVE ANY ATTACK ITEMS!?
CHIRIN
OH!
ZUGAGAGA (VOOM)
WHAT!? IT'S GOING AFTER GARNET!
OH NO YOU DON'T!
BA (WHOOSH)

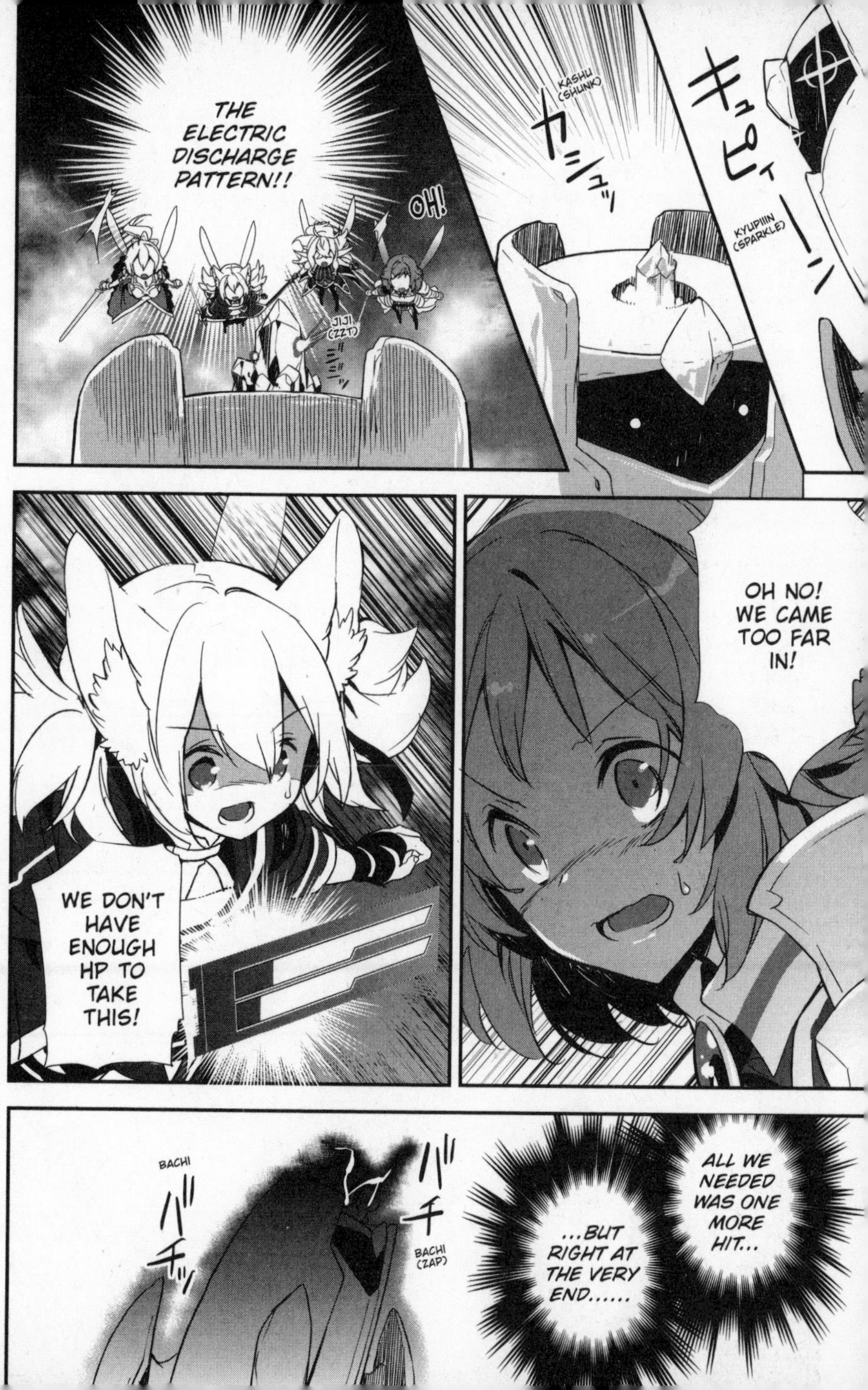
キュピィーン
KYUPIIIN (SPARKLE)
カシュッ
KASHU (SHUNK)
OH!
THE ELECTRIC DISCHARGE PATTERN!!
JIJI (ZZT)
OH NO! WE CAME TOO FAR IN!
WE DON'T HAVE ENOUGH HP TO TAKE THIS!
ALL WE NEEDED WAS ONE MORE HIT...
...BUT RIGHT AT THE VERY END......
バチ
BACHI (ZAP)
バチッ
BACHI

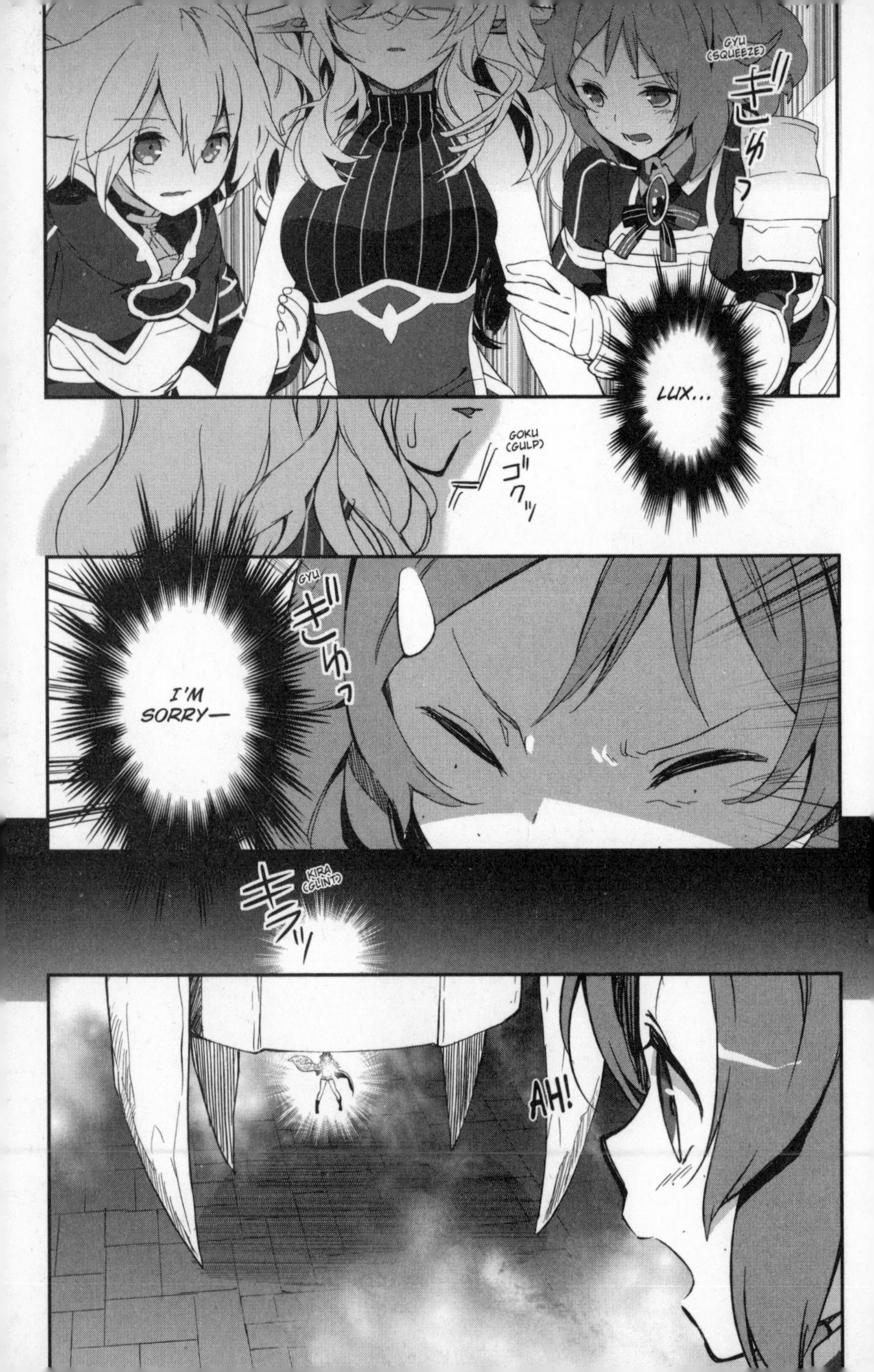
GYU (SQUEEZE)
ぎゅッ
LUX...
GOKU (GULP)
ゴクッ
GYU
ぎゅっ
I'M SORRY—
KIRA (GLINT)
キラッ
AH!

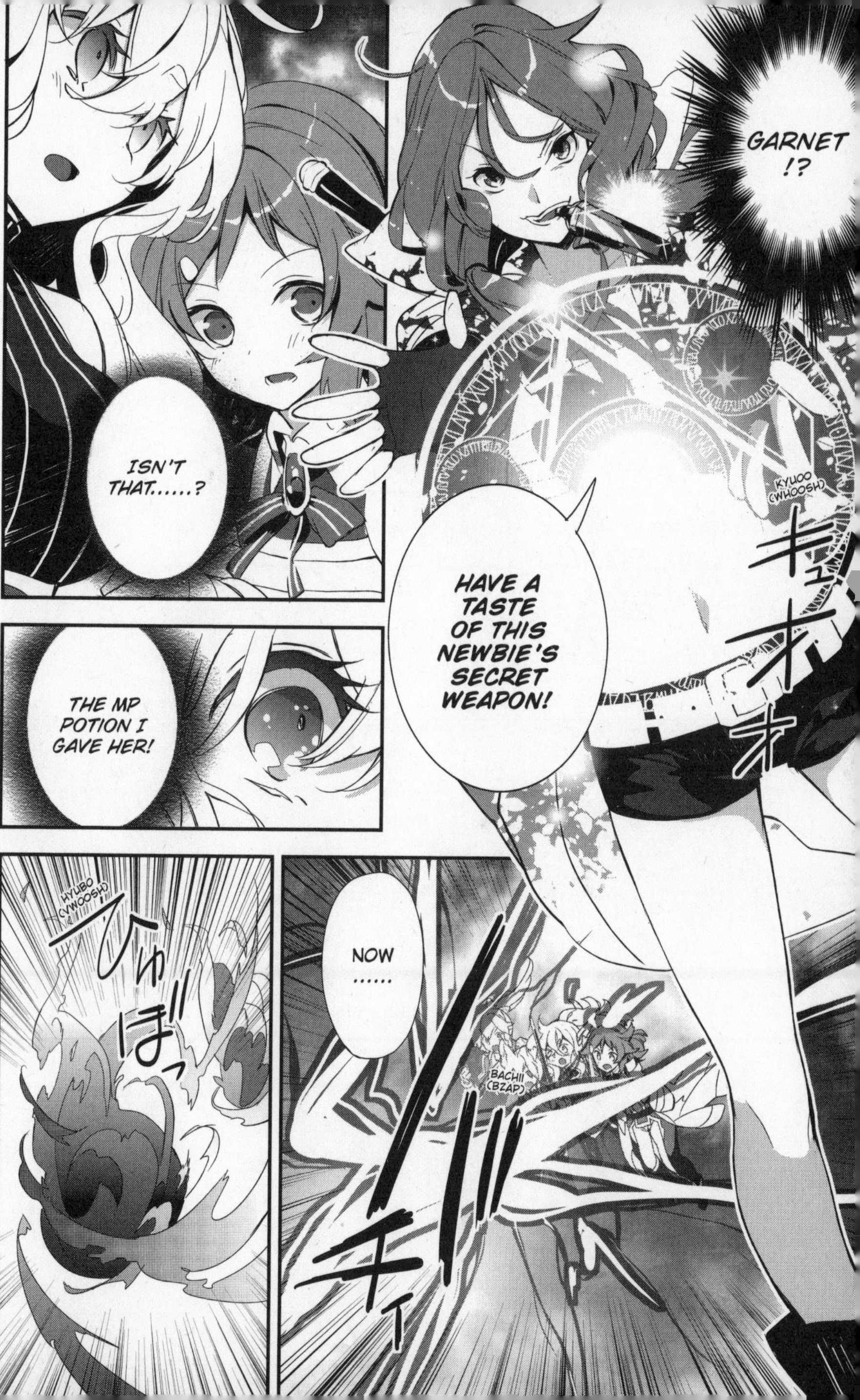

GARNET !?
ISN'T THAT......?
HAVE A TASTE OF THIS NEWBIE'S SECRET WEAPON!
KYUOO (WHOOSH)
キュオオ
THE MP POTION I GAVE HER!
NOW ......
BACHII (BZAP)
HYUBO (VWOOSH)
ひゅぼっ

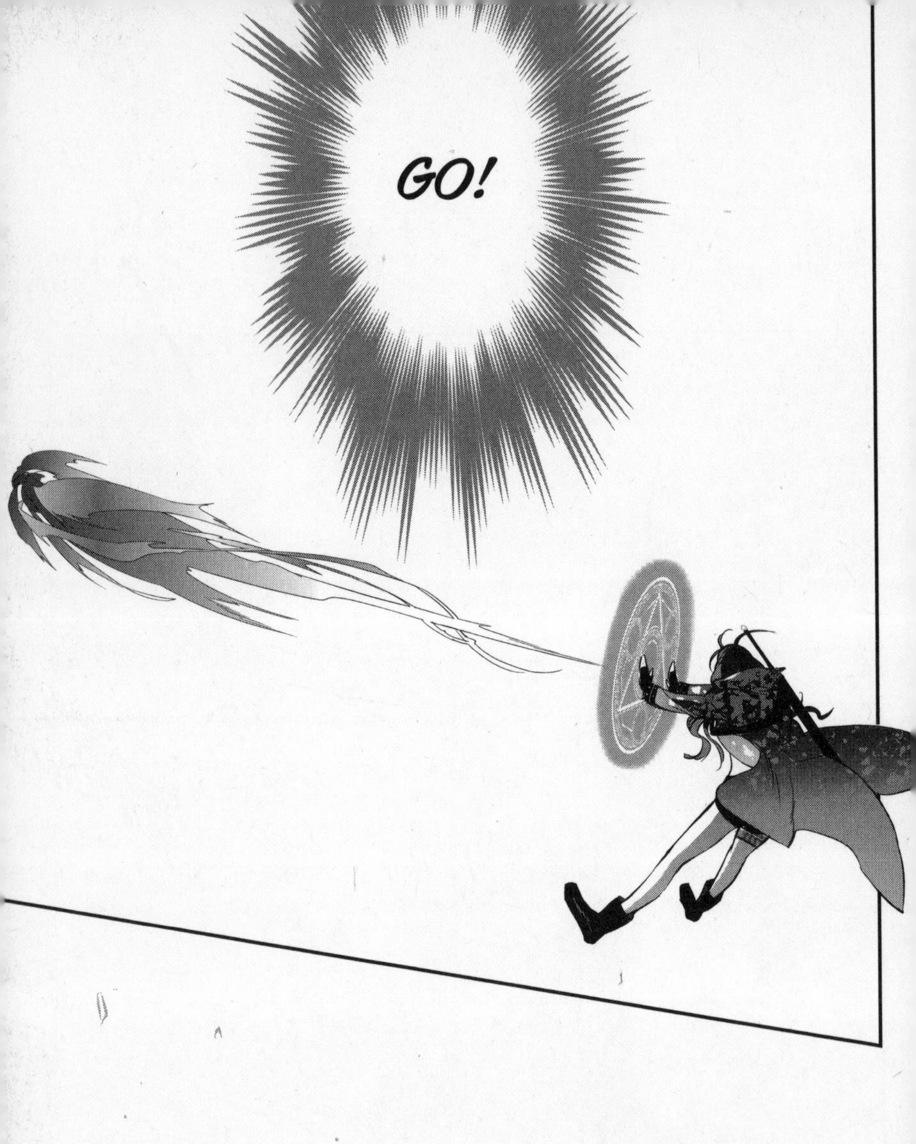
GO!

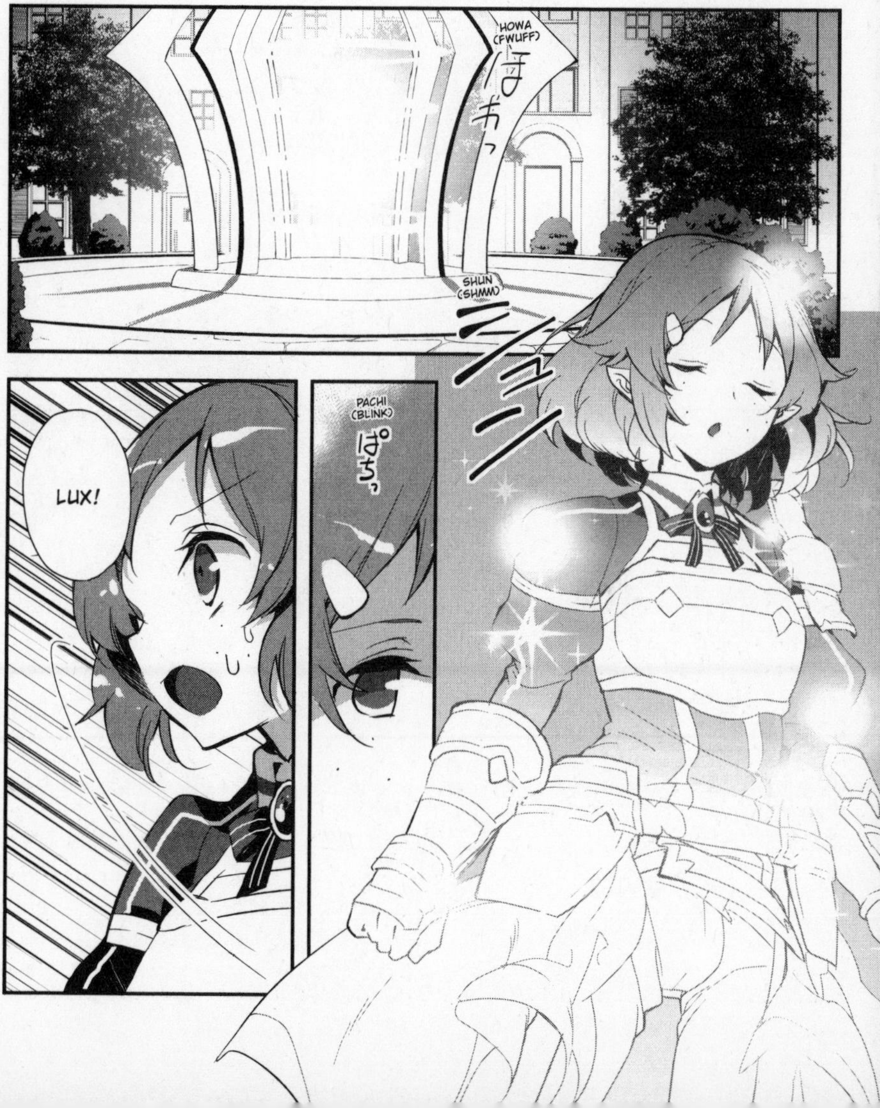
HOWA (FWUFF)
ほわっ
SHUN (SHMM)
シュン
PACHI (BLINK)
ぱちっ
LUX!

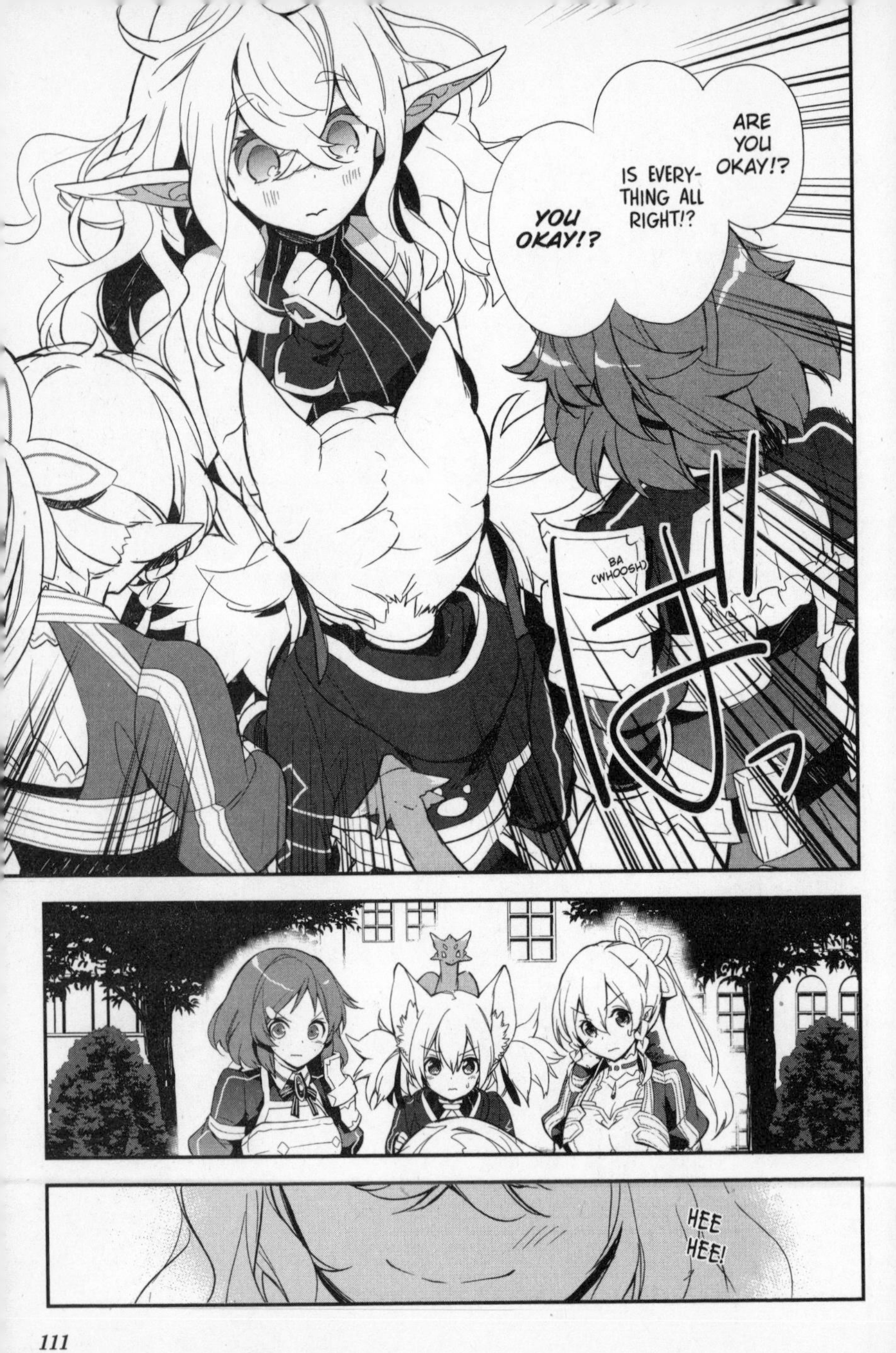
ARE YOU OKAY!?
IS EVERY-THING ALL RIGHT!?
YOU OKAY!?
BA (WHOOSH)
HEE HEE!

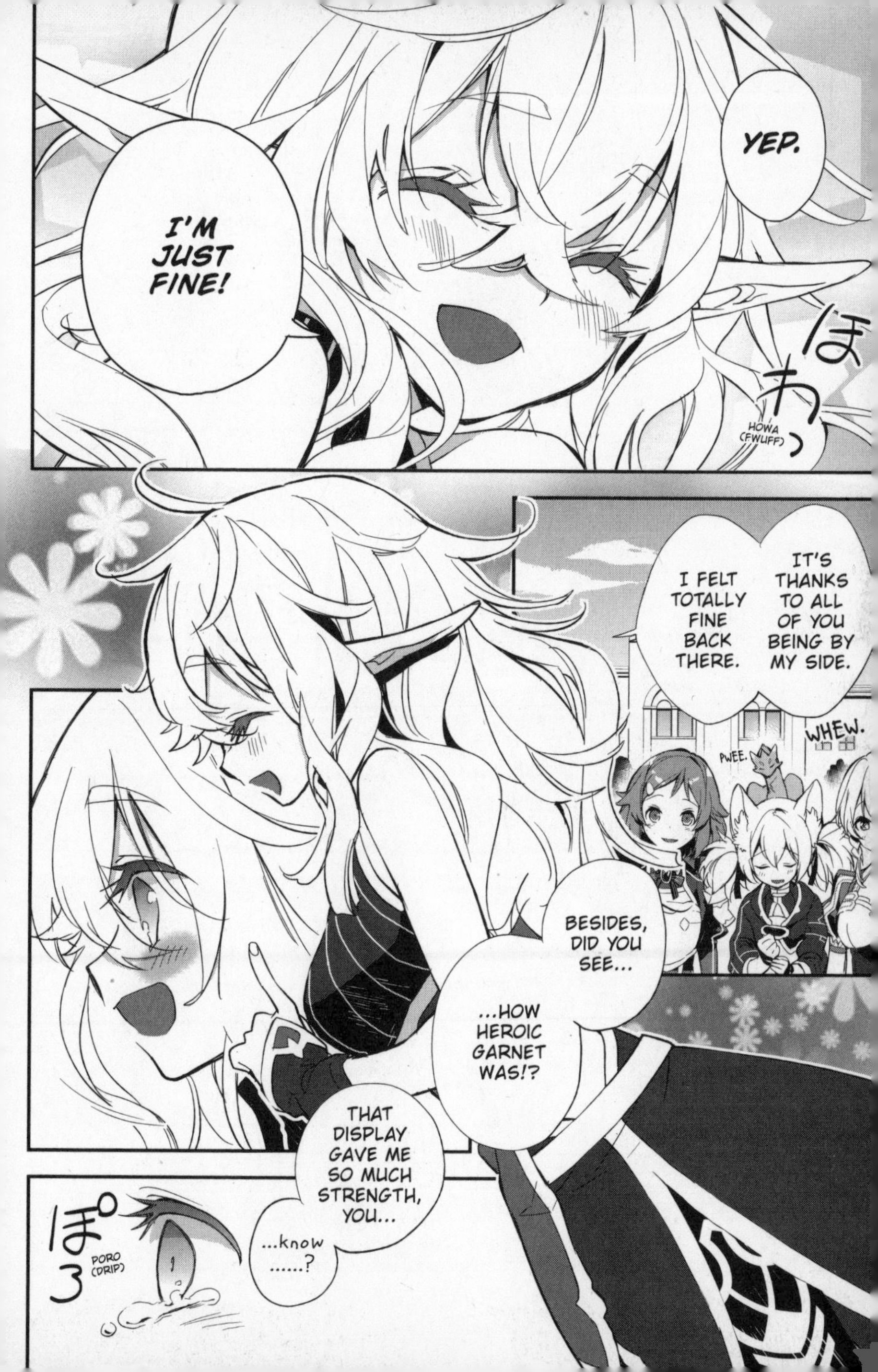
YEP.
I'M JUST FINE!
ほわっ
HOWA (FWUFF)
IT'S THANKS TO ALL OF YOU BEING BY MY SIDE.
I FELT TOTALLY FINE BACK THERE.
WHEW.
PWEE.
BESIDES, DID YOU SEE...
...HOW HEROIC GARNET WAS!?
THAT DISPLAY GAVE ME SO MUCH STRENGTH, YOU...
...know ......?
ぽろ
PORO (DRIP)

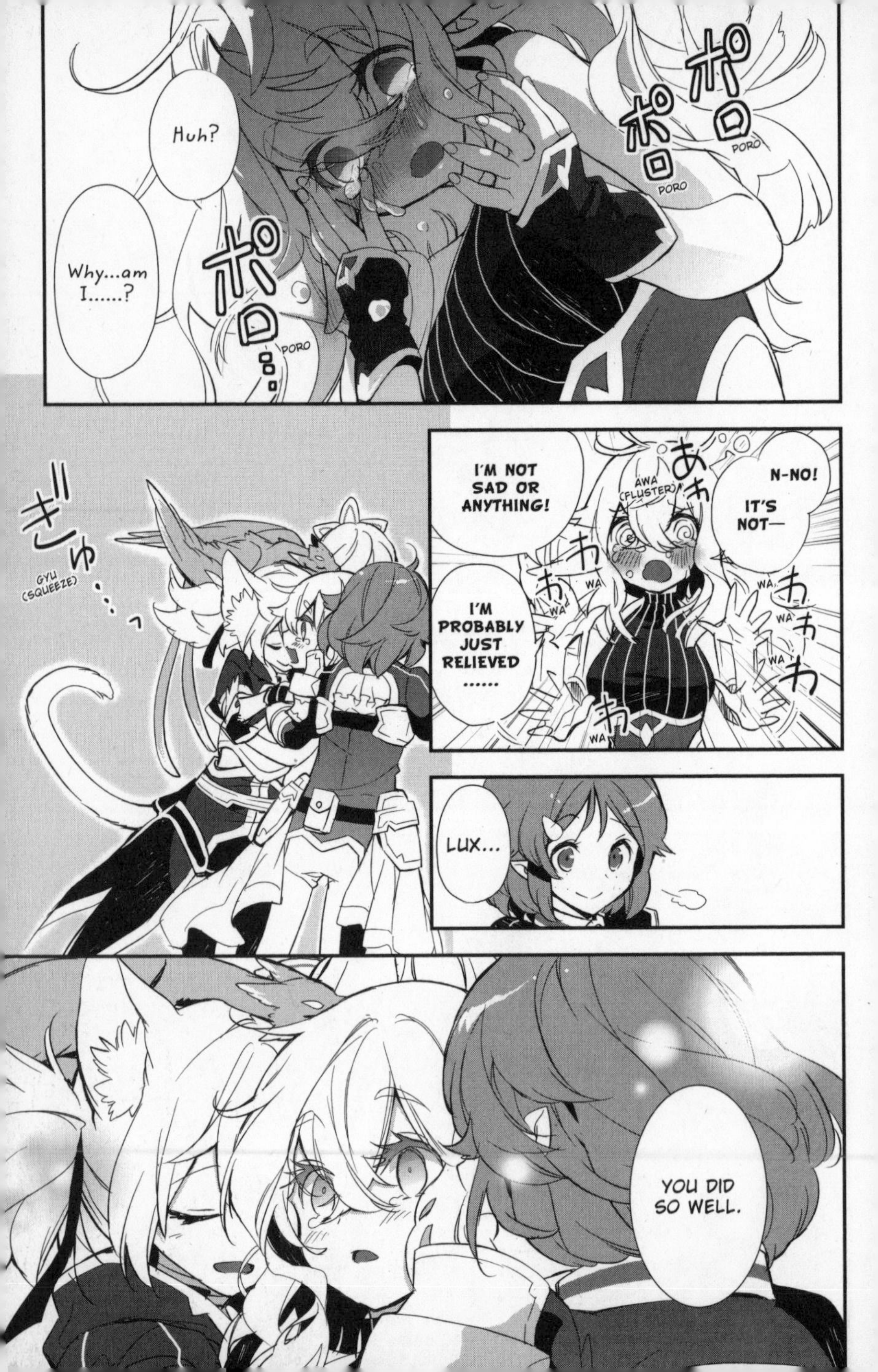
ポロ
PORO
ポロ
PORO
Huh?
ポロ...
PORO
Why...am I......?
N-NO! IT'S NOT—
あわ
AWA (FLUSTER)
I'M NOT SAD OR ANYTHING!
わ
WA
I'M PROBABLY JUST RELIEVED......
LUX...
ぎゅ...っ
GYU (SQUEEZE)
YOU DID SO WELL.

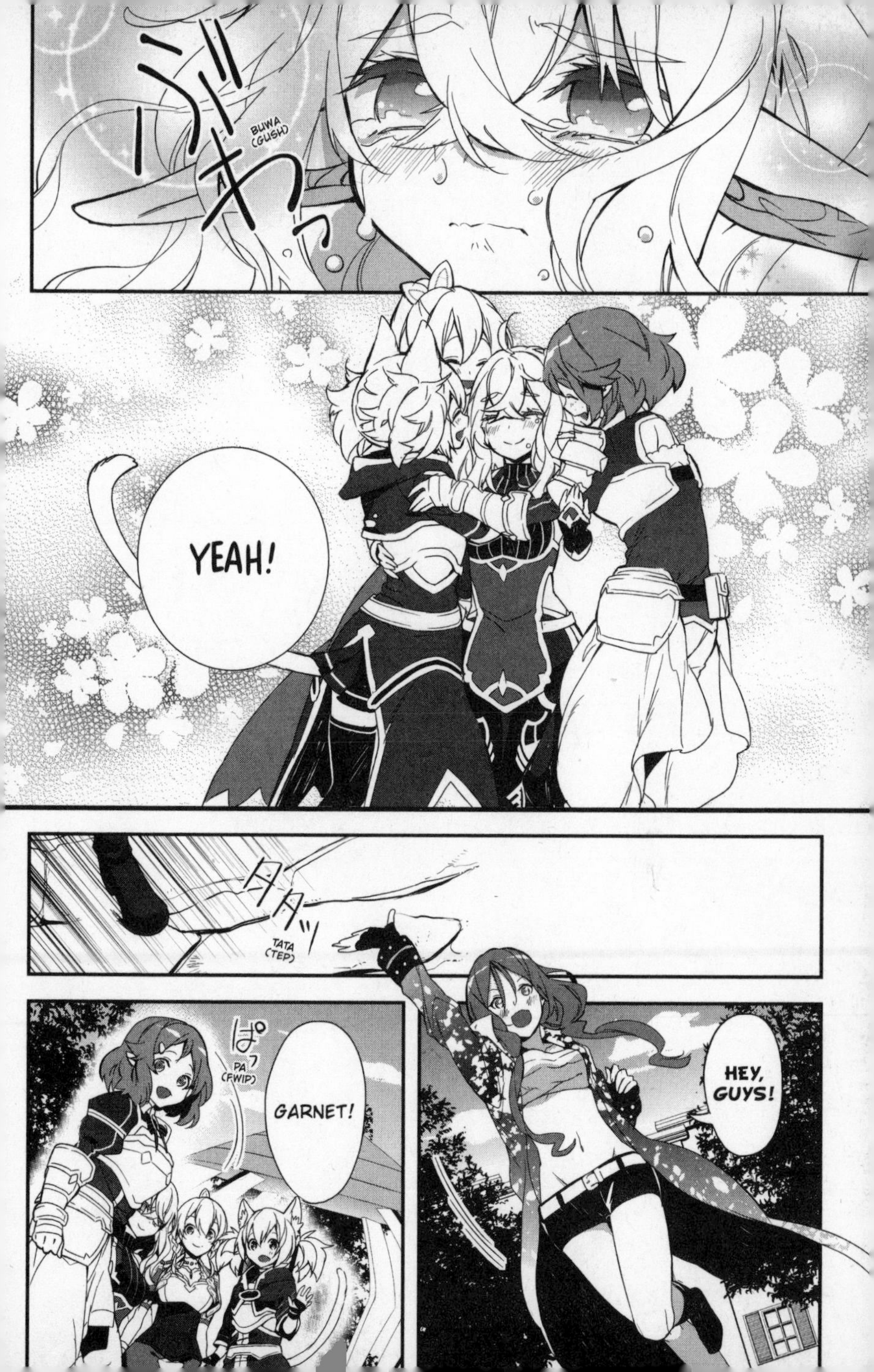
ぶわっ
BUWA (GUSH)
YEAH!
タタッ
TATA (TEP)
HEY, GUYS!
GARNET!
ぱっ
PA (FWIP)

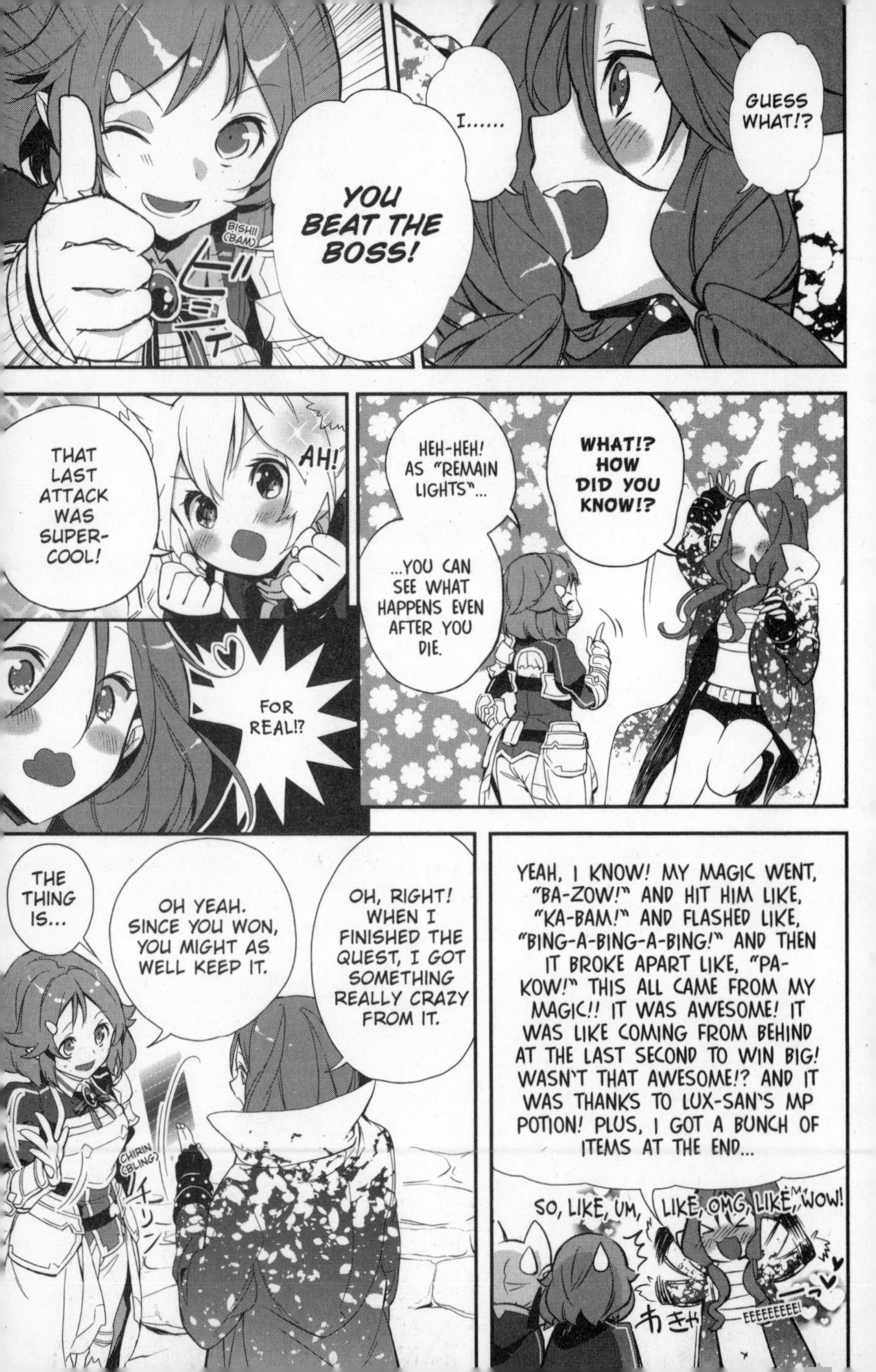
GUESS WHAT!?
I......
YOU BEAT THE BOSS!
BISHII (BAM)
WHAT!? HOW DID YOU KNOW!?
HEH-HEH! AS "REMAIN LIGHTS"...
...YOU CAN SEE WHAT HAPPENS EVEN AFTER YOU DIE.
AH!
THAT LAST ATTACK WAS SUPER-COOL!
FOR REAL!?
YEAH, I KNOW! MY MAGIC WENT, "BA-ZOW!" AND HIT HIM LIKE, "KA-BAM!" AND FLASHED LIKE, "BING-A-BING-A-BING!" AND THEN IT BROKE APART LIKE, "PA-KOW!" THIS ALL CAME FROM MY MAGIC!! IT WAS AWESOME! IT WAS LIKE COMING FROM BEHIND AT THE LAST SECOND TO WIN BIG! WASN'T THAT AWESOME!? AND IT WAS THANKS TO LUX-SAN'S MP POTION! PLUS, I GOT A BUNCH OF ITEMS AT THE END...
SO, LIKE, UM,
LIKE, OMG, LIKE, WOW!
EEEEEEEEE!
OH, RIGHT! WHEN I FINISHED THE QUEST, I GOT SOMETHING REALLY CRAZY FROM IT.
OH YEAH. SINCE YOU WON, YOU MIGHT AS WELL KEEP IT.
THE THING IS...
CHIRIN (BLING)

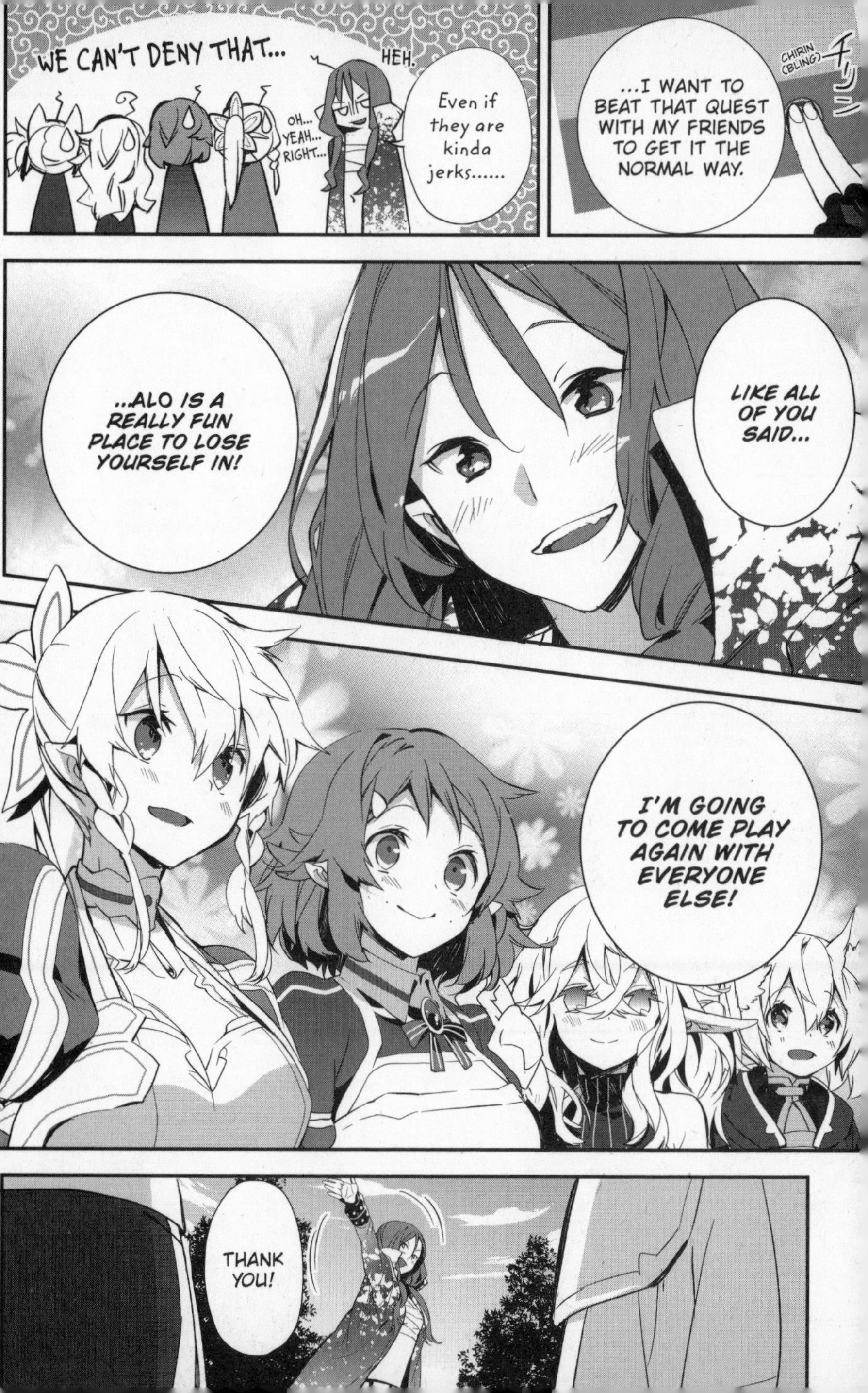
...I WANT TO BEAT THAT QUEST WITH MY FRIENDS TO GET IT THE NORMAL WAY.
CHIRIN (BLING)
Even if they are kinda jerks......
HEH.
WE CAN'T DENY THAT...
OH... YEAH... RIGHT...
LIKE ALL OF YOU SAID...
...ALO IS A REALLY FUN PLACE TO LOSE YOURSELF IN!
I'M GOING TO COME PLAY AGAIN WITH EVERYONE ELSE!
THANK YOU!

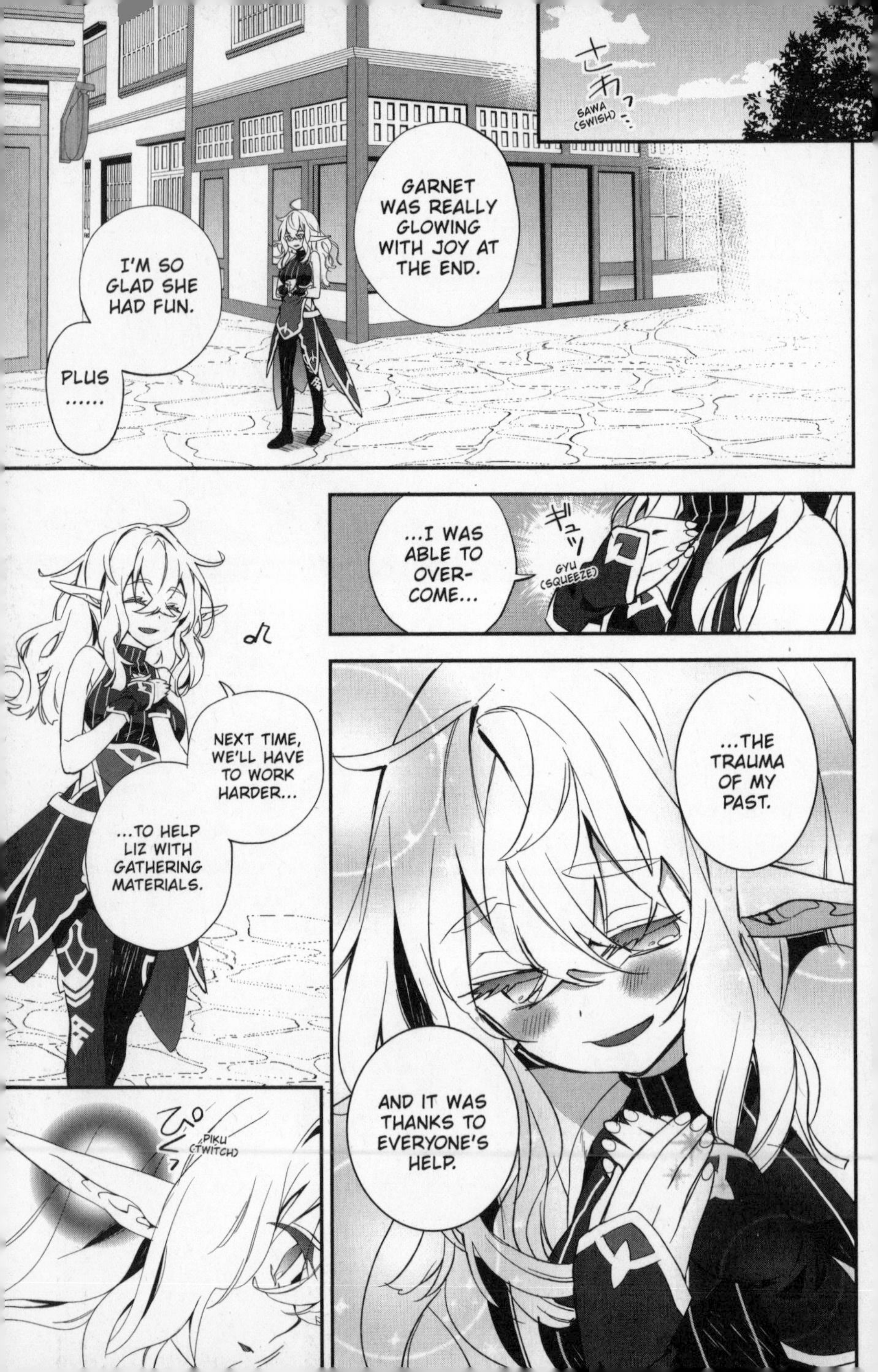
さわっ
SAWA (SWISH)
GARNET WAS REALLY GLOWING WITH JOY AT THE END.
I'M SO GLAD SHE HAD FUN.
PLUS ......
ギュッ
GYU (SQUEEZE)
...I WAS ABLE TO OVERCOME...
...THE TRAUMA OF MY PAST.
AND IT WAS THANKS TO EVERYONE'S HELP.
NEXT TIME, WE'LL HAVE TO WORK HARDER...
...TO HELP LIZ WITH GATHERING MATERIALS.
ぴくっ
PIKU (TWITCH)

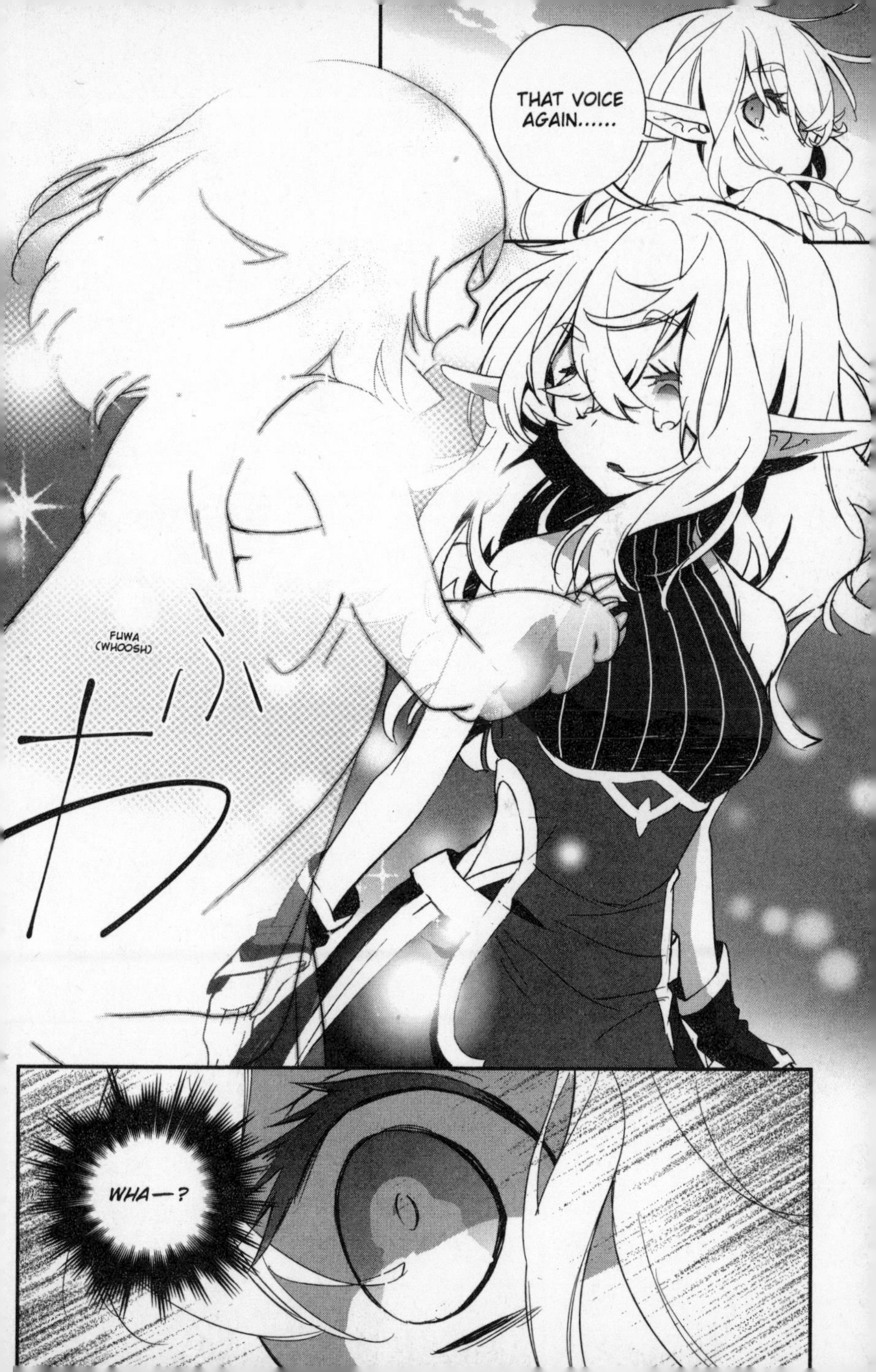
THAT VOICE AGAIN......
FUWA (WHOOSH)
ふわ
WHA—?

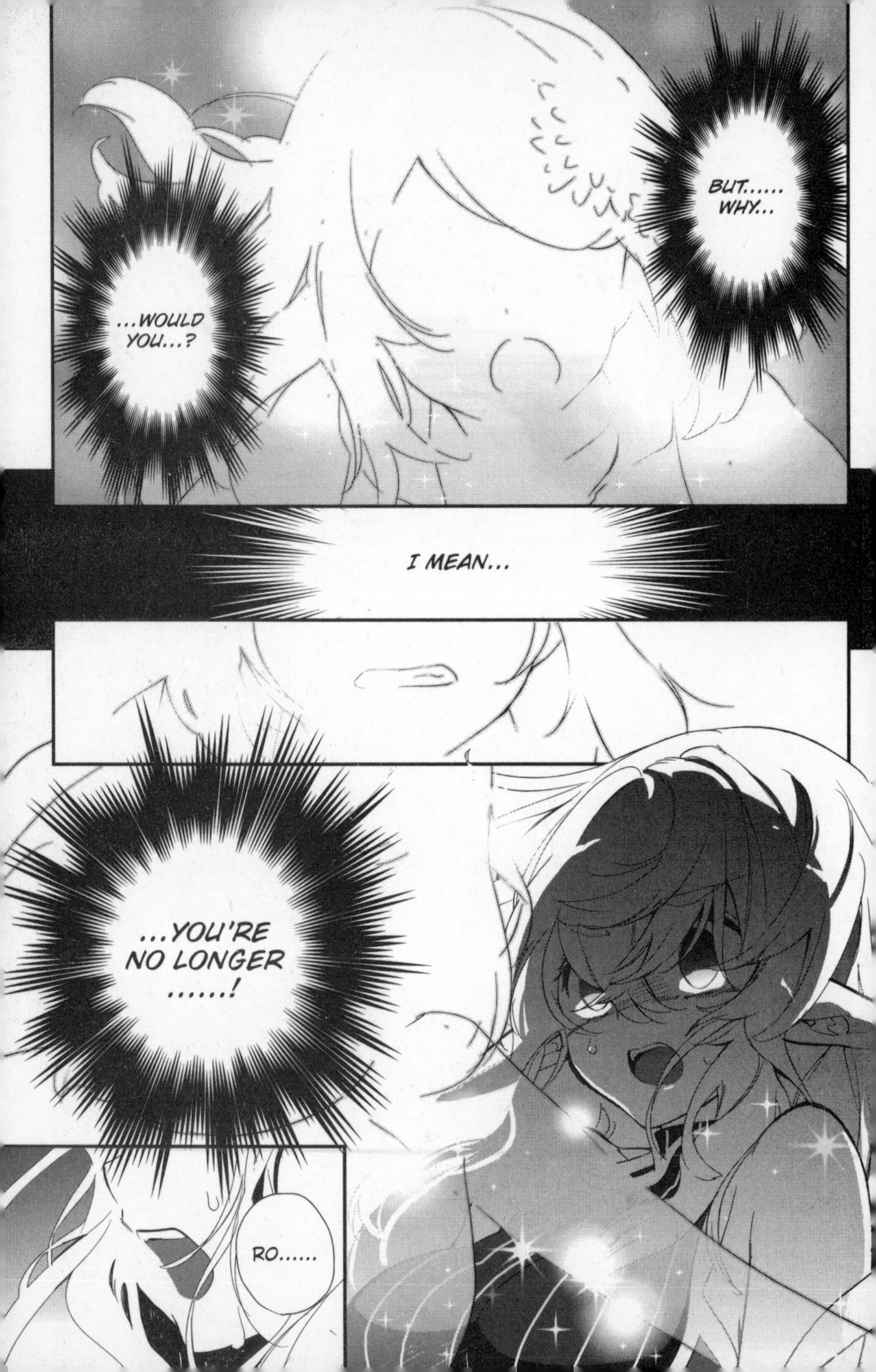
BUT...... WHY...
...WOULD YOU...?
I MEAN...
...YOU'RE NO LONGER ......!
RO......

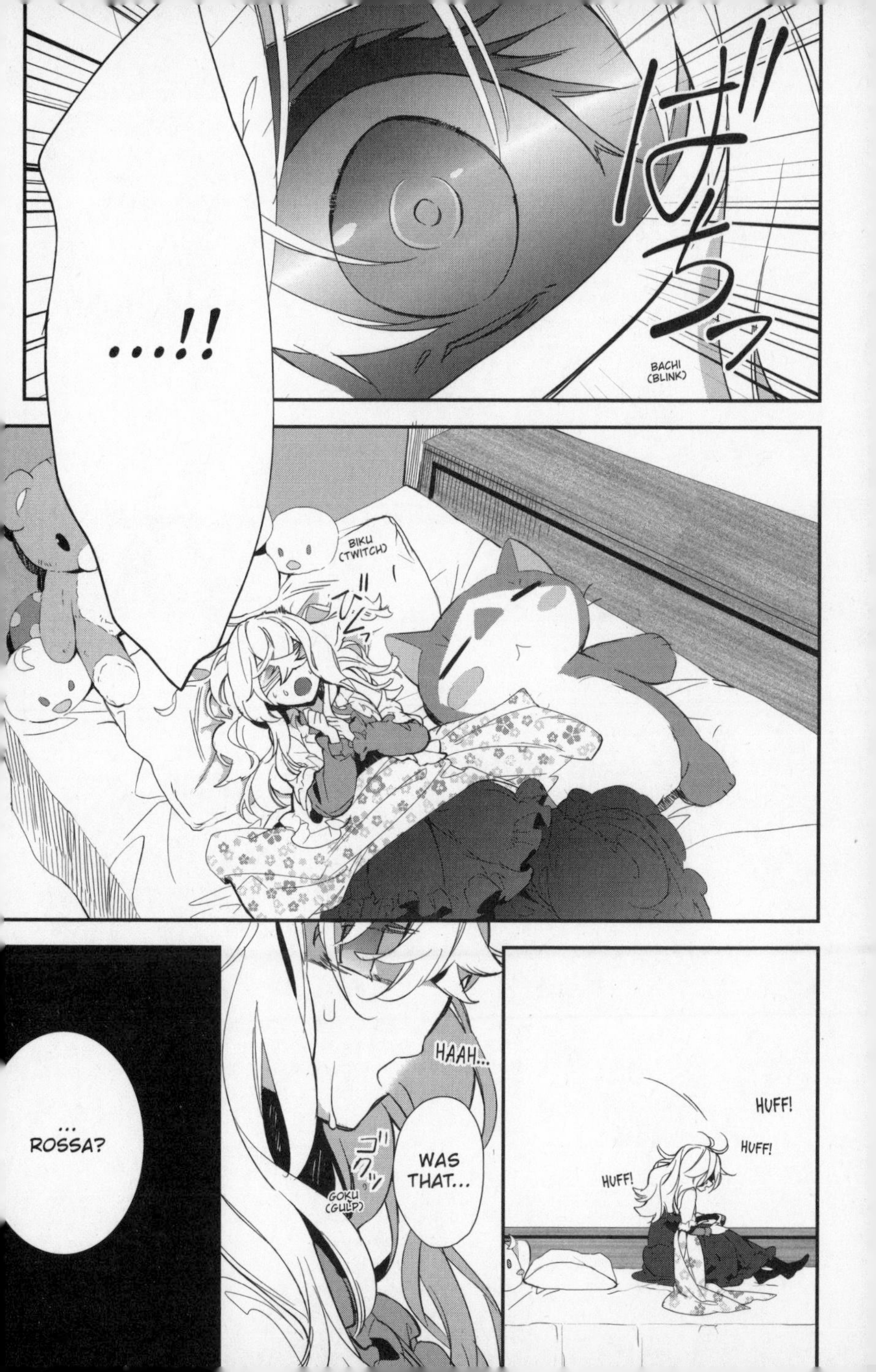
BACHI (BLINK)
...!!
BIKU (TWITCH)
HUFF!
HUFF!
HUFF!
HAAH...
GOKU (GULP)
WAS THAT...
... ROSSA?

SWORD ART ONLINE
GIRLS' OPS

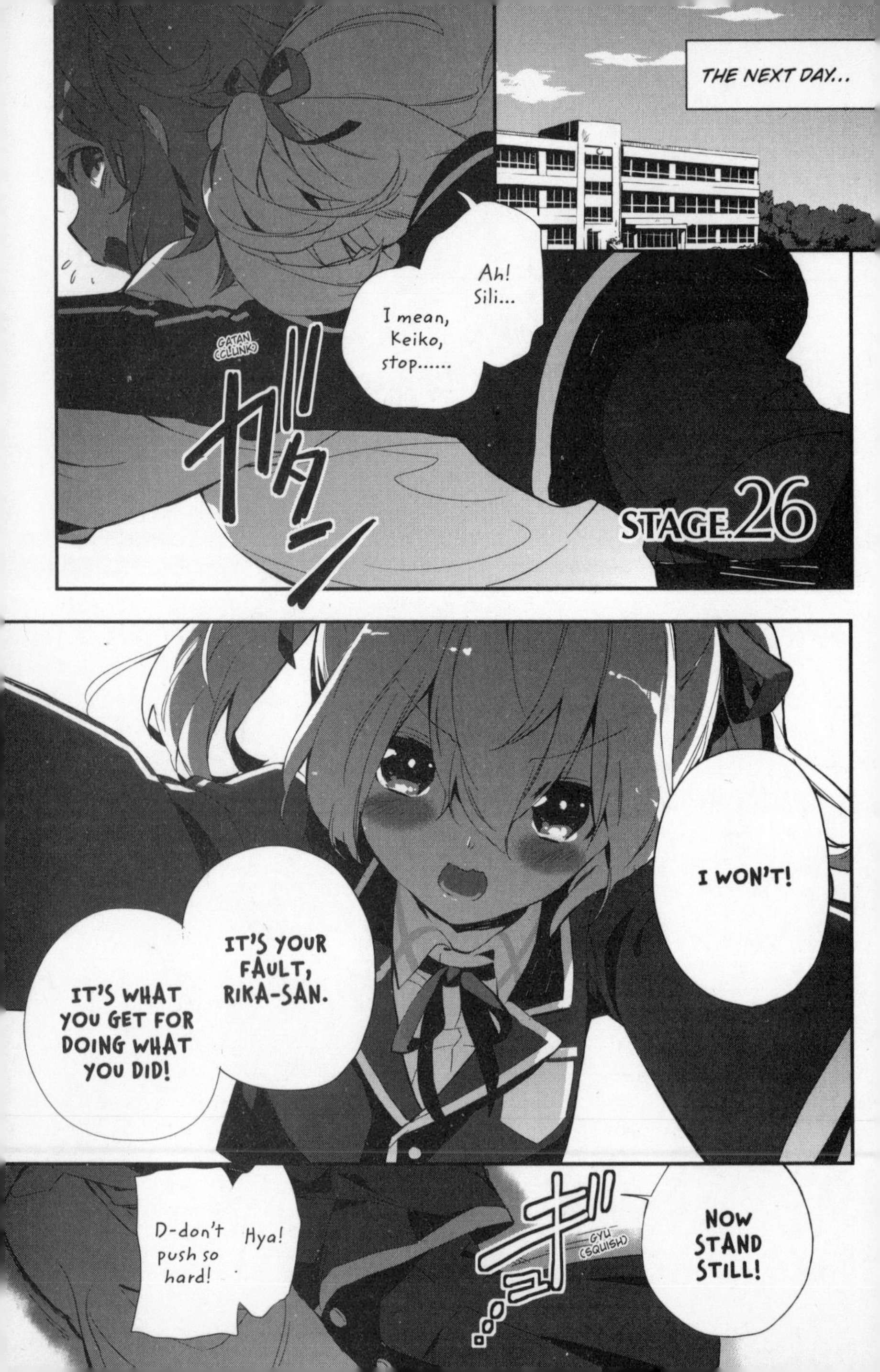
THE NEXT DAY...
Ah! Sili...
I mean, Keiko, stop......
GATAN (CLUNK)
STAGE.26
I WON'T!
IT'S YOUR FAULT, RIKA-SAN.
IT'S WHAT YOU GET FOR DOING WHAT YOU DID!
NOW STAND STILL!
GYU (SQUISH)
Hya!
D-don't push so hard!

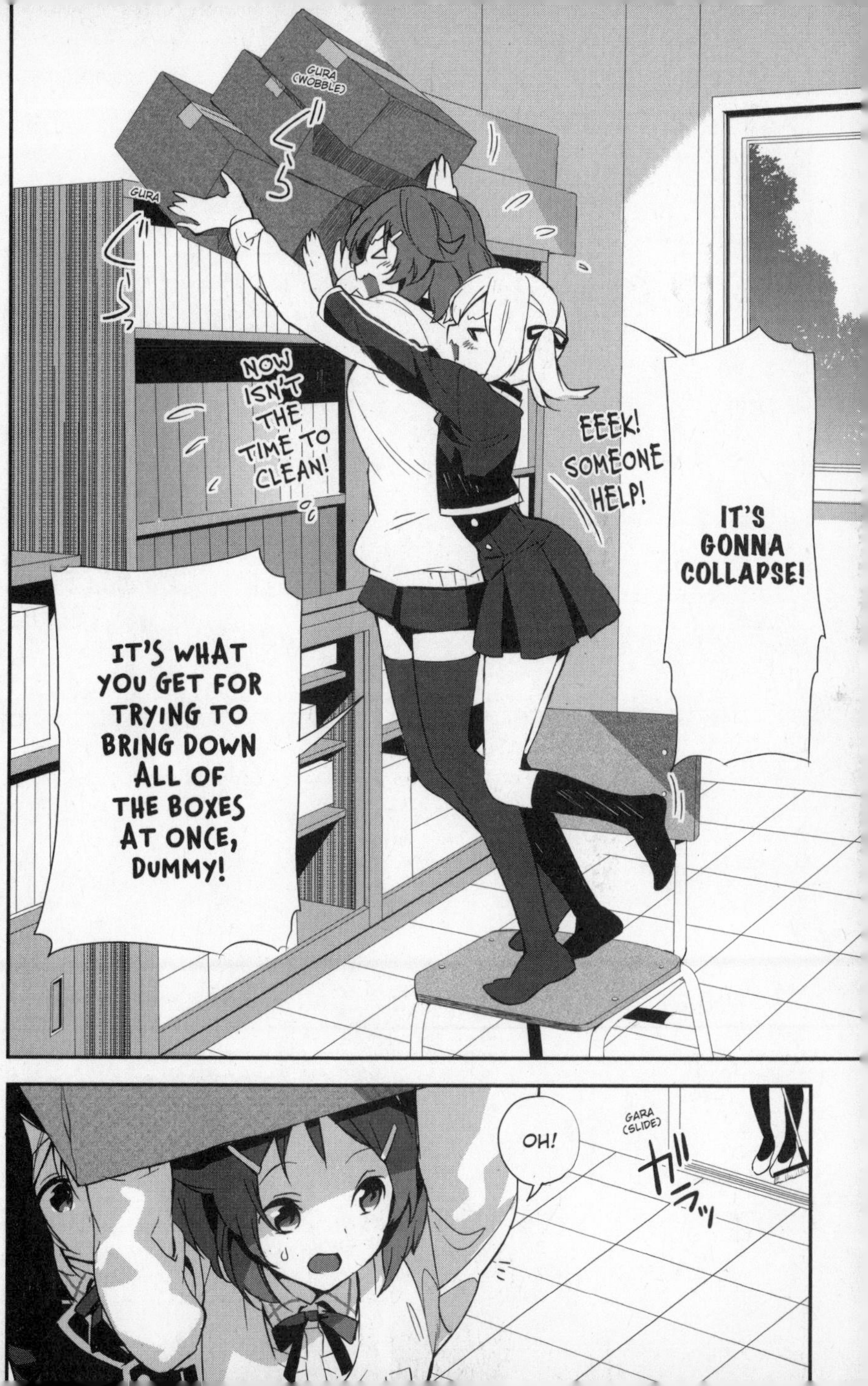
IT'S GONNA COLLAPSE!
EEEK! SOMEONE HELP!
GURA (WOBBLE)
GURA
NOW ISN'T THE TIME TO CLEAN!
IT'S WHAT YOU GET FOR TRYING TO BRING DOWN ALL OF THE BOXES AT ONCE, DUMMY!
GARA (SLIDE)
OH!

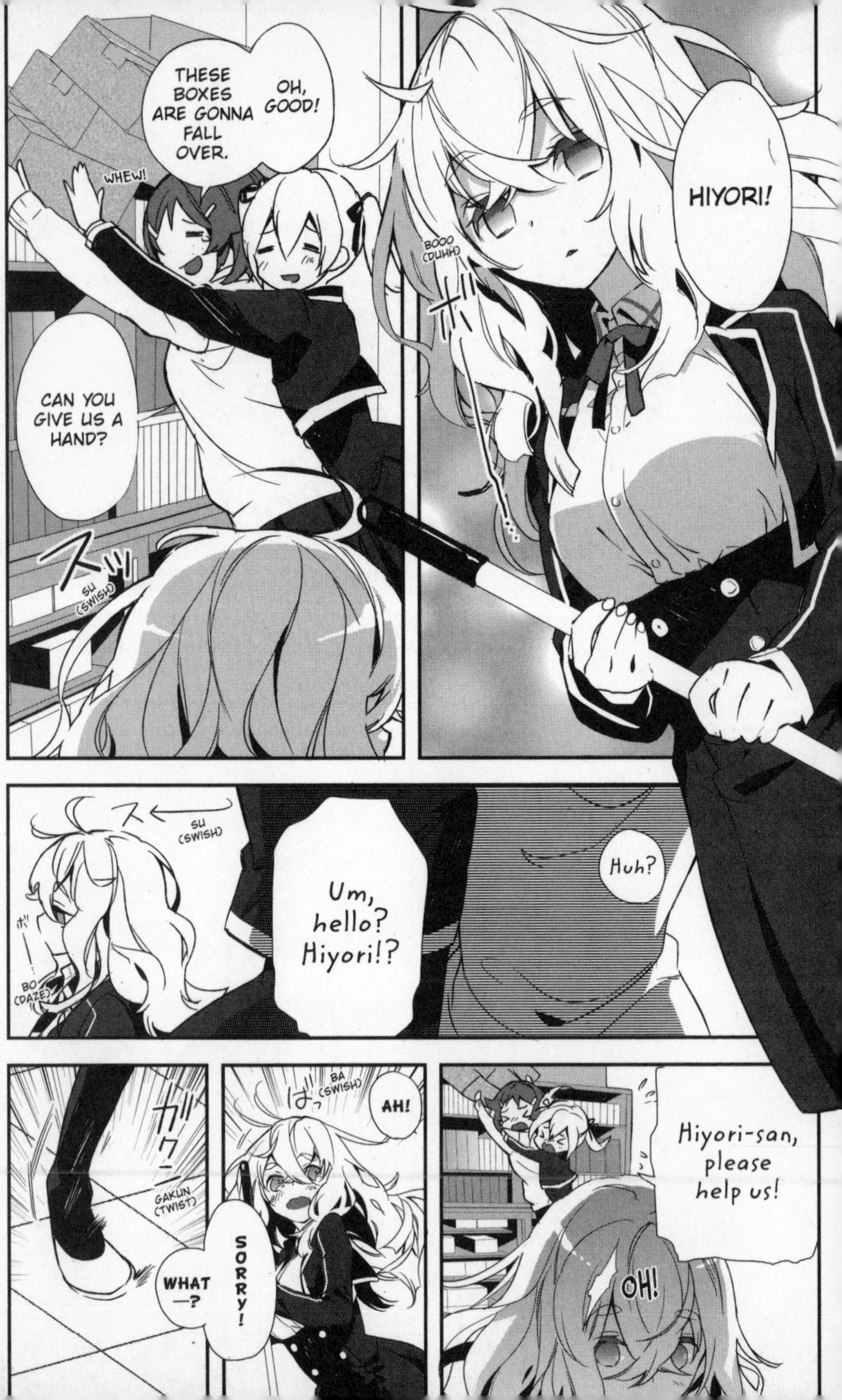
HIYORI!
BOOO (DUHH)
OH, GOOD!
THESE BOXES ARE GONNA FALL OVER.
WHEW!
CAN YOU GIVE US A HAND?
SU (SWISH)
Huh?
Um, hello? Hiyori!?
SU (SWISH)
BO (DAZE)
Hiyori-san, please help us!
OH!
AH!
BA (SWISH)
SORRY!
WHAT—?
GAKUN (TWIST)

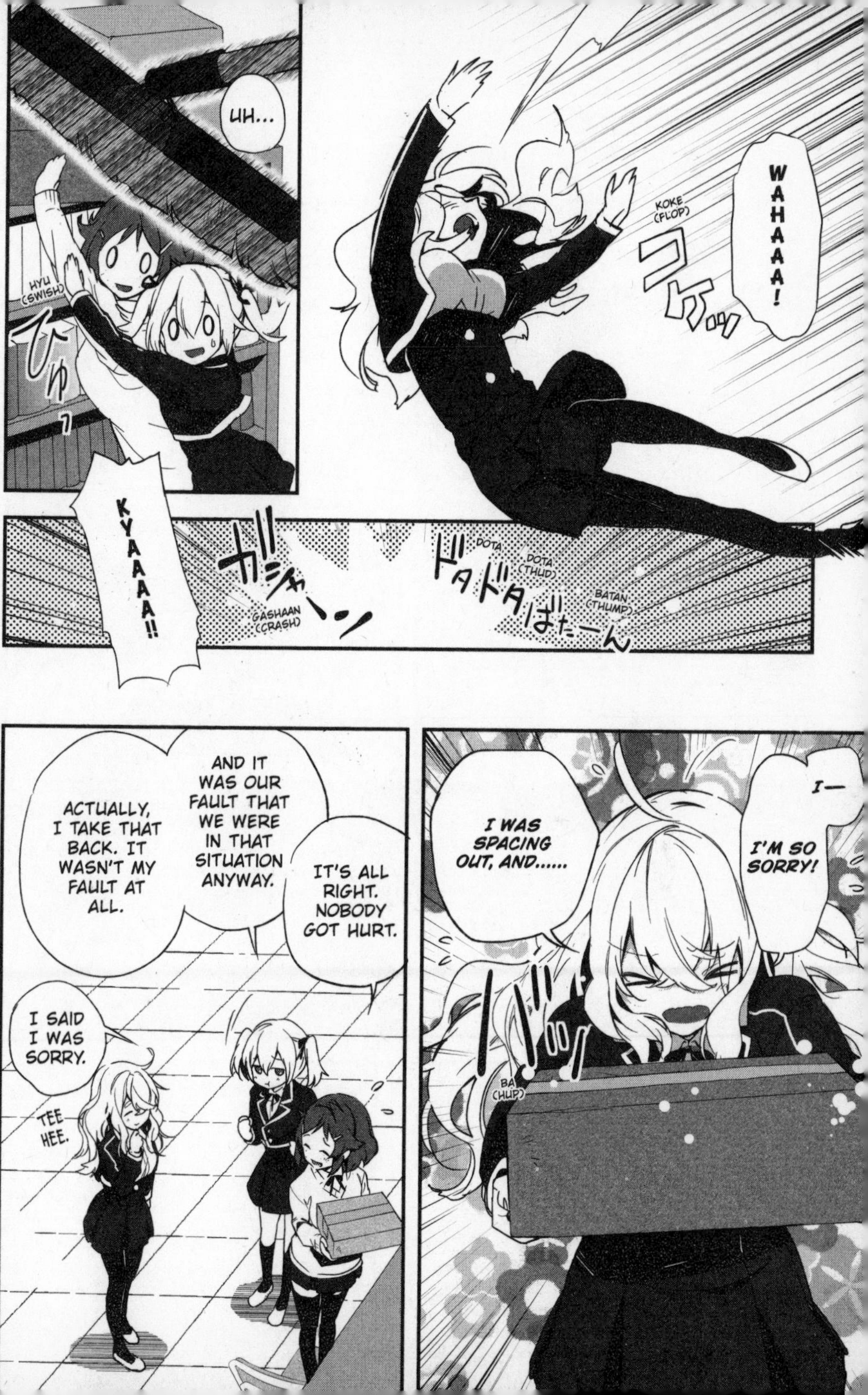
WAHAAAA!
KOKE (FLOP)
UH...
HYU (SWISH)
KYAAAAA!!
DOTA DOTA (THUD)
BATAN (THUMP)
GASHAAN (CRASH)
I—
I'M SO SORRY!
I WAS SPACING OUT, AND......
BA (CHUP)
IT'S ALL RIGHT. NOBODY GOT HURT.
AND IT WAS OUR FAULT THAT WE WERE IN THAT SITUATION ANYWAY.
ACTUALLY, I TAKE THAT BACK. IT WASN'T MY FAULT AT ALL.
I SAID I WAS SORRY.
TEE HEE.

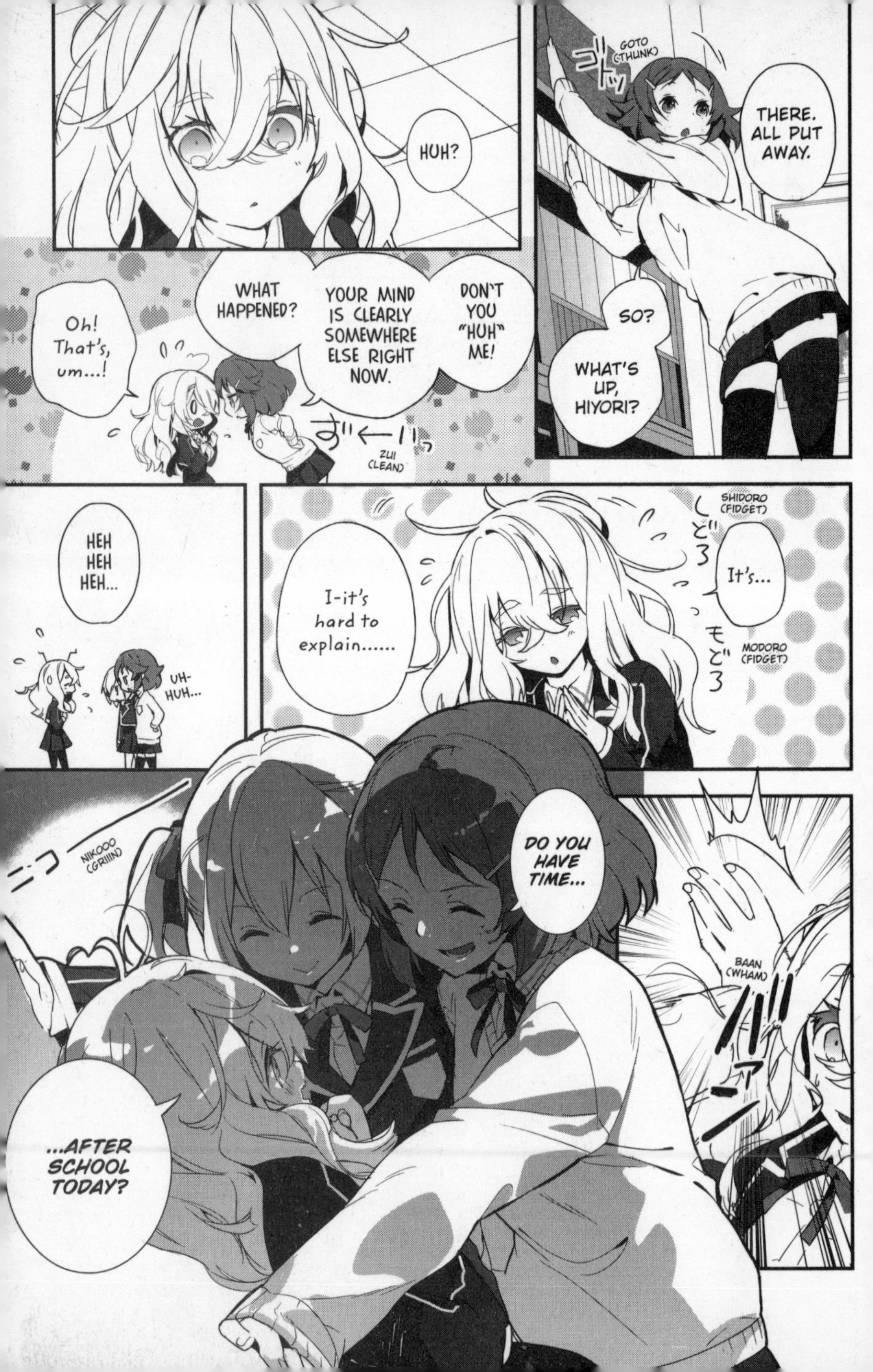

ゴトッ
GOTO (THUNK)
THERE. ALL PUT AWAY.
SO?
WHAT'S UP, HIYORI?
HUH?
DON'T YOU "HUH" ME!
YOUR MIND IS CLEARLY SOMEWHERE ELSE RIGHT NOW.
WHAT HAPPENED?
ずい
ZUI (LEAN)
Oh! That's, um...!
しどろ
SHIDORO (FIDGET)
It's...
もどろ
MODORO (FIDGET)
I-it's hard to explain......
HEH HEH HEH...
UH-HUH...
BAAN (WHAM)
DO YOU HAVE TIME...
NIKOOO (GRIIIN)
...AFTER SCHOOL TODAY?

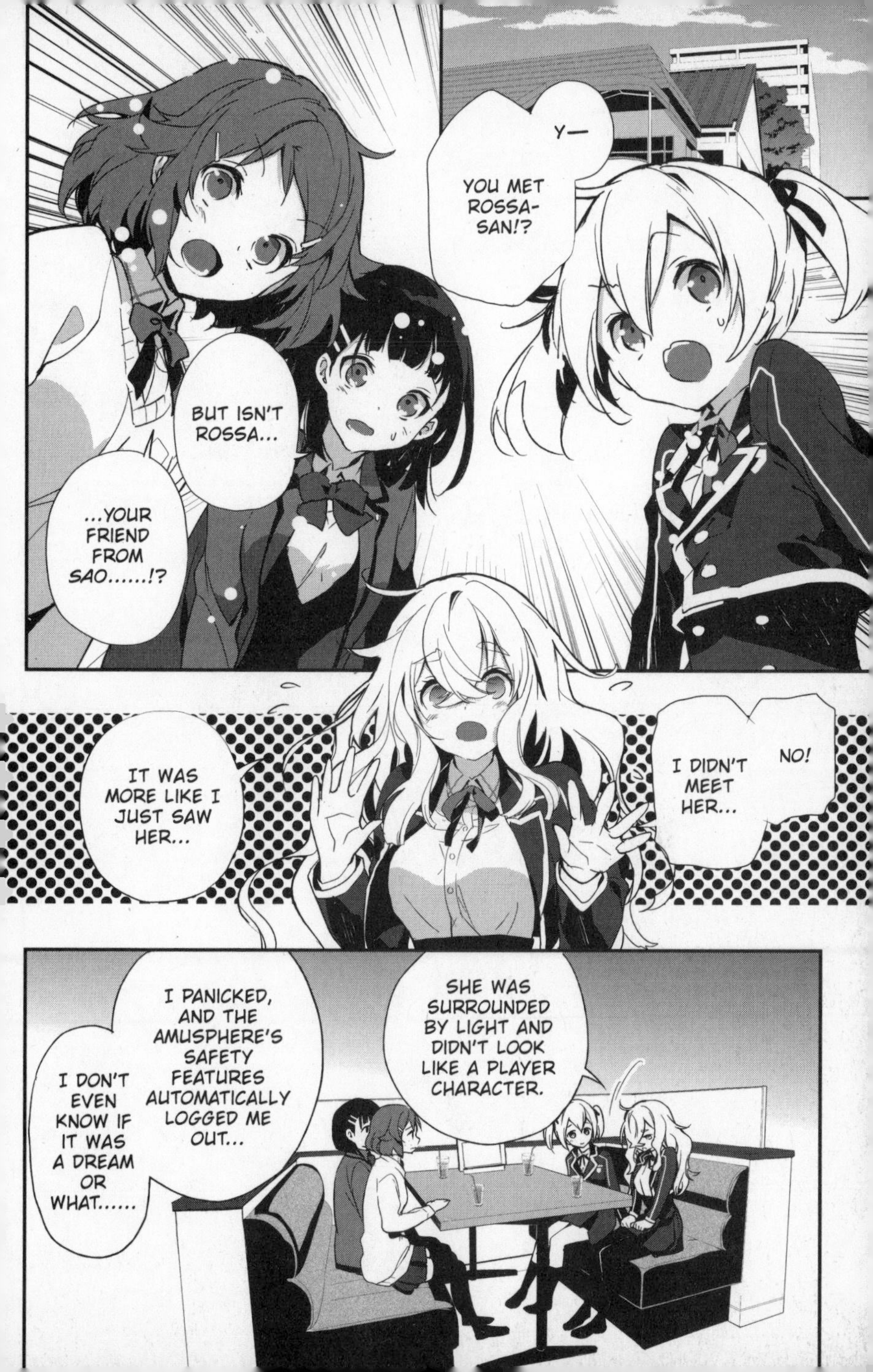
Y—
YOU MET ROSSA-SAN!?
BUT ISN'T ROSSA...
...YOUR FRIEND FROM SAO......!?
NO!
I DIDN'T MEET HER...
IT WAS MORE LIKE I JUST SAW HER...
SHE WAS SURROUNDED BY LIGHT AND DIDN'T LOOK LIKE A PLAYER CHARACTER.
I PANICKED, AND THE AMUSPHERE'S SAFETY FEATURES AUTOMATICALLY LOGGED ME OUT...
I DON'T EVEN KNOW IF IT WAS A DREAM OR WHAT......

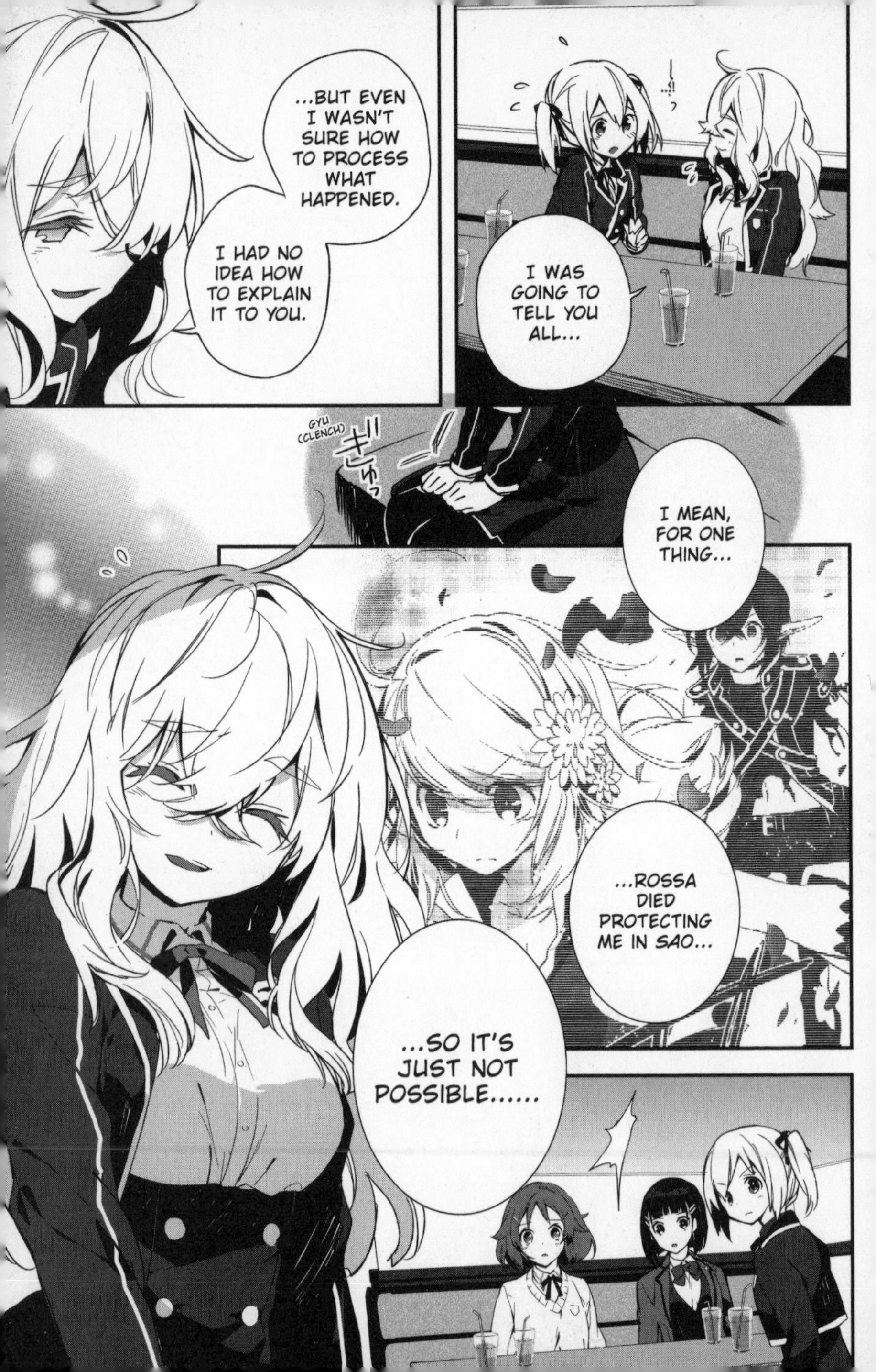
I WAS GOING TO TELL YOU ALL...
...BUT EVEN I WASN'T SURE HOW TO PROCESS WHAT HAPPENED.
I HAD NO IDEA HOW TO EXPLAIN IT TO YOU.
GYU (CLENCH)
I MEAN, FOR ONE THING...
...ROSSA DIED PROTECTING ME IN SAO...
...SO IT'S JUST NOT POSSIBLE......

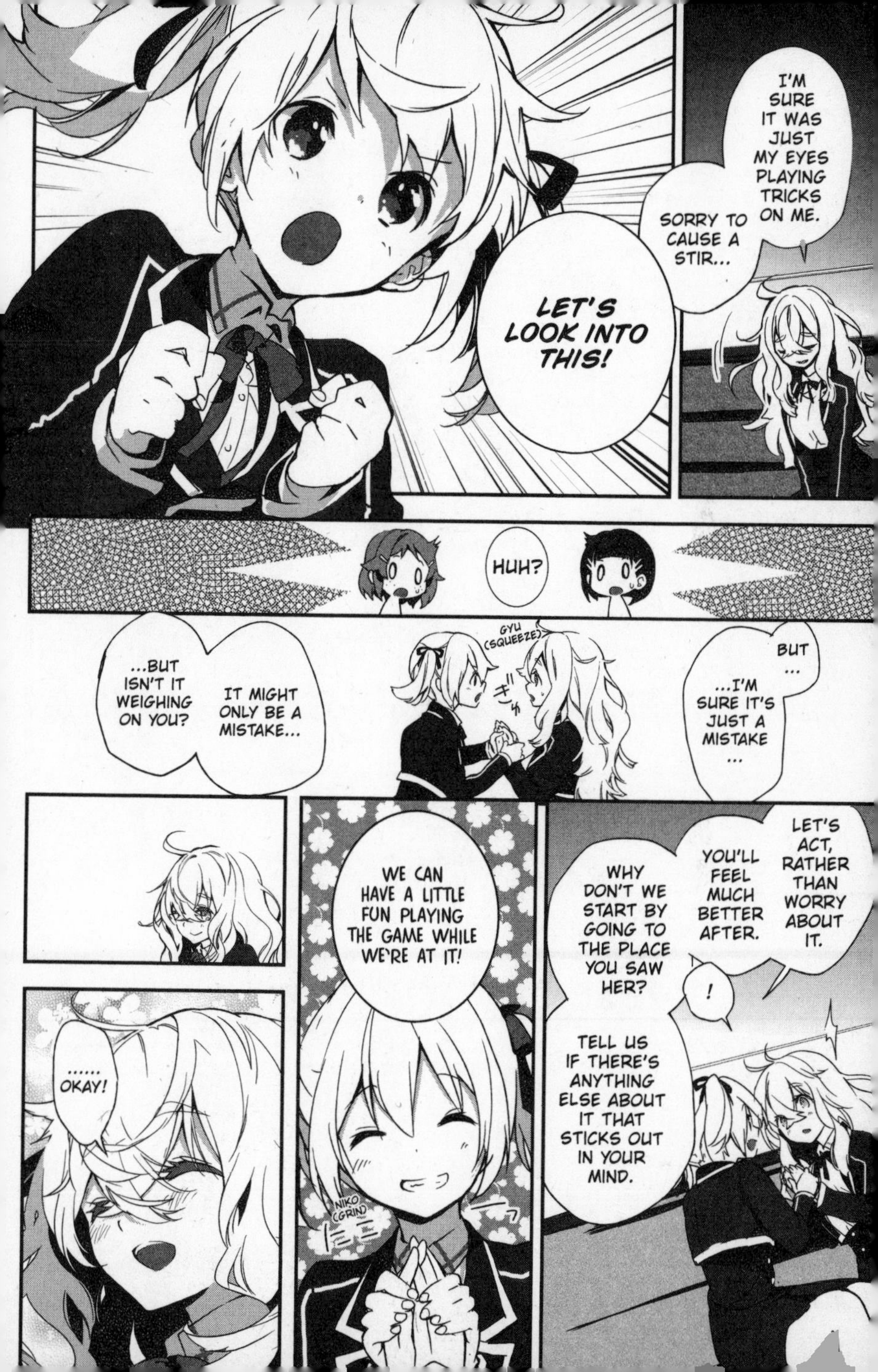
I'M SURE IT WAS JUST MY EYES PLAYING TRICKS ON ME.
SORRY TO CAUSE A STIR...
LET'S LOOK INTO THIS!
HUH?
BUT ...
...I'M SURE IT'S JUST A MISTAKE ...
GYU (SQUEEZE)
IT MIGHT ONLY BE A MISTAKE...
...BUT ISN'T IT WEIGHING ON YOU?
LET'S ACT, RATHER THAN WORRY ABOUT IT.
YOU'LL FEEL MUCH BETTER AFTER.
WHY DON'T WE START BY GOING TO THE PLACE YOU SAW HER?
!
TELL US IF THERE'S ANYTHING ELSE ABOUT IT THAT STICKS OUT IN YOUR MIND.
WE CAN HAVE A LITTLE FUN PLAYING THE GAME WHILE WE'RE AT IT!
NIKO (GRIN)
......OKAY!

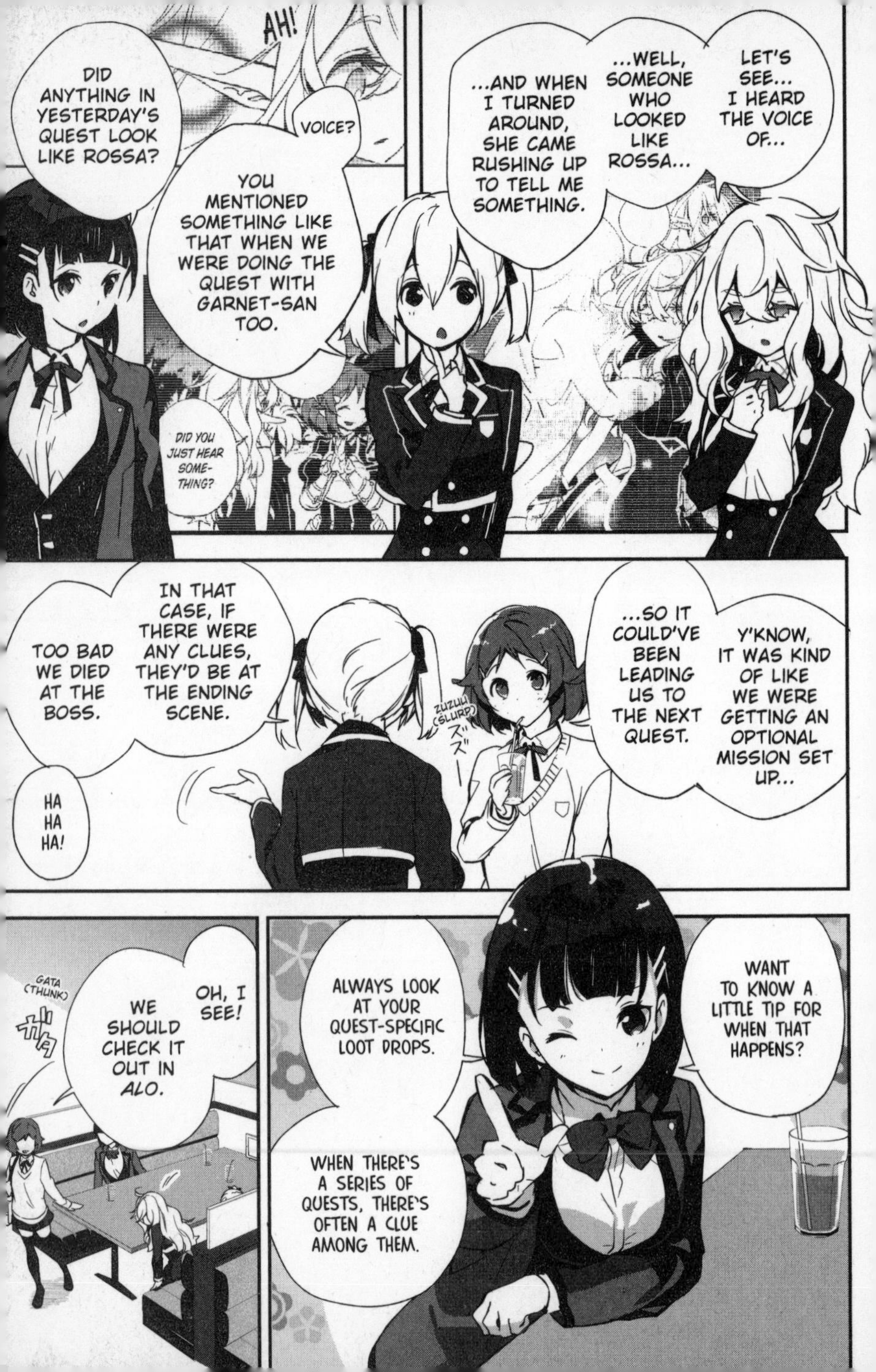
LET'S SEE... I HEARD THE VOICE OF...
...WELL, SOMEONE WHO LOOKED LIKE ROSSA...
...AND WHEN I TURNED AROUND, SHE CAME RUSHING UP TO TELL ME SOMETHING.
AH!
VOICE?
DID ANYTHING IN YESTERDAY'S QUEST LOOK LIKE ROSSA?
YOU MENTIONED SOMETHING LIKE THAT WHEN WE WERE DOING THE QUEST WITH GARNET-SAN TOO.
DID YOU JUST HEAR SOME-THING?
Y'KNOW, IT WAS KIND OF LIKE WE WERE GETTING AN OPTIONAL MISSION SET UP...
...SO IT COULD'VE BEEN LEADING US TO THE NEXT QUEST.
ZUZUU (SLURP)
IN THAT CASE, IF THERE WERE ANY CLUES, THEY'D BE AT THE ENDING SCENE.
TOO BAD WE DIED AT THE BOSS.
HA HA HA!
WANT TO KNOW A LITTLE TIP FOR WHEN THAT HAPPENS?
WHEN THERE'S A SERIES OF QUESTS, THERE'S OFTEN A CLUE AMONG THEM.
ALWAYS LOOK AT YOUR QUEST-SPECIFIC LOOT DROPS.
OH, I SEE!
WE SHOULD CHECK IT OUT IN ALO.
GATA (THUNK)

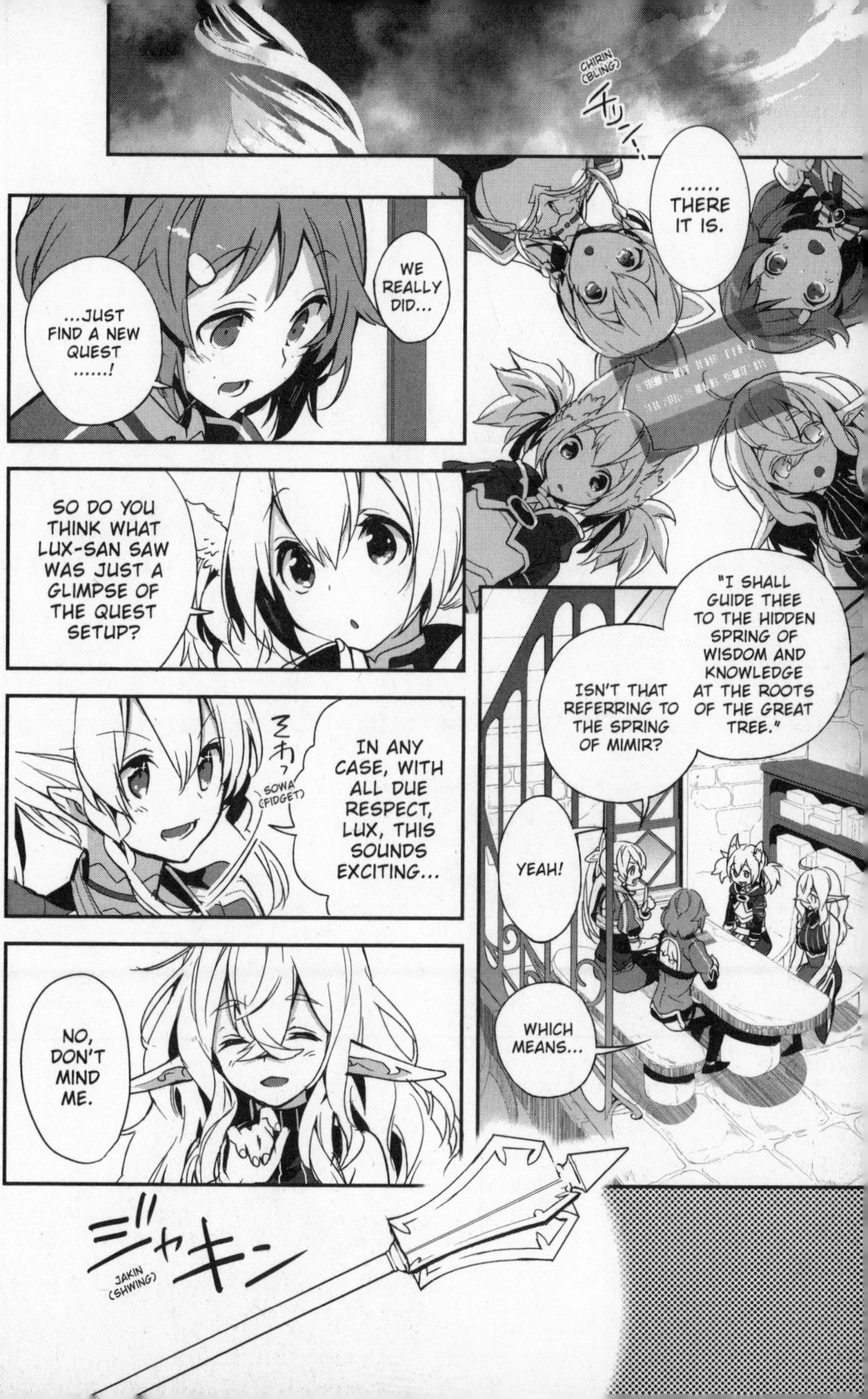

CHIRIN (BLING)
......THERE IT IS.
WE REALLY DID...
...JUST FIND A NEW QUEST......!
"I SHALL GUIDE THEE TO THE HIDDEN SPRING OF WISDOM AND KNOWLEDGE AT THE ROOTS OF THE GREAT TREE."
ISN'T THAT REFERRING TO THE SPRING OF MIMIR?
YEAH!
WHICH MEANS...
SO DO YOU THINK WHAT LUX-SAN SAW WAS JUST A GLIMPSE OF THE QUEST SETUP?
SOWA (FIDGET)
IN ANY CASE, WITH ALL DUE RESPECT, LUX, THIS SOUNDS EXCITING...
NO, DON'T MIND ME.
JAKIN (SHWING)

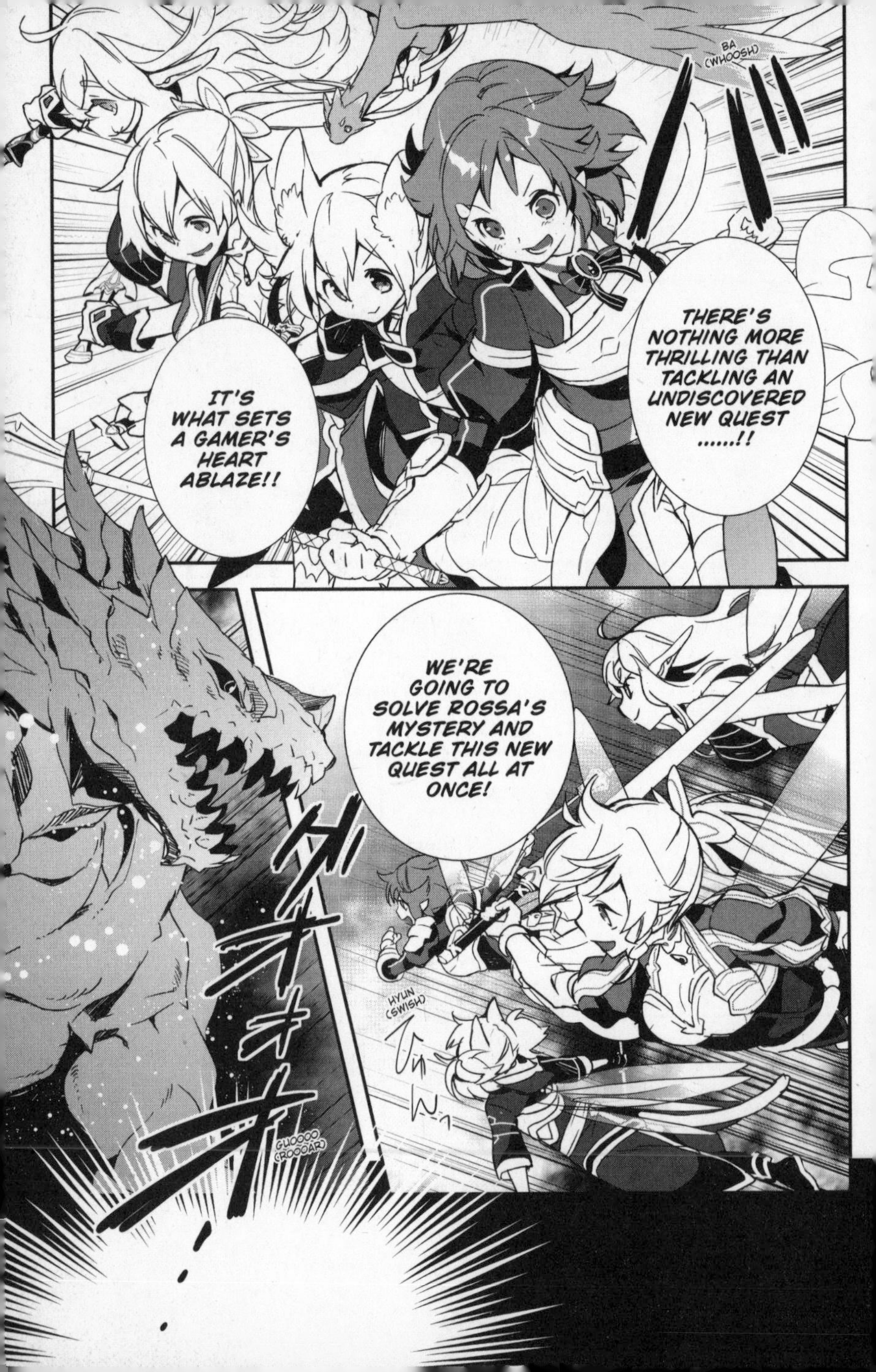

BA (WHOOSH)
THERE'S NOTHING MORE THRILLING THAN TACKLING AN UNDISCOVERED NEW QUEST ......!!
IT'S WHAT SETS A GAMER'S HEART ABLAZE!!
WE'RE GOING TO SOLVE ROSSA'S MYSTERY AND TACKLE THIS NEW QUEST ALL AT ONCE!
HYUN (SWISH)
GUOOOO (ROOOAR)

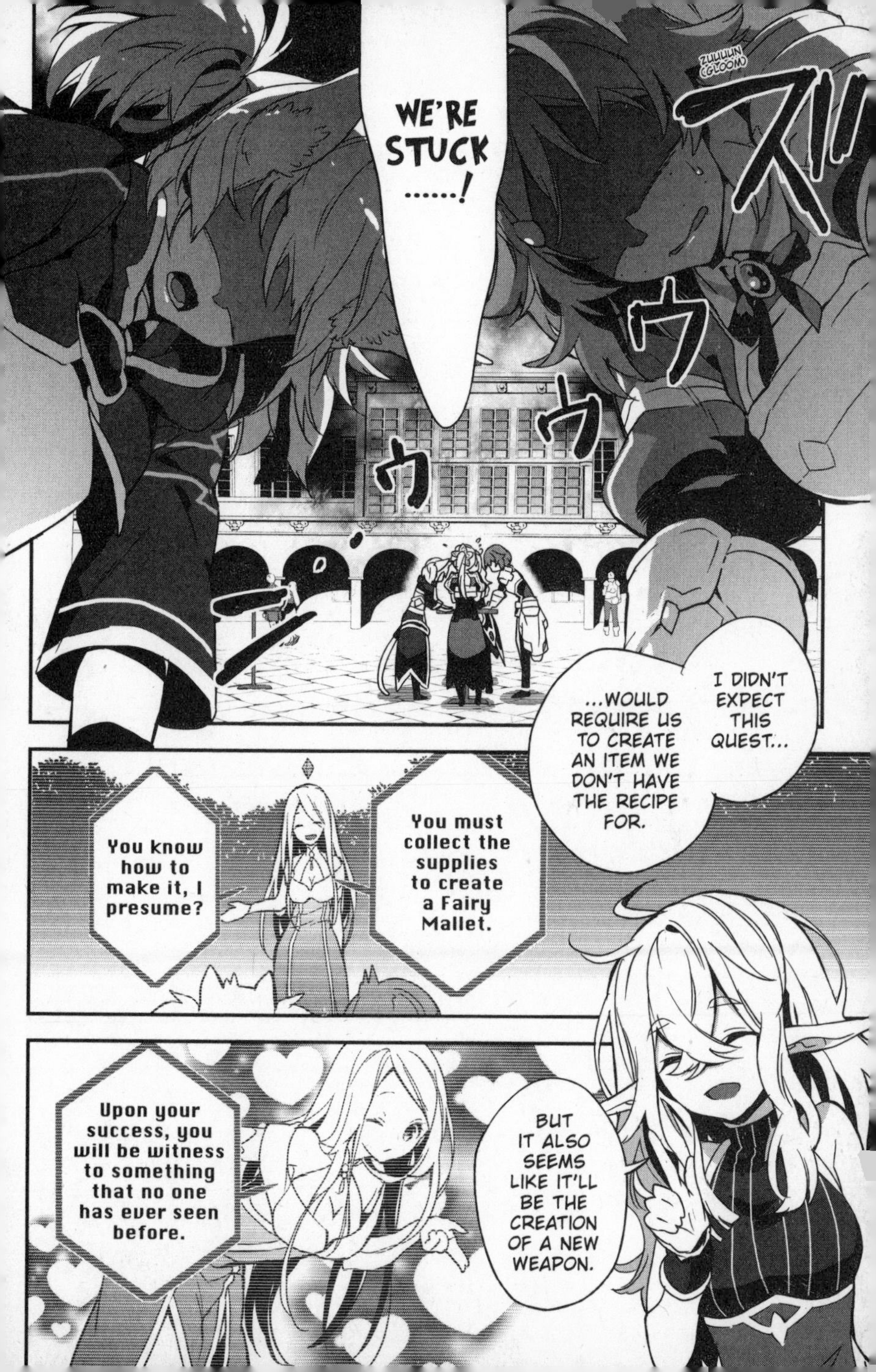
ZUUUUN (GLOOM)
WE'RE STUCK ......!
I DIDN'T EXPECT THIS QUEST...
...WOULD REQUIRE US TO CREATE AN ITEM WE DON'T HAVE THE RECIPE FOR.
You must collect the supplies to create a Fairy Mallet.
You know how to make it, I presume?
BUT IT ALSO SEEMS LIKE IT'LL BE THE CREATION OF A NEW WEAPON.
Upon your success, you will be witness to something that no one has ever seen before.

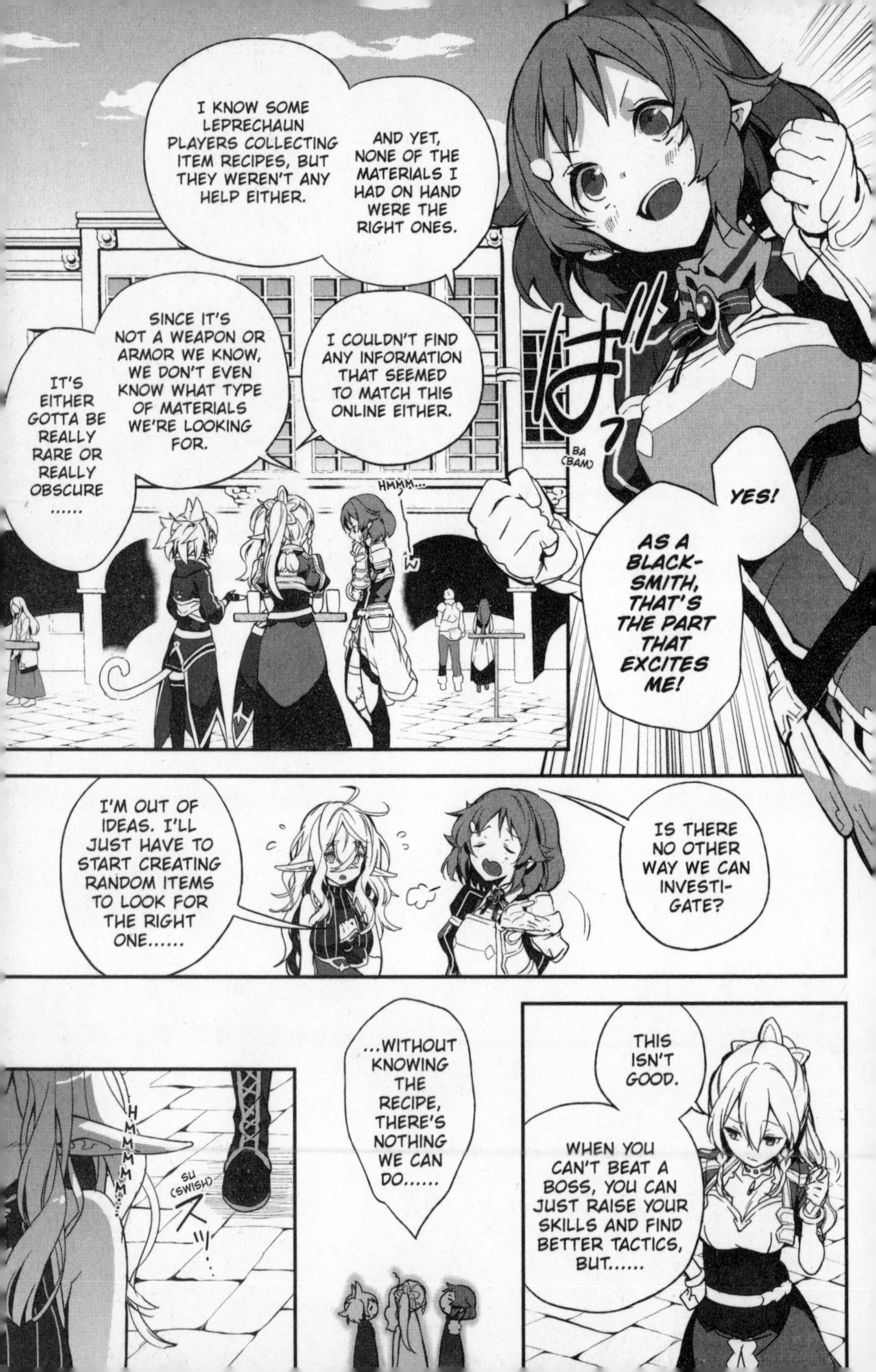

AND YET, NONE OF THE MATERIALS I HAD ON HAND WERE THE RIGHT ONES.
I KNOW SOME LEPRECHAUN PLAYERS COLLECTING ITEM RECIPES, BUT THEY WEREN'T ANY HELP EITHER.
I COULDN'T FIND ANY INFORMATION THAT SEEMED TO MATCH THIS ONLINE EITHER.
SINCE IT'S NOT A WEAPON OR ARMOR WE KNOW, WE DON'T EVEN KNOW WHAT TYPE OF MATERIALS WE'RE LOOKING FOR.
IT'S EITHER GOTTA BE REALLY RARE OR REALLY OBSCURE ......
HMMM...
BA (BAM)
YES!
AS A BLACK-SMITH, THAT'S THE PART THAT EXCITES ME!
IS THERE NO OTHER WAY WE CAN INVESTI-GATE?
I'M OUT OF IDEAS. I'LL JUST HAVE TO START CREATING RANDOM ITEMS TO LOOK FOR THE RIGHT ONE......
THIS ISN'T GOOD.
WHEN YOU CAN'T BEAT A BOSS, YOU CAN JUST RAISE YOUR SKILLS AND FIND BETTER TACTICS, BUT......
...WITHOUT KNOWING THE RECIPE, THERE'S NOTHING WE CAN DO......
HMMMM...
SU (SWISH)

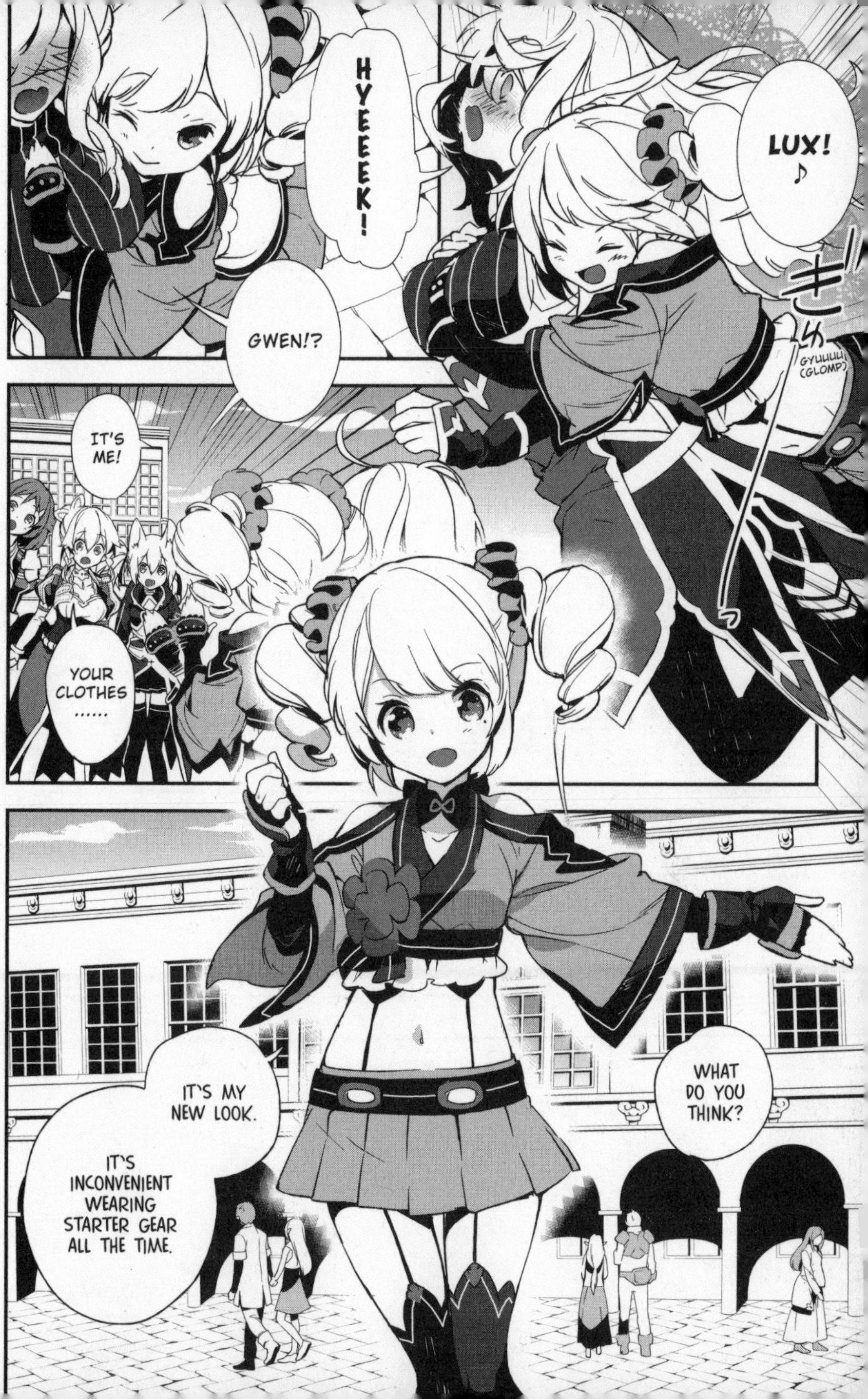
LUX! ♪
ぎゅ
GYUUUUU (GLOMP)
HYEEEK!
GWEN!?
IT'S ME!
YOUR CLOTHES ......
WHAT DO YOU THINK?
IT'S MY NEW LOOK.
IT'S INCONVENIENT WEARING STARTER GEAR ALL THE TIME.

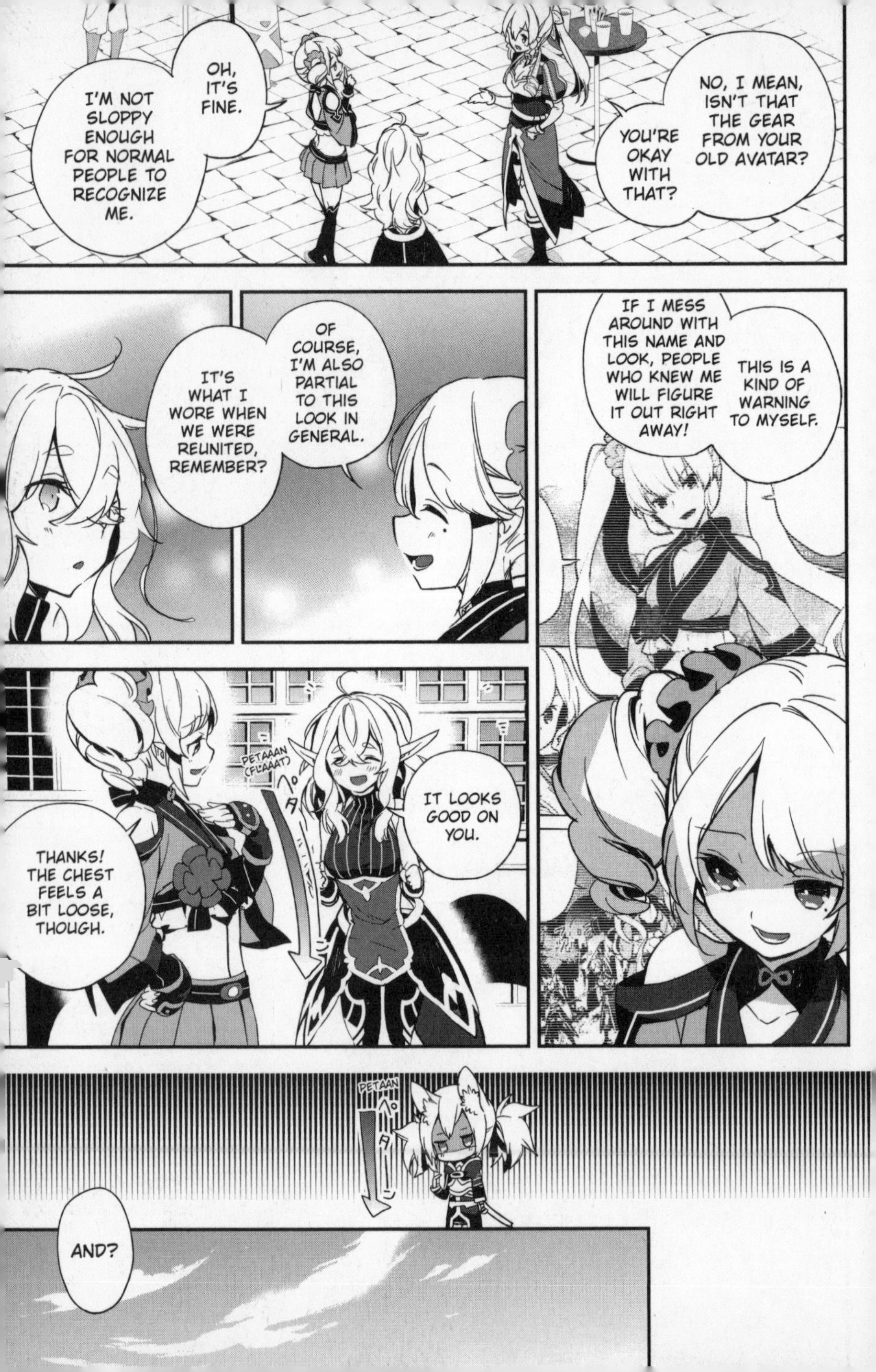
NO, I MEAN, ISN'T THAT THE GEAR FROM YOUR OLD AVATAR?
YOU'RE OKAY WITH THAT?
OH, IT'S FINE.
I'M NOT SLOPPY ENOUGH FOR NORMAL PEOPLE TO RECOGNIZE ME.
IF I MESS AROUND WITH THIS NAME AND LOOK, PEOPLE WHO KNEW ME WILL FIGURE IT OUT RIGHT AWAY!
THIS IS A KIND OF WARNING TO MYSELF.
OF COURSE, I'M ALSO PARTIAL TO THIS LOOK IN GENERAL.
IT'S WHAT I WORE WHEN WE WERE REUNITED, REMEMBER?
IT LOOKS GOOD ON YOU.
PETAAAN (FLAAAT)
THANKS! THE CHEST FEELS A BIT LOOSE, THOUGH.
PETAAN
AND?

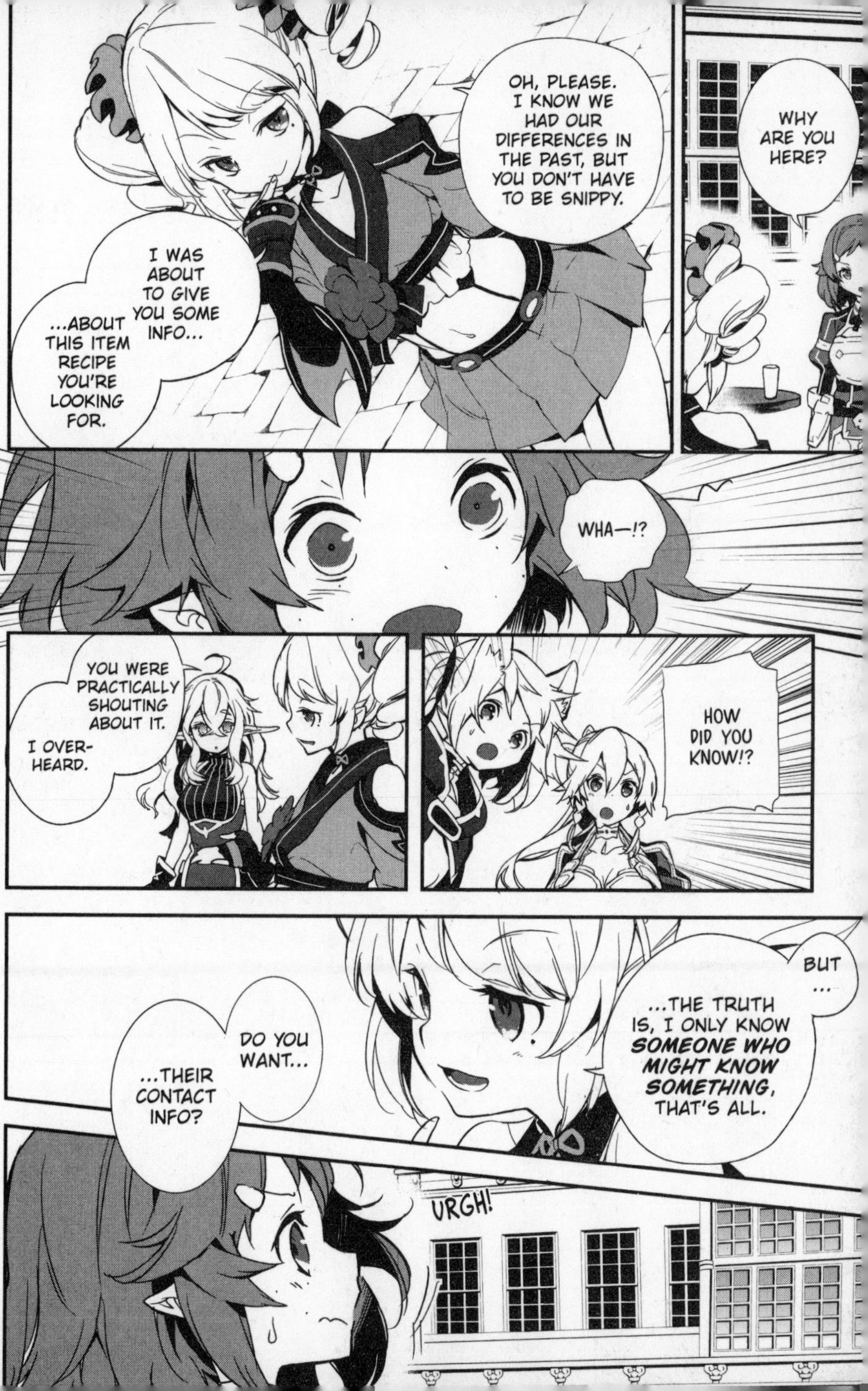
WHY ARE YOU HERE?
OH, PLEASE. I KNOW WE HAD OUR DIFFERENCES IN THE PAST, BUT YOU DON'T HAVE TO BE SNIPPY.
I WAS ABOUT TO GIVE YOU SOME INFO...
...ABOUT THIS ITEM RECIPE YOU'RE LOOKING FOR.
WHA—!?
HOW DID YOU KNOW!?
YOU WERE PRACTICALLY SHOUTING ABOUT IT.
I OVER-HEARD.
BUT ...
...THE TRUTH IS, I ONLY KNOW ***SOMEONE WHO MIGHT KNOW SOMETHING***, THAT'S ALL.
DO YOU WANT...
...THEIR CONTACT INFO?
URGH!

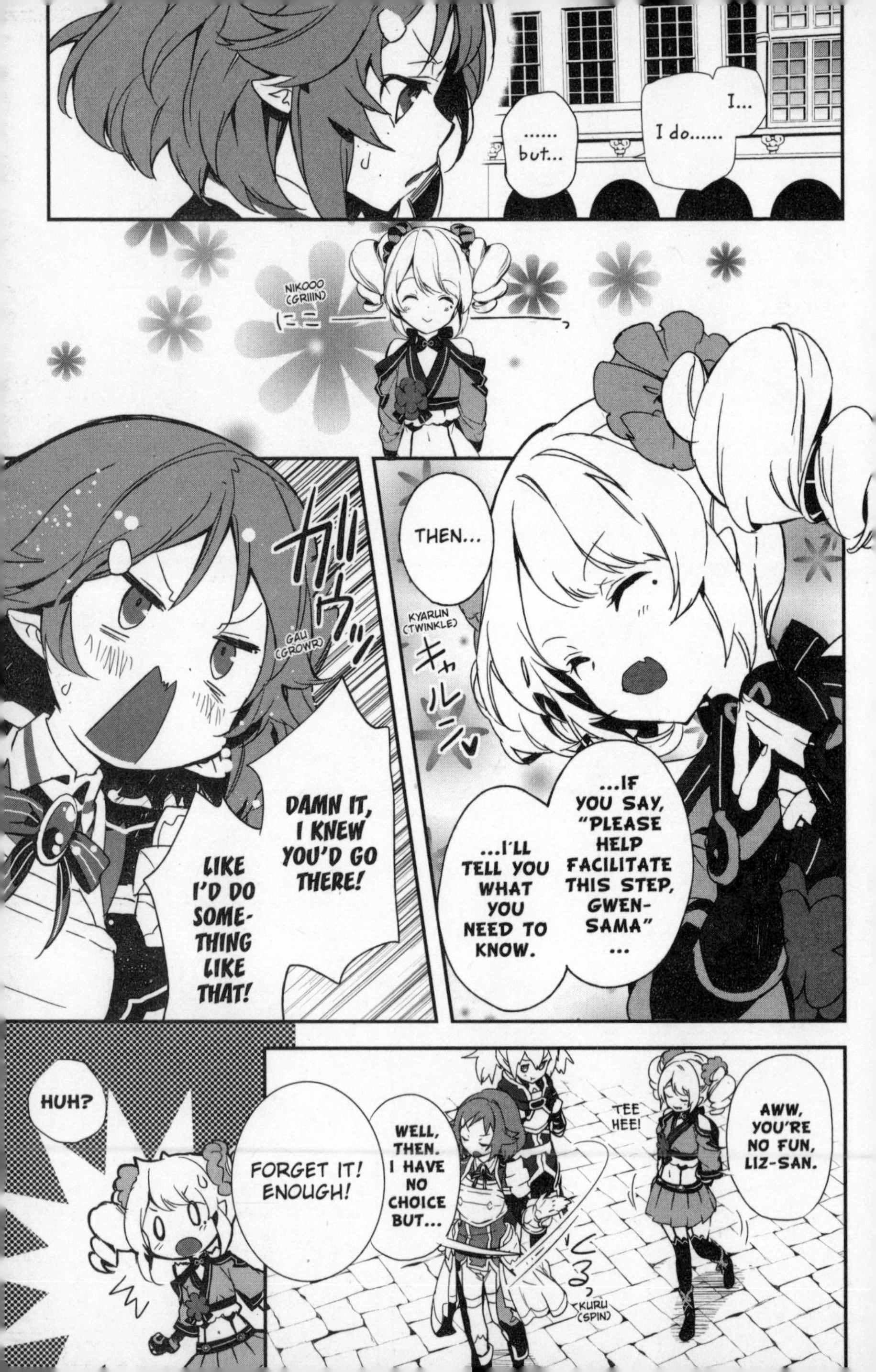
I...
I do......
......
but...
NIKOOO (GRIIIN)
にこ——
THEN...
KYARUN (TWINKLE)
キャルーン
...IF YOU SAY, "PLEASE HELP FACILITATE THIS STEP, GWEN-SAMA"...
...I'LL TELL YOU WHAT YOU NEED TO KNOW.
GAU (GROWR)
ガゥヴッ
DAMN IT, I KNEW YOU'D GO THERE!
LIKE I'D DO SOME-THING LIKE THAT!
AWW, YOU'RE NO FUN, LIZ-SAN.
TEE HEE!
KURU (SPIN)
くるっ
WELL, THEN. I HAVE NO CHOICE BUT...
FORGET IT! ENOUGH!
HUH?

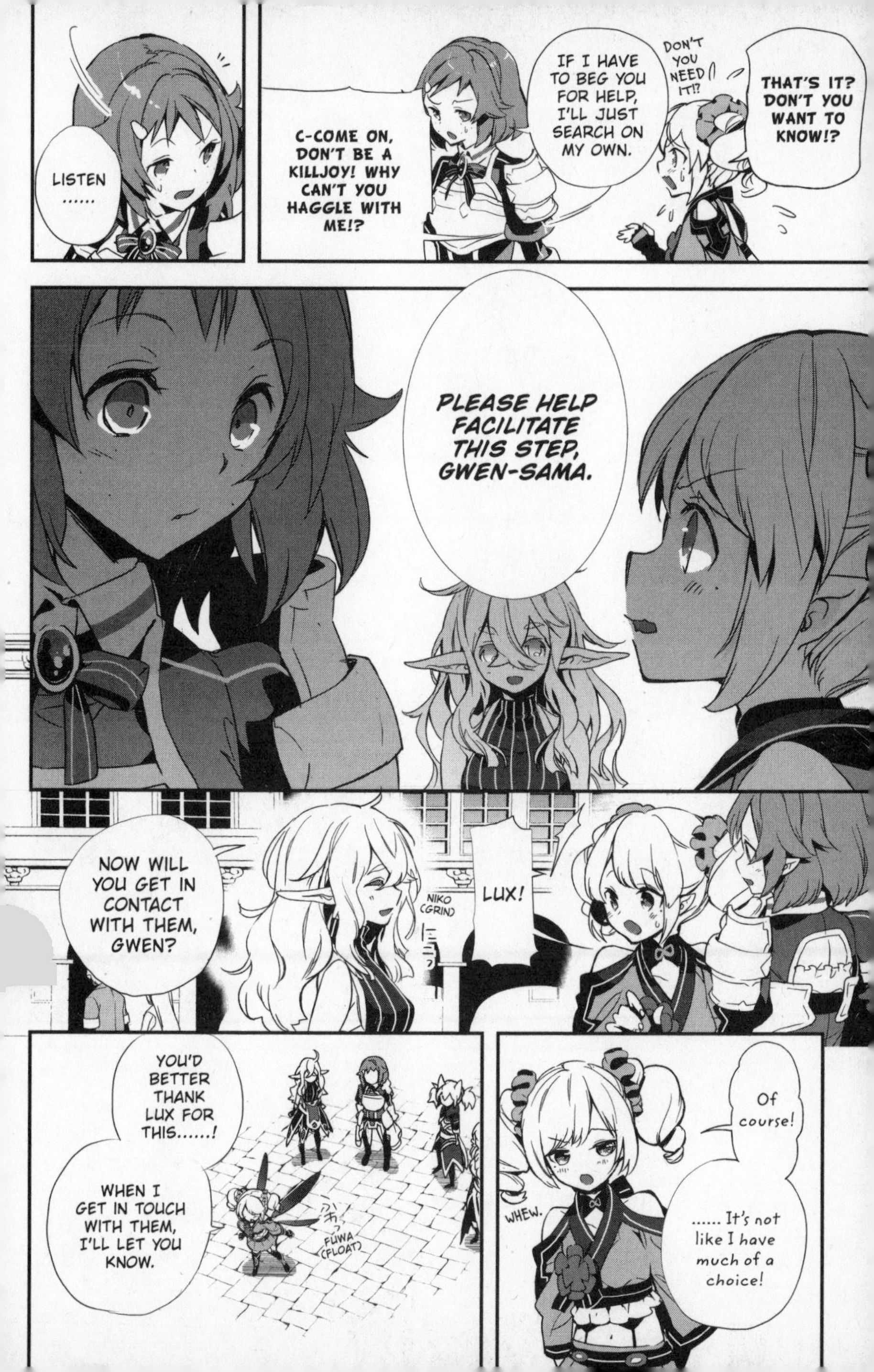
THAT'S IT? DON'T YOU WANT TO KNOW!?
DON'T YOU NEED IT!?
IF I HAVE TO BEG YOU FOR HELP, I'LL JUST SEARCH ON MY OWN.
C-COME ON, DON'T BE A KILLJOY! WHY CAN'T YOU HAGGLE WITH ME!?
LISTEN ......
PLEASE HELP FACILITATE THIS STEP, GWEN-SAMA.
LUX!
NIKO (GRIN)
NOW WILL YOU GET IN CONTACT WITH THEM, GWEN?
Of course!
WHEW.
...... It's not like I have much of a choice!
YOU'D BETTER THANK LUX FOR THIS......!
WHEN I GET IN TOUCH WITH THEM, I'LL LET YOU KNOW.
FUWA (FLOAT)

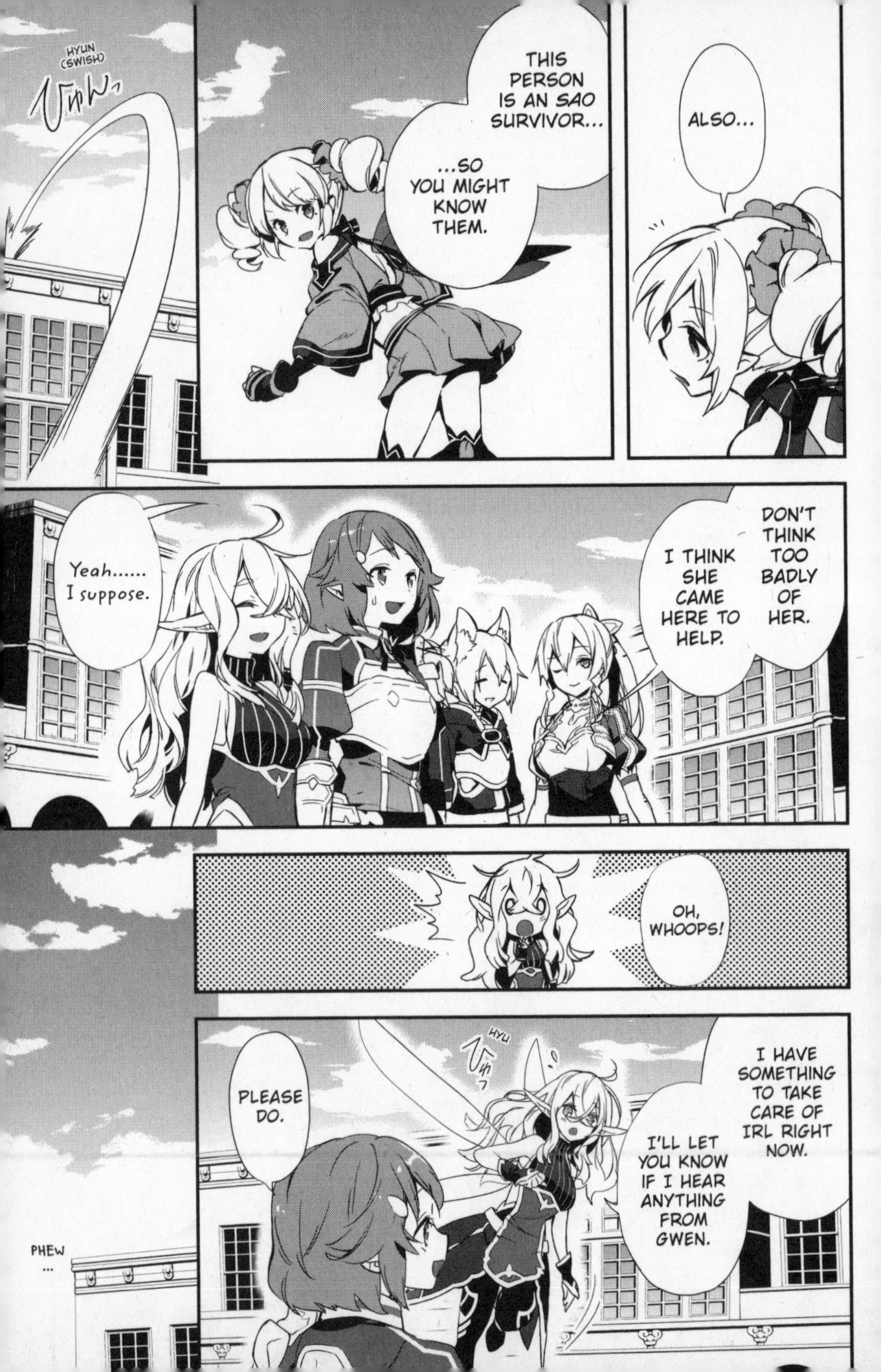
HYUN (SWISH)
ひゅんっ
THIS PERSON IS AN SAO SURVIVOR...
...SO YOU MIGHT KNOW THEM.
ALSO...
DON'T THINK TOO BADLY OF HER.
I THINK SHE CAME HERE TO HELP.
Yeah...... I suppose.
OH, WHOOPS!
I HAVE SOMETHING TO TAKE CARE OF IRL RIGHT NOW.
I'LL LET YOU KNOW IF I HEAR ANYTHING FROM GWEN.
HYU
ひゅっ
PLEASE DO.
PHEW ...

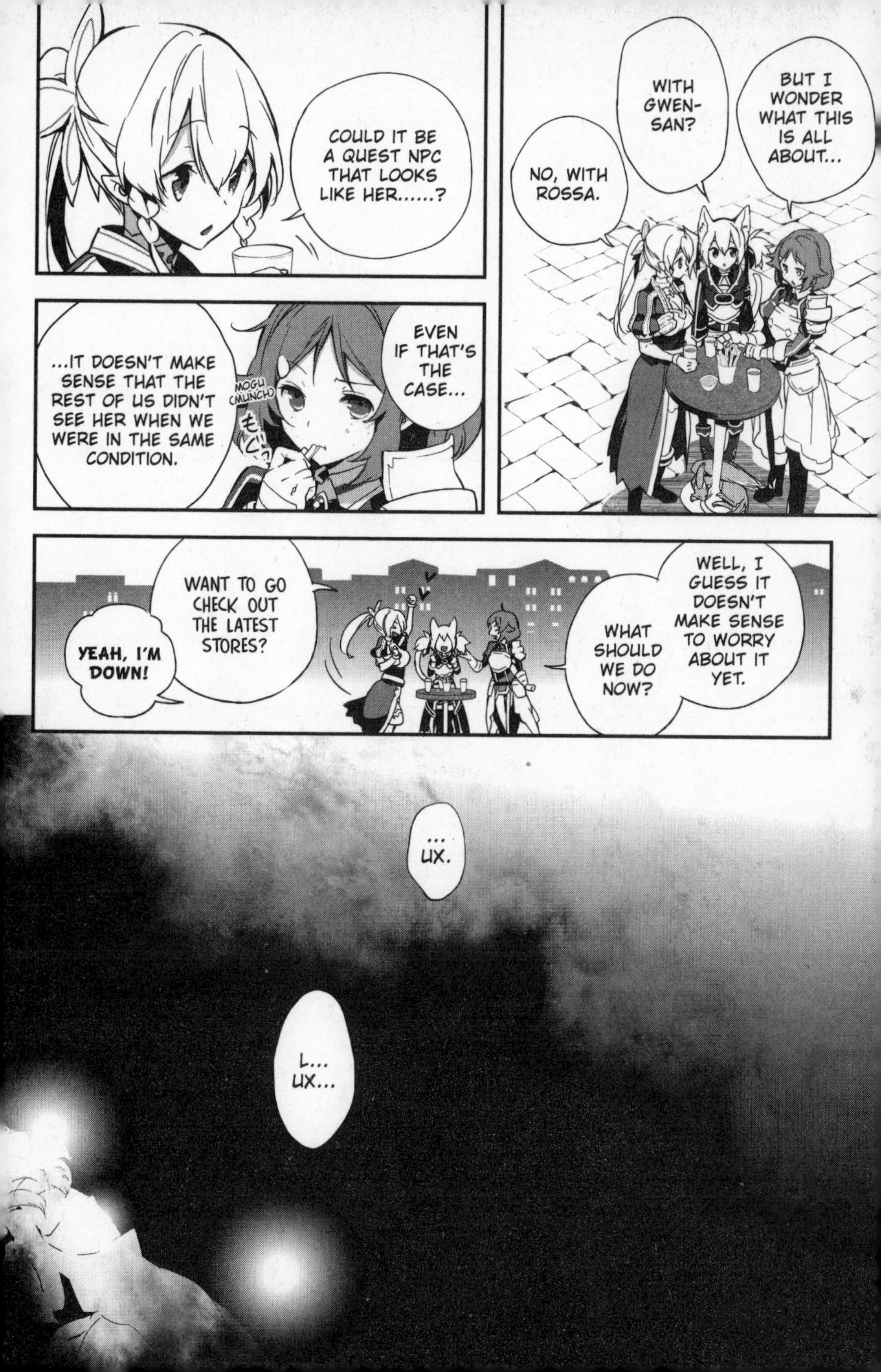
BUT I WONDER WHAT THIS IS ALL ABOUT...
WITH GWEN-SAN?
NO, WITH ROSSA.
COULD IT BE A QUEST NPC THAT LOOKS LIKE HER......?
EVEN IF THAT'S THE CASE...
...IT DOESN'T MAKE SENSE THAT THE REST OF US DIDN'T SEE HER WHEN WE WERE IN THE SAME CONDITION.
MOGU (MUNCH)
WELL, I GUESS IT DOESN'T MAKE SENSE TO WORRY ABOUT IT YET.
WHAT SHOULD WE DO NOW?
WANT TO GO CHECK OUT THE LATEST STORES?
YEAH, I'M DOWN!
... UX.
L... UX...

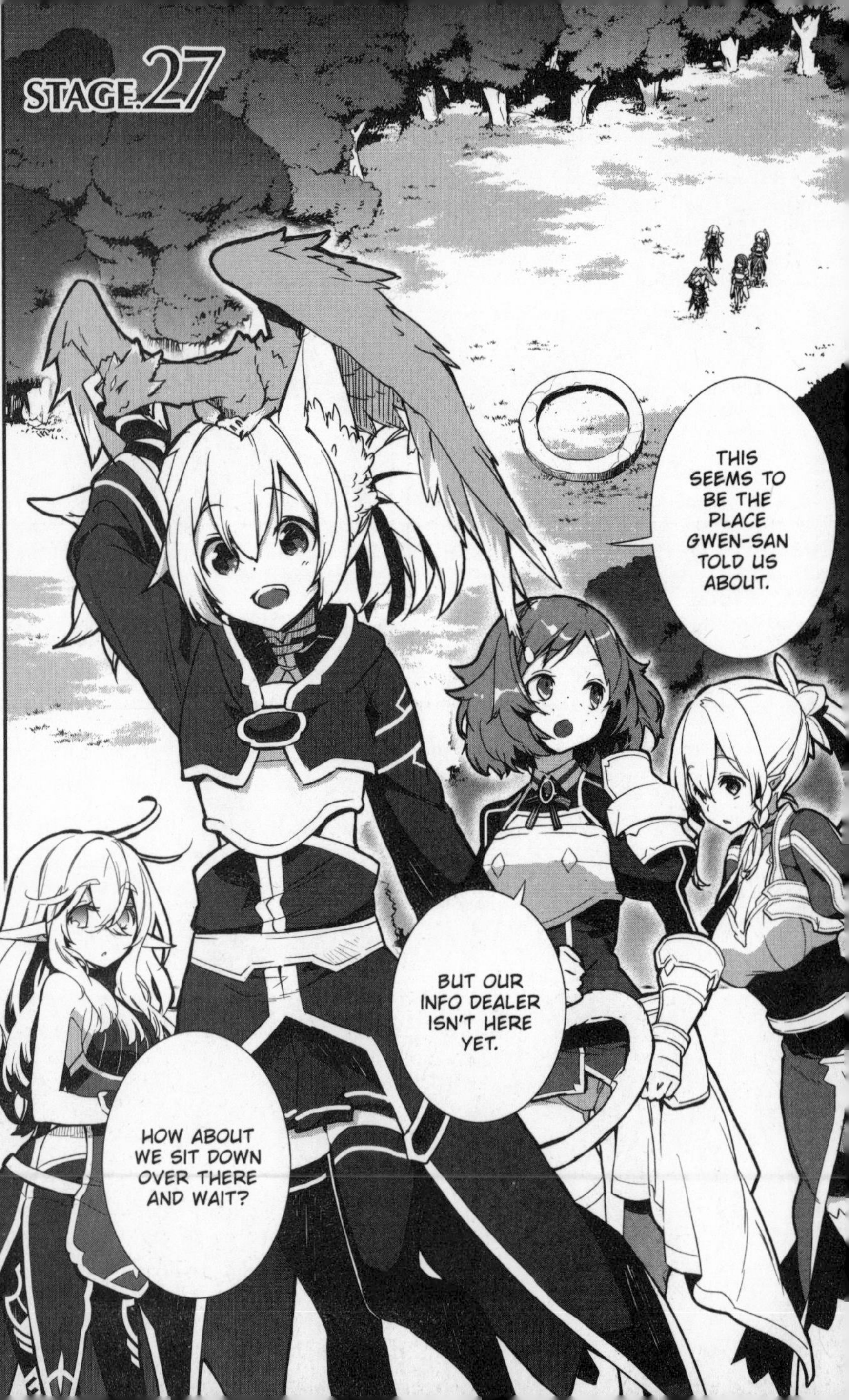
STAGE.27
THIS SEEMS TO BE THE PLACE GWEN-SAN TOLD US ABOUT.
BUT OUR INFO DEALER ISN'T HERE YET.
HOW ABOUT WE SIT DOWN OVER THERE AND WAIT?

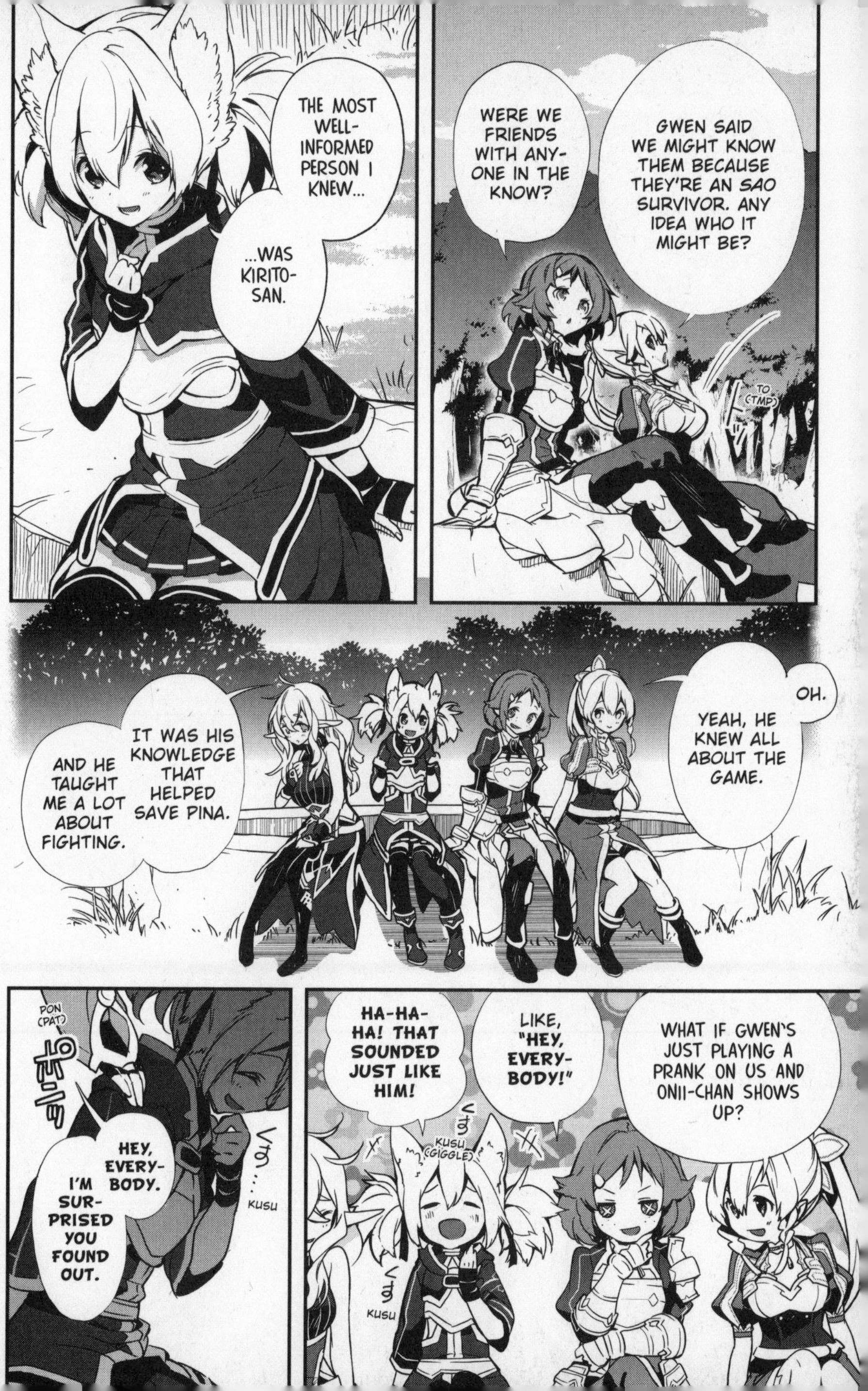
GWEN SAID WE MIGHT KNOW THEM BECAUSE THEY'RE AN SAO SURVIVOR. ANY IDEA WHO IT MIGHT BE?
WERE WE FRIENDS WITH ANY-ONE IN THE KNOW?
TO (TMP)
THE MOST WELL-INFORMED PERSON I KNEW...
...WAS KIRITO-SAN.
OH.
YEAH, HE KNEW ALL ABOUT THE GAME.
IT WAS HIS KNOWLEDGE THAT HELPED SAVE PINA.
AND HE TAUGHT ME A LOT ABOUT FIGHTING.
WHAT IF GWEN'S JUST PLAYING A PRANK ON US AND ONII-CHAN SHOWS UP?
LIKE, "HEY, EVERY-BODY!"
HA-HA-HA! THAT SOUNDED JUST LIKE HIM!
KUSU (GIGGLE)
KUSU
PON (PAT)
HEY, EVERY-BODY. I'M SUR-PRISED YOU FOUND OUT.
KUSU

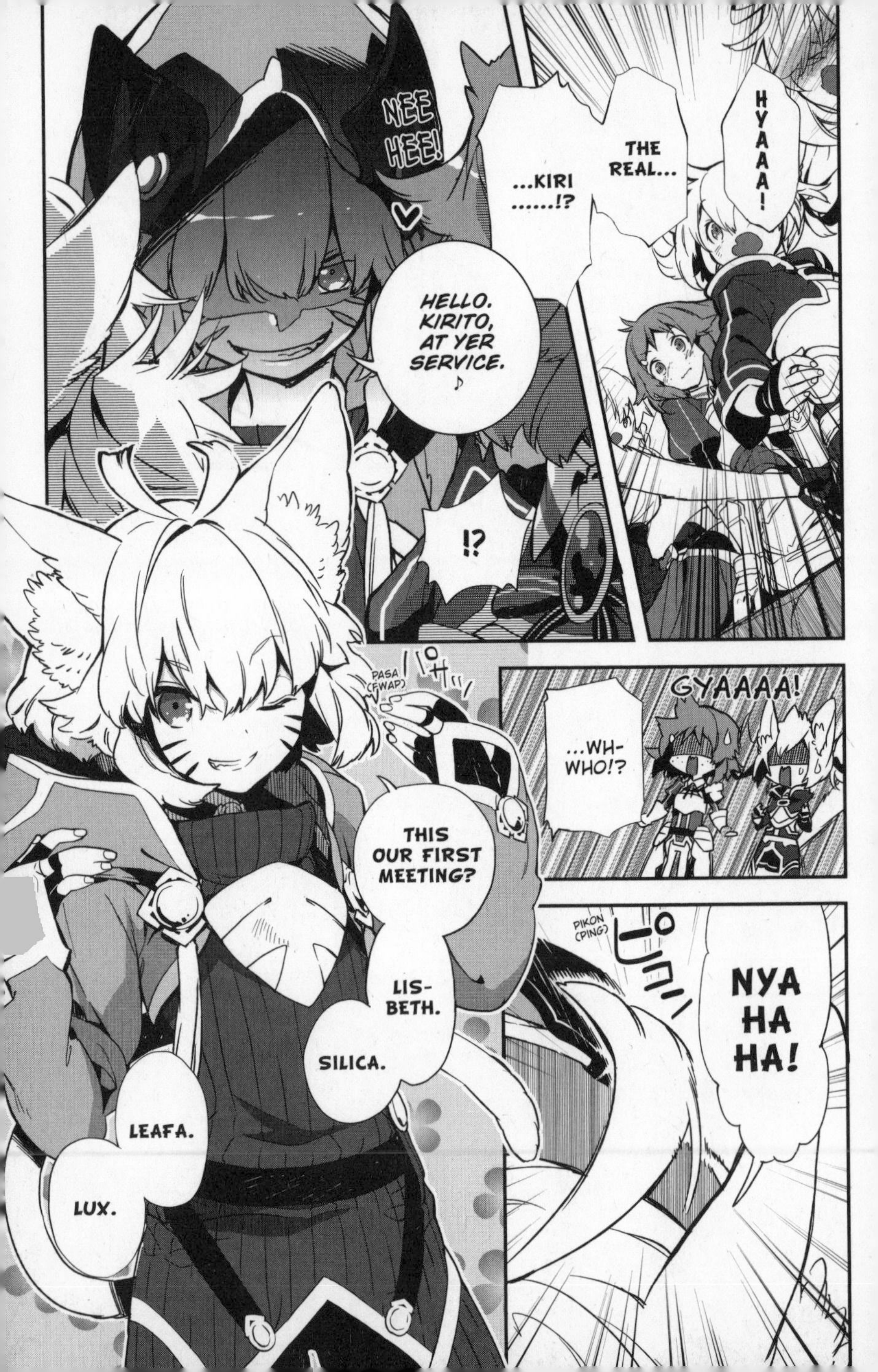
HYAAAA!
THE REAL...
...KIRI ......!?
NEE HEE!
HELLO. KIRITO, AT YER SERVICE. ♪
!?
GYAAAA!
...WH-WHO!?
PIKON (PING)
NYA HA HA!
PASA (FWAP)
THIS OUR FIRST MEETING?
LIS-BETH.
SILICA.
LEAFA.
LUX.

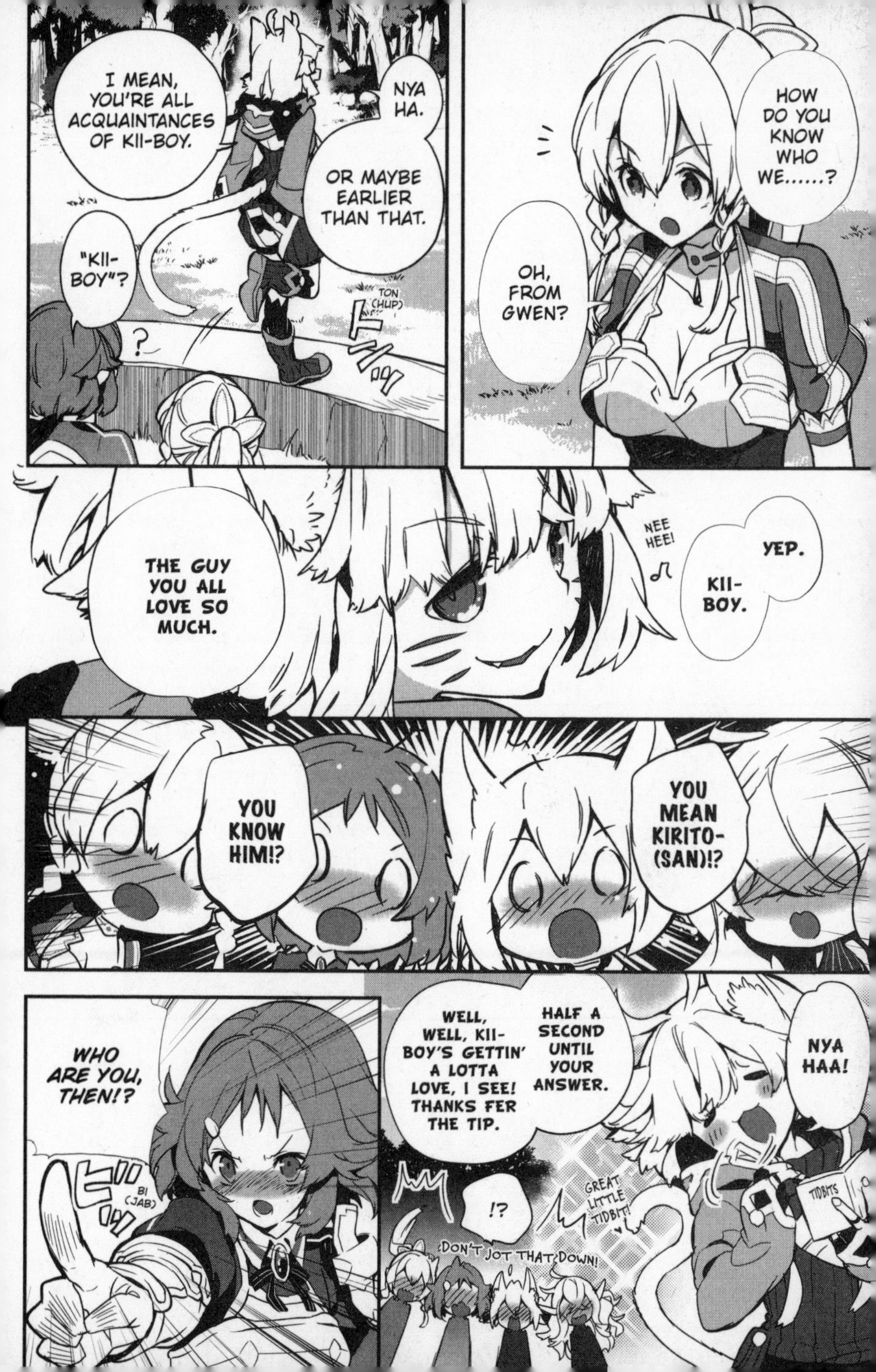
HOW DO YOU KNOW WHO WE......?
OH, FROM GWEN?
NYA HA.
OR MAYBE EARLIER THAN THAT.
I MEAN, YOU'RE ALL ACQUAINTANCES OF KII-BOY.
TON (CHUP)
"KII-BOY"?
?
NEE HEE! ♪
YEP.
KII-BOY.
THE GUY YOU ALL LOVE SO MUCH.
YOU MEAN KIRITO-(SAN)!?
YOU KNOW HIM!?
NYA HAA!
HALF A SECOND UNTIL YOUR ANSWER.
WELL, WELL, KII-BOY'S GETTIN' A LOTTA LOVE, I SEE! THANKS FER THE TIP.
TIDBITS
GREAT LITTLE TIDBIT!
!?
DON'T JOT THAT DOWN!
WHO ARE YOU, THEN!?
BI (JAB)

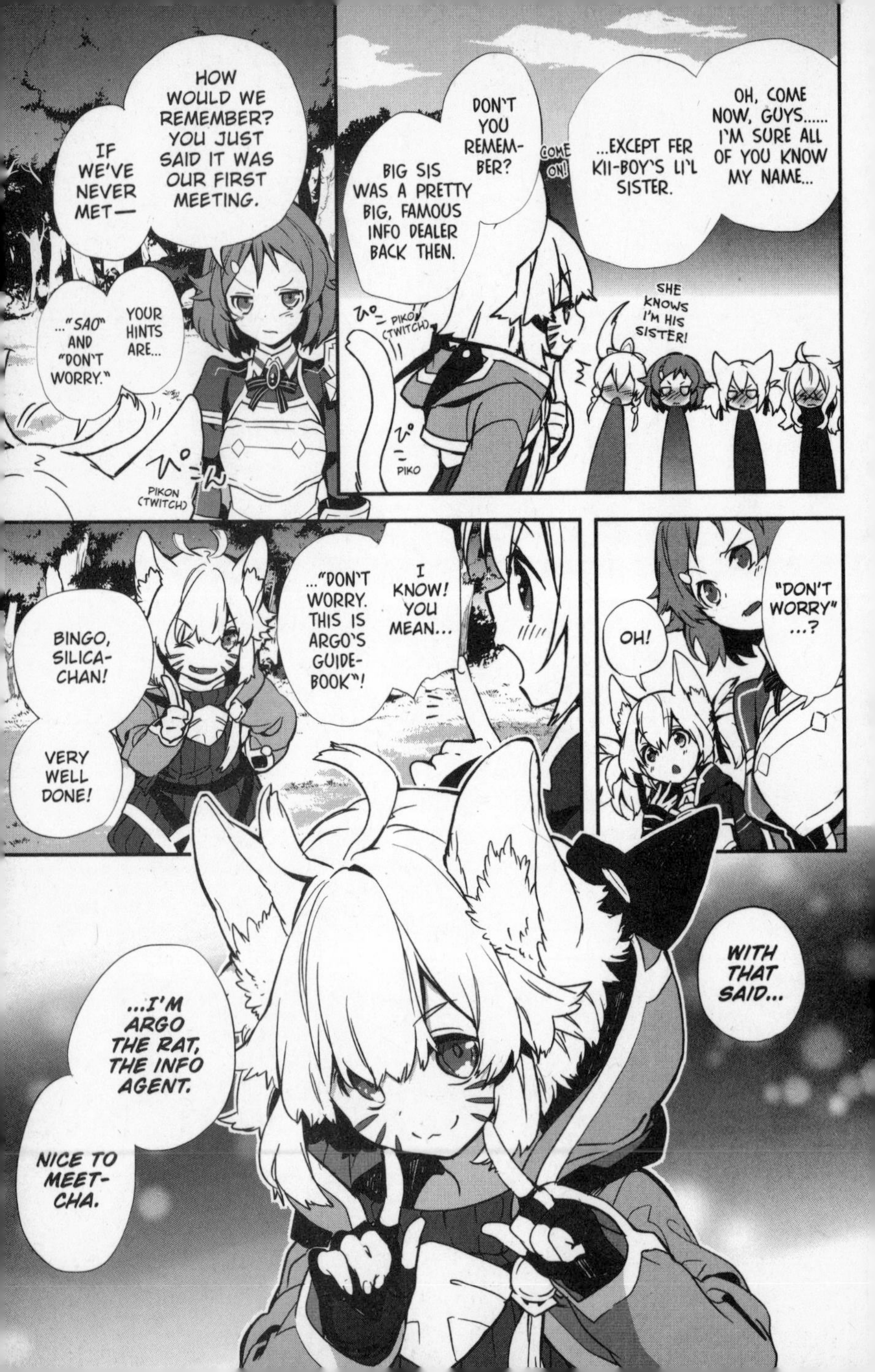
OH, COME NOW, GUYS...... I'M SURE ALL OF YOU KNOW MY NAME...
...EXCEPT FER KII-BOY'S LI'L SISTER.
COME ON!
SHE KNOWS I'M HIS SISTER!
DON'T YOU REMEMBER?
BIG SIS WAS A PRETTY BIG, FAMOUS INFO DEALER BACK THEN.
PIKO (TWITCH)
PIKO
HOW WOULD WE REMEMBER? YOU JUST SAID IT WAS OUR FIRST MEETING.
IF WE'VE NEVER MET—
YOUR HINTS ARE...
..."SAO" AND "DON'T WORRY."
PIKON (TWITCH)
"DON'T WORRY" ...?
OH!
I KNOW! YOU MEAN...
..."DON'T WORRY. THIS IS ARGO'S GUIDEBOOK"!
BINGO, SILICA-CHAN!
VERY WELL DONE!
WITH THAT SAID...
...I'M ARGO THE RAT, THE INFO AGENT.
NICE TO MEET-CHA.

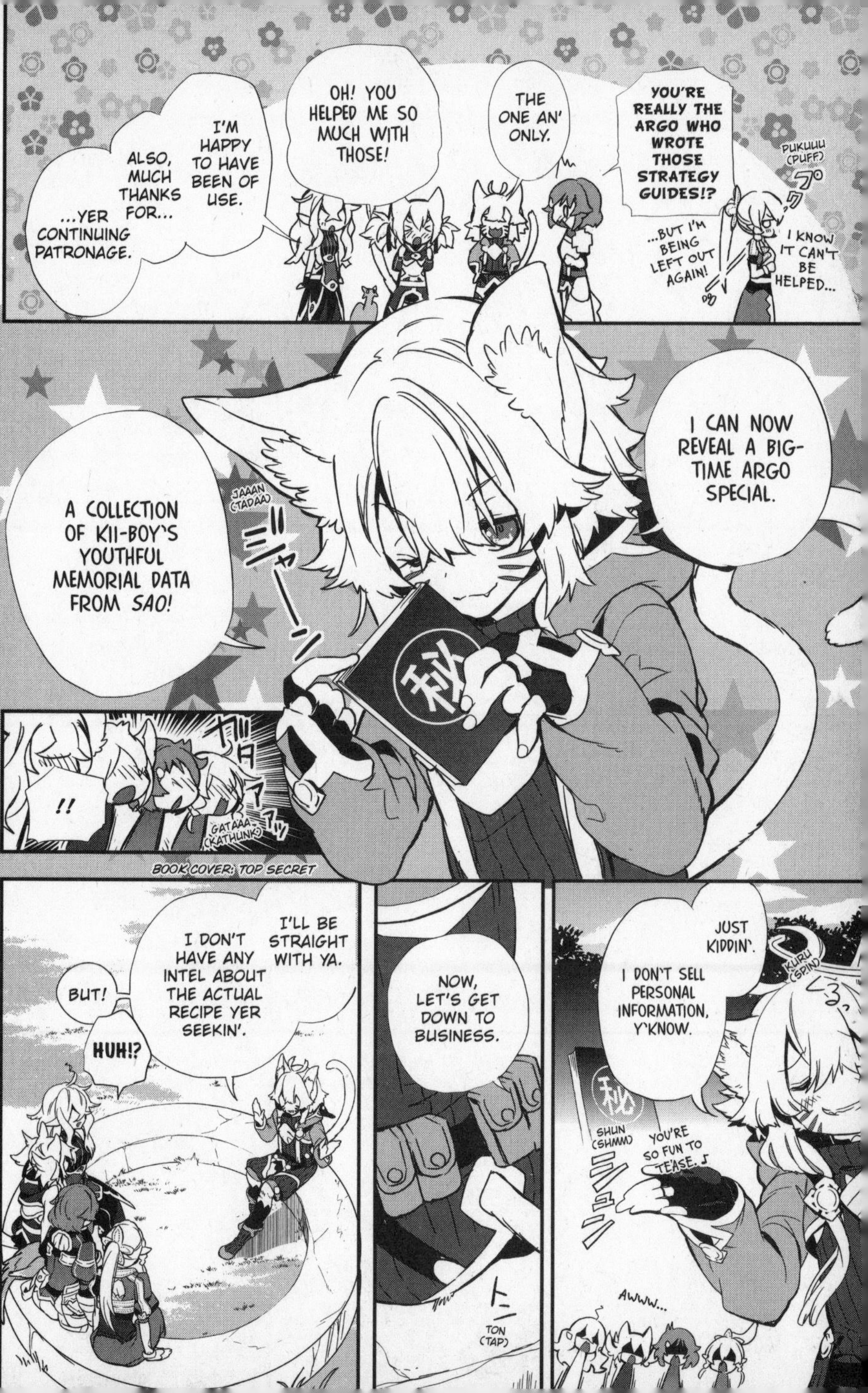
YOU'RE REALLY THE ARGO WHO WROTE THOSE STRATEGY GUIDES!?
PUKUUU (PUFF)
I KNOW IT CAN'T BE HELPED...
...BUT I'M BEING LEFT OUT AGAIN!
THE ONE AN' ONLY.
OH! YOU HELPED ME SO MUCH WITH THOSE!
I'M HAPPY TO HAVE BEEN OF USE.
ALSO, MUCH THANKS FOR...
...YER CONTINUING PATRONAGE.
I CAN NOW REVEAL A BIG-TIME ARGO SPECIAL.
JAAAN (TADAA)
A COLLECTION OF KII-BOY'S YOUTHFUL MEMORIAL DATA FROM SAO!
GATAAA (KATHUNK)
!!
BOOK COVER: TOP SECRET
JUST KIDDIN'.
KURU (SPIN)
I DON'T SELL PERSONAL INFORMATION, Y'KNOW.
SHUN (SHMM)
YOU'RE SO FUN TO TEASE. ♪
AWWW...
NOW, LET'S GET DOWN TO BUSINESS.
TON (TAP)
I'LL BE STRAIGHT WITH YA.
I DON'T HAVE ANY INTEL ABOUT THE ACTUAL RECIPE YER SEEKIN'.
BUT!
HUH!?

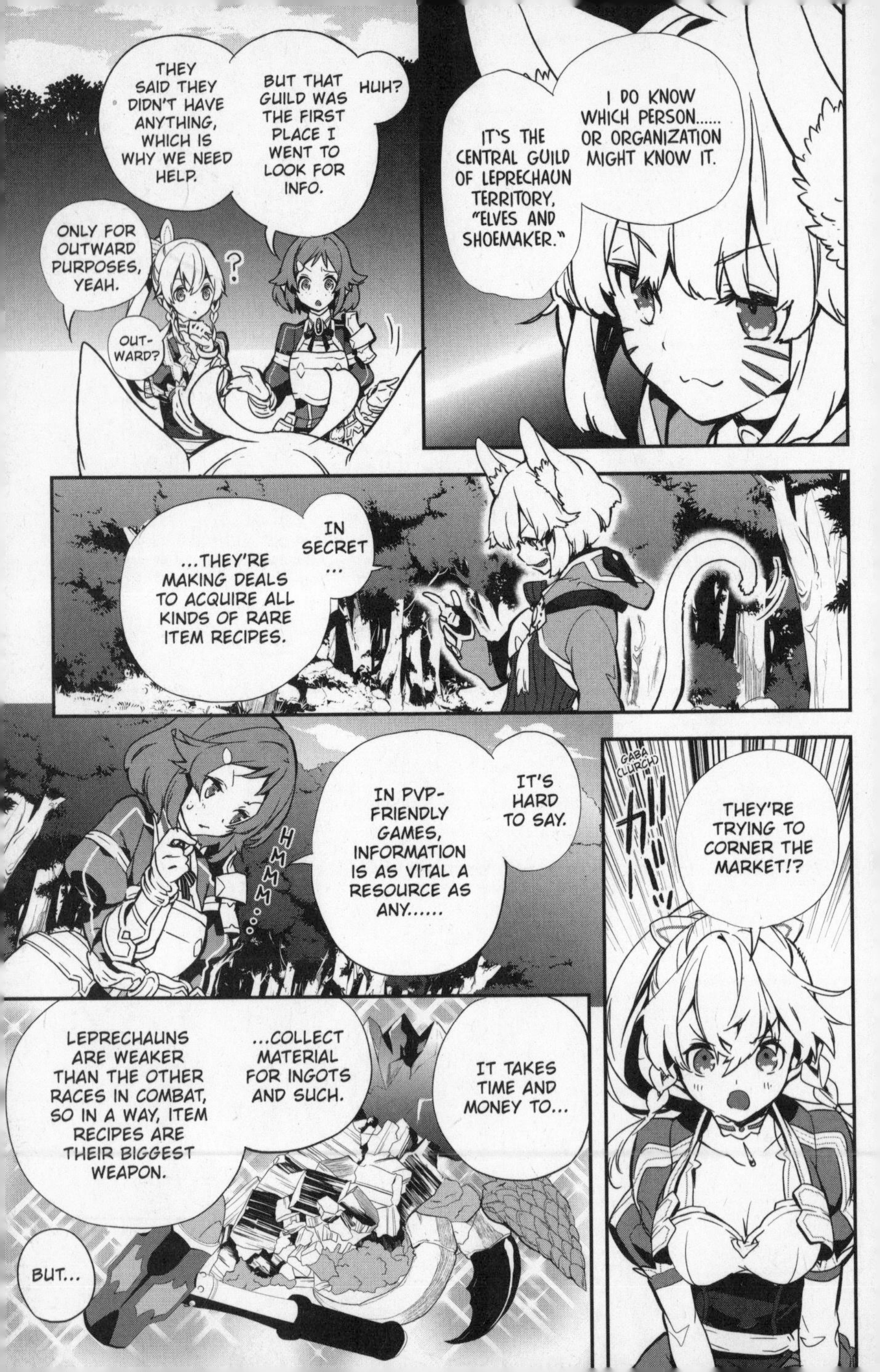
I DO KNOW WHICH PERSON...... OR ORGANIZATION MIGHT KNOW IT.
IT'S THE CENTRAL GUILD OF LEPRECHAUN TERRITORY, "ELVES AND SHOEMAKER."
HUH?
BUT THAT GUILD WAS THE FIRST PLACE I WENT TO LOOK FOR INFO.
THEY SAID THEY DIDN'T HAVE ANYTHING, WHICH IS WHY WE NEED HELP.
ONLY FOR OUTWARD PURPOSES, YEAH.
?
OUT-WARD?
IN SECRET ...
...THEY'RE MAKING DEALS TO ACQUIRE ALL KINDS OF RARE ITEM RECIPES.
GABA (CLURCH)
THEY'RE TRYING TO CORNER THE MARKET!?
IT'S HARD TO SAY.
IN PVP-FRIENDLY GAMES, INFORMATION IS AS VITAL A RESOURCE AS ANY......
HMMMM
IT TAKES TIME AND MONEY TO...
...COLLECT MATERIAL FOR INGOTS AND SUCH.
LEPRECHAUNS ARE WEAKER THAN THE OTHER RACES IN COMBAT, SO IN A WAY, ITEM RECIPES ARE THEIR BIGGEST WEAPON.
BUT...

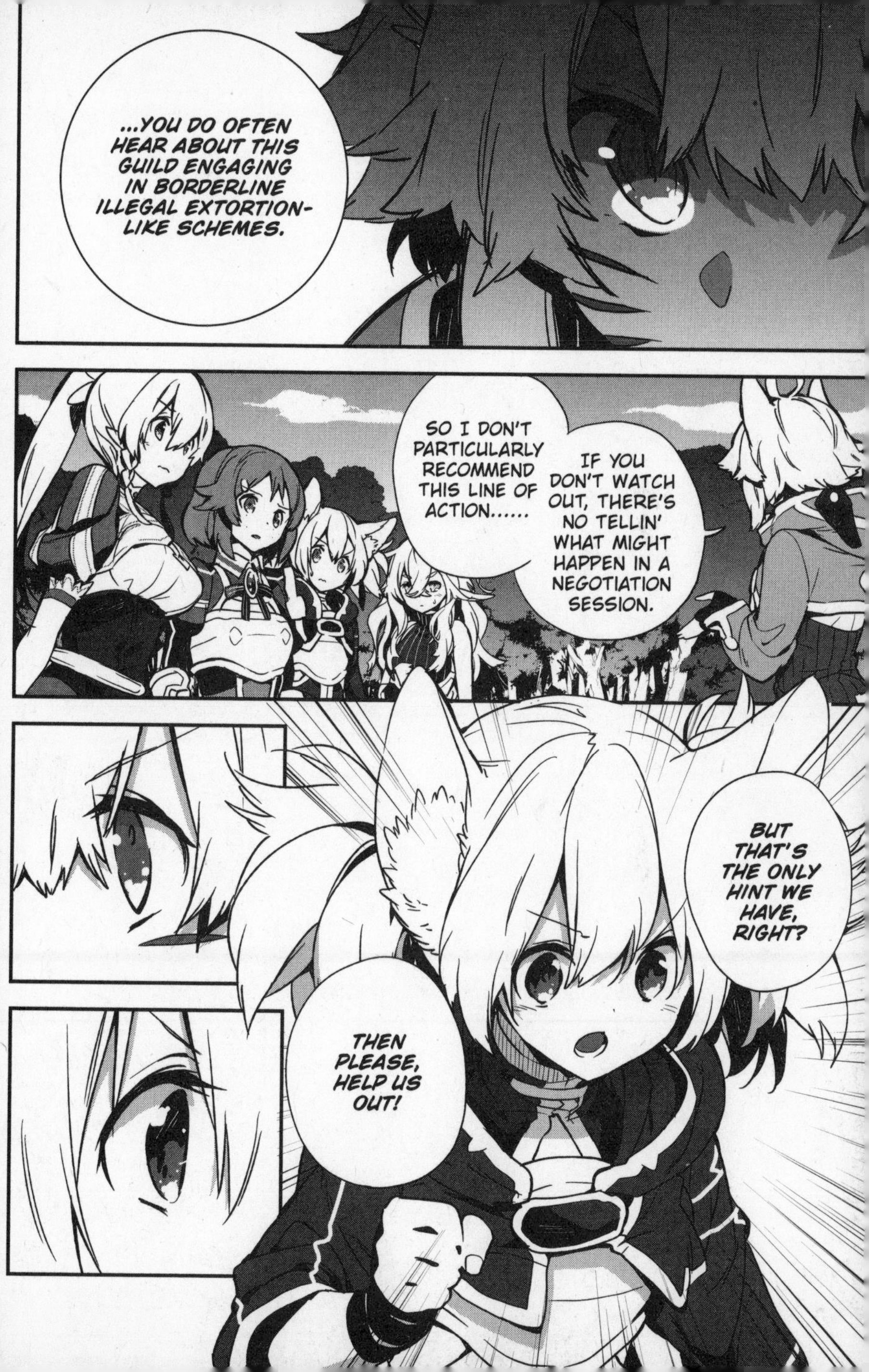
...YOU DO OFTEN HEAR ABOUT THIS GUILD ENGAGING IN BORDERLINE ILLEGAL EXTORTION-LIKE SCHEMES.
IF YOU DON'T WATCH OUT, THERE'S NO TELLIN' WHAT MIGHT HAPPEN IN A NEGOTIATION SESSION.
SO I DON'T PARTICULARLY RECOMMEND THIS LINE OF ACTION......
BUT THAT'S THE ONLY HINT WE HAVE, RIGHT?
THEN PLEASE, HELP US OUT!

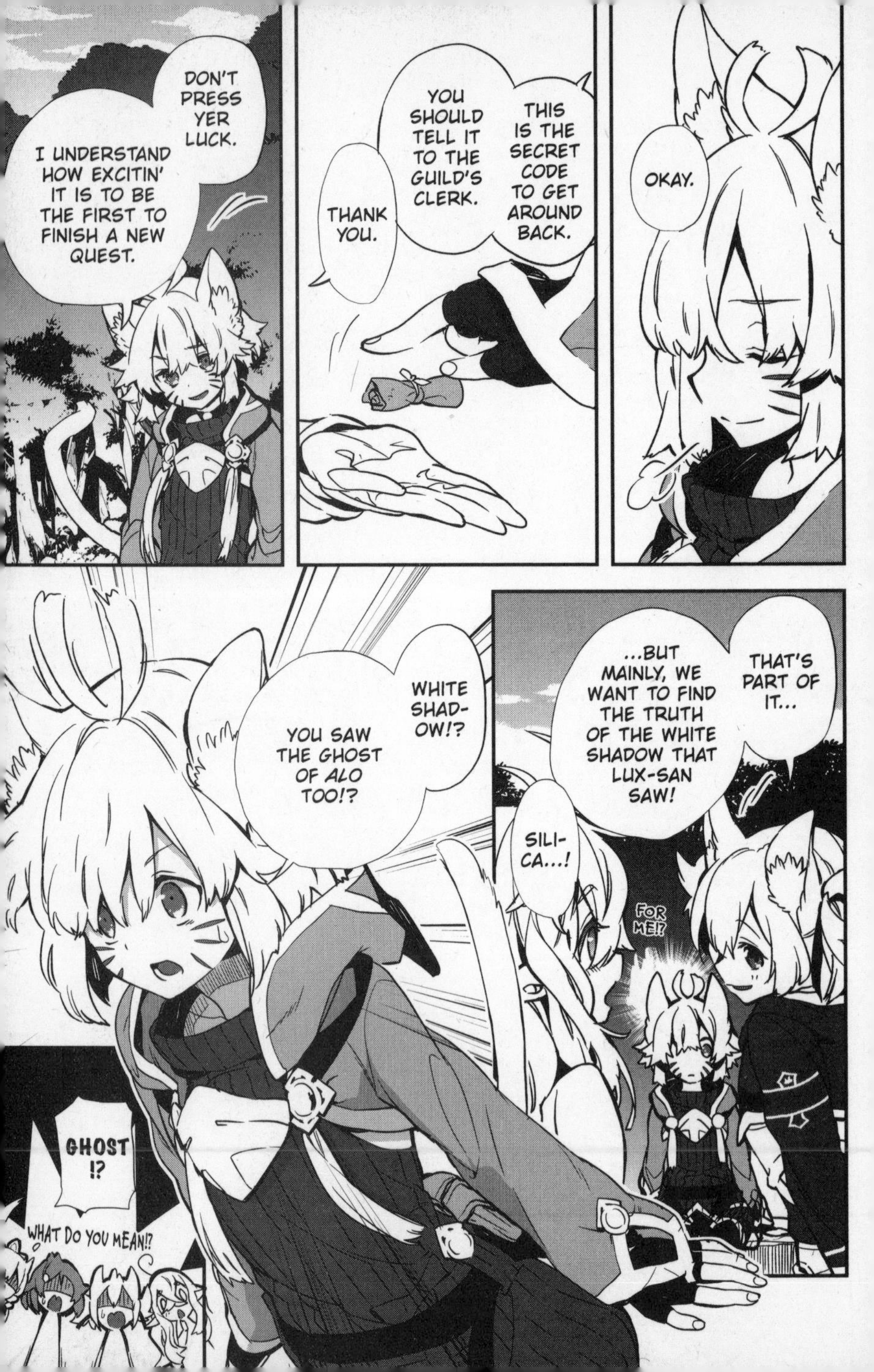

OKAY.
THIS IS THE SECRET CODE TO GET AROUND BACK.
YOU SHOULD TELL IT TO THE GUILD'S CLERK.
THANK YOU.
DON'T PRESS YER LUCK.
I UNDERSTAND HOW EXCITIN' IT IS TO BE THE FIRST TO FINISH A NEW QUEST.
THAT'S PART OF IT...
...BUT MAINLY, WE WANT TO FIND THE TRUTH OF THE WHITE SHADOW THAT LUX-SAN SAW!
SILI-CA...!
FOR ME!?
WHITE SHADOW!?
YOU SAW THE GHOST OF ALO TOO!?
GHOST!?
WHAT DO YOU MEAN!?

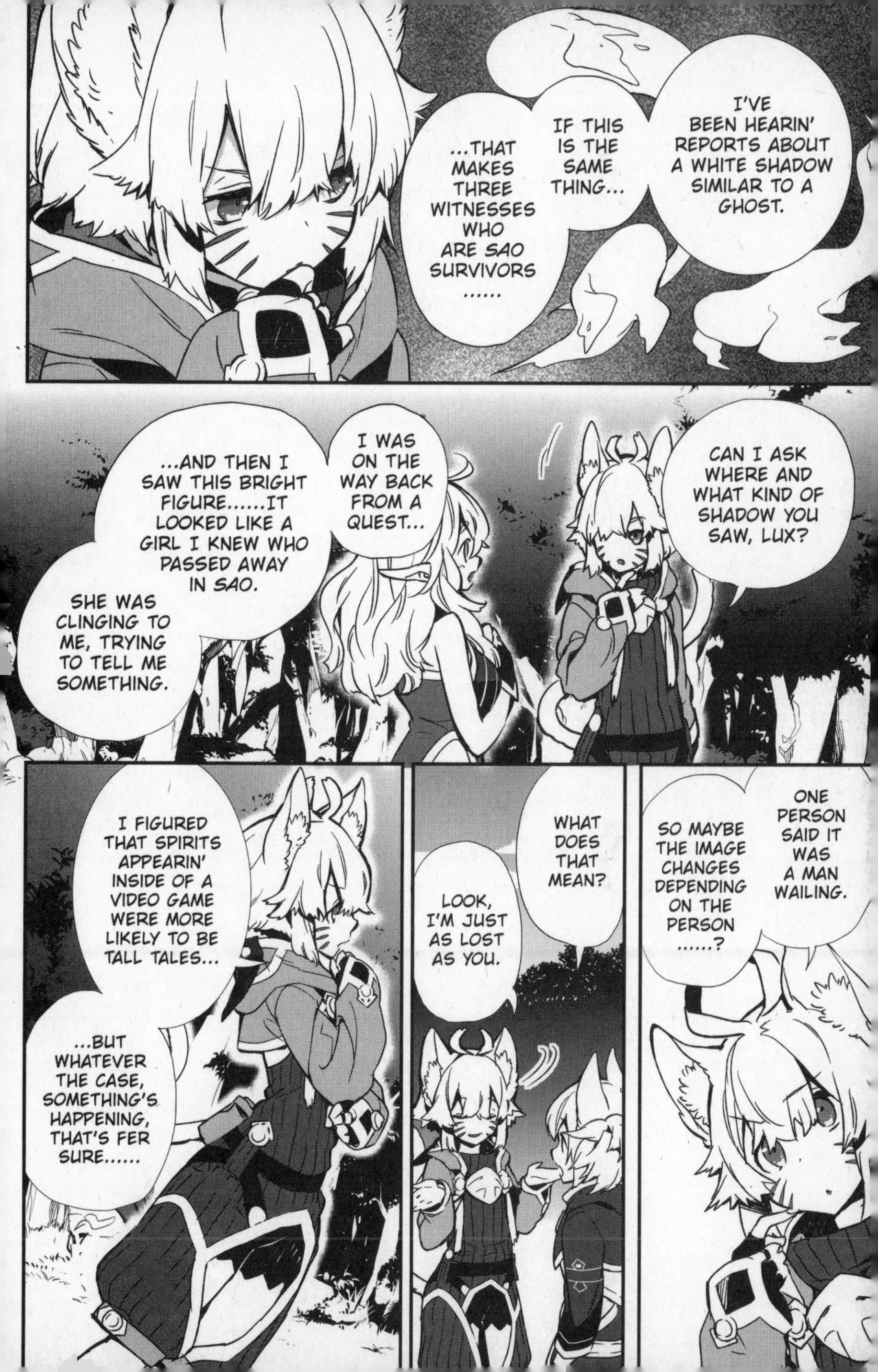
I'VE BEEN HEARIN' REPORTS ABOUT A WHITE SHADOW SIMILAR TO A GHOST.
IF THIS IS THE SAME THING...
...THAT MAKES THREE WITNESSES WHO ARE SAO SURVIVORS ......
CAN I ASK WHERE AND WHAT KIND OF SHADOW YOU SAW, LUX?
I WAS ON THE WAY BACK FROM A QUEST...
...AND THEN I SAW THIS BRIGHT FIGURE......IT LOOKED LIKE A GIRL I KNEW WHO PASSED AWAY IN SAO.
SHE WAS CLINGING TO ME, TRYING TO TELL ME SOMETHING.
ONE PERSON SAID IT WAS A MAN WAILING.
SO MAYBE THE IMAGE CHANGES DEPENDING ON THE PERSON ......?
WHAT DOES THAT MEAN?
LOOK, I'M JUST AS LOST AS YOU.
I FIGURED THAT SPIRITS APPEARIN' INSIDE OF A VIDEO GAME WERE MORE LIKELY TO BE TALL TALES...
...BUT WHATEVER THE CASE, SOMETHING'S HAPPENING, THAT'S FER SURE......

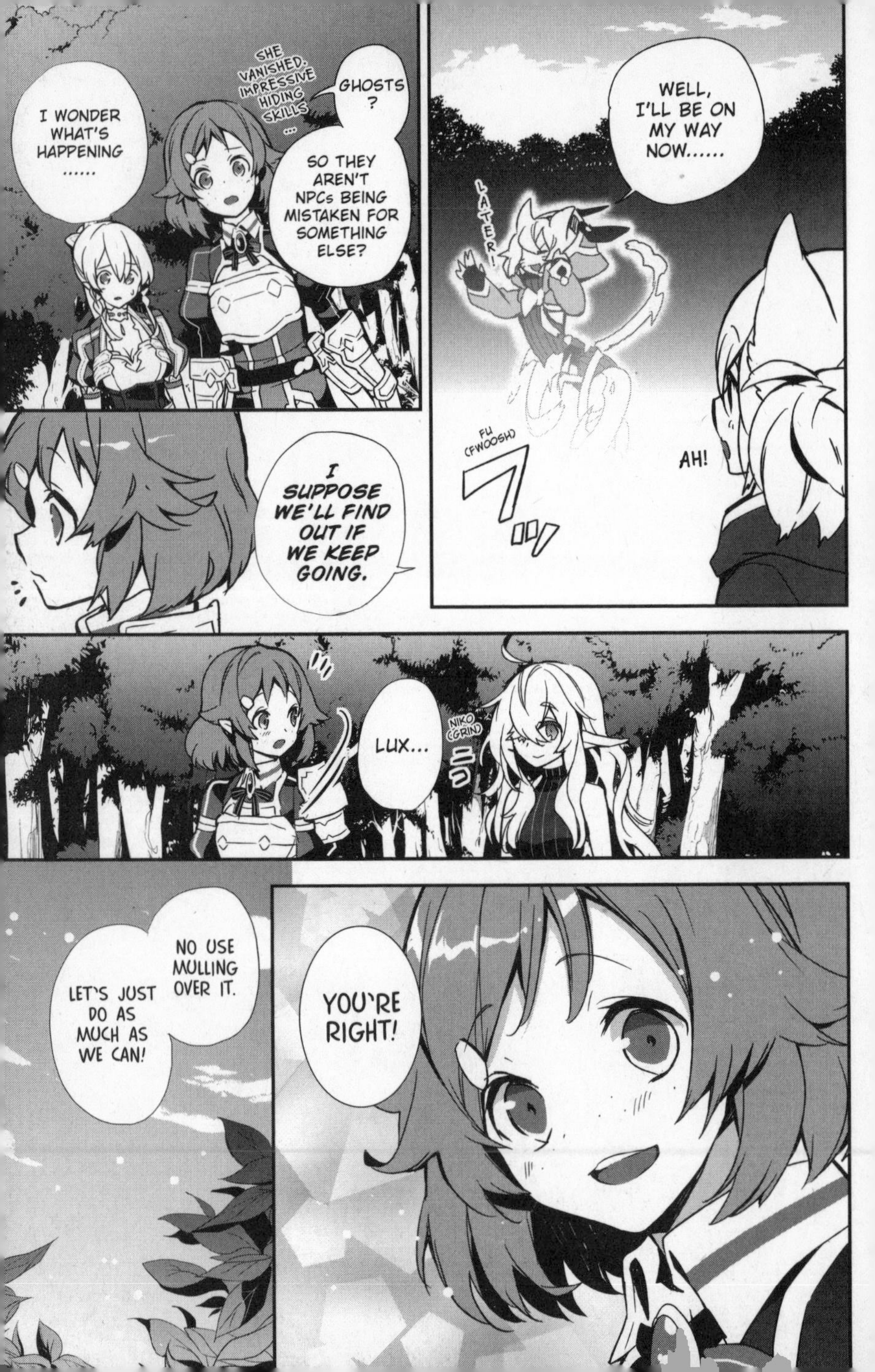

WELL, I'LL BE ON MY WAY NOW......
LATER!
FU (FWOOSH)
AH!
SHE VANISHED. IMPRESSIVE HIDING SKILLS...
GHOSTS?
SO THEY AREN'T NPCs BEING MISTAKEN FOR SOMETHING ELSE?
I WONDER WHAT'S HAPPENING......
I SUPPOSE WE'LL FIND OUT IF WE KEEP GOING.
NIKO (GRIN)
LUX...
YOU'RE RIGHT!
NO USE MULLING OVER IT.
LET'S JUST DO AS MUCH AS WE CAN!

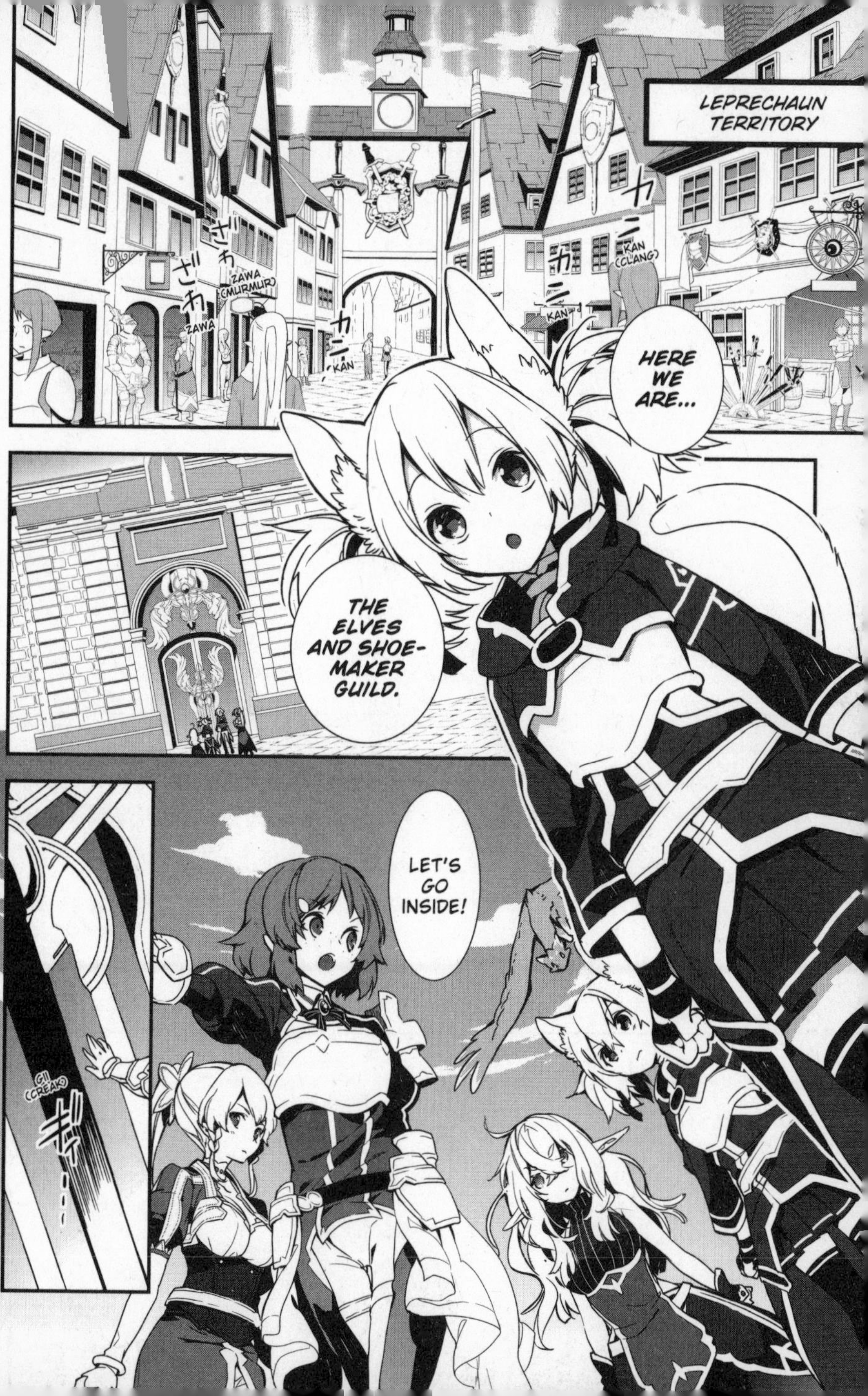

LEPRECHAUN TERRITORY
KAN (CLANG)
KAN
ZAWA (MURMUR)
ZAWA
KAN
HERE WE ARE...
THE ELVES AND SHOE-MAKER GUILD.
LET'S GO INSIDE!
GII (CREAK)

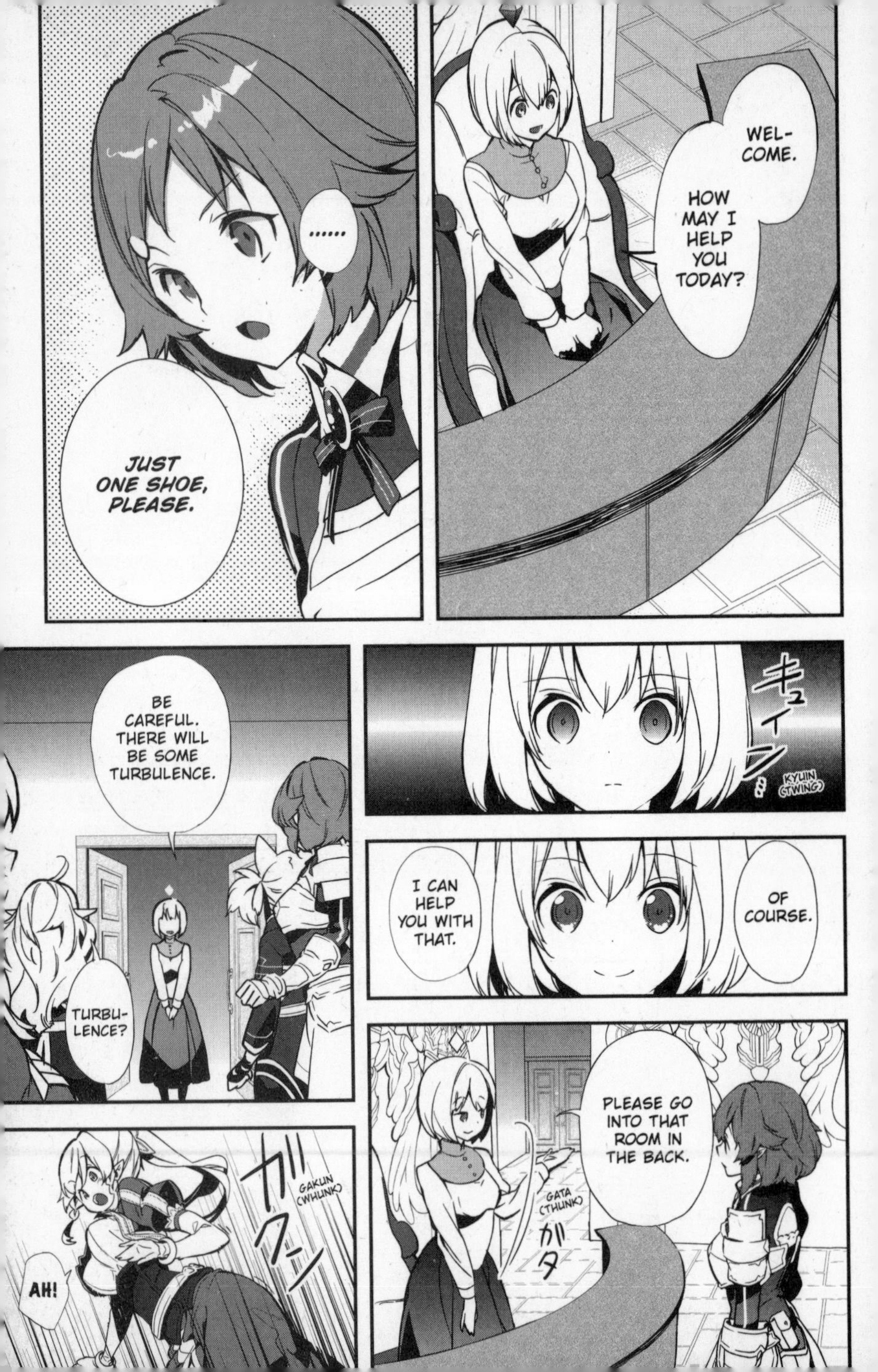
WEL-COME.
HOW MAY I HELP YOU TODAY?
......
JUST ONE SHOE, PLEASE.
キュイン
KYUIN (TWING)
OF COURSE.
I CAN HELP YOU WITH THAT.
PLEASE GO INTO THAT ROOM IN THE BACK.
ガタ
GATA (THUNK)
BE CAREFUL. THERE WILL BE SOME TURBULENCE.
TURBU-LENCE?
ガクン
GAKUN (WHUNK)
AH!

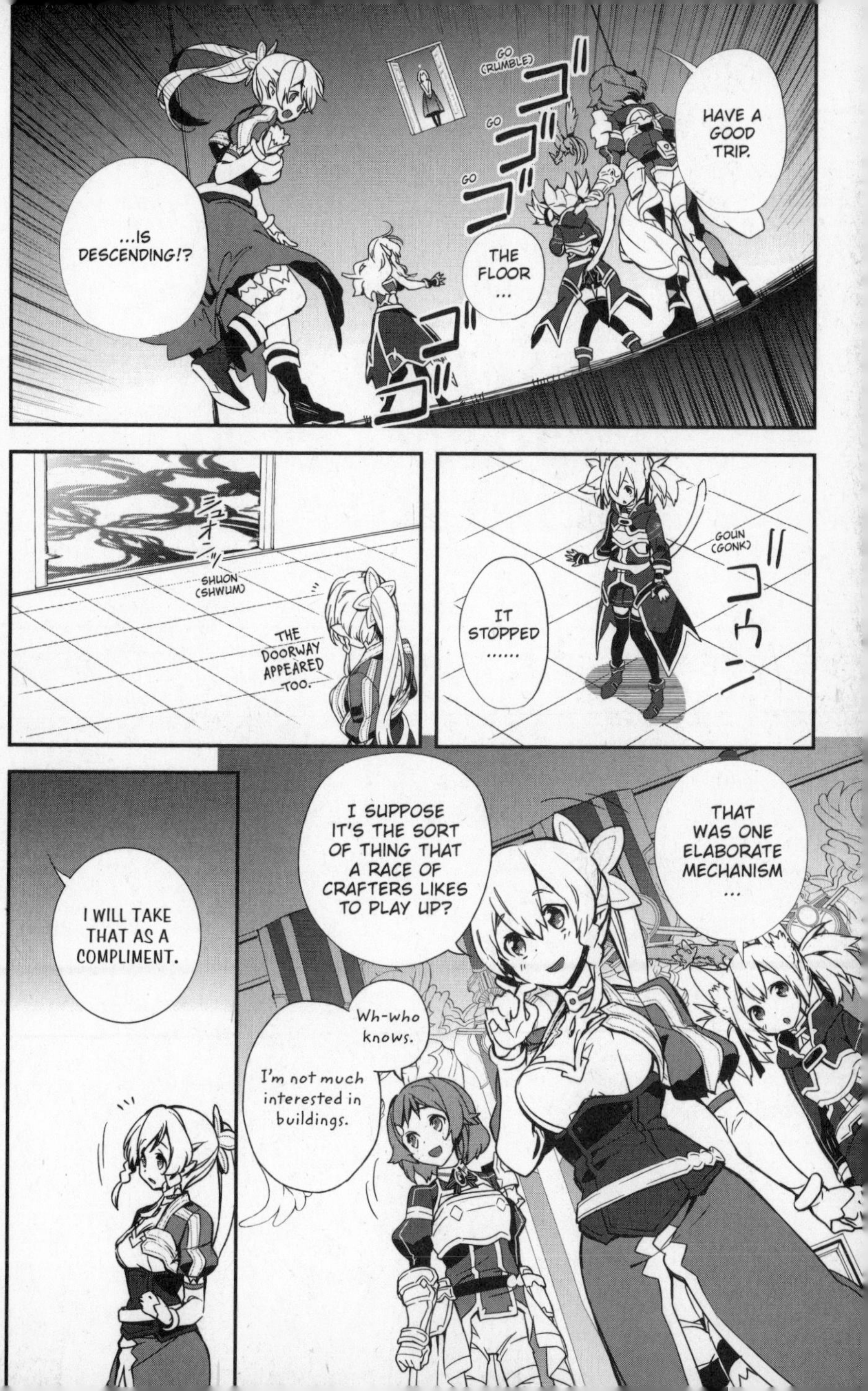
HAVE A GOOD TRIP.
GO (RUMBLE)
GO
GO
ゴゴゴ
THE FLOOR ...
...IS DESCENDING!?
GOUN (GONK)
ゴウン
IT STOPPED ......
シュオンッ
SHUON (SHWUM)
THE DOORWAY APPEARED TOO.
THAT WAS ONE ELABORATE MECHANISM ...
I SUPPOSE IT'S THE SORT OF THING THAT A RACE OF CRAFTERS LIKES TO PLAY UP?
Wh-who knows.
I'm not much interested in buildings.
I WILL TAKE THAT AS A COMPLIMENT.

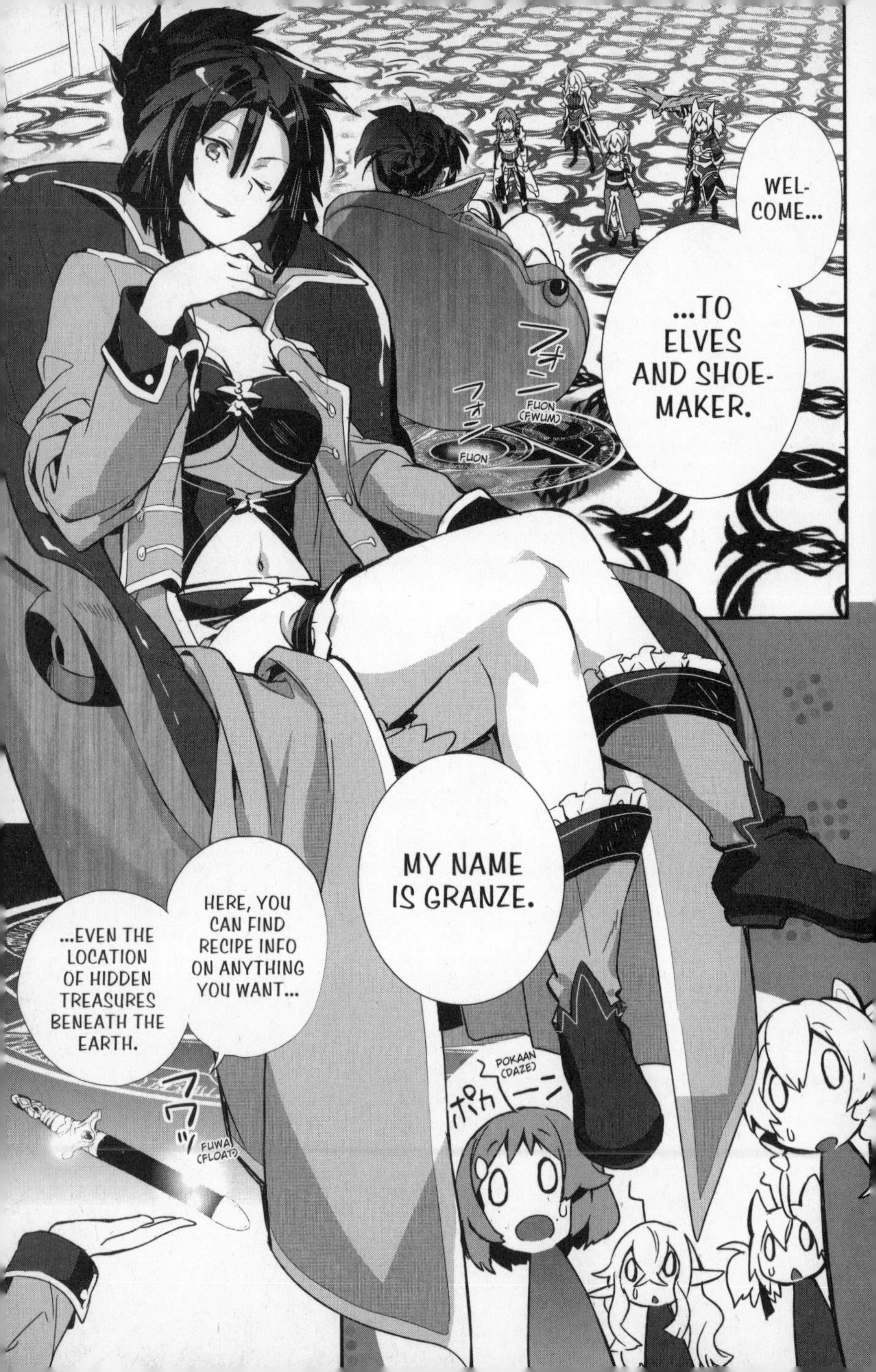
WEL-
COME...
...TO ELVES AND SHOE-MAKER.
フォン FUON (FWUM)
フォン FUON
MY NAME IS GRANZE.
HERE, YOU CAN FIND RECIPE INFO ON ANYTHING YOU WANT...
...EVEN THE LOCATION OF HIDDEN TREASURES BENEATH THE EARTH.
ポカーン POKAAN (DAZE)
フワッ FUWA (FLOAT)

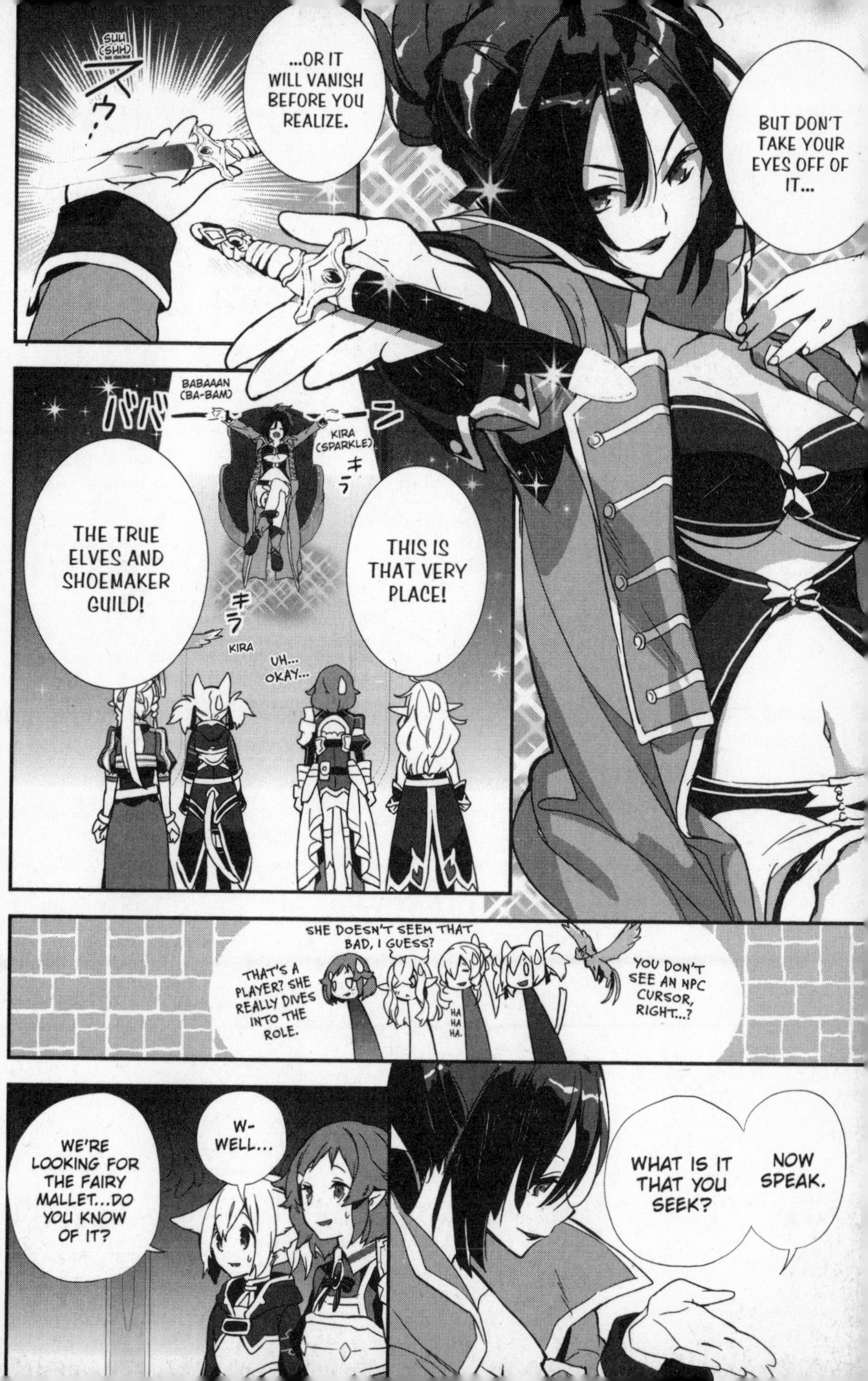
BUT DON'T TAKE YOUR EYES OFF OF IT...
...OR IT WILL VANISH BEFORE YOU REALIZE.
SUU (SHH)
BABAAAN (BA-BAM)
KIRA (SPARKLE)
THIS IS THAT VERY PLACE!
THE TRUE ELVES AND SHOEMAKER GUILD!
KIRA
UH... OKAY...
YOU DON'T SEE AN NPC CURSOR, RIGHT...?
SHE DOESN'T SEEM THAT BAD, I GUESS?
HA HA HA.
THAT'S A PLAYER? SHE REALLY DIVES INTO THE ROLE.
NOW SPEAK.
WHAT IS IT THAT YOU SEEK?
W-WELL...
WE'RE LOOKING FOR THE FAIRY MALLET...DO YOU KNOW OF IT?

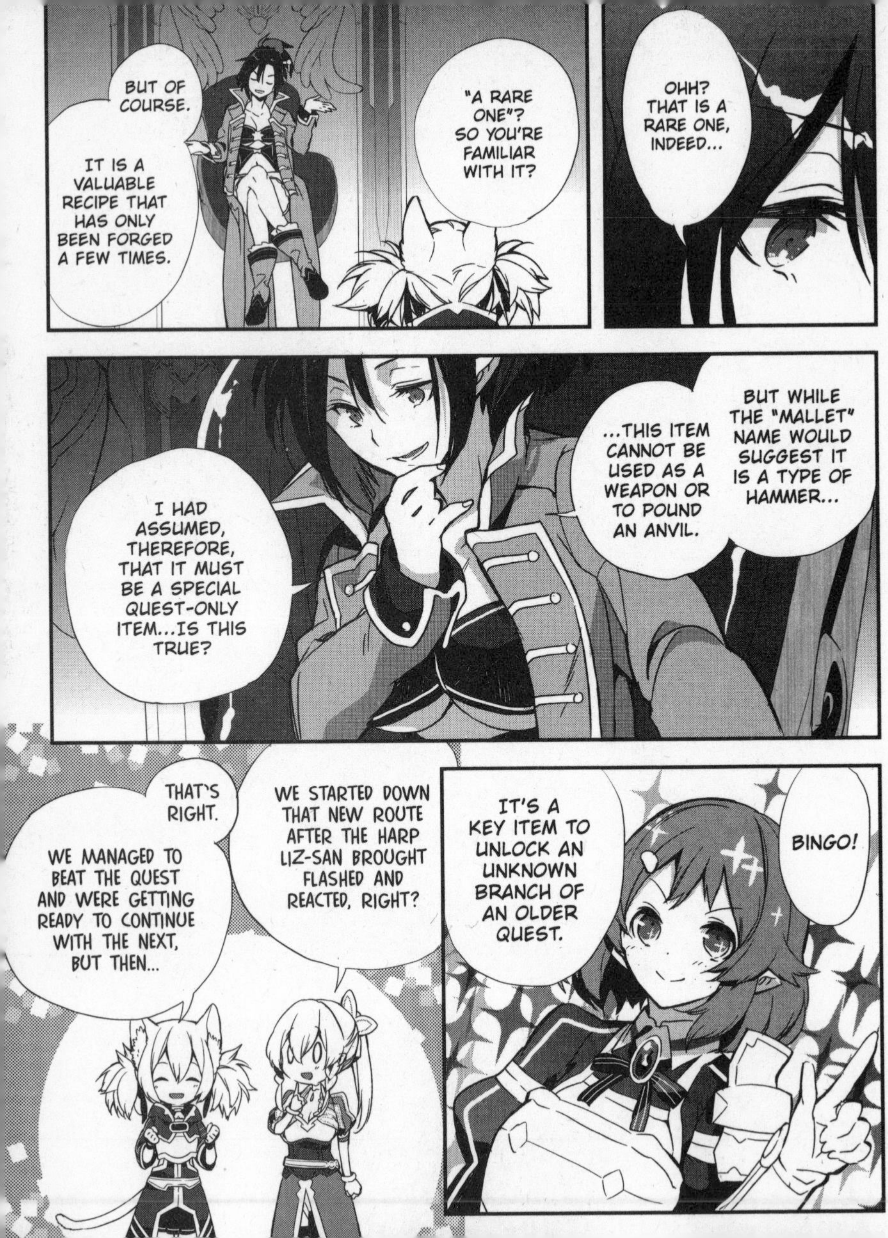
OHH? THAT IS A RARE ONE, INDEED...
"A RARE ONE"? SO YOU'RE FAMILIAR WITH IT?
BUT OF COURSE.
IT IS A VALUABLE RECIPE THAT HAS ONLY BEEN FORGED A FEW TIMES.
BUT WHILE THE "MALLET" NAME WOULD SUGGEST IT IS A TYPE OF HAMMER...
...THIS ITEM CANNOT BE USED AS A WEAPON OR TO POUND AN ANVIL.
I HAD ASSUMED, THEREFORE, THAT IT MUST BE A SPECIAL QUEST-ONLY ITEM...IS THIS TRUE?
BINGO!
IT'S A KEY ITEM TO UNLOCK AN UNKNOWN BRANCH OF AN OLDER QUEST.
WE STARTED DOWN THAT NEW ROUTE AFTER THE HARP LIZ-SAN BROUGHT FLASHED AND REACTED, RIGHT?
THAT'S RIGHT.
WE MANAGED TO BEAT THE QUEST AND WERE GETTING READY TO CONTINUE WITH THE NEXT, BUT THEN...

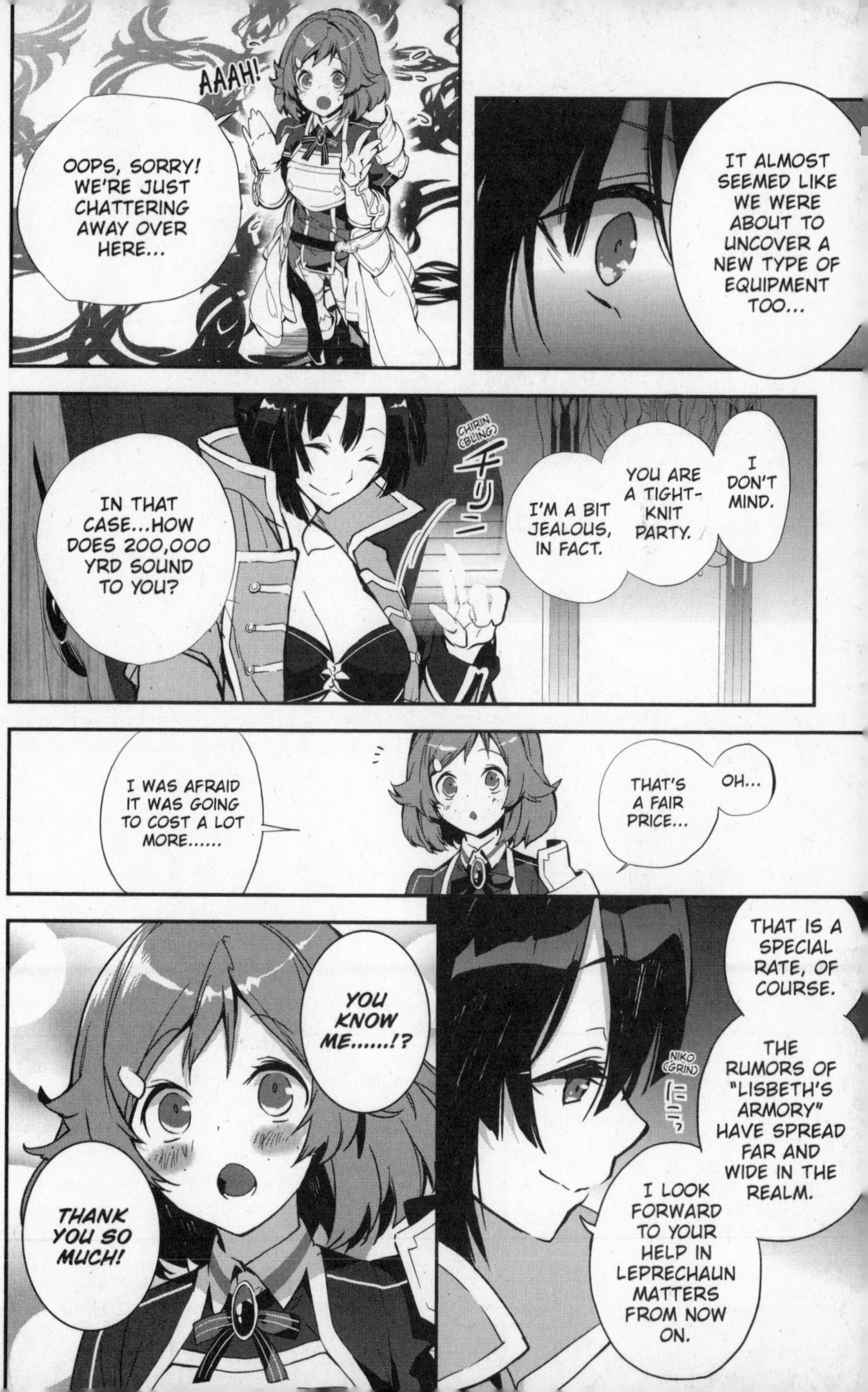
IT ALMOST SEEMED LIKE WE WERE ABOUT TO UNCOVER A NEW TYPE OF EQUIPMENT TOO...
AAAH!
OOPS, SORRY! WE'RE JUST CHATTERING AWAY OVER HERE...
I DON'T MIND.
YOU ARE A TIGHT-KNIT PARTY.
I'M A BIT JEALOUS, IN FACT.
CHIRIN (BLING)
IN THAT CASE...HOW DOES 200,000 YRD SOUND TO YOU?
OH...
THAT'S A FAIR PRICE...
I WAS AFRAID IT WAS GOING TO COST A LOT MORE......
THAT IS A SPECIAL RATE, OF COURSE.
THE RUMORS OF "LISBETH'S ARMORY" HAVE SPREAD FAR AND WIDE IN THE REALM.
NIKO (GRIN)
I LOOK FORWARD TO YOUR HELP IN LEPRECHAUN MATTERS FROM NOW ON.
YOU KNOW ME......!?
THANK YOU SO MUCH!

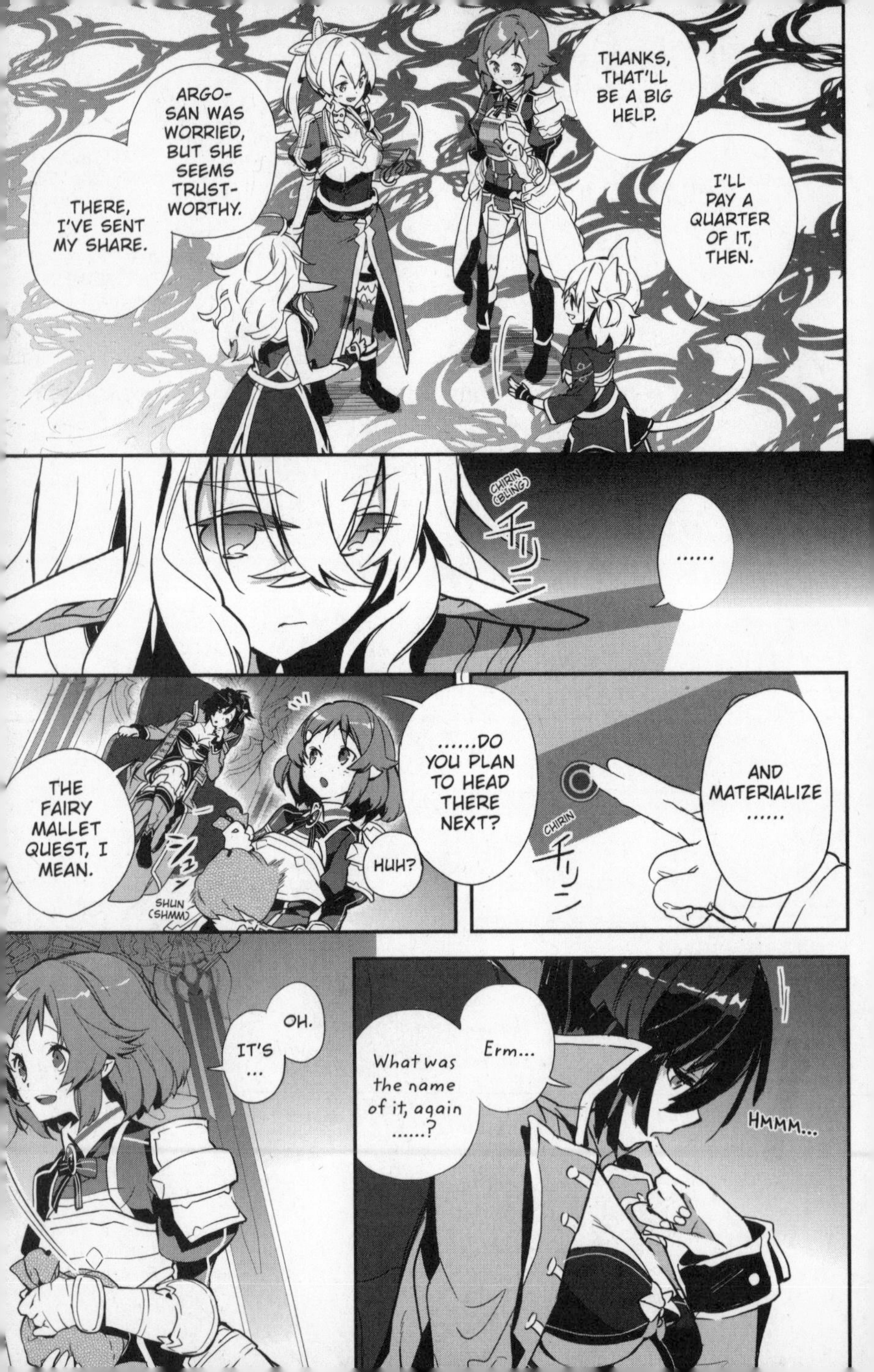
THANKS, THAT'LL BE A BIG HELP.
I'LL PAY A QUARTER OF IT, THEN.
ARGO-SAN WAS WORRIED, BUT SHE SEEMS TRUST-WORTHY.
THERE, I'VE SENT MY SHARE.
CHIRIN (BLING)
チリーン
......
AND MATERIALIZE ......
CHIRIN
チリン
......DO YOU PLAN TO HEAD THERE NEXT?
HUH?
THE FAIRY MALLET QUEST, I MEAN.
SHUN (SHMM)
HMMM...
Erm...
What was the name of it, again ......?
OH.
IT'S ...

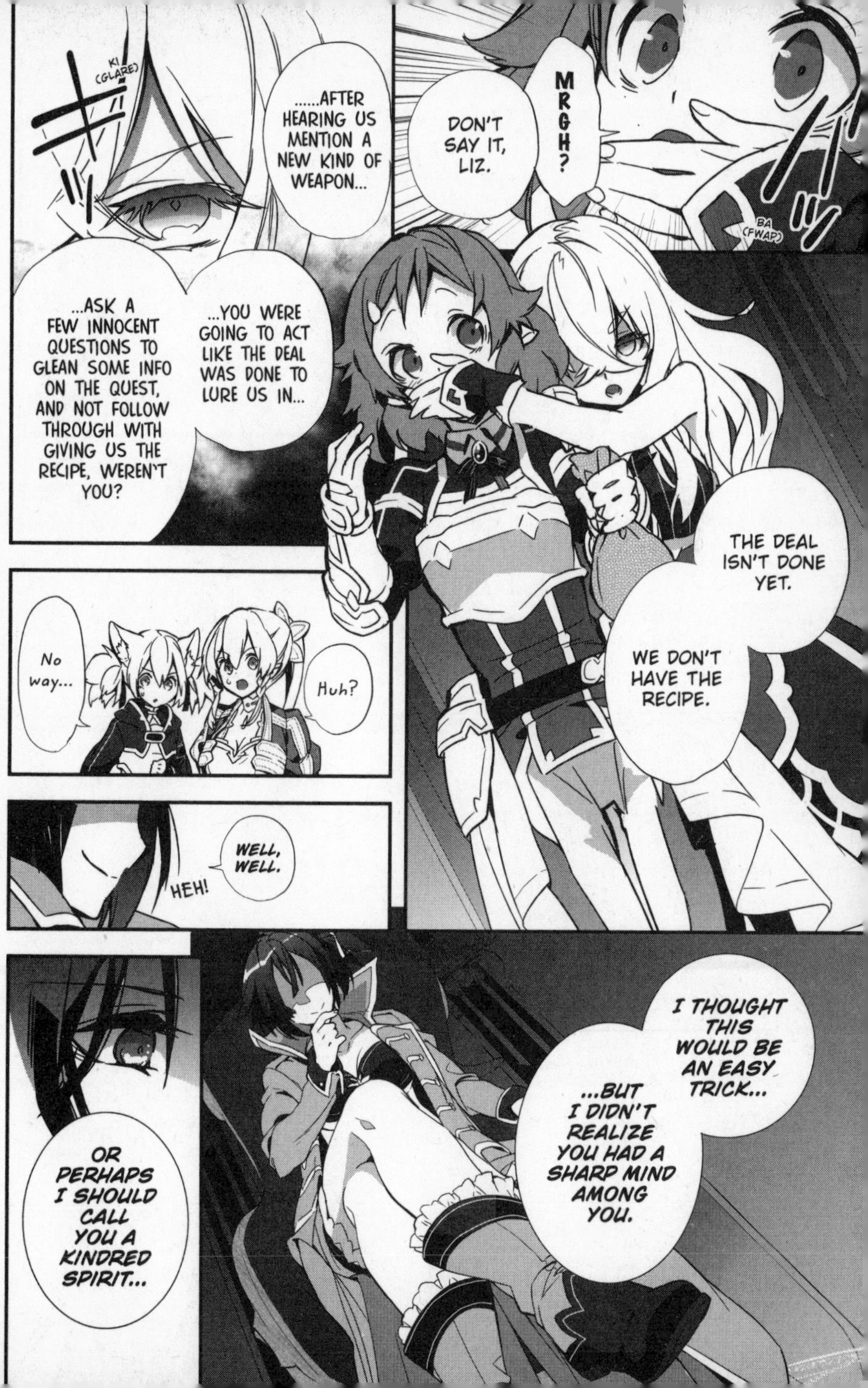
MRGH?
BA (FWAP)
DON'T SAY IT, LIZ.
......AFTER HEARING US MENTION A NEW KIND OF WEAPON...
KI (GLARE)
...YOU WERE GOING TO ACT LIKE THE DEAL WAS DONE TO LURE US IN...
...ASK A FEW INNOCENT QUESTIONS TO GLEAN SOME INFO ON THE QUEST, AND NOT FOLLOW THROUGH WITH GIVING US THE RECIPE, WEREN'T YOU?
THE DEAL ISN'T DONE YET.
WE DON'T HAVE THE RECIPE.
Huh?
No way...
WELL, WELL.
HEH!
I THOUGHT THIS WOULD BE AN EASY TRICK...
...BUT I DIDN'T REALIZE YOU HAD A SHARP MIND AMONG YOU.
OR PERHAPS I SHOULD CALL YOU A KINDRED SPIRIT...

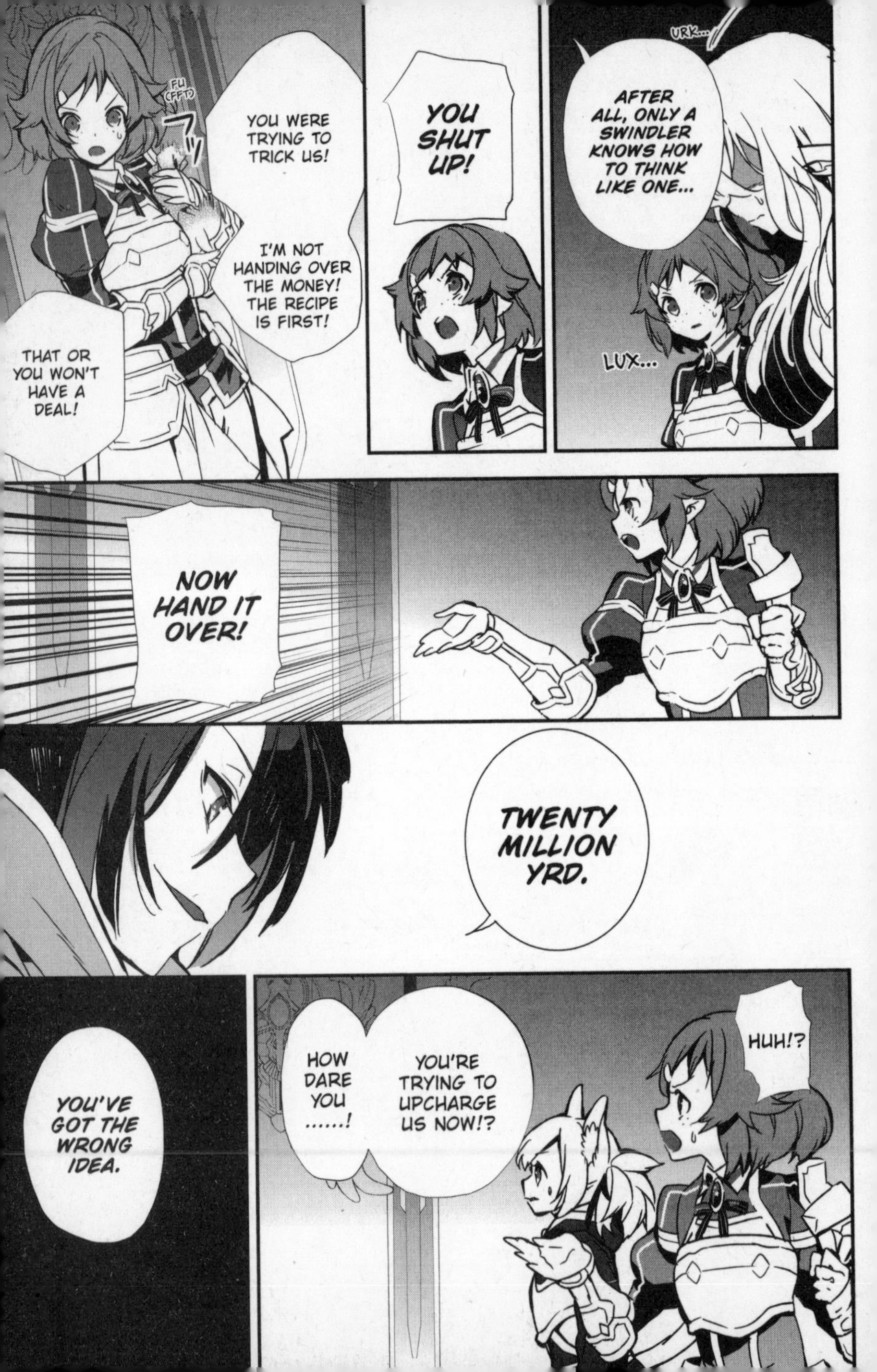
URK...
AFTER ALL, ONLY A SWINDLER KNOWS HOW TO THINK LIKE ONE...
LUX...
YOU SHUT UP!
FU (FFT)
YOU WERE TRYING TO TRICK US!
I'M NOT HANDING OVER THE MONEY! THE RECIPE IS FIRST!
THAT OR YOU WON'T HAVE A DEAL!
NOW HAND IT OVER!
TWENTY MILLION YRD.
HUH!?
YOU'RE TRYING TO UPCHARGE US NOW!?
HOW DARE YOU ......!
YOU'VE GOT THE WRONG IDEA.

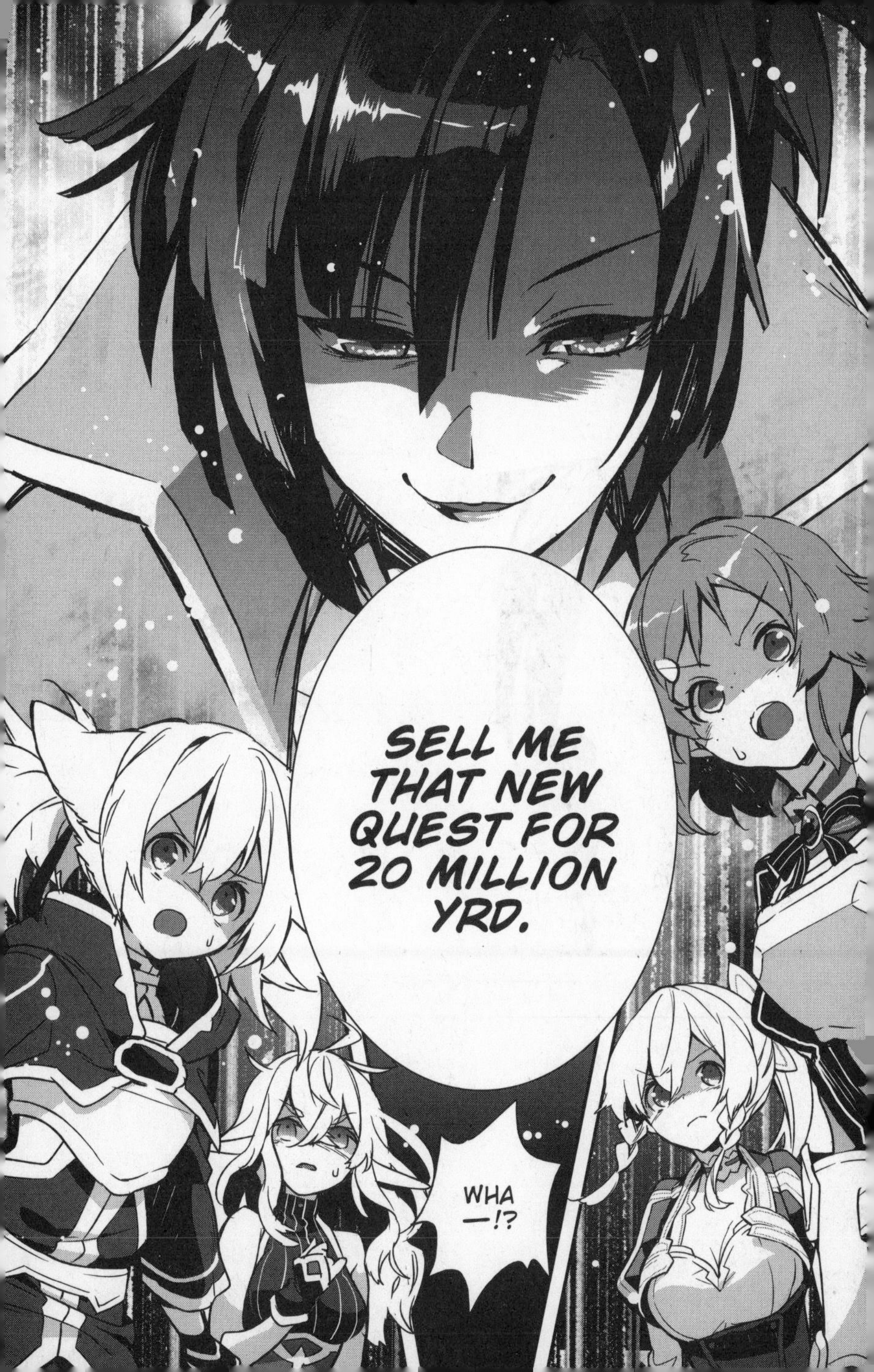
SELL ME THAT NEW QUEST FOR 20 MILLION YRD.
WHA—!?

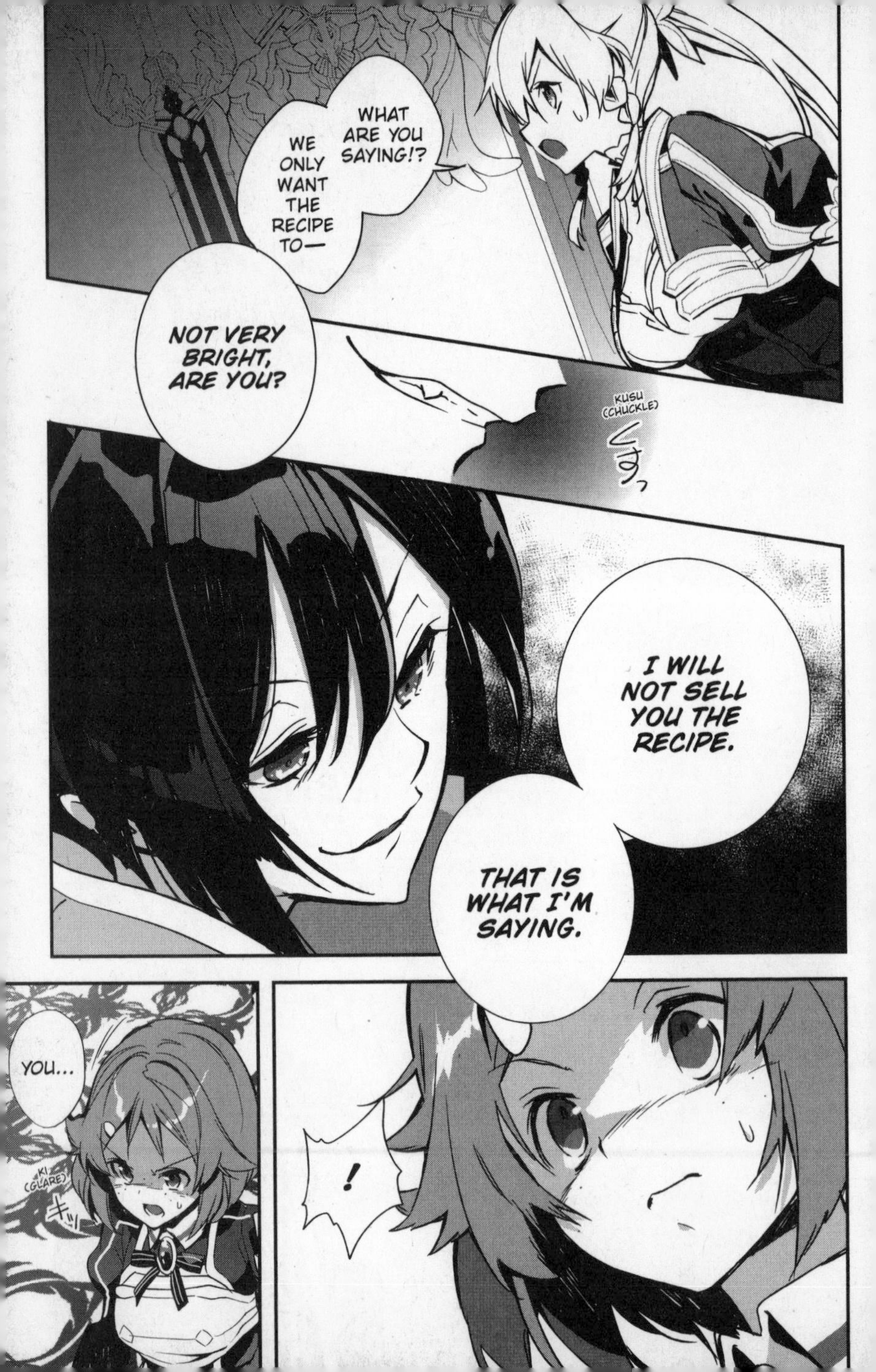
WHAT ARE YOU SAYING!?
WE ONLY WANT THE RECIPE TO—
NOT VERY BRIGHT, ARE YOU?
KUSU (CHUCKLE)
I WILL NOT SELL YOU THE RECIPE.
THAT IS WHAT I'M SAYING.
!
YOU...
KI (GLARE)

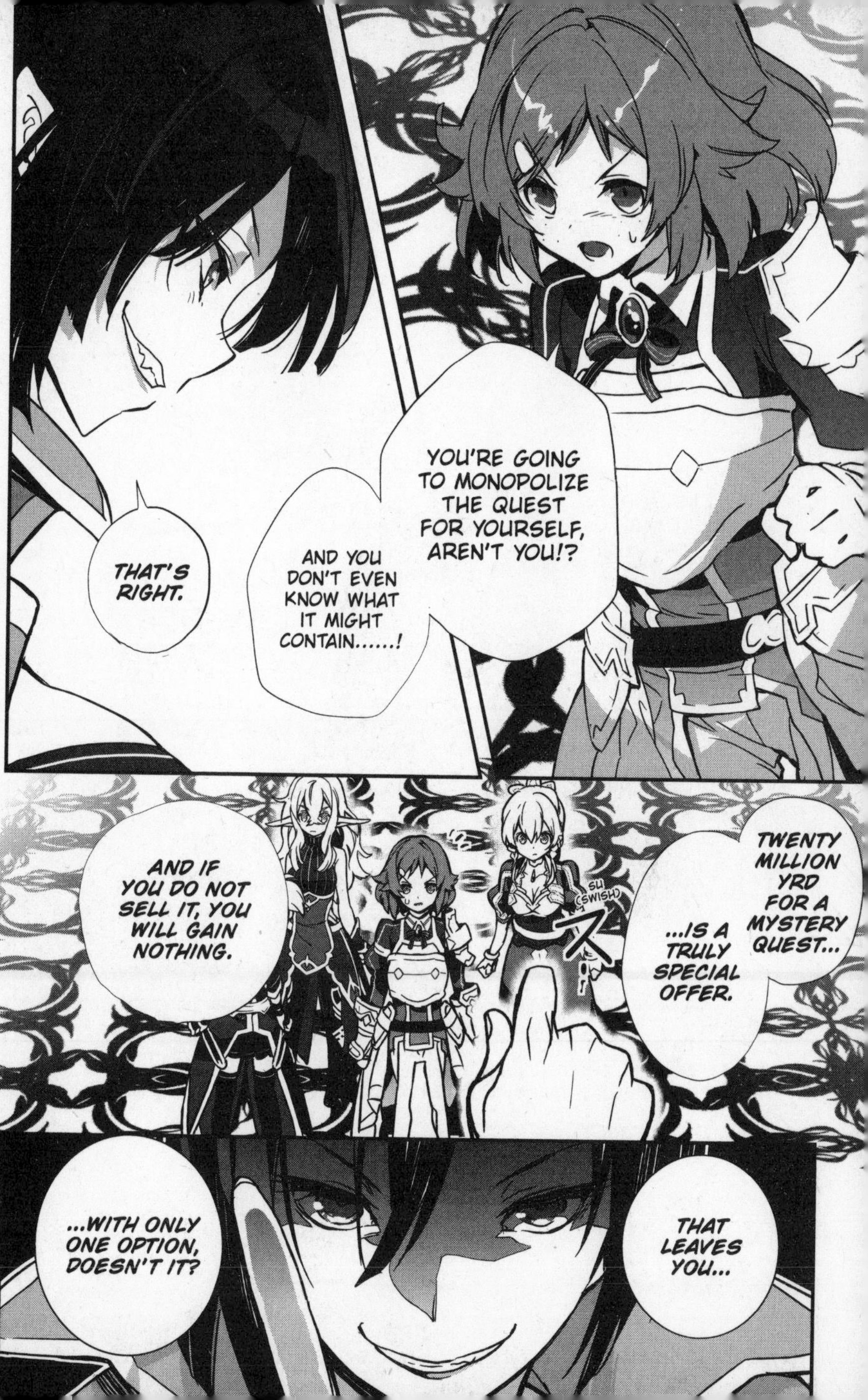
YOU'RE GOING TO MONOPOLIZE THE QUEST FOR YOURSELF, AREN'T YOU!?
AND YOU DON'T EVEN KNOW WHAT IT MIGHT CONTAIN......!
THAT'S RIGHT.
TWENTY MILLION YRD FOR A MYSTERY QUEST...
...IS A TRULY SPECIAL OFFER.
SU (SWISH)
AND IF YOU DO NOT SELL IT, YOU WILL GAIN NOTHING.
THAT LEAVES YOU...
...WITH ONLY ONE OPTION, DOESN'T IT?

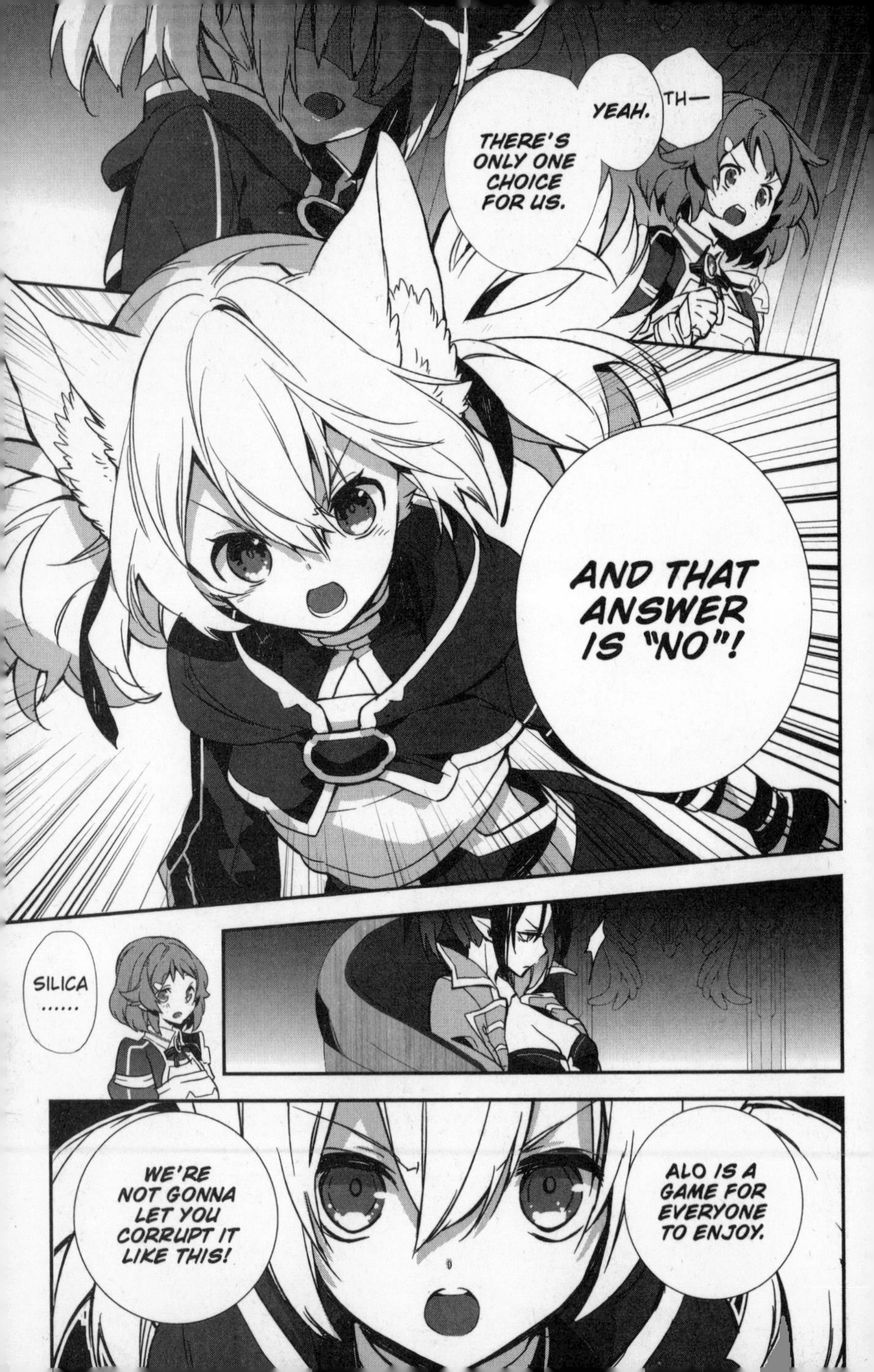
TH—
YEAH.
THERE'S ONLY ONE CHOICE FOR US.
AND THAT ANSWER IS "NO"!
SILICA ......
ALO IS A GAME FOR EVERYONE TO ENJOY.
WE'RE NOT GONNA LET YOU CORRUPT IT LIKE THIS!

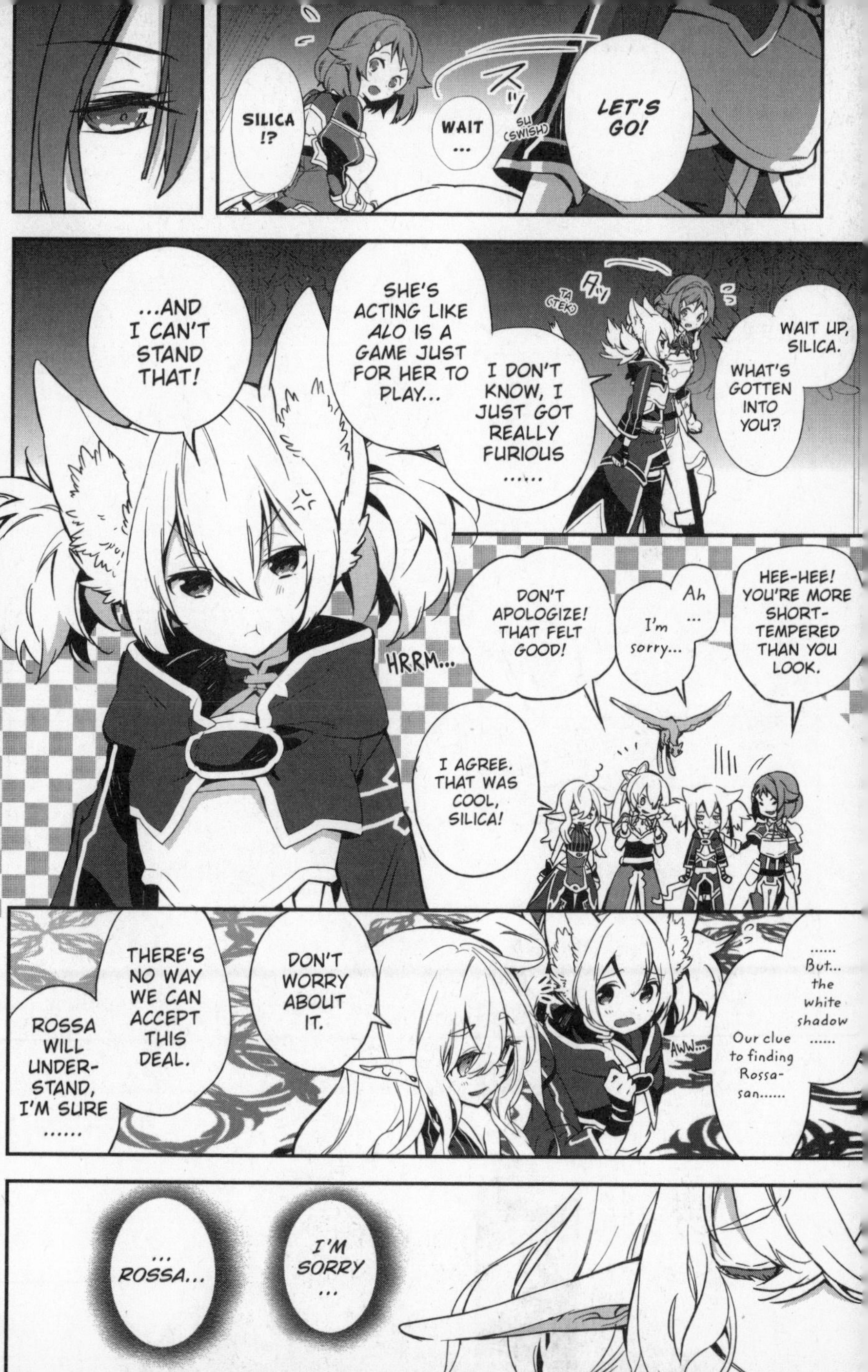
LET'S GO!
SU (SWISH)
WAIT ...
SILICA !?
WAIT UP, SILICA.
WHAT'S GOTTEN INTO YOU?
TA (TEK)
I DON'T KNOW, I JUST GOT REALLY FURIOUS ......
SHE'S ACTING LIKE ALO IS A GAME JUST FOR HER TO PLAY...
...AND I CAN'T STAND THAT!
HEE-HEE! YOU'RE MORE SHORT-TEMPERED THAN YOU LOOK.
Ah ... I'm sorry...
DON'T APOLOGIZE! THAT FELT GOOD!
I AGREE. THAT WAS COOL, SILICA!
HRRM...
...... But... the white shadow ......
Our clue to finding Rossa-san......
AWW...
DON'T WORRY ABOUT IT.
THERE'S NO WAY WE CAN ACCEPT THIS DEAL.
ROSSA WILL UNDERSTAND, I'M SURE ......
I'M SORRY ...
... ROSSA...

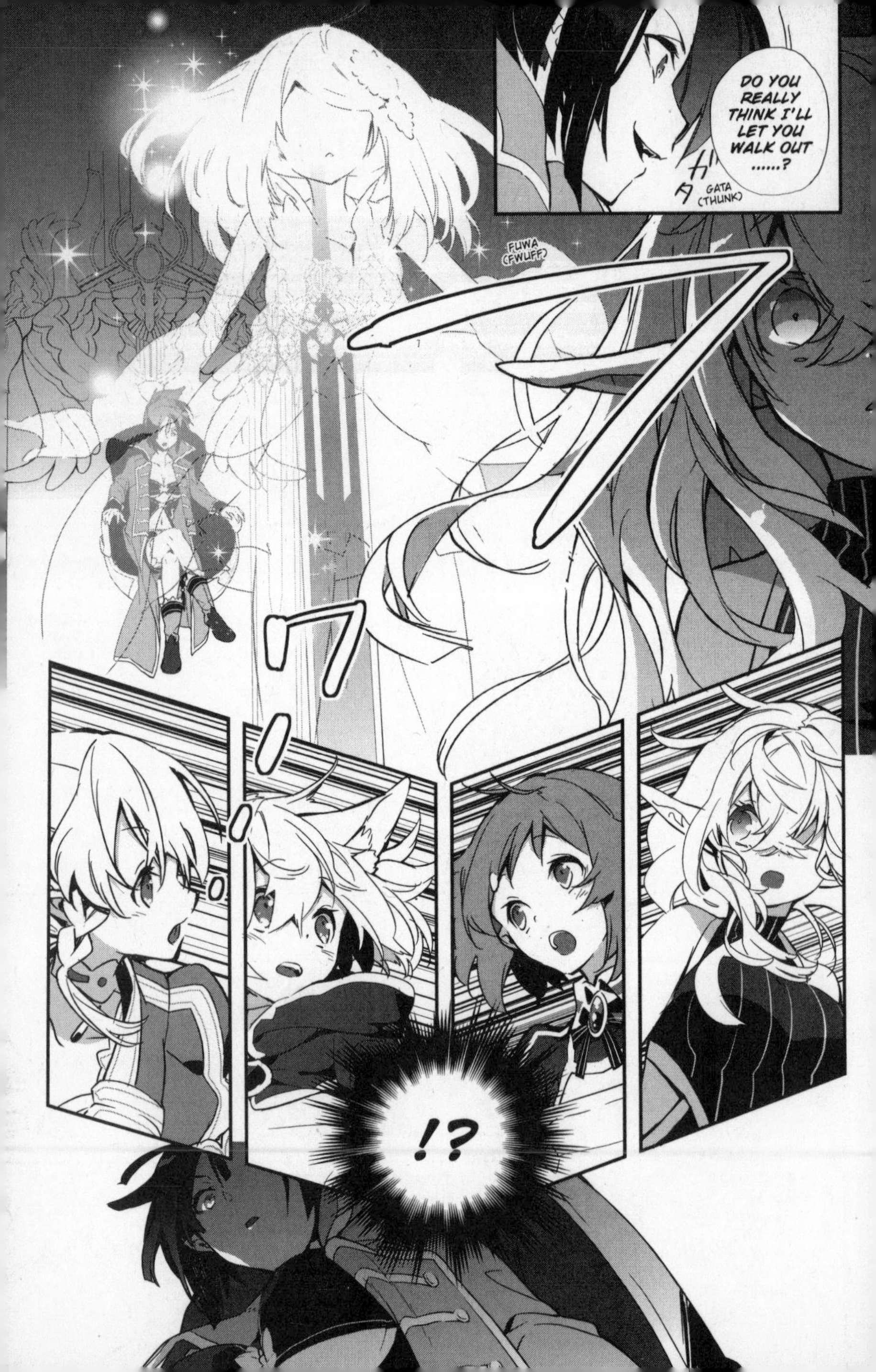
DO YOU REALLY THINK I'LL LET YOU WALK OUT ......?
GATA (THUNK)
FUWA (FWUFF)
!?

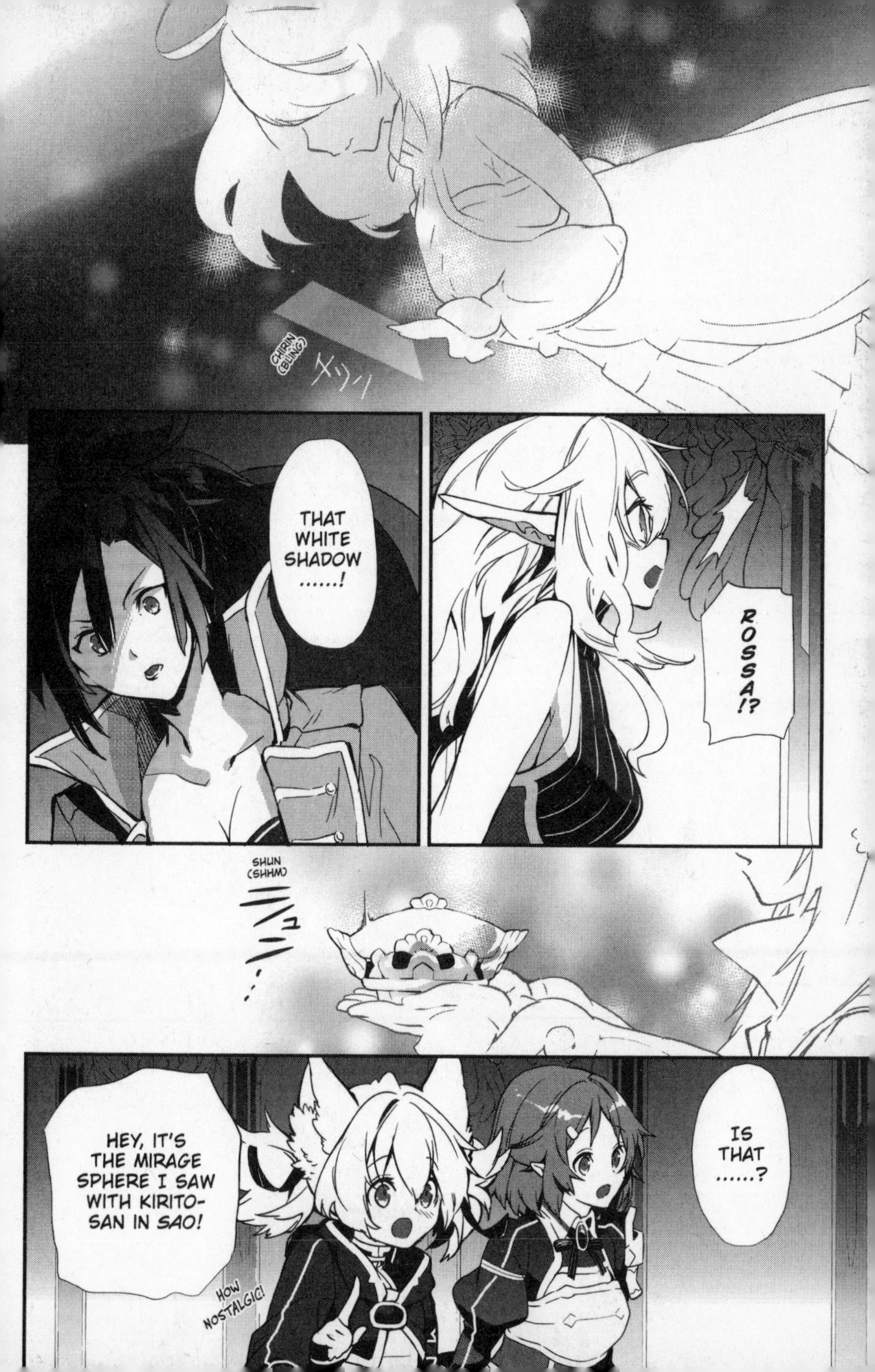
CHIRIN (BLING)
ROSSA!?
THAT WHITE SHADOW ......!
SHUN (SHHM)
IS THAT ......?
HEY, IT'S THE MIRAGE SPHERE I SAW WITH KIRITO-SAN IN SAO!
HOW NOSTALGIC!

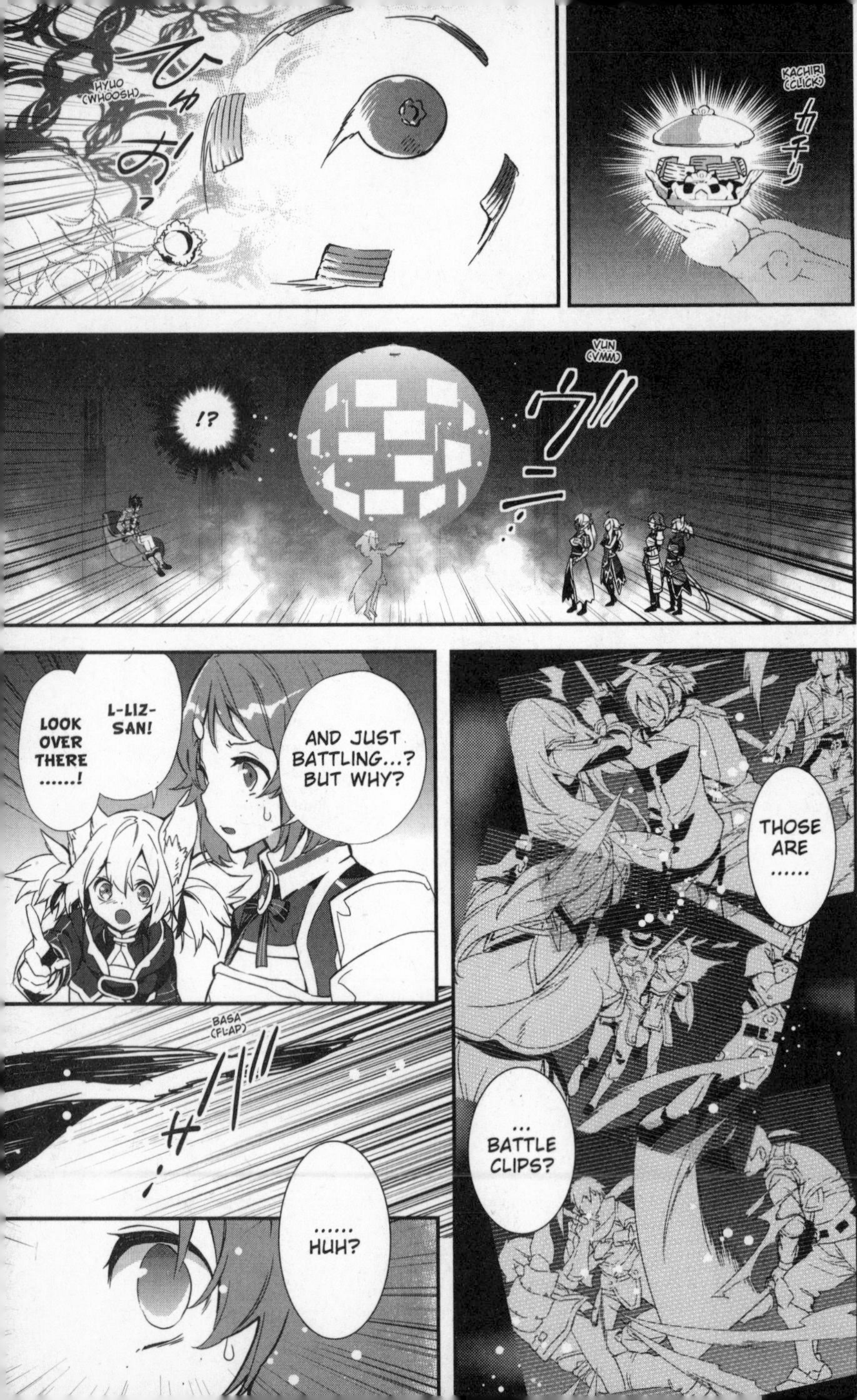
KACHIRI (CLICK)
カチリ
HYUO (WHOOSH)
ひゅおっ
VUN (VMM)
!?
THOSE ARE ......
AND JUST BATTLING...? BUT WHY?
L-LIZ-SAN!
LOOK OVER THERE ......!
... BATTLE CLIPS?
BASA (FLAP)
...... HUH?

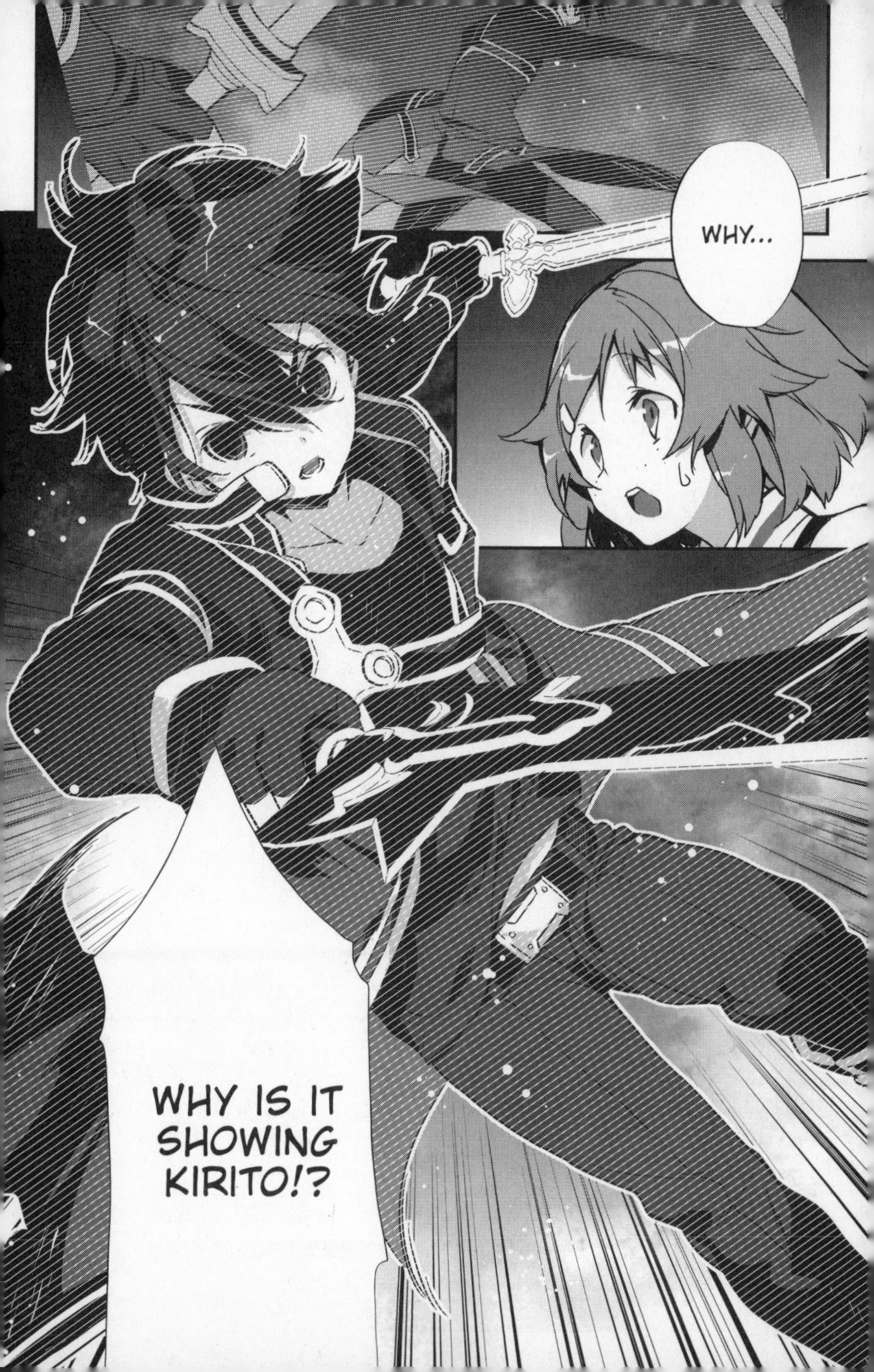
WHY...
WHY IS IT SHOWING KIRITO!?

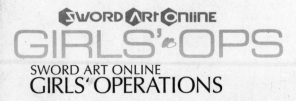

SWORD ART ONLINE
GIRLS' OPS

SWORD ART ONLINE
GIRLS' OPERATIONS

To be continued in the next volume!

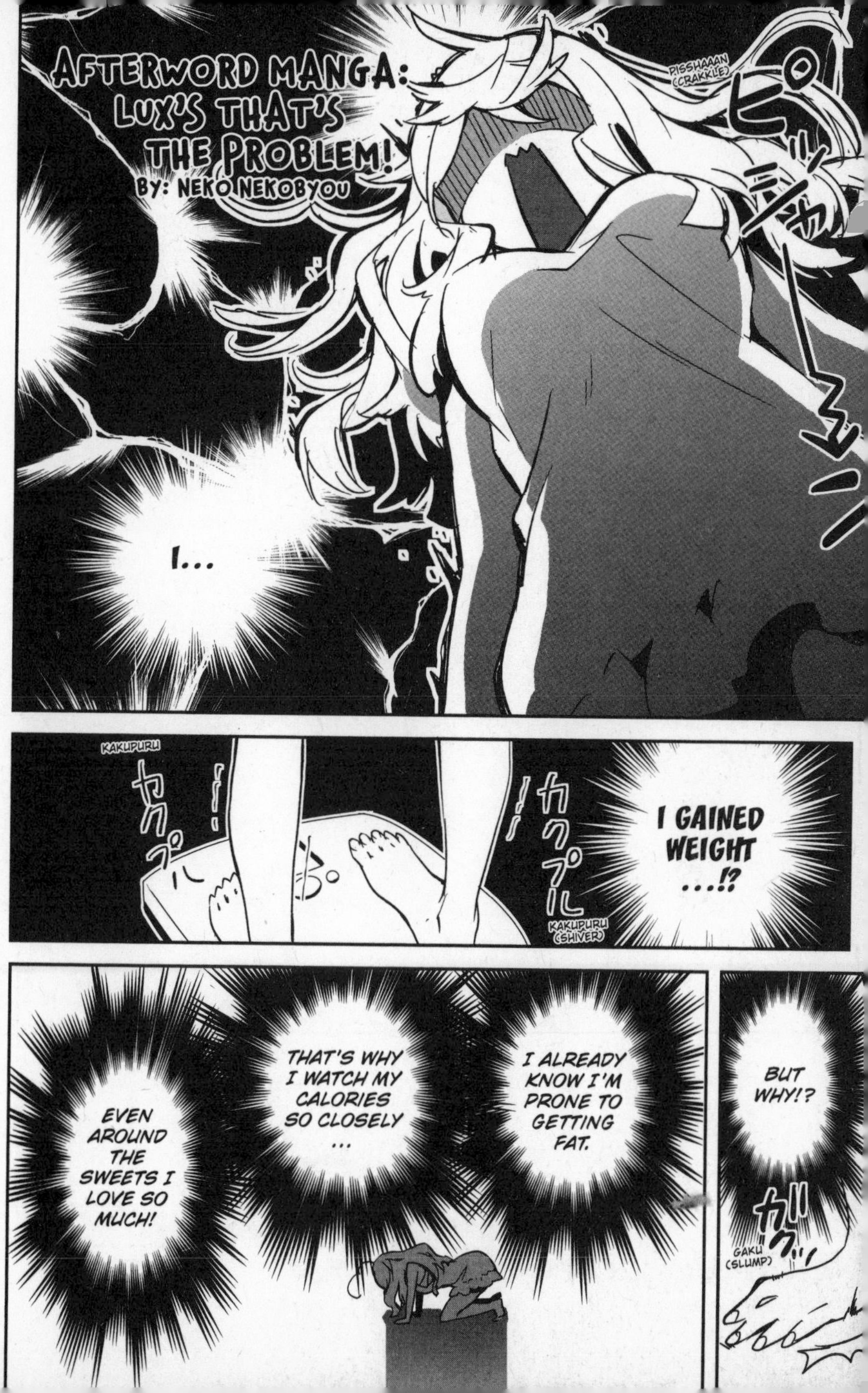
Afterword Manga: Lux's That's the Problem!
By: Neko Nekobyou
Pisshaaan (crakkle)
I...
Kakupuru (shiver)
I gained weight ...!?
Kakupuru
But why!?
Gaku (slump)
I already know I'm prone to getting fat.
That's why I watch my calories so closely ...
Even around the sweets I love so much!

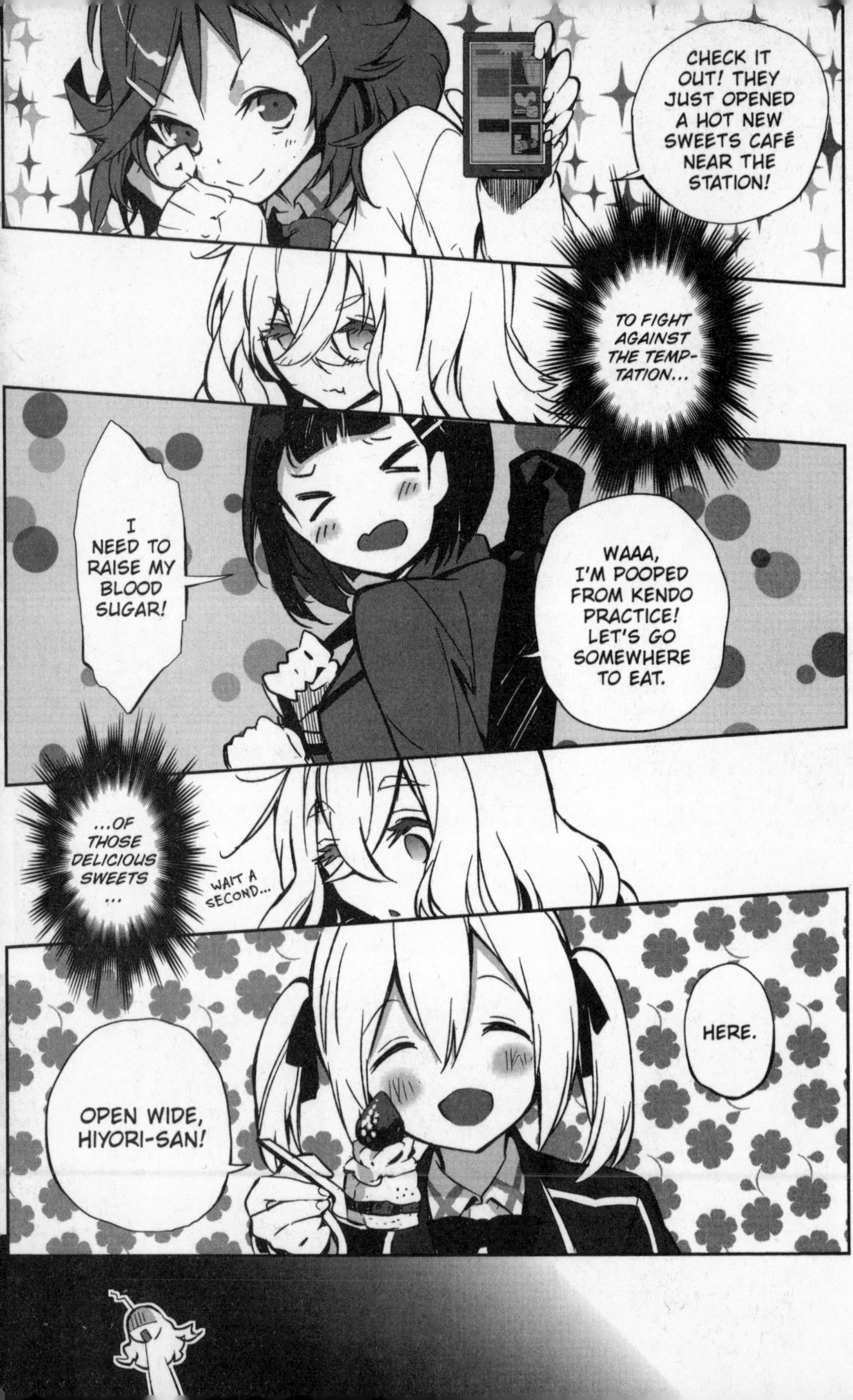

CHECK IT OUT! THEY JUST OPENED A HOT NEW SWEETS CAFÉ NEAR THE STATION!
TO FIGHT AGAINST THE TEMPTATION...
WAAA, I'M POOPED FROM KENDO PRACTICE! LET'S GO SOMEWHERE TO EAT.
I NEED TO RAISE MY BLOOD SUGAR!
WAIT A SECOND...
...OF THOSE DELICIOUS SWEETS...
HERE.
OPEN WIDE, HIYORI-SAN!

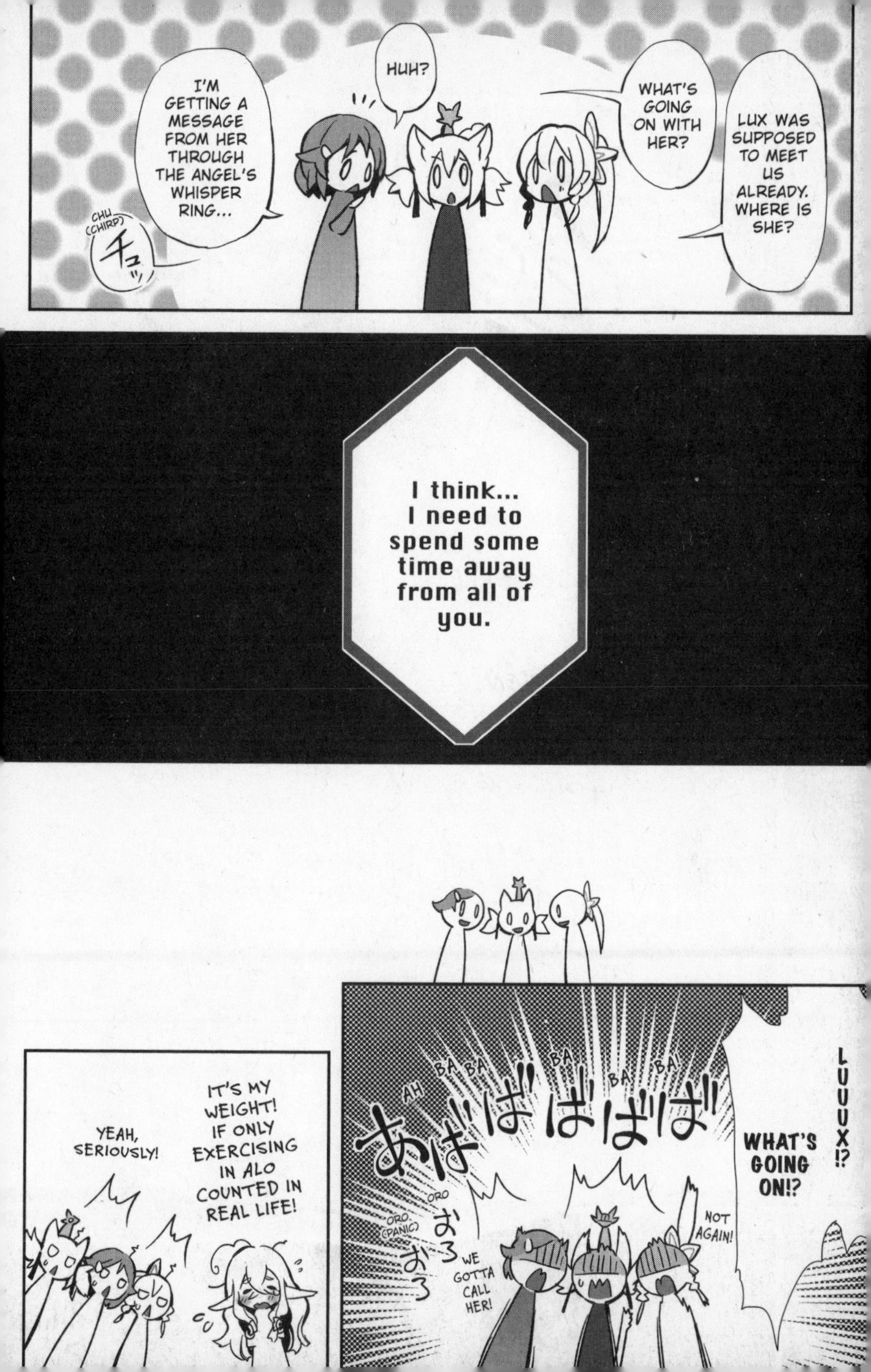
LUX WAS SUPPOSED TO MEET US ALREADY. WHERE IS SHE?
WHAT'S GOING ON WITH HER?
HUH?
I'M GETTING A MESSAGE FROM HER THROUGH THE ANGEL'S WHISPER RING...
CHU (CHIRP)
チュッ
I think... I need to spend some time away from all of you.
LUUUUX!?
WHAT'S GOING ON!?
AH BA BA BA BA BA
あばばばばば
NOT AGAIN!
WE GOTTA CALL HER!
ORO ORO (PANIC)
おろおろ
IT'S MY WEIGHT! IF ONLY EXERCISING IN ALO COUNTED IN REAL LIFE!
YEAH, SERIOUSLY!